NEO1
PHILOSOPHY

Introductory Readings

NEOPLATONIC PHILOSOPHY

Introductory Readings

John Dillon
Lloyd P. Gerson

Hackett Publishing Company, Inc.
Indianapolis/Cambridge

Copyright © 2004 by Hackett Publishing Company, Inc.

All rights reserved
Printed in the United States of America

10 09 08 07   2 3 4 5 6 7

For further information, please address:

   Hackett Publishing Company, Inc.
   P.O. Box 44937
   Indianapolis, IN 46244-0937

   www.hackettpublishing.com

Cover design by Abigail Coyle
Text design by Jennifer Plumley
Composition by Professional Book Compositors, Inc.
Printed at Edwards Brothers, Inc.

Library of Congress Cataloging-in-Publication Data

Neoplatonic philosophy : introductory readings/[edited by] John Dillon, Lloyd P. Gerson.
   p. cm.
   Includes bibliographical references and index.
   ISBN 0-87220-708-0 (cloth) — 0-87220-707-2 (paper)
   1. Neoplatonism.   I. Dillon, John M.   II. Gerson, Lloyd P.
B517.N443 2004
186'.4—dc22   2003056868

ISBN-13: 978-0-87220-708-0 (cloth)
ISBN-13: 978-0-87220-707-3 (pbk.)

The paper used in this publication meets the minimum requirements of
American National Standard for Information Sciences—
Permanence of Paper for Printed Library Materials,
ANSI Z39.48-1984

TABLE OF CONTENTS

Preface ... ix
Introduction ... xiii
Principal Texts Used in This Anthology ... xxiii

Plotinus

Enneads

I 1 (53) On What Is the Living Being and What Is the Human Being (complete) ... 1
I 4 (46) On Happiness ... 12
§§ 1–4
I 6 (1) On Beauty (complete) ... 18
I 8 (51) On What Evils Are and Where They Come From ... 30
§§ 1–5
III 8 (30) On Nature and Contemplation and on the One (complete) ... 35
IV 7 (2) On the Immortality of the Soul ... 49
§§ 1; 9–15
IV 8 (6) On the Descent of the Soul Into Bodies (complete) ... 56
V 1 (10) On the Three Principal Hypostases (complete) ... 66
V 2 (11) On the Generation and Order of the Things That Come after the First (complete) ... 83
V 3 (49) On the Knowing Hypostases and on That Which Is Transcendent ... 86
§§ 1–9; 13–17
V 5 (32) That the Intelligibles Are Not Outside the Intellect, and on the Good ... 105
§§ 1–2
VI 4 (22) On the Presence of Being, One and the Same Simultaneously Existing Everywhere as a Whole—Part One ... 109
§§ 1–11

VI 7 (38) How the Multitude of Ideas Came to Exist, and On the One §§ 1–23; 37–42	122
VI 8 (39) On the Free Will and the Volition of the One §§ 1–8; 12–16	159

Porphyry

Launching-Points to the Intelligible §§ 10, 11, 13, 16, 22, 25, 26, 32, 41, 43, 44	178
Inquiries Into Various Topics Frs. 259, 261	195
On the Return of the Soul Frs. 284, 285, 287, 300	199
The History of Philosophy Frs. 220–223	202
Commentary on Parmenides Frs. IV, V, VI	205
Commentary on Timaeus Fr. LXXIX	212
Commentary on Categories	214
On Principles Fr. 232	217
From Damascius *On Principles (De Principiis)* Fr. 367	217
From Iamblichus *On the Soul (De Anima)* §§ 6, 17, 23, 37	218

Iamblichus

On the Mysteries of the Egyptians Book I 1–3; 10; Book II 2; 11; Book III 25; Book V 26; Book VII 4–5; Book VIII 2; Book X 1–8	221
On the Soul (De Anima) §§ 7, 18, 19, 37, 38	241
Letter to Macedonius, On Fate Frs. 1–7	244
Commentary on Parmenides Fr. 2B	248

CONTENTS

Commentary on Timaeus	249
Frs. 7, 29, 50, 53, 54, 81, 87	
Commentary on Phaedrus	256
Fr. 6	
Commentary on Philebus	257
Frs. 4, 7	
From Proclus' *Commentary on Parmenides*	258
From Proclus' *Platonic Theology*	259
From Damascius' *On Principles (De Principiis)*	260
From Pseudo-Simplicius' *Commentary on the Soul (De Anima)*	262

Proclus

Elements of Theology	264
Props. 1, 7, 11, 15, 16, 17, 20, 21, 25, 35, 41, 53, 57, 64, 67, 123, 186, 187, 194, 195, 211	
Platonic Theology	280
I 1–3	
Commentary on Parmenides	292
Book I 617–659	
Book VI 1043–1051	
Commentary on Timaeus	331
Prologue	
Book I 4–9, 24	
Book II 276, 30–277, 14	
Book III 234, 8–235, 9	
Commentary on Book I of Euclid's Elements	344
The Nature and Origin of Evil	345
§§ 1–5; 8–9; 30–33; 36–37; 51	

Glossary	360

PREFACE

Neoplatonic Philosophy: Introductory Readings aims to provide a starting point for the serious study of a relatively neglected period in the history of philosophy. It was originally loosely conceived to be a sort of companion to R. T. Wallis' monograph *Neoplatonism* (1972, 2nd edition with updated bibliography, Hackett, 1992) It picks up roughly where *Hellenistic Philosophy: Introductory Readings* by B. Inwood and L. P. Gerson (1988, 2nd edition, Hackett, 1997) leaves off. The present work contains many, though by no means all, of the texts referred to by Wallis. For anyone unfamiliar or only vaguely familiar with Neoplatonism, the use of the two books together should provide a basic orientation.

In selecting material for inclusion in this book, we were guided by a number of principles in addition to the one mentioned above. The foremost among these was the decision to include mainly philosophical material, broadly speaking. We are aware that, regrettably, this will leave the reader with a somewhat incomplete picture of the last great flowering of Hellenic culture. We have also refrained from including translations of any of the 15,000 or so extant pages of Neoplatonic Aristotelian commentary in recognition of the soon-to-appear three volume collection including selections of that material, edited by Richard Sorabji. Finally, in our selection we strove to include the material that would enable the reader to begin to form a judgment about the philosophical distinctness of each of the four major figures. In order to achieve this goal, we chose to include complete or, at any rate, lengthy, continuous texts, rather than to chop up material thematically. Although there is considerable justification for treating Neoplatonism as a unified philosophy, nevertheless disagreement among Neoplatonists was far from uncommon, and shifting perspectives, sometimes the result of literally centuries of debate, produced in fact many unique philosophical positions.

The study of Neoplatonism throws up a number of challenges. For one, the Neoplatonists were expositors, interpreters, and champions of a tradition going back to Plato himself and the Academy. Accordingly, one must be constantly aware of the relevant historical background of the Neoplatonic writings. We have tried to indicate this extensively in the footnotes. The reader should also be aware that, as evidenced by the enormous number of their Aristotelian commentaries, Neoplatonists were engaged in constant dialogue with Plato's greatest pupil.

The translations of Plotinus were the primary responsibility of Lloyd Gerson. The translations of the other Neoplatonists were the primary responsibility of John Dillon. Some of the latter were excerpted from already published works. Extensive collaboration and revision by both authors followed initial drafts. The authors wish to acknowledge their gratitude to Princeton University Press for allowing us to use the Morrow-Dillon translation of Proclus' *Parmenides Commentary*, and to the Society for Biblical Literature of Atlanta for allowing us to use Dillon's translation of Iamblichus' *De Mysteriis*, and to Vrin for permission to use portions of Dillon's forthcoming translations of Porphyry's *Sententiae*. Although we have striven to be consistent in the translations of technical terms within each author, we have not attempted to harmonize completely translations of terminology among the authors. We hope that the glossary and the index will help serve to reduce possible confusion.

The authors are conscious of a considerable debt to earlier published English translations of the writings of the Neoplatonic philosophers. In particular, A. H. Armstrong's magisterial translation of all of Plotinus in the Loeb series, Stephen MacKenna's earlier vivid and inspired version of Plotinus, and E. R. Dodds' great edition of Proclus' *Elements of Theology* have been immensely useful. The translation of and commentary on Proclus' *On the Existence of Evils* by J. Opsomer and C. Steel (Ithaca, 2003), appeared too late for us to avail ourselves of its riches.

In translating the Neoplatonists, we have been especially conscious of the needs of nonspecialists. Accordingly, we have adopted a number of conventions that we hope will be of assistance in reading these most powerful though difficult and even obscure thinkers. Among these are paragraphs used to organize the flow of argument; replacement of pronouns by their nouns when the reference is certain, and brackets in which is placed the probable reference when there is no certainty; capitalization of the words referring to the first principle of all (the One, the Good), to the second principle (Intellect), as distinct from individual intellects, and to the third principle (Soul), when distinguished from individual souls, including the soul of the universe. Square brackets indicate additions by the translators; angle brackets indicate translations of additions to the text by various editors. We have also capitalized the reference to Forms or Ideas, when Plotinus and others are speaking about the principles of Plato's theory of Forms; otherwise, in the discussions of form, it is left in lower case. For the later Neoplatonists, this convention is extended to the terms "Being," "Life," etc., when these are used as the names of principles. Generally, the Greek word for "god" is not used as a proper noun and is treated accordingly. We have also been free in breaking up long (sometimes *very* long) sentences into shorter English sentences, always trying to retain the logical connections in thought. We have tried to meet the perennial challenge to the translator of ancient philosophical material, which is to combine accuracy with readability. There are a number of works traditionally attributed to Plato and to some Neoplatonic philosophers whose authenticity, though generally accepted in antiquity, have been seriously questioned in modern times. We indicate with "[?]" those works. Finally, we have provided extensive cross-references in the notes, though many of these are to works not included in this volume. We trust that the reader will be able to make his or her way to the relevant editions or translations, most of which are listed in the bibliography to Wallis' book.

A number of colleagues and friends have helped us from the inception of this project. We are particularly grateful to Professor Anne Sheppard, who served as a reader for Hackett and made numerous extremely helpful suggestions regarding translations and organization of material. Professors John Bussanich and Sara Rappe gave us helpful advice regarding the inclusion of material. The index was prepared by Ian Bell, who also rescued us from a number of stylistic blunders.

INTRODUCTION

I

The four philosophers represented in this collection are the dominant figures in what has come to be known as Neoplatonism. Plotinus (204/5–270 C.E.) is recognized as the founder of Neoplatonism, and, accordingly, it is to him that we devote the most space. His most famous disciple was Porphyry (234–c.305 C.E.). Most of his wide-ranging philosophical works are extant only in fragmentary form. Nevertheless it is clear from the material we do possess that he aimed to build on and in a way systematize Plotinus' interpretation of Platonism. We are also at a disadvantage in fully appreciating the contribution of Iamblichus (c.245–325 C.E.) to Platonic philosophy, for apart from the first four volumes of a nine- or ten-volume work on Pythagoreanism and his *Reply of Abammon to Porphyry's Letter to Anebo* (known since the Renaissance as *On the Egyptian Mysteries*), we possess only fragments of his impressive array of commentaries on the works of Plato and Aristotle. It is clear, however, that Iamblichus was a central figure in the shaping of later Neoplatonism, in both its philosophical and its religious dimensions. We possess far more, though by no means all, of the improbably vast output of Proclus (412–485 C.E.), whose *Elements of Theology* constitutes a sort of *summa* of ancient Platonism. In its Latin version, known as *Liber de Causis* and transmitted through an Arabic translation, it was enormously influential on medieval philosophy's thinking about ancient Greek philosophy. Proclus' works constitute the most complete expression of Platonism that we possess. Space constraints prohibit us from including any material from the Neoplatonic philosophers after Proclus, especially John Philoponus (c.490–570 C.E.), Olympiodorus (before 510–after 565 C.E.), Simplicius (c.490–560 C.E.), and Damascius (c.462–after 538 C.E.), though they each have unique contributions to make in the development of the Platonic tradition.

The term "Neoplatonism" is an artifact of 19th-century Germanic scholarship and reflects a contemporary academic trend to systematize history into nameable periods. Although the prefix "neo-" is intended to suggest that something significantly new is to be found in the thought of this period, it is worth stressing at the outset that Plotinus, Porphyry, Iamblichus, and Proclus would all have probably preferred to identify themselves as "paleo"-Platonists; that is, as non-innovating expositors and defenders of Platonic philosophy.[1] We need not of course accept such protestations of absence of originality at face value. There is admittedly a fine line between saying what one thinks the master meant and saying something, in fact, new. Still, a good deal of what is generally recognized as original among the Neoplatonists is owing to factors other than a self-conscious desire to seek out "new beginnings" in philosophy. In order to appreciate what is and what is not "neo" in the writings of the Neoplatonists we need to try to look briefly at the history of ancient Greek philosophy through their eyes.

Let us begin with the Platonic corpus as the Neoplatonists knew it. As Diogenes Laertius reports,[2] Thrasyllus (d.36 C.E.) divided the works of Plato into nine tetralogies, or groups of four. To these he appended a number of works he judged to be spurious. There is considerable controversy today over the question of whether Thrasyllus originated the division into tetralogies. There is even greater dispute regarding Thrasyllus' division of authentic and spurious material. From our perspective, what is most important is that the Thrasyllan scheme established the authentic corpus of Platonic writings for the Neoplatonists.

The nine tetralogies include thirty-five dialogues and thirteen *Epistles* or *Letters*, which are all counted as one work. Not all of these are today universally recognized as genuine. Of the dialogues of doubted authenticity, *Alcibiades I* is the one that was most important for Neoplatonists because that dialogue was apparently read first among the works of Plato in the Neoplatonic curriculum. Among the *Epistles* of doubted authenticity, the second and the philosophical portion of the seventh are unquestionably the most significant for the Neoplatonists, who used them regularly to bolster their interpretations of the dialogues.

Among the thirty-six works recognized by the Neoplatonists as genuine, some were naturally selected as having more doctrinal significance than others. Apparently there was, at least by the time of Iamblichus, a well-established order of study of the dialogues. After lectures on Plato's life, a series of ten questions were to be answered: (1) What sort of philosophy is found in Plato? (2) Why did Plato believe it was his duty to write down his philosophy? (3) Why did he employ a literary form in his dialogues? (4) What are the elements of the dialogues? (5) What is the source of the titles of the dialogues? (6) What is the principle of division

---

[1] See *infra* pp. 281–3, the extract from *Platonic Theology* where Proclus provides a brief history of Neoplatonism as exegesis of the Platonic "revelation." In later antiquity generally, originality was certainly not viewed as an unalloyed virtue.

[2] See D.L. III 56.

of the dialogues? (7) In what manner are the topics of the dialogues introduced? (8) What are the criteria for determining the aim of the dialogues? (9) What is the order of the dialogues? (10) What is the manner of teaching of the dialogues? Discussion of these topics was followed by introductions to the twelve dialogues contained in the syllabus of Plato's works: *Alcibiades I, Gorgias, Phaedo, Cratylus, Theaetetus, Sophist, Statesman, Phaedrus, Symposium, Philebus, Timaeus, Parmenides.*

The selection of these twelve dialogues does not in any obvious way correspond to any tetralogical order. In addition, the above curriculum does not give a full picture of Neoplatonic interest in the genuine works. In fact, the most glaring omission, *Republic,* is of the utmost importance to Neoplatonists, especially its central metaphysical portion. Also surprising is the omission from the list of works to be studied of any of the so-called "Socratic" dialogues (with the exception of *Alcibiades I*). Their omission reflects several features of the Neoplatonic approach to Plato. First, since this approach was thoroughly non-developmentalist, the Neoplatonists did not recognize a Socratic, or early, phase of Plato's philosophy, and so the dialogues today held to represent such a phase were not relevant to revealing it. Nor was it supposed that there was development of Plato's thought away from the constructive period of the so-called "middle dialogues." Second, the aporetic or inconclusive character of these dialogues was not directly relevant to anything like a systematic representation of Platonism. Third, the Neoplatonic ethical preoccupation was addressed by the more elaborate treatments in the dialogues included in the introductory twelve.

Another important feature of the curriculum is that it culminated in the two works, *Timaeus* and *Parmenides,* the former being Plato's ultimate and most comprehensive statement of the structure of the sensible world and the latter containing the corresponding statement for the intelligible world.[3] Reading *Timaeus* in this way, though by no means universally accepted, is far less controversial than reading *Parmenides* in this way.[4]

---

[3] See Proclus *In Tim.* I 13, 15–17, who quotes Iamblichus as saying that the entirety of Plato's thought is contained in *Timaeus* and *Parmenides.*

[4] See *infra* pp. 302–13. Proclus, *In Parm.* 630, 15–645, 8, who gives a most valuable history of types of interpretation of *Parmenides*—especially its second part—within the Platonic tradition. The basic division is between a logical and a metaphysical interpretation. The logical interpretation that takes *Parmenides* as an exercise in reasoning, was held, for example, by Albinus (*Isag.*, chapter 4), Alcinous (*Didask.*, chapter 6), and Thrasyllus (D.L. III 58). The metaphysical interpretation, of which there are several varieties, was normative for the

Part of the reason for the Neoplatonic consensus that *Parmenides* contained an expression of Plato's most profound thoughts about the structure of intelligible reality was that the Neoplatonists did not rely solely on the dialogues for their understanding of Platonism. They relied on Aristotle's and others' testimony about Plato's unwritten teachings. The view that Plato *had* unwritten teachings and that these differed in any way from what is said in the dialogues is a matter of intense and even bitter controversy. It is rather less a matter of contention that Aristotle does refer to unwritten teachings of the Academy that contain some sort of a theory about ultimate metaphysical principles. The relation between the theory of Forms as presented in the dialogues and the alleged theory of ultimate principles presented in Aristotle's account is far from clear in the Neoplatonists. But they took Aristotle, not unreasonably, to be a faithful reporter of Plato's views, including views that do not for the most part make an explicit appearance in the dialogues.[5] In this regard, two well-known passages in *Phaedrus* and the *7th Epistle* with others in *Republic* and the *2nd Epistle*, supported the case for the existence of an unwritten teaching and its identification as a theory of first principles.[6]

Apart from the Platonic corpus and Aristotle's testimony, Neoplatonists were the inheritors of more than 500 years of Platonic and anti-Platonic philosophizing. The former group includes the works of the immediate disciples of Plato in the so-called "Old Academy," Speusippus, Xenocrates, Polemo, et al., as well as the vast corpus of material rather unhelpfully labeled "Middle Platonic," which covers the period roughly from 80 B.C.E. to 220 C.E.[7] The latter, or anti-Platonic, group includes the writings of Stoics, Epicureans, and Pyrrhonian skeptics.

In addition to the use of the writings of self-declared Academics and Platonists, Neoplatonists assumed that Plato was not the first to express the truths contained in what later came to be called "Platonism." For

---

Neoplatonists. See Plotinus V 1. 8, 23 ff. As Dodds famously argued ("The *Parmenides* of Plato and the Origin of the Neoplatonic One," *Classical Quarterly* 22 (1928), 129–42), the positive, metaphysical interpretation may well antedate Plotinus.

[5] This has been strenuously disputed, especially by Harold Cherniss in his *Aristotle's Criticism of Plato and the Academy* (New York, 1944) and *The Riddle of the Early Academy* (New York, 1945).

[6] See *Phdr.* 274C–277A; *7th Ep.* 341B ff.

[7] See John Dillon, *The Middle Platonists*. 2nd Edition (London, 1996); *The Heirs of Plato* (Oxford, 2003).

example, Plotinus supposed that Egyptian, Persian, and perhaps Indian philosophers had expressed insights into intelligible reality akin to those of Plato. Iamblichus, in part owing to his acknowledgement of Aristotle's testimony, supposed that Plato belonged to the great Pythagorean tradition. Proclus, too, supposed that Plato was the greatest expositor of truths contained in the Greek mystery religions. The rejection of what no doubt would have seemed to Neoplatonists as the hopelessly naive view that Plato was utterly original contributed to their unwavering focus on what they thought Plato *meant* rather than on what they perfectly well knew Plato *said*.

The writings of Aristotle himself, as well as those of his Peripatetic successors (especially the great commentator Alexander of Aphrodisias [second–early third century C.E.]) have a unique role to play in the development of what is distinctive about Neoplatonism. It is perhaps to Iamblichus that we owe the introduction of the study of the works of Aristotle into the Platonic curriculum. This was done on the assumption—shared by virtually all Neoplatonists—that at a fundamental level, Aristotle's philosophy was in harmony with Platonism. The manifest differences, particularly expressed in Aristotle's unrelenting criticisms of Platonic doctrines, were variously explained or explained away. The principal feature of the harmony was that Aristotle was thought to be authoritative for the sensible world and Plato for the intelligible world, and that Aristotle's doctrine pertaining to the former could be, with certain reservations, fitted into Plato's doctrines pertaining to the latter much as, for example, Newtonian mechanics can be fitted into quantum mechanics. Whatever one thinks of the assumption of harmony, it is incontestable that Neoplatonists took Aristotle seriously as providing insights into Platonism. That is exactly why we have today some 15,000 pages of *Neoplatonic* commentary on the works of Aristotle.[8]

Even before the formal introduction of Aristotle into the Neoplatonic curriculum, Plotinus was, as Porphyry tells us, deeply engaged in what we might call the "appropriation" of Aristotle on behalf of Platonism. Plotinus did not hesitate to criticize Aristotle when he thought that he had misunderstood Plato. But Plotinus also did not hesitate to incorporate Aristotelian terminology and arguments into his own expression of Platonism. This was done with such naturalness that Neoplatonists who

---

[8] The ongoing project of translating this vast body of philosophy into English under the direction of Richard Sorabji is of the greatest importance for the understanding of Neoplatonism. Sorabji has recently edited a three-volume sourcebook, including selections of this commentary material.

came after Plotinus and followed him were perhaps not always conscious that frequently they spoke Platonism with an Aristotelian voice.

Three examples of this important feature of Neoplatonism must suffice. Plato's term for the activity of thinking is "intellect's motion" (κίνησις νοῦ).[9] Aristotle introduced the technical term ἐνέργεια (activity) and distinguished it from κίνησις. The distinction is that the latter implies potency or imperfection inherent in change whereas the former does not. Aristotle describes the thinking of the Prime Mover as ἐνέργεια νοῦ and identifies that activity as the best life (ζωή), thus claiming that the highest activity, that of thinking, does not involve change.[10] Neoplatonists accepted the distinction between κίνησις and ἐνέργεια as an important contribution to *Platonic* philosophy, for the activity of the intelligible world has a fundamental explanatory function. The presence of activity, as opposed to *im*mobility, makes significantly more plausible the idea that the intelligible world produces effects in the sensible world.

The second and related example is found in Aristotle's claim that intellect is a kind (γένος) different from soul (ψυχή).[11] It is only the former that is separable from the body and immortal. Plato, however, seems to hold that intellect can only exist in soul precisely because it is inseparable from life.[12] Aristotle, identifying life with the activity of intellect, thus seems to use the term "soul" more narrowly than Plato; he makes it the "first actuality of a body."[13] The relationship between intellect, intellectual activity, and soul is a deep puzzle both for Aristotle and for the Neoplatonists. But the crucial point is that in trying to understand the Platonic commitment to the immortality of the soul, Neoplatonists did so with the Aristotelian specification that this immortality belonged to intellect. In other words, they took Aristotle as expressing or clarifying a Platonic position.

The third example concerns the Neoplatonic (and Peripatetic) use of the expression ἔνυλα εἴδη (enmattered forms) to indicate the forms of sensibles, that which answers to Aristotle's "formal cause."[14] Neopla-

---

[9] See *Lg.* 897E4.
[10] See *Met.* Λ 7, 1072b27.
[11] See *De An.* B 2, 413b24–6.
[12] See *Soph.* 249A–B. Cf. *Tim.* 30B2; 46D5–6.
[13] See *De An.* B 1, 412a27.
[14] Cf. Plotinus I 8. 8, 13–16; VI 1. 29, 11–14; VI 7. 4, 19; Simplicius *In Phys.* 1, 16; Proclus *In Parm.* 705, 37; 839, 33; 1053, 11; *In Tim.* I 3, 2; I 10, 14; II 25, 2; II 36, 29.

tonists took this term as a generalization of examples of Platonic usage. In *Phaedo* Plato speaks of "the largeness in us" as distinct from "Largeness itself," and in *Parmenides* he speaks of "the likeness in us" as opposed to "likeness itself."[15] Thus Aristotelian sensible form is integrated into the Platonic doctrine of separate Forms in the sense that once a distinction is made, say, between "likeness in us" and "Likeness," a commitment to the former, far from precluding a commitment to the latter, may actually be thought to entail it implicitly. In addition, taking "enmattered form" as a legitimate Platonic concept allowed Neoplatonists to accept the concept of matter (ὕλη) as legitimately Platonic, too. This was particularly important in their understanding of the "Receptacle" of becoming in Plato's *Timaeus* as well as in their reflections on Platonic ideas about evil and its association with material or sensible reality.

The point of these examples is that Neoplatonists believed that Aristotle could serve as a guide to a more profound understanding of Platonism. The questions of whether this is in fact true or not and whether the originality of Neoplatonism should be counted as comprising this more profound understanding or else rejected as a *misunderstanding* are commended to the reader's attention.

One other factor in the development of Neoplatonism should not be discounted, and that is its increasing confrontation with the philosophizing of the new religion, Christianity. If Neoplatonism may be said to begin with Plotinus, it is typically held to end with the "closing" of the Platonic school in Athens by the Byzantine Christian emperor Justinian in 529 C.E. This event certainly does not mark the end of Platonism as such. Christianity, Judaism, and Islam all appropriate elements of Platonism for their various theologies. But it does more or less mark the beginning of the end of "pagan" Neoplatonism, that is, Platonism untouched by the revealed, monotheistic religions. It is clear enough, starting with the works of Porphyry, that Neoplatonists were aware of the threat Christianity posed to what they regarded, with considerable justification, as the *philosophia perennis* of Greek civilization. The consequence of this awareness was that efforts were repeatedly made to systematize and reconcile diverging interpretations of Platonism in order to make the best case for it. In addition, the soteriological aspect of Christianity, an undoubted "plus" in proselytizing pagans, was countered with an increasing integration of theurgical elements into Neoplatonism. Iamblichus stands out as the first of the Neoplatonists in

---

[15] See *Phd.* 102E; *Parm.* 130E.

whom the philosophical and practical religious sides of his thinking are inseparable. And this is owing, in no small part, to the challenge posed by Christianity.

All of the above factors constitute signposts on the road leading from Plato to the construction of something called Platonism or, if one insists, Neoplatonism.

II

As is the case with all philosophical schools, increasing complexity of conceptual distinctions and argument is the mark of ongoing vitality. This is especially the case for Platonism, which by 529 C.E. had a more or less continuous 900-year history. But beneath the layers of complexity and the inevitable disagreements that this entailed, there are core principles adhered to by all Neoplatonists. The first of these is based on a distinction between what is available to our senses and what is available to our intellects, between the sensible and the intelligible. To dismiss this as a crude form of "dualism" would be unfortunate, principally because the sensible world was never supposed to be bereft of intelligibility altogether. On the contrary, such intelligibility as it possesses is to be explained by the unqualifiedly intelligible world. This is the first of the core principles. As in the examples above drawn from *Phaedo* and *Parmenides*, the largeness and likeness of physical bodies are accounted for by Largeness and Likeness themselves. Thus, the priority of the intelligible to the sensible in the order of explanation is held to require a hierarchy of ontological principles, since explanations, at least causal explanations, are impossible unless in each case the *explanans* exists. In general, if A is ontologically prior to B, that is because A can exist without B, but not vice versa. The atemporal explanations of intelligibility in the sensible world—if there be such—are clearly prior in this sense.[16]

The second, and related, core principle is that the intelligible world itself is a hierarchy, ordered according to the idea that the simpler is prior to the more complex. What this means above all is that there must be an absolutely first principle of all, and it must be absolutely simple. The notions of relative and absolute simplicity are difficult ones, and Neoplatonists diverged on their understanding of these and what they entailed. They agreed in both identifying the absolutely first principles

---

[16] Cf. Aristotle *Met.* Δ 11, 1019a2–4 and Θ 8, 1050b6–8, who attributes this sense of priority to Plato and then himself endorses the priority of the eternal to the temporal.

with Plato's Idea of the Good in *Republic* and accepting Aristotle's testimony that Plato equated this Idea with a first principle he called "the One."[17] But Neoplatonists also agreed that the intelligible world could not consist solely in an absolutely simple first principle, whether it be called "Good" or "One." For that which is intelligible (or, in the case of the sensible world, equivocally intelligible) is intrinsically complex, and so the principles of intelligibility must be similarly complex. For example, the Largeness and Likeness that explain the very possibility of their images or reflections in the sensible world are themselves complex in their structure, as any attempt to analyze them would presume.

There is another sort of complexity, apart from that of the structure of intelligibles, and that is the complexity of thinking itself. All Neoplatonists recognized that a principle of Intellect was required both to sustain the articulated complexity of the intelligible world and to account for the qualified presence of this in the sensible world. In the first instance, the complexity that is inseparable within, say, Threeness must be eternally sustained by thinking it. It would be misleading to call this conceptual complexity, since Neoplatonists assumed that concepts are representations and hence hierarchically inferior to what Intellect must do, which is to be eternally identical with the intelligible complexity. In the second instance, Intellect, here basically identified with the Demiurge of Plato's *Timaeus*, serves as the explanatory entity in a design argument; that is, an argument that the intelligibility found in the sensible world could not otherwise be accounted for than by a primary Intellect.

Although Intellect is, as we have seen, a principle of life as well as thinking, the presence of entities with souls "here below" required the postulation of a principle, Soul. We might call this a principle not of life but of non-intellectual life or of non-intellectual striving. All things with souls desire in some way to attain things that are outside of themselves at the moment of desiring, including other psychic states. What in general do they desire? The Neoplatonic answer is: wholeness, completeness, integrity, continuity. All of these are versions of the unity that is ultimately found in the first principle of all. Everything strives, insofar as possible given the kind of thing it is, to *return* to the first principle. This return does not amount to an annihilation of the "returnee," although some mystical versions of Neoplatonism may tend to speak in this way. Nothing produced by the One with the instrumentality of In-

---

[17] See especially *Met.* A 6, 987a29–988a17; N 4, 1091b13–15; *EE* A 8, 1218a15–28.

tellect could be annihilated anyway. It amounts to a reconnection of some sort with the intelligible world.

Seeing the "horizontal" striving of embodied souls "here below" as really a reflection of the "vertical" striving for return to the intelligible world, which is "above," is one of the most distinctive features of Neoplatonism. It is the key to understanding the moral psychology and even the aesthetics of Neoplatonists.

The hierarchy of One, Intellect, and Soul, first developed in detail among the Neoplatonists by Plotinus, is not so much a fixed doctrine as a conceptual framework for exploring Platonism. If some of the writings of the Neoplatonists give the impression of a kind of scholastic rigidity, this is perhaps somewhat misleading. The impression owes more to what, at least after Plotinus, came to be the recognized style of philosophical expression than to substance. In fact, the very considerable diversity of opinion among Neoplatonists in regard to fundamental philosophical issues as well as to matters of interpretation testifies to Neoplatonism's vitality.

Platonism is arguably the central tradition in the history of philosophy. If one considers the history of philosophy relevant to contemporary philosophical concerns, one can hardly ignore the serious study of Platonism. We hope in this collection of translations to assist readers in the understanding of Platonism via the understanding of a major interpretation or version of it. Even if one comes to reject Neoplatonism as an interpretation of Platonic philosophy, it can hardly be doubted that much of the history of philosophy has seen Platonism through Neoplatonic eyes.

PRINCIPAL TEXTS USED IN THIS ANTHOLOGY

Plotinus

Plotini Opera. Edited by P. Henry and H.-R. Schwyzer, 3 v. (Oxford, 1964, 1977, 1983) (= H-S$_2$, the so-called *editio minor*). The so-called *editio maior* is referred to as H-S$_1$. A reference to H-S without subscripts indicates that both versions agree.

Porphyry

Sententiae. Edited by E. Lamberz (Leipzig, 1975)
Porphyre Sentences. Edited by L. Brisson, et al. (Paris, 2004)
Fragmenta. Edited by A. Smith (Leipzig, 1993)
In Platonis Timaeum Commentariorum Fragmenta. Edited by A. R. Sodano (Napoli, 1964)
The Anonymous Commentary on Plato's Parmenides. Edited by G. Bechtle (Bern, 1999)
In Aristotelis Categorias. Edited by A. Busse (CAG Vol. IV) (Berlin, 1887)

Iamblichus

Les Mystères d'Égypte. Edited by É. Des Places (Paris, 1966)
De Anima. Edited by J. Finamore and J. Dillon (Leiden, 2002)
Letters. Edited by J. Dillon (Atlanta, forthcoming).
In Platonis Dialogos Commentariorum Fragmenta. Edited by J. Dillon (Leiden, 1973)

Proclus

The Elements of Theology. 2nd edition. Edited by E. R. Dodds (Oxford, 1963)

Commentarium in Platonis Parmenidem. Edited by V. Cousin (Paris, 1864).

In Platonis Timaeum Commentarii. Edited by E. Diehl, 3 v. (Leipzig, 1903–1906)

Théologie Platonicienne. Edited by H. D. Saffrey and L. G. Westerink, 6 v. (Paris, 1968–1997)

De l'existence du mal. Vol. III of *Trois études sur la providence.* Edited by D. Isaac (Paris, 1982).

OTHER EDITIONS USED WITH ABBREVIATIONS

Anth. = John Stobaeus, *Antholgium.* See W-H

Atkinson, M. *Ennead V I* (Oxford, 1983)

CH = *Corpus Hermeticum.* Edited by A.D. Nock and A.J. Festugière (Paris, 1972)

D-K = H. Diels and W. Kranz, *Die Fragmente der Vorsokratiker* (Berlin, 7th edition, 1954)

D.L. = Diogenes Laertius, *Lives of Eminent Philosophers* 2 v. Edited by R.D. Hicks (Cambridge, Mass., London, 1925)

Hadot, P. *Traité (VI 7).* (Paris, 1994)

LSJ = *A Greek English Lexicon.* Edited by H. Liddell, R. Scott, and H.S. Jones (Oxford, 9th edition with supplement, 1996)

M = Sextus Empiricus, *Adversus Mathematicos* in *Sexti Empirici Opera.* 2 v. Edited by H. Mutschmann and J. Mau (Leipzig, 1958)

Morani, M. *Nemesii Emeseni De natura hominis* (Leipzig, 1987)

Nauck, A. *Tragicorum Graecorum Fragmenta* (Leipzig, 2nd edition, 1964)

PH = Sextus Empiricus, *Outlines of Pyrrhonism.*

PGM = *Papyri Magicae Graecae.* Edited by K. Preisendanz. (Stuttgart, 1973–1973)

SVF = *Stoicorum Veterum Fragmenta.* Edited by H. von Arnim 3 v. (Leipzig, 1903–1905)

S-W = *Théologie Platonicienne.* Edited by H.D. Saffrey and L.G. Westerink.

W-H = John Stobaeus, *Anthologium.* Edited by C. Wachsmuth and O. Hense, 5 v. (Berlin, 1884, reprinted 1958)

VP = *Vita Plotini* by Porphyry

PLOTINUS

Enneads

I 1 (53) On What Is the Living Being and What Is the Human Being[1] (complete)

In this work, one of the last Plotinus wrote, he reflects on the relationship between the human being and the soul-body composite. The human being, the true self or person, is separable from the composite and identifiable with the subject of thinking. The title might be making an allusion to Rep. 589A7, where Plato refers to the "human being within the human being," or the rational faculty of the soul. Plotinus is thus faced with the problem of how embodiment affects persons, if at all.

§1. Pleasures and pains, fears and feelings of boldness, appetites and aversions and distress—to what do these belong?[2] In fact, they belong either to the soul or to a soul using a body[3] or to some third thing that arises from a combination of both of these. In fact, the last mentioned can be understood in two ways: either as a mixture or as [5] something different that arises from the mixture. The alternatives are the same for what arises from these states—namely, actions and beliefs. And so we must investigate discursive thinking and belief to determine whether they belong to that to which the states belong or whether some of them are like this and some are not. And we should also consider how acts of thinking occur and to what they belong, as well as that itself [10] which is considering the investigation of these questions and making the judgment about what they are. Before that, we should investigate that to

---

[1] The number in parentheses refers to the chronological ordering of the treatises as attested to Porphyry. He tells us further (*VP* 4, 17–19) that the titles were not given by Plotinus but rather were those that "prevailed" (κρατήσασαι), presumably among those who had copies of the works.

[2] See Plato *Rep.* 429C–D; 430A–B; *Phd.* 83B; *Tim.* 69D; *Lg.* 897A and Aristotle *De An.* A 4, 408b1–29, where the question of the subject of affective and cognitive states is addressed in various ways.

[3] See Plato [?] *Alc.* I 129E.

which the act of sense-perception belongs. It is appropriate to begin from there, since the states are either certain kinds of acts of sense-perception or else they do not occur without sense-perception.[4]

§2. First, we need to understand if it is the case that soul is one thing and the essence of soul another.[5] For if it is, soul will be something composite, and there will at once be nothing absurd in its being subject, I mean, of these kinds of states [5] and, in general, in its being subject of better and worse habits and dispositions, that is, assuming the argument will turn out this way. In fact, however, if soul and the essence of soul were identical, soul would be a certain form incapable of being subject of all these activities, which it imparts to something else, instead having an activity that is natural to itself in itself, whatever the argument reveals this to be. In this case, it will be [10] true to say that the soul is immortal, if it is necessary to say that the immortal and indestructible is impassive,[6] somehow giving what belongs to itself to another while it gets nothing from another or only so much as is present in the things prior to it,[7] from which, since they are superior, it is not cut off.

Now what would something of this sort fear, since it is not subject of anything external to it? [15] Let's agree, then, that that which is afraid is that which is capable of being affected. Then does it not feel courageous, for do not such feelings belong to that to which things that are fearful happen not to be present? And how can it have appetites, which are satisfied by means of the emptied body being filled up, since that which is emptied and filled up is different from it?

And how could soul be a mixture? In fact, its essential nature is unmixed.[8] How could other things be [20] introduced into it? If this were to occur, it would be hastening towards not being what it is. Distress is

---

[4] See Plato *Tim.* 61C8–D2.

[5] See Aristotle *Met.* Z 6, 1037a17–b3 and H 3, 1042b2–3, where Aristotle says that "soul and the essence of soul are the same, but human being and the essence of human being are not the same, unless the soul is said to be a human being." See *infra* §10, where Plotinus argues that the rational part of the soul is the human being.

[6] See Aristotle *De An.* Γ 4, 429a15 on the impassivity of the soul; 430a23 on its immortality; and B 2, 413b26, on the indestructibility of *intellect* which Aristotle variously treats as a "part of soul" and a "genus different from soul."

[7] Plotinus means "ontologically prior," referring to Intellect and the One. In general, an inferior is not "cut off" from its superior, since it depends on it for its being.

[8] See Plato *Phil.* 59C4.

even more remote from it. For how can something be pained except in regard to something? But that which is simple in its essence is self-sufficient, in a way stabilized in its own essence. Will it be pleased if something is added to it when there is nothing, not even any good, that can accrue to it? For what it is, [25] it is always.

Further, it will perceive nothing nor will there be discursive thinking or belief in it. For sense-perception is the reception of a form or also of a bodily state,[9] and discursive thinking and belief supervene on sense-perception. Regarding thinking, if we are going to understand this as being in soul, we should examine how this happens, and regarding pleasure, I mean, pure pleasure,[10] if it has this when it is by itself.

§3. In regard to the soul that is [presently] in the body, we should also examine whether it exists prior to this or [only] in this, since it is from this [combination] that "the entire living being is named."[11] If, then, on the one hand, it uses the body as an instrument,[12] it is not forced to be subject of the states that come through the body, [5] just as craftsmen are not subjects of the states of their instruments.[13] On the other hand, perhaps it would of necessity be a subject of sense-perception, supposing it must use this instrument [the body] for cognizing the states arising from sense-perception of what is external. Seeing is, after all, the instrumental use of the eyes. But there are possible damages associated with seeing, so that there are also pains and distress in the soul, as is [10] generally the case for everything that happens to the body. So, too, there are desires in one looking for a remedy for the [pains, etc.] of his [bodily] instrument.

But how will the states come from the body into it? For though body will transfer its own states to another body, how will body transfer anything to the soul? For this would be equivalent in a way to saying that when one thing has an experience another thing [15] has that experience. For so long as one thing is using the instrument and another is the instrument it uses, each is separate.[14] At least, anyone who posits the soul as using the body separates them.

---

[9] See Aristotle *De An.* B 12, 424a18. Plotinus means that the soul perceives the presence of the form or the bodily state owing to the presence of the form.
[10] See Plato *Phil.* 52C.
[11] See Plato *Phdr.* 246C5.
[12] See Plato [?] *Alc.* I 129C5–130A1.
[13] See Aristotle *EE* H 9, 1241b18 for the analogy.
[14] See Plato [?] *Alc.* I 129D11–E7, where the difference of soul and body is deduced from the fact that one uses the other.

But prior to their separation by philosophy,[15] how were they related to each other? In fact, they were mixed. But if they were mixed, there was either some composing, or some "interweaving,"[16] or it was like a [20] form not separated from [body] or a form controlling [body] like the pilot [of a ship],[17] or one part of it was like this and another part was in some other way [related to the body].[18] I mean that one part is separated— the part that uses the body—and that one part is somehow mixed and itself belongs to the arrangement of that which is used. Thus philosophy would turn this part to the part that uses the body and divert [25] the part that uses the body, to the extent that its presence is not entirely necessary, from that part that it uses, so that it does not always use it.

§4. Let us suppose, then, that they have been mixed. But if they are mixed, the inferior element, the body, will be made better, and the superior element, the soul, will be made worse. The body will be made better by partaking in life and the soul will be made worse by partaking in death and nonrationality. But in what way [5] would that which has been deprived of life acquire the added power of sense-perception? On the contrary, this body, by receiving life, would be partaking in sense-perception and the states that arise from sense-perception. It is this, then, that will desire—for this is what will enjoy the objects of its desires—and fear for itself. For it is this that will not acquire the [10] pleasures and will be destroyed.

And we should investigate the manner of the mixture to see if it is in fact impossible, as it would be if someone said that a line was mixed with white, that is, one nature mixed with another of a different sort.[19] The concept of "interweaving"[20] does not imply that the things interwoven are affected in the same way. It is possible for that which is interwoven to be unaffected, that is, for the soul [15] to pass through and not experience the states of the body, just like light, especially if it is in this way woven through the whole. In this way, it will not experience the states of the body just because it is interwoven.[21]

---

[15] On the separation of soul from body by (the practice of) philosophy see Plato *Phd.* 67C–D.

[16] See Plato *Tim.* 36E2.

[17] See Aristotle *De An.* B 1, 413a9 where, however, Aristotle says "sailor."

[18] Plotinus is here alluding to the distinction of intellect and soul or the other parts of soul.

[19] See Aristotle *GC* 7, 323b25–7 for the analogy.

[20] See *supra* 3, 19.

[21] See Plato *Tim.* 36E.

But will it then be in the body in the way that a form is in matter?[22] If so, then first it will be like a form that is separate, supposing it is the essence [of the composite], and [20] even more so if it is that which uses the body. But if we assume it to be like the shape of an axe that is imposed on the iron, and the axe that is thus constituted will do what it does having been shaped in this way, according to its shape, we would in that case be even more inclined to attribute to the body such states that are common, that is, to this sort of body, to the "natural [25] instrumental body having life potentially."[23] For Aristotle says that it is absurd to say that "the soul is doing the weaving,"[24] so that it is also absurd to say that it has desires and is in pain. These belong rather to the living being.

§5. What we should say is that the living being is either a certain kind of body [living], or the sum [of body and soul], or some other third thing that arises from both of these.[25] But whatever is the case, either it is necessary to preserve the soul's unaffected state while it is the cause of something else being affected, or it must be affected [5] along with the body. And [in the latter case], it experiences either the identical state that the body does or a similar one— for example, if the living being has appetites in one way and the appetitive part of the soul acts or is affected in another. The body that is of this kind should be examined later.[26]

How, for example, is the composite able to feel pain?[27] Is it, then, because the body [10] is disposed in this way and the state penetrates up to sense-perception, which has its culmination in the soul? But it is not yet clear how sense-perception would do this. But whenever the pain has its origin in a belief or judgment of some evil being present either to oneself or to what belongs to him, is there then a painful change in the body [15] and, generally, in the entire living being?[28] But it is also not yet clear whether someone's belief is the belief of the soul or of the composite.

---

[22] See Aristotle *De An.* B1, 412b10–13.

[23] Ibid. 412a27–8, not an exact quotation.

[24] Ibid. A4, 408b12–13.

[25] The term τὸ κοινόν is usually used by Plotinus as equivalent to τὸ συναμφότερον (the composite) but here Plotinus seems to be making a distinction between the mere "sum" of body and soul and the product that arises from their being combined in some way.

[26] See *infra* §7.

[27] See Plato [?] *Alc.* I 130A9.

[28] See *SVF* III 459 for the Stoic view that Plotinus is considering.

Further, the belief about some evil does not include the state of pain. For it is possible that when the belief is present, the feeling of pain is completely absent; or, again, it is possible for the feeling of anger not to be present [20] when the belief that we have been slighted is present; or, again, for a belief about what is good not to move one's desire. How, then, are the states common [to body and soul]? In fact, it is the case that appetite belongs to the appetitive part of the soul, and spirit belongs to the spirited part of the soul, and, generally, the inclination towards something belongs to the desiring part of the soul.[29] In this way, though, they will no longer be common, but belong to the soul alone. Or else they belong to the [25] body as well, because it is necessary for blood and bile to boil and somehow for the body to be disposed to move desire, for example, in the direction of sexual objects.

Let us agree that the desire for that which is good is not a common state but belongs to the soul [alone], as is the case with others, and no account will attribute all of these to both. But the human being who has the appetite will be [30] the one having the desire for the sexual objects, though in another way it will be the appetitive part of the soul that has the appetite. How? Will the human being initiate the appetite and the appetitive part follow after? But in general, how could a human being have an appetite when the appetitive part has not been moved? In that case, it will be the appetitive part that is the starting point. But where will it start from if the body is not previously disposed in this way?

§6. Perhaps it is better to say generally that it is owing to the presence of the potentialities in the things that have them that they act according to them, while these potentialities are themselves immobile, providing to the things that have them the ability to act. But if this is the case, when the living being is being affected, the [5] cause that endows the composite with life is itself unaffected by the states and activities that belong to that which has these. But if this is so, living will in every way not belong to the soul, but to the composite.

In fact, the living of the composite will not be that of the soul. And the potentiality for sense-perception will [10] not perceive, but rather that which has the potentiality. But if sense-perception is a motion

---

[29] Plotinus here follows Aristotle in dividing "desire" into three: "appetitive," "spirited," and "wish." See Aristotle *De An.* B 3, 414b2. At *EN* A 13, 1102a27 ff. Aristotle distinguishes between two parts of soul: the part that reasons and the part that "obeys reason." But the tripartite division of the soul into appetitive, spirited, and calculative or deliberative is Plato's. See *Rep.* 435B9 ff. Plato does, however, attribute to the calculative part its own type of appetite. See 580D7–8.

through the body having its culmination in the soul,[30] how will the soul not perceive? In fact, when the potentiality for sense-perception is present, it is by its presence that the composite perceives what it perceives. But if the potentiality will [15] not be moved, how will the composite still perceive when neither the soul nor the psychic potentiality are counted together with it?

§7. In fact, assume that it is the composite that perceives, owing to the presence of the soul, which is not the sort of thing that can make itself an attribute of the composite or of the other part [the body] but can make from this type of body and from a sort of light, which it gives to the composite [along with its presence] another sort of thing, the nature of the [5] living being, to which sense-perception and other such states of the living being are said to belong.

But, then, how is it that *we* perceive? In fact, it is because we are not cut off from such a living being, even if other things more honorable than we are present in the whole essence of the human being, which is made of many parts. But the potentiality of soul for sense-perception should [10] not be for sense-perception of sensibles, but rather for the impressions that arise from sense-perception and are graspable by the living being. For these are already intelligible. So, sense-perception of externals is a reflection of this, but this is truer in essence, since it contemplates forms alone without being affected. From these [15] forms, from which the soul alone has already received its leadership over the living being, acts of discursive reasoning, beliefs, and acts of thinking occur. And this is especially where we are. The things that come before these are ours,[31] whereas we, directing the living being, are located from there [thinking] upward.

But there is nothing against calling the whole "living being," with the lower parts being mixed, [20] while the true human being begins about there [with thinking]. Those lower parts are the "lion-like" and, generally, the "multifaceted beast."[32] Given that the human being coincides with the rational soul, whenever human beings reason, it is we who are reasoning with the acts of reasoning that are psychic products.

§8. But how are we related to the Intellect? By "Intellect" I mean not that which the soul has when it is in the habitual condition derived from the Intellect, but the Intellect itself. In fact, not only do we have

---

[30] See Plato *Phil.* 34A; *Tim.* 43C; 45D.

[31] "Before" in time. Sense-perception precedes higher thought.

[32] See Plato *Rep.* 588C7; 590A9–B1. The "lion-like" part refers to the spirited part of the soul and the "multifaceted beast" to the appetitive part.

this, but also it transcends ourselves. But we have it either collectively or individually, or both collectively and individually. We have it collectively, [5] because it is indivisible and everywhere one and identical; we have it individually, because each one of us has the whole of it in the primary part of the soul.[33] We, then, have the Forms in two ways, in the soul in a way unfolded and separated, but in Intellect "all of them altogether."[34]

But how are we related to god [the first principle of all, the One]? In fact, he is "astride the intelligible nature,"[35] that is, over true [10] essence[36] whereas we [our souls] are in third place, being made, Plato says, from the "indivisible essence," which is above us, and from the "divisible essence found in bodies."[37] We should think of this as divided among bodies in the sense that it gives itself to bodily magnitudes in whatever amount is appropriate for each living being, since, being [15] one, it gives itself to the whole, or else because it is imagined to be present to bodies as shining on them and makes living beings not out of itself and body, but while remaining in itself, giving off reflections of itself, like a face in a multiplicity of mirrors.

The first reflection is sense-perception, which is in the composite. Next after this comes everything [20] <which is>[38] said to be another type of soul, each always coming from the other. It ends in the generative and vegetative souls or, generally, in what is productive and perfective of what is other than what productive soul makes, while the productive soul is directed to its own product.

§9. The nature of that soul of ours, then, will be freed from being the cause of the evils that a human being does and suffers. These belong to the living being, the composite, that is, composite in the manner stated.[39] But if belief and discursive thinking belong to the soul, how is it without error? [5] For belief can be false, and many evils are committed on the basis of false belief. In fact, evils are done when we are overcome by what is inferior to us—for we are complexes—by either appetite or spirit or an evil mental image. That which is said to be thinking of falsities is imagination that has not waited for the judgment of the

---

[33] See V 3. 3, 23–9.
[34] See Anaxagoras Fr. B 1 D–K.
[35] See Numenius Fr. 2 Des Places.
[36] See Plato *Soph.* 248A11.
[37] See Plato *Tim.* 35A1–3.
[38] Reading πᾶν <ὅ> ἄλλο with Igal.
[39] See I 1. 7, 1–6.

discursive reasoning faculty, but in that case [10] we acted by being persuaded by our inferiors; just as in the case of sense-perception, we seem to see falsely by our general faculty of sense-perception before the discursive faculty makes a judgment. The intellect has either been in contact with its object or not, so that it is without error.[40] In fact, we are, in this way, either in contact with the intelligible in Intellect or we are not. Actually, it is in contact with the intelligible in us. [15] For it is possible to have them [the intelligibles] but not to have them at hand.[41]

We have distinguished what belongs to the composite and what belongs uniquely to soul;[42] what belongs to the composite are the things that are bodily or do not exist without a body, whereas what does not need a body for its activity belongs uniquely to the soul. Discursive reasoning, when it makes a judgment on the impressions that come from sense-perception, is at that moment [20] contemplating forms, that is, contemplating them with a sort of awareness; this is, at any rate, primarily so for the discursive reasoning of the true soul. For true discursive reasoning is an activity of thinking, and there is often a similarity and association of things external and internal. Then the soul will be no less quiet and turned inward, that is, into itself. The changes and the [25] tumult in us coming from the things that are entangled with us, that is, from the states of the composite, whatever exactly that is, are as we have said.[43]

§10. But if we are the soul, and we experience these things, the soul would experience them and, again, it will do what we do. In fact, we said that the composite is a part of us, especially when we are not yet separated from it, since we say that what our body experiences [5] we experience. The term "we," then, is used in two ways, referring either to that which includes the beast or to that which is at the same time above this. The beast is the body that has been vivified. But the true human being is other, purified of these [bodily states] and possessing the virtues that are found in the activity of thinking that is situated in the separated soul, separate and separable [10] even when it is here below. For whenever it

---

[40] See Aristotle *De An.* Γ 6, 430a26–8; *Met.* Θ 10, 1051b17–33. The idea is that intellect only operates as such when it is grasping its objects. Then there is no possibility of its thinking falsely.

[41] See Plato *Tht.* 198D5–8, where the distinction is between "having" knowledge and "possessing" it by recovering from within what is known.

[42] See Aristotle *De An.* A 1, 403a4.

[43] See Plato *Phd.* 66D6 and *Tim.* 43B6, where the "tumult" is owing to our embodiment.

removes itself completely, the soul that receives its illumination goes away too, following after it.[44] But the virtues that do not belong to thought apply to the custom and training of the composite.[45] For the vices belong to this, since types of envy and jealousy and compassion are there. What do types of love belong to? In fact, some belong to [15] this, and some belong to the "interior human being."[46]

§11. When we are children, [the powers] of the composite are active. There is little illumination of it from the things above. Whenever they are inactive in us, they act in relation to that which is above. But they act in us whenever they enter the middle part. What then? Is not the "we" prior to this middle, too?[47] [5] Yes, but there has to be an apprehension of it. For we do not always use that which we have, but we only do so whenever we arrange the middle, either in relation to that which is above or in relation to its opposites or to such things as we actualize from potentiality or habit.

But how do beasts have life? In fact, if the souls in them are human, as it is said [by Plato],[48] [10] and have committed errors, the [separable part] of the soul does not belong to the beasts, but while it is present, it is not present to them. Rather, the awareness that belongs to the soul of each is a reflection that it has along with the body. Such a body has been in a way made by a reflection of soul. But if the soul of a human being has not entered it, it becomes the kind of living being it is owing to the illumination [15] coming from the soul of the universe.

§12. But if the soul is without error, how can there be punishments for it? For this line of reasoning is inconsistent with every one that says that it both errs and acts correctly and undergoes punishments, both in Hades and via reincarnation. One ought to associate oneself with whichever [5] line of reasoning one wishes. But perhaps we can discover a way in which they do not conflict.

The line of reasoning that attributes infallibility to the soul assumes that it is one and totally simple, claiming that the soul and essence of soul are identical. The one that attributes fallibility to it interweaves and

---

[44] That is, the lower types of soul referred to in 8, 18–23.

[45] See Plato *Rep.* 518E1–2.

[46] Ibid. 589A7–B1, the "man within the man."

[47] See I 1. 7, 9–18; IV 8. 8, 9–11; V 3. 3, 32–46. The "middle" refers to the powers of embodied cognition.

[48] See Plato *Phd.* 81E2–82b7; *Phdr.* 249B3–5; *Rep.* 618A3; 620A2–D5; *Tim.* 42C1–D8.

adds to it another form of soul having these terrible states.⁴⁹ [10] So, the soul is then composed of all these and is affected as a whole, and it is the composite that errs; and it is this which undergoes punishment, not the other.⁵⁰ Hence Plato says, "we have seen soul like those who have seen the sea-god Glaucus."⁵¹ [15] But if someone wants to see its nature, he says, he must "knock off the accretions"⁵² and look at "its philosophy" to see "that to which it adheres" and "owing to its affinity to what," is it the sort of thing it is.⁵³

There is, then, another life belonging to soul and other activities, and it is a different one that is punished. The withdrawal and separation is not only from this body, but also from everything that has been added to it. [20] For the addition is in the coming-to-be [in the body]. In fact, the coming-to-be is of another form of soul entirely. How the coming-to-be takes place has already been explained.⁵⁴ It is because of the soul's descent when something else arises from it owing to its inclination. Does it, then, abandon its reflection? And how is the inclination itself not an error? But if the [25] inclination is an illumination of what is below, it is not an error, just as casting a shadow is not an error; what is illuminated is responsible for the error. For if that did not exist, it would not have anything to illuminate.⁵⁵

To descend or to incline, then, means that that which is illuminated by it is so owing to its living with it. It then abandons its reflection if there is nothing near to receive it. But it abandons it [30] not by being cut off, but owing to the reflection no longer existing. And it no longer exists if the whole soul is looking to the intelligible world. The poet seems to be separating the reflection in the case of Heracles when he puts it in Hades, but Heracles among the gods.⁵⁶ Maintaining both stories, namely, that Heracles was among the gods and that he was in Hades, [35] the poet then divided him. Perhaps in this way the account would be plausible, because Heracles had practical virtue and was thought worthy of being a god owing to that excellence. But because his

---

⁴⁹ See Plato *Tim.* 69C7–D1.

⁵⁰ See Plato *Rep.* 611B5 for the description of the soul as a composite.

⁵¹ Ibid. 611C7–D1. Cf. *Gorg.* 523A1–6; *Phd.* 107D2–4.

⁵² Ibid. 611E1–612A4.

⁵³ Plotinus here, following Plato is not talking about a particular soul, but the nature of soul separated from human life.

⁵⁴ See IV 8.

⁵⁵ Plotinus is here talking about matter.

⁵⁶ See Homer *Od.* XI 601–2.

virtue was practical and not theoretical (in which case he would have been entirely in the intelligible world), he *is* above, though a part of him is also still below.

§13. That which has investigated these matters: is it we or the soul? In fact, it is we, but by means of the soul. How have we done this by means of the soul? Is it, then, by having that which was investigated [soul]? In fact, it is insofar as we are soul. Is it, then, in motion? In fact, we should attribute to it the sort of motion that is not bodily [5] but belongs to its life. And our thinking is like this because the soul is intellectual, and thinking is its better life, whenever soul thinks, that is, whenever intellect acts in us. For this is also a part of us, and it is to this that we ascend.

I 4 (46) On Happiness (§§ 1–4)

In the first four chapters of this treatise, Plotinus argues against Peripatetic and Epicurean conceptions of happiness. Plotinus concludes that the happiness of a person follows a determination of what a person is. Since a person is an intellect, not a composite of soul and body, the happiness of a person is found in intellectual activity. The achievement of this is to be preceded by the recognition of one's true identity.

§1. If we suppose that living well and being happy consist in the same thing, will we be endowing other living things with these, too?[1] For if it is natural for them to live their lives in an unimpeded fashion, what prevents us from saying that they also live well?[2] [5] One will suppose that living well is either being in a good state or completing the work appropriate to oneself, and in both cases, this will be the case for other living things;[3] for it would be possible to be in a good state or to complete one's work by nature, for example, musically disposed animals, who are otherwise in a good state, sing naturally, that is, [10] have a life that is in this respect selected by them.

If we suppose, then, that being happy is a certain goal,[4] that is, the ultimate goal of natural desire,[5] we would in that case be endowing with happiness those who achieve this, that is, those who arrive at their ulti-

---

[1] See Aristotle *EN* A 8, 1098b21; *SVF* III 17.
[2] Aristotle *EN* H 4, 1153b11.
[3] Ibid. B 5, 1106a23–4; K7, 1177a16–17.
[4] Ibid. K 6, 1176a31.

mate goal, their nature having traversed their entire life or [15] completed it from beginning to end. But if one disapproves of the act of extending happiness to other living things—for to do this is to endow with happiness even the basest living things,[6] and plants, too, since they are themselves alive, that is, they have a life that also unfolds to a goal— first, [20] why will it not seem absurd for him to be saying that other living beings do not live well because they do not seem to be worth much to *him*? One would, however, not be forced to give to plants that which one gives to living beings in general, because they have no sense-perception.[7]

But there is perhaps someone who would include plants just because they are alive. There is [on this view] life that is good and life that is [25] the opposite, which in the case of plants is being in a good state or not, for example, bearing fruit or not bearing fruit. Then, if pleasure is the goal and living well consists in this,[8] it is absurd for someone to deny that other living things live well. The same applies to freedom from disturbance.[9] And it applies to living according to nature if one were to say that this is living well.[10]

§2. Those who do not include plants because they do not have sense-perception will by that then risk not including all living beings,[11] for if they say that [actual] sense-perception is this—the state of being aware— then it is necessary for the state to be good prior to [5] being aware.[12] For example, being in a natural state is good even if one is not aware of being in that state, and similarly, being in one's proper state, even if one is not yet aware that it is proper and that it is pleasurable, for it should be pleasurable. So if the state is good and it is present, that which has it is at once living well. So why should we add sense-perception [the state of being aware]?

We should not, unless in response they attribute good not to a state or [10] condition that has come to be, but to the awareness, or sense-

---

[5] See SVF III 3; 65.

[6] See Sextus Empiricus M XI 97, where this objection is raised against the Epicureans.

[7] See Aristotle EN A 6, 1097b33–1098a2.

[8] Probably, given the above, a reference to the Epicurean view.

[9] See D. L. X 128, quoted from Epicurus' *Ep. to Menoeceus*.

[10] A reference to the Stoic position. See SVF I 183; III 16.

[11] See Aristotle EN K 9, 1178b28.

[12] See Plato *Phil.* 33D8–9.

perception, of this.[13] But if they say this, they will be saying that it is the sense-perception itself that is good, that is, the actuality of the perceptual life regardless of what things are apprehended. But if they attribute good to the combination of both, so that it is the sense-perception of a certain type of object, [15] how can they say that the combination is good when each member of the combination is neutral?[14] But if it is the state that is good, and living well is the condition where someone is aware that that which is good is present to him, we ought to ask them if such a one lives well just by being aware that this is present to him, or if he should also be aware not only that it is pleasurable but also that it is good, too.

But if he must be aware that it is [20] good, living well is at once no longer the function of sense-perception but of an ability different from and greater than sense-perception. Then living well will not belong to those who are experiencing pleasure, but to one who has the ability to recognize that the good is pleasure. But, then, the cause of living well will not be pleasure, but being able to discern that pleasure is good. And [25] that which does the discerning is better than that which is in the state, for it is reason or intellect. But pleasure is a state, and nowhere is the nonrational superior to reason.

How, then, will reason, segregating itself, suppose something else located in a contrary genus to be superior to it? Actually, it seems that those who deny that plants live well and those who claim that living well consists in a certain type of awareness [30] conceal from themselves the fact that they are seeking living well in something greater and that they are supposing the better life to consist in a more transparent life.[15]

Those who say that living well exists in the rational life, not simply in life, nor even perceptual life, would perhaps be correct.[16] But it is appropriate [35] to ask them why they thus place happiness only in the rational living being: "Do you add the qualification 'rational' because reason is more efficient and is able easily to discover and procure the basic natural needs, or [would you still insist on this qualification] even if it were not able to discover or procure these? But if you say this be-

---

[13] The word αἴσθησις covers both sensations (of which we might not be aware) and perception or awareness that a sensation is occurring.

[14] See SVF III 122 on "things indifferent" or "neutral."

[15] See VI 7. 5, 27.

[16] See SVF III 687. Diogenes Laertius says here that, according to the Stoics, "the rational life" is the basis for "the contemplative life" as well as "the practical life."

cause reason is better able [than anything else] to discover these, happiness will belong even to living beings [40] without reason provided they are able to acquire the basic natural needs. And then reason would become subordinate and would not be choiceworthy in itself, nor in turn would its perfection, which we call 'virtue.'[17]

"But if you say that reason is more honorable not because it is better at getting the basic natural needs, but because it is desirable in itself, [45] you should say what other function it has and what its nature is and what makes it perfect, for it should not be theorizing about these basic natural needs that makes it perfect but something else that is of another nature that makes it perfect and is itself not one of these basic natural needs nor from the source from which these basic [50] natural needs arise nor generally of this kind, but better than all these." Otherwise, I do not see how they will account for its being honorable. But until they find a better nature than that at which they are now arrested, let them remain at this level, where they wish to remain, being at a loss to say [55] how living well belongs to those capable of acquiring this from these [basic natural needs].[18]

§3. Let us state from the beginning what we suppose happiness to be. Having supposed that happiness is something that is found in life,[19] if we made "living" mean the same thing in all cases, we would be claiming that all living things are receptive of happiness and that those who are [5] actually living well are those in whom is present one and the same thing, which all living beings are receptive of by nature. In doing this, we would not be endowing rational beings with the ability to live well and denying it to nonrational beings, for life was assumed to be something common to both and something which, by being receptive of the same thing, was intended to be capable of achieving happiness, if, that is, happiness was to exist in some kind of life.

Hence [10] I think that those who say that happiness arises [only] in a rational life, by not supposing that it is found in life in general, are unaware that they are presuming it not to be life. They would be forced to say that the rational capacity upon which happiness is built is a quality of life. But that which they hypothesized was rational [15] life [not rationality], for it is on the whole [rationality plus life] that happiness is built, so that it is actually built on a particular form of life and not just on life. I mean this not in the sense of a distinction of reason [within a

---

[17] See Aristotle *Phys.* H 2, 247a2.
[18] See V 9. 1, 10–16.
[19] See Aristotle *Met.* Θ 8, 1050b1–2.

genus] but in the sense in which we [Platonists] speak of one thing being prior and another being posterior.[20]

The term "life" is, then, spoken of in many ways, differentiated according to the primary way, the secondary way, and [20] so on in order. The term "living" is said homonymously, that is, it is said in one way of a plant and in another of a nonrational animal, according to the clarity and dimness of the lives they have. And it is clear that "living well" is said analogously. And if one sense of the term "living" is a reflection of another, it is also clear that one sense of "living well" is a reflection of another.

If, then, happiness belongs to something living fully—[25] meaning to something that is in no way deficient in life—it will belong only to one living fully, for the best will belong to this, if that which is really best in life, that is, the perfect life, is among the things that are real; for in this way, the goodness that exists [in happiness] would not be something superadded nor will something else from somewhere else [30] provide the basis for its being good, for what, added to a perfect life, would turn it into the best life? But if someone will say that what does this is the nature of the Good, that is our own approach, whereas now we are not seeking the cause [of goodness] but that in which it exists.

It has been said many times that the perfect life and the true and real life is in that intellectual nature [35] and that the others are imperfect and reflections of life and not existing perfectly nor purely and no more lives than the opposite.[21] And now let it be said summarily that so long as all living beings are from one source and they do not have life in the same way that it does, it is necessary that the source is the primary life and the [40] most perfect life.

§4. If, then, it is possible for a human being to have the perfect life, a human being who has this life is happy. If not, one would suppose happiness to be found among the gods, if such a life is found among them alone. But since we are now saying that this happiness is found [5] among human beings, we should examine how this is so.

What I mean is this: It is clear also from other considerations that the fact that a human being has a perfect life does not mean that he only has a perceptual life, but rather that he has a reasoning capacity or a genuine intellect as well. But is it therefore the case that he is one thing and his

---

[20] See Aristotle *Cat.* 13, 14b33–15a1. In a Platonic scheme, "life" is logically and ontologically prior to "rational life."

[21] See VI 6. 18; VI 7. 15 and Plato *Soph.* 248E6–249A1, where Plato is interpreted here as holding that life exists within intelligible reality.

having this, another? In fact, he is not a human being at all if he has [10] this neither in potency nor in actuality, where we locate happiness.

But will we say that he has this perfect form of life in himself as a part of himself? In fact, one who has it in potency has it as a part, whereas the one who is at once happy is the one who is this actually and [15] has transformed himself in the direction of being identical with this.[22] Everything else is something he is carrying around at the same time, which no one would suppose to be a part of him, since he does not want to carry these things around. They would be parts of him if they were connected to him according to his will.

What, then, is the good for this human being? In fact, he is, for himself, what he has. And the transcendent cause of goodness in him [the Good], which is [20] good in one way, is present to him in another. Evidence for the fact that this is so is that one who is like this does not seek to be anything else. What else would he seek? It would, of course, not be something worse, and the best is already with him. The life of one living in this way, then, is self-sufficient.[23] And if he is virtuous, he has what he needs in order to be happy and to possess [25] good, for there is no good that he does not have.

What he seeks he seeks as something necessary and not for himself but for some one of the things that belong to him, for he is seeking something for the body that is attached to him. And even if that body is alive, and what belongs to it belongs to this living being [the body], it does not belong to a human being of this sort. He knows these things [what the body needs] and gives what he gives to it [30] without taking anything away from his own life. His happiness, then, will not be diminished by adverse fortune, for this sort of life remains as it is. And when relatives and friends are dying, he knows what death is, as do those dying, if they are virtuous. Even if the dying of relatives and close ones [35] causes grief, it does not grieve him, but only that in him which is apart from intellect, that whose pains he will not experience.

---

[22] That is, the human being is happy when he identifies himself exclusively as the agent of the best human activity.

[23] See Aristotle *EN* K 6, 1176b5–6.

I 6 (1) On Beauty (complete)

This is presumably the first treatise Plotinus composed. The work is primarily concerned with exploring the moral dimension of beauty. Plotinus argues that the recognition that beauty is to be found in form should lead to an affective attachment to the source of all form, the intelligible realm of intellect. Attainment of the beautiful proceeds by assimilating oneself to the object of intelligible desire.

§1. Beauty is found for the most part in what is seen, but it is also found in sounds, when these are composed into words, and in all the arts generally.[1] For songs and rhythms are also beautiful. And beauty is also found by those who turn away from sense-perception towards the higher region; that is, practices,[2] [5] actions, habits, and types of knowledge are beautiful, to say nothing of the beauty of the virtues.[3] If there is some beauty prior to these, this discussion will show it.

What, then, is it that has made us imagine bodies to be beautiful and our sense of hearing incline to sounds, finding them beautiful? And as for the things that depend directly on the soul, how are all of these beautiful? Is it because all of them are beautiful by [10] one and the same beauty, or is it that there is one sort of beauty in the body and another in other things? And what, then, are these sorts of beauty, or what is this beauty?

For some things, such as bodies, are not beautiful owing to what they are in themselves, but rather by participation, whereas some things are beautiful in themselves, such as the nature that virtue is. This is so because bodies themselves sometimes appear beautiful and sometimes [15] do not[4] since the body and the beauty are distinct. What is it, then, that is present in the bodies [that makes them beautiful]? It is this that we must examine first. What is it, then, that moves the eyes of spectators

---

[1] Literally, in all that is governed by the Muses, including poetry, literature, music, and dance. Later, these also included philosophy, astronomy, and intellectual practices generally.

[2] Moral practices that lead to the acquisition of virtue are meant here. See Plato *Rep.* 444E; *Lg.* 793D.

[3] See Plato *H. Ma.* 287E–298B; *Symp.* 210C. Plotinus does not follow exactly Plato's hierarchy of types of beauty here. The central point is the superiority of intellectual to physical beauty.

[4] See Plato *Symp.* 211A3.

and turns them[5] towards it and draws them on and makes them rejoice at the sight? By finding this and using it as a [20] stepping-stone,[6] we might also be in a position to see the rest.

Practically everyone claims that proportion of parts in relation to each other and to the whole added to fine coloration makes something beautiful to see.[7] And, generally, in regard to the objects of sight and all other things, their beauty consists in their proportion [25] or measure. For those who hold this view, no simple thing will be beautiful; necessarily, beauty will exist only in the composite. The whole will be beautiful for them, while each of the parts will not have its own beauty but will be a contributing factor in making the whole beautiful. But it should be the case that if the whole is beautiful, the parts are also beautiful. For beauty is not made up out of ugly things; all of its parts are beautiful.

[30] For these people, the beauty of colors, for example, and the light of the sun, since they are simple, do not have proportion and so will be excluded from being beautiful. But, then, how is gold beautiful? And how about lightning in the night and the stars, which are beautiful to see? And as for the beauty of sounds, [35] the simple ones will be eliminated for the same reason, although it is frequently the case that in the beauty of a whole [composition], each sound is itself beautiful. Further, when a face sometimes appears beautiful and sometimes not, though the proportion remains the same, would we not have to say that beauty is other than the proportion and [40] that the proportion is beautiful because of something other than itself?

If they pass on to beautiful practices and expressions and attribute their beauty to proportion, what does it mean to say that there is proportion in beautiful practices or laws or studies or types of knowledge?[8] For how could theories be proportional to [45] each other? If it is because they are in harmony, it is also the case that there is agreement and harmony among bad theories. For example, to say that "self-control is stupidity" and "justice is silly nobility" is to say two things that are harmonious, or in concord, or agree with each other.[9]

---

[5] The word ἐπιστρέφει, a central term in Plotinus' philosophy and in Neoplatonism generally, indicates a reorienting of the soul in the direction of the One, away from other objects of desire. See I 2. 4, 16; II 4. 5, 34;V 2. 1, 10.

[6] See Plato *Symp.* 211C3.

[7] This is the Stoic view. See *SVF* III 278; 472.

[8] See Plato *Symp.* 210C3–7; 211C6.

[9] See Plato *Rep.* 348C11–12; 560D2–3.

And then every type of virtue is a beauty in the soul and a beauty that is [50] truer than the previous ones. But how are these proportioned? It is not as magnitudes or numbers[10] that they are proportioned. And since there are several parts of the soul, what is the formula for the combination or the mixture of the parts or of the theories? And what would be the beauty of intellect taking it in isolation?[11]

§2. Taking up the matter again, let us say what, then, is the primary beauty in bodies. There is, of course, something that is perceived at first glance, and the soul speaks about it as it does about that with which it is familiar, and takes it in as something that it recognizes and, in a way, it finds itself in concord with it. [5] But when it encounters the ugly, it holds back and rejects it and recoils from it as something with which it is not in harmony and as something that is alien to it.[12] We say, then, that the soul, having the nature it does and turned in the direction of the greater essence in the realm of true reality, when it sees something to which it has an affinity[13] or something that is a trace of that to which it has an affinity, is both delighted and thrilled and [10] returns to itself and recalls itself and what belongs to itself.

What likeness is there, then, between the things here in relation to the things that are beautiful in the intelligible world? For if there is a likeness, then we assume that there are like things. How, then, are things here and there both beautiful? We say that these are beautiful by participation in Form. For everything that is shapeless but is by nature capable of receiving shape or form is, having no share [15] in an expressed principle or form, ugly and stands outside of divine reason. This is complete ugliness.

But something is also ugly if it has not been mastered by shape and an expressed principle owing to the fact that its matter has not allowed itself to be shaped completely according to form.[14] The form, then, approaches [the matter] and orders that which is to be a single composite from many parts, and guides it [20] into being a completed unity and makes it one by the parts' acceptance of this; and since the form is one,

---

[10] Magnitude and number are the two species of quantity. Hence Plotinus is implying that if beauty is a type of proportion, it is not a proportion of quantities.

[11] That is, intellect, which is distinct from the soul. See e.g., Aristotle *De An.* Γ 4, 429b5.

[12] See Plato *Symp.* 206D6.

[13] On the affinity of the soul to intelligible reality, see Plato *Phd.* 79D3; *Rep.* 611E2; *Tim.* 90A5–7.

[14] See Aristotle *GC* Δ 3, 769b12; Δ 4, 770b16–17.

that which is shaped had to be one, to the extent possible for that which is composed of many parts.

Beauty is, then, situated over that which is shaped at the moment when, the parts having been arranged into one whole, it gives itself to the parts and to the wholes. Whenever beauty takes hold of something that is one and uniform in its parts, [25] it gives the same thing to the whole. It is, in a way, like art, that sometimes gives beauty to a whole house along with its parts and sometimes like some nature that gives beauty to a single stone. Thus, a body comes to be beautiful by its association with an expressed principle coming from the divine [Forms].

§3. The power [in the soul][15] corresponding to beauty recognizes it, and there is nothing more authoritative in judging its own concerns, especially when the rest of the soul judges along with it. Perhaps the rest of the soul also expresses itself by bringing into concord the beautiful object with the form inside itself, using that for judgment like [5] a ruler used to judge the straightness of something.[16]

But how does the beauty in the body harmonize with that which is prior to body? How can the architect, harmonizing the external house with the form of the house internal to him, claim that the former is beautiful? In fact, it is because the external house is, apart from the stones, the inner form divided by the external mass of matter. Being in fact undivided, it appears divided into many parts. Then, [10] whenever sense-perception sees the form in the bodies binding together and mastering the contrary nature, which is shapeless—that is, whenever it sees an overarching shape on top of other shapes—it gathers together as one that which was in many places and brings it back and collects it into the soul's interior as something without parts and at that moment gives it to the interior [judging power of the soul] as something having the harmony and [15] concord that is dear to it. This is just as when a good man sees in the fresh face of a youth a trace of the virtue that is in harmony with the truth that is inside himself.

The simple beauty of a color resides in shape and in the mastery of the darkness in matter by the presence of incorporeal light[17] and of an expressed principle and a form. This is the reason why fire itself, among all the other bodies, [20] is beautiful: it has the role of form in relation to the other elements, highest in position, finest of the other bodies, being as close as possible to the incorporeal, and alone is not receptive

---

[15] Plotinus here means the "calculative" or "rational" part of the entire soul.
[16] See I 8. 9, 3; V 3. 4, 16.
[17] On light as incorporeal, see IV 5. 6 and 7.

of the other [elements], though the others receive it. For it heats them, but is itself not cooled, and is primarily colored, [25] whereas the others get the form of color from it. So it shines and glows as if it were form. That [color] which fades in a fire's light, unable to master [the matter], is no longer beautiful, since it does not partake of the whole form of the color. As for the imperceptible harmonies in sounds that make the perceptible ones, they make the soul [30] grasp them so as to have comprehension of beauty in the same way, showing the same thing in another way.

It is logical that perceptible harmonies be measured by numbers, though not by every formula but only by one that serves in the production of form for the purpose of mastering. And so regarding perceptible beauties, which are reflections and shadows that come to matter as if they were making a dash there to beautify it and thrill us when they appear, enough said.

§4. Regarding the more elevated beauties that sense-perception is not fated to see, soul sees them and speaks about them without the instruments of sense-perception, but it has to ascend to contemplate them, leaving sense-perception down below. But just as in the case of the beauties perceived by the senses, [5] it is not possible to speak about them to those who have not seen them or to those who have never grasped them for what they are, for example, those who have been blind since birth; in the same way, it is not possible to speak about the beauty of practices to those who have not accepted their beauty nor that of types of knowledge and other such things. Nor can one speak about the "splendor"[18] of virtue [10] to those who have not even imagined for themselves the beauty of the visage of justice and self-control, "not even the evening nor the morning star are so beautiful."[19]

But such a sight must be reserved for those who see it with that in the soul by which it sees such things, and seeing it are delighted and shocked and overwhelmed much more than in the previous cases, since we are now speaking of [15] those who have already got hold of true beauties.[20] For these are the emotions one should experience in regard to that which is [truly] beautiful: astonishment, and a sweet shock, and longing, and erotic thrill, and a feeling of being overwhelmed with

---

[18] See Plato *Phdr.* 250B3.

[19] See Aristotle *EN* E 3, 1129b28–9 quoting Euripides *Melanippe* Fr. 486 Nauck$_2$. See also VI 6. 6, 37–42.

[20] See VI 7. 36, 4; 39, 19; VI 9. 4, 27. The metaphor of direct contact with intelligibles has roots in both Plato and Aristotle. See *Phd.* 65B9; *Rep.* 572A8; 600C6; 608A7 and *Met.* Θ 10, 1051b24–5; Λ 7, 1072b20–1.

pleasure. It is possible to have these emotions, and practically all souls do have them in regard to all the unseen beauties, so to say, but in particular those souls who are more enamored of these. [20] It is the same with regard to the [beautiful] bodies that all can see, though not everyone is "stung"[21] equally by their beauty. Those who are stung especially are those who are called "lovers."

§5. We should next ask those who are enamored of the beauties not available to the senses: "What is it you experience in regard to the practices said to be beautiful and to beautiful ways of being in the world and to self-controlled characters and, generally, to the products of virtue and dispositions, I mean the beauty of souls?"[22] [5] And "When you see your own 'interior beauty,'[23] what do you feel?" And "Can you describe the frenzied[24] and excited state you are in and your longing to be with your [true] selves, when extricating yourselves from your bodies?" For this is how those who are truly enamored feel.

But what is it that makes them feel this way? It is not shapes or colors [10] or some magnitude, but rather they feel this way about soul, it being itself "without color"[25] and having self-control that is also without color and the rest of the "splendor"[26] of virtues. You feel this way whenever you see in yourselves or someone else greatness of soul or a just character or sheer self-control or the awe-inspiring visage of courage[27] or [15] dignity and reserve circling around a calm and untroubled disposition with divine intellect shining on them all.

So, we love and are attracted to these qualities, but what do we mean when we say that they are beautiful? For they are real and appear to us so, and no one who has ever seen them says anything else but that they are really real. What does [20] "really real" mean? In fact, it means that they are beautiful things. But the argument still needs to show why real things have made the soul that of which they are enamored. What is that striking thing shining on all the virtues like a light?

Would you like to consider the opposites, the ugly things that come to be in the soul, and contrast them with the beauties? For perhaps a consideration of what ugliness is and [25] why it appears as such would

---

[21] See Plato *Phdr.* 251D5.
[22] See Plato *Symp.* 210B–C.
[23] See Plato *Phdr.* 279B9.
[24] See VI 7. 22, 7–10; Plato *Phd.* 69D1.
[25] See Plato *Phdr.* 247C6.
[26] Ibid. 250B3.
[27] See Homer *Il.* VII 212.

contribute to our achieving what we are seeking. Well, then, let there be an ugly soul,[28] one that is unrestrained and unjust, filled with all manner of appetites and every type of dread, mired in fear owing to cowardice and envy owing to pettiness, thinking that everything it can think of is mortal and base, deformed in every way, a lover of impure pleasures, [30] that is, one who lives a life in which bodily pleasures are measured by their vileness.

Shall we not say, therefore, that this very vileness supervenes on his soul just as would a beauty added to it, which both harmed it and made it impure, "mixed with much evil"[29] no longer having a life or perceptions that are pure, [35] but rather living a murky life by an evil adulteration that includes much death in it, no longer seeing what a soul should see, no longer even being allowed to remain in itself owing to its always being dragged to the exterior and downward into darkness?[30]

This is what I regard as an impure soul, [40] dragged in every direction by its chains towards whatever it happens to perceive with its senses, with much of what belongs to the body adulterating it, deeply implicating itself with the material element and, taking that element into itself owing to that adulteration that only makes it worse, it exchanges the form it has for another. It is as if someone fell into mud or slime and the beauty he had is no longer evident, [45] whereas what is seen is what he wiped on himself from the mud or slime. But the ugliness that has been added to him has come from an alien source, and his job, if he is again to be beautiful, is to wash it off and to be clean[31] as he was before.

So we would be speaking correctly in saying that the soul becomes ugly by a mixture or adulteration and by an inclination in the direction of the body and matter. [50] And this is ugliness for a soul: not being pure or uncorrupted like gold, but filled up with the earthly which, were someone to remove that from it, would just be gold and would be beautiful, isolated from other things and being just what it is itself. In the same way, the soul — being isolated from appetites, [55] which it acquires because of that body with which it associates too much — when it is separated from other affections and is purified of what it has that is

---

[28] See Plato *Gorg.* 524E7–525A6 for a similar description of the ugly soul.
[29] See Plato *Phd.* 66B5.
[30] Ibid. 79C2–8.
[31] The word καθηραμένῳ indicates both physical cleanliness and moral or spiritual purity.

bodily, remains just what it is when it has put aside all the ugliness that comes from that other nature.

§6. For it is the case, as the ancient doctrine[32] has it, that self-control and courage and, indeed, every virtue is a purification and is wisdom itself. For this reason, the mysteries correctly offer the enigmatic saying that one who has not been purified will lie in Hades in slime, [5] because one who is not pure likes slime owing to his wickedness. They are like pigs that, with unclean bodies, like such things.[33]

What would true self-control be, besides not having anything to do with the pleasures of the body and fleeing them as impure, as not belonging to one who is pure? And what is courage but the absence of fear of death? But death is the separation [10] of the soul from the body.[34] And this is not feared by one who loves to be isolated.[35] And greatness of soul[36] is contempt for the things here below. And wisdom is the process of thought consisting in a turning away from the things below, leading the soul to the things above.

The soul, then, when it is purified, becomes a form, and an expressed principle, and entirely incorporeal and intellectual and wholly [15] divine, which is the source of beauty and of all things that have an affinity to it. Soul then, being borne up to Intellect, becomes even more beautiful. And Intellect and the things that come from Intellect are soul's beauty, since they belong to it, that is, they are not alien to it, because it is then really soul alone.[37] For this reason, it is correctly said that goodness and being beautiful for the soul consist in [20] "being assimilated to god"[38] because it is there that beauty is found as well as the rest of the destiny of real beings. Or rather, true being is beauty personified[39] and ugliness is the other nature, primary evil itself, so that for god,

---

[32] See Plato *Phd.* 69C1–6.
[33] See Heraclitus Fr. B. 13 D–K; Sextus Empiricus *PH* I 56.
[34] See Plato *Phd.* 64C5–7.
[35] That is, from whatever is alien to him.
[36] See Aristotle *EN* B 7, 1107b22; Δ 7, 1123a34–b4.
[37] That is, when soul rises to Intellect, it realizes its true self.
[38] See Plato *Rep.* 613B1; *Tht.* 176B1; *Lg.* 716C6–D4.
[39] The word used here is ἡ καλλονή instead of τὸ καλόν. See Plato *Symp.* 206D2 for the personification of beauty. Plotinus is using the term here to refer to the One, or the Good, the source of all intelligible beauty or goodness. So in a way, since the One is beyond all intelligible reality, the essence of beauty is beyond beauty.

"good," and "beautiful" are the same, or rather goodness and beauty are the same.[40]

In a similar way, then, we should seek out what is beautiful and [25] good and ugly and evil. And first we should posit Beauty,[41] which is the Good from which Intellect comes, which is identical with the Form of Beauty. And soul is beautiful by Intellect. Other things are beautiful as soon as they are shaped by soul, including the beauties in actions and in practices. And the bodies that are said to be beautiful are so as soon as [30] soul makes them so. Since it is divine and, in a way, a part of beauty, it makes all that it grasps and masters beautiful insofar as it is possible for them to partake in beauty.

§7. We must, then, ascend to the Good, which every soul desires.[42] If someone then has seen it, he knows[43] what I mean when I say how beautiful it is. For it is desired as good,[44] and the desire is for this, though the attainment of it is for those who ascend upward and [5] revert to it and who divest themselves of the garments they put on when they descended. It is just like those who ascend to the sacred religious rites where there are acts of purification and the removal of the cloaks they had worn before they went inside naked.[45] One proceeds in the ascent, passing by all that is alien to the god until one sees by oneself alone that which is itself alone uncorrupted, simple, [10] and pure,[46] that upon which everything depends[47] and towards which one looks and is and lives and thinks.[48] For it is the cause of life and intellect and

---

[40] That is, for Intellect, but also for the One or the Good itself.

[41] See n. 39.

[42] See Plato *Rep.* 517B4–5 on the ascent from the cave to the intelligible world and *Symp.* 210A–211C on the ascent of the soul to Beauty in the higher mysteries of love.

[43] Plotinus here is playing on the similarity of the words for "see" (εἶδεν) and for "know" (οἶδεν).

[44] See VI 8. 7, 3–4.

[45] See Plato *Gorg.* 523C–E.

[46] See Plato *Symp.* 211E1.

[47] See V 5. 3, 6; VI 4. 14, 16; VI 8. 7, 8; VI 8. 18, 7; Aristotle *Ca.* A 9, 279a28–30; *Met.* Λ 7, 1072b14 on the dependence of everything else, on a first principle. It is only when one strips off in oneself all that is other than intellect and uses the "eye" of intellect alone that one sees one's dependence on the One.

[48] To say that one "is and lives and thinks" *in relation* to the Good or the One is to indicate that these activities depend on the One.

being.[49] And then if someone see this, what pangs of love will he feel, what longings and, wanting to be united with it, how would he <not> be overcome with pleasure?[50]

For though it is possible for one who has not yet seen it [15] to desire it as good, for one who has seen it, there is amazement and delight in beauty, and he is filled with pleasure and he undergoes a painless shock, loving with true love and piercing longing. And he laughs at other loves and is disdainful of the things he previously regarded as beautiful. It is like the experience of those who have happened upon apparitions of gods [20] or daemons after which they can no longer look at the beauty of other bodies in the same way.

What, then, should we think if someone sees pure beauty itself by itself, not contaminated by flesh or bodies, not on the earth or in heaven, in order that it may remain pure?[51] For all these things are added on and have been mixed in and are [25] not primary; rather, they come from that [the Good]. If, then, one sees that which orchestrates[52] everything, remaining by itself while it gives everything, though it does not receive anything into itself, if he remains in sight of this and enjoys it by making himself like it, what other beauty would he need? For this, since it is itself supremely beautiful and the primary beauty, makes [30] its lovers beautiful and lovable.

And with the Good as the prize, the greatest and "ultimate battle is set before souls,"[53] in which battle our entire effort is directed to not being deprived of the most worthy vision. And the one who attains this is "blessed,"[54] since he is seeing a blessed sight, whereas the one who does not is without luck. It is not the one who does not attain beautiful colors or bodies [35] or power or ruling positions or a kingship who is without luck, but the one who does not attain this and this alone. For the sake of this he ought to cede the attainment of kingship and ruling positions over the whole earth, sea, and heaven, if by abandoning these things and ignoring them he could revert to the Good and see it.

---

[49] See III 8. 8; V 3. 5; V 5. 1; V 9. 10; VI 7. 8 on the three aspects of Intellect: being, life, and thinking.

[50] Reading ἂν <οὐκ> ἐκπλαγείη with the *addenda ad textum* of H-S$_2$. See VI 7. 27, 24–8.

[51] See Plato *Symp.* 211A8; 211D8–E2.

[52] See VI 9. 8, 35–45.

[53] See Plato *Phdr.* 247B5–6.

[54] Ibid. 250B6.

§8. How, then, can we do this? What technique should we employ? How can one see the "inconceivable beauty"[55] as it remains within the sacred temple, not venturing outside, lest the uninitiated should see it? Let he who is able go and follow inside leaving outside the sight of his [5] eyes, not allowing himself to turn back to the splendor of the bodies he previously saw. When he does see beautiful bodies, he should not run after them, but realizing that they are images and traces and shadows, he should flee them in the direction of that of which these are images.[56] For if someone runs towards the image, wanting to grasp it as something true like one wanting to grasp [10] a beautiful reflection in water (as some story has it, in a riddling way, I think) and falls into the water and disappears, in the same way, the one holding on to beautiful bodies and not letting them go plunges down, not with his body but with his soul, into the depths, where there is no joy for intellect and where he stays, [15] blind in Hades, spending time with shadows everywhere he turns.

Someone would be better advised to say "Let us flee to our beloved fatherland."[57] But what is this flight, and how is it accomplished? Let us set sail in the way Homer, in a riddling way, I think, tells us Odysseus did from the sorceress Circe or from Calypso. Odysseus was not satisfied to remain there, even though he had [20] visual pleasures and passed his time with sensual beauty. Our fatherland, from where we have come, and our father are both in the intelligible world.[58]

What is our course, and what is our means of flight? We should not rely on our feet to get us there, for our feet just take us everywhere on earth, one place after another. Nor should you saddle up a horse or prepare some sea-going vessel. You should put aside [25] all such things and stop looking; just shut your eyes, and change your way of looking, and wake up. Everyone has this ability, but few use it.

§9. What, then, is that inner way of looking? Having just awakened, the soul is not yet able to look at the bright objects before it.[59] The soul must first be accustomed to look at beautiful practices, then beautiful works—not those works that the arts produce, but those that [5] men who are called "good" produce— then to look at the soul of those who produce these beautiful works.[60]

---

[55] See Plato *Rep.* 509A6; *Symp.* 218E2.
[56] See Plato *Tht.* 176B1 on the image of "flight" from this world.
[57] See Homer *Il.* II 140.
[58] See V 1. 1, 1; V 8. 1, 3. "Father" variously refers to the One and to Intellect.
[59] See Plato *Rep.* 515E–516A.
[60] See Plato *Symp.* 210B–C.

How, then, can you see the kind of beauty that a good soul has? Go back into yourself and look. If you do not yet see yourself as beautiful, then be like a sculptor, making a statue that is supposed to be beautiful, who removes a part here and polishes a part there so that he makes the latter smooth [10] and the former just right until has given the statue a beautiful face. In the same way, you should remove superfluities and straighten things that are crooked, work on the things that are dark, making them bright, and not stop "working on your statue"[61] until the divine splendor of virtue shines in you, until you see [15] "self-control enthroned on the holy seat."[62]

If you have become this and have seen it and find yourself in a purified state, you have no impediment to becoming one in this way[63] nor do you have something else mixed in with yourself, but you are entirely yourself, true light alone, neither measured by magnitude nor reduced by a circumscribing shape [20] nor expanded indefinitely in magnitude but being unmeasured everywhere, as something greater than every measure and better than every quantity. If you see that you have become this, at that moment you have become sight, and you can be confident about yourself, and you have at this moment ascended here, no longer in need of someone to show you. Just open your eyes and see, [25] for this alone is the eye that sees the great beauty.

But if the eye approaches that sight bleary with evils and not having been purified or weak and, owing to cowardice, is not able to see all the bright objects, it does not see them even if someone else shows it that they are present and able to be seen. For the one who sees has an affinity to that which is seen, and he must [30] make himself like it if he is to attain the sight. For no eye has ever seen the sun without becoming sunlike,[64] nor could a soul ever see beauty without becoming beautiful. You must become wholly godlike and wholly beautiful if you intend to see god and beauty.

For first, the soul will come in its ascent to Intellect, and [35] in the intelligible world it will see all the beautiful Forms and will declare that these Ideas are what beauty is.[65] For all things are beautiful, owing to

---

[61] See Plato *Phdr.* 252D7.
[62] Ibid. 254B7.
[63] See Plato *Rep.* 443E1.
[64] Ibid. 508B3; 509A1.
[65] The words here, "Forms" (τὰ εἴδη) and "Ideas" (τὰ ἰδεαί), are used by Plotinus synonymously.

these by the products of Intellect, that is, by essence.[66] But we say that that which "transcends"[67] Intellect is the Idea of the Good, a nature that holds beauty in front of itself. So roughly speaking, the Good is the primary [40] beauty. But if one distinguishes the intelligibles apart, one will say that the "place" of the Forms[68] is intelligible beauty, whereas the Good transcends that and is the "source and principle"[69] of beauty. Otherwise, one will place the Good and the primary beauty in the same thing.[70] In any case, beauty is in the intelligible world.

I 8 (51) On What Evils Are and Where They Come From (§§ 1–5)

In this treatise, Plotinus addresses the question of how it is possible for evil to exist alongside an all-powerful first principle, the Good. He identifies evil with matter or absolute formlessness. Soul is implicated in evil only when it consorts with matter.

§1. Those who are investigating where evils come from—whether they pass into reality in general or into a particular class of things—would be making an appropriate start to their investigation if they first offered a hypothesis as to what evil is, that is, what its nature is. For in this way it would [5] also be understood where evil comes from and where it is located and in what sort of thing it occurs, and, in general, some agreement could be arrived at as to whether it does exist among things.

But if it should be the case that we understand each thing by being like it, we would be at a loss to know by what capacity we know the nature of evil,[1] for intellect and soul, being Forms, [10] would produce the

---

[66] Here, the Forms are treated as the products of Intellect, though Intellect is, in actuality, not prior to the Forms. See V 3. 5, 44–5; V 9. 7, 14–17.

[67] See Plato *Rep.* 509B9. Simplicius *In Ca.* 485, 22 (= Fr. 49 Rose, p. 57 Ross) says that Aristotle held that the first principle of all is "above intellect" (ἐπέκεινα νοῦ).

[68] See Plato *Rep.* 517B5; Aristotle *De An.* Γ 4, 429a27–8.

[69] See Plato *Phdr.* 245C9.

[70] See Plato [?] *Alc.*I 116C1–2.

---

[1] See Aristotle *De An.* A 2, 404b17–18.

understanding of Forms, and would have a desire for these.[2] But how could one imagine that evil is a Form, when it is situated in the absence of all good? But owing to the fact that the same understanding applies to opposites, and evil is opposite to the Good, if the knowledge of good will be of evil,[3] too, then it is necessary [15] for those who intend to understand evils to comprehend good, since the better precedes the worse, that is, among Forms, and some [of the worse] are not Forms but rather a privation [of Form]. It is, all the same, a matter for investigation how the Good is opposite to evil, with perhaps one a beginning and the other an end or the one as form, the other privation. [20] But these questions will be addressed later.[4]

§2. Now we should say what the nature of the Good is, to the extent that is appropriate for the present discussion. The Good is that upon which all things depend and that "which all things desire";[5] they have it as their principle and are also in need of it. It itself lacks nothing, being sufficient [5] unto itself and in need of nothing. It is also the measure and limit of all things, giving from itself Intellect and essence and Soul and life and the activity of Intellect. And all of these up to the Good are beautiful, but it itself is beyond beauty and is the transcendent ruler of all that is best, all that is in the intellectual world.[6] Intellect there is not like the intellects we [10] might be believed to have, intellects that are filled with propositions and are capable of understanding things said and of observing things, as if they were observing consequences that were not previously there but which were empty before learning them [15] even though they were intellects.

Intellect there is not like that; rather, it has all things and is all things and is present with them when it is present to itself and has all things while not having them, for they are not one thing and it, another. Nor is each thing separate in it. For each is the whole, and everything is everywhere. Yet they are not mixed up, but each is in its turn separate. [20] At

---

[2] Perhaps Plotinus here has in mind not that an individual intellect or soul is a separate Form, but that it is a form in the sense in which Aristotle notes at *De An.* Γ 8, 432a2–3, where he says that intellect is the "form of forms" and sense-perception the "form of sensibles."

[3] See Plato *Phd.* 97D4–5; Aristotle *APr.* A 1, 24a22.

[4] See §3 and following.

[5] See I 7. 1, 21–2; Plato *Phil.* 20D8; Aristotle *Met.* Λ 7, 1072b14; *EN* A 1, 1094a3.

[6] See Plato *Rep.* 509D2.

least, that which shares in the others is not all the others in the same way, but rather in the way that it is able to share.

[Intellect] is the primary activity[7] from the Good and the primary essence from that which remains in itself. But Intellect is active around the Good, in a way living around it. Soul dances outside this looking at it and, [25] in contemplating its interior, looks at god through itself.[8]

And "this is the life of the gods,"[9] carefree and blessed, and evil is nowhere there. And if [procession] had stopped there, there would be no evil but only the first and the second and third order of goods. "All things are around the king of all, and that is the cause [30] of all beauties, and all things come from that, and second things are around the second, and third things around the third."[10]

§3. If, then, these are the things that are real, and this is what transcends them, evil would not be present in them or in that which transcends them. For these are good. It remains, then, that if evil does exist, it exists in nonbeings as a sort of form of [5] nonbeing and is involved in some way with that which is mixed or associated with nonbeing. "Nonbeing" does not mean "that which is completely nonexistent" but only something different from real being.[11] Nor does it refer to the nonbeing that motion and rest have in relation to being but rather to an image of being or to something that has even more nonbeing than that.[12]

This is [the manner of existing] of every sensible object and [10] every state in relation to sensibles, whether as something posterior to these and accidental to them or as a principle of these or as some one of the things that together comprise that which is this kind of [non]being. On this basis, someone might immediately arrive at a conception of evil as a sort of absence of measure in relation to measure, or absence of limit in relation to limit, or absence of form in relation to what is productive of form, or what is always in need [15] in relation to what is self-sufficient, always indeterminate, in no way stable, entirely passive, insatiable, and completely impoverished. And these properties are not

---

[7] See V 3. 5, 36; VI 7. 40, 18.

[8] See VI 9. 8, 36-45.

[9] See Plato *Phdr.* 248A1.

[10] See Plato [?] *2nd Ep.* 312E1–4.

[11] See Plato *Parm.* 162A4–B3 and *Soph.* 257B3–4. As Plato argues, if A is different from B, then A has "nonbeing" with respect to B. Thus, to say that A has nonbeing does not mean that A does not exist; indeed, having nonbeing in this way entails that A exists.

[12] See Plato *Soph.* 240B11.

accidental to it, but in a way its essence. Whatever part of it you might look at, it is all these. All other things that partake of evil and are likened to it become evil, though they are not what [20] evil is.

What is the sort of existent in which these properties are present, not as being something different from it, but as being identical with what it is? For, indeed, if evil occurs in something else, it is necessary for it to be something prior to this, even if it is not a substance. For just as the Good itself is one thing and the property of being good another, so evil is one thing and the property of being evil, which immediately derives from that, another.

[25] What, then, is absence of measure if it is not just that which is in that which is without measure? But just as there is measure that is not in that which is measured, so there is absence of measure that is not in that which is without measure. For if it is in another, either it is in that which is without measure—but in this case it should not have an absence of measure in it, since it is unmeasured—or it is in that which is measured. But it is not possible for [30] that which is measured to have absence of measure to the extent that it is measured.

And so, then, there must be something that is absence of limit in itself and, again, absence of form in itself and all the other properties mentioned, which characterize the nature of evil. And if there is something like it that comes after it, either it has evil mixed in with it, or it regards evil and so is like it, or it is productive of this sort of thing. [35] So [the nature] that underlies figures and forms and shapes and measures and limits and whatever is ordered by an ordering alien to it, not having good from itself but like a reflection in relation to real beings, is the essence of evil if indeed some [nature] is able to be the essence of evil. The argument has found this to be primary evil, that is, [40] evil itself.

§4. But it is the nature of bodies, insofar as they partake of matter, to be evil but not to be primary evil. For they have some form, though it is not genuine, and they are deprived of life, and they destroy each other by a disordered motion that comes from them, and they are an "impediment"[13] to the soul in regard to its own activity, and they recoil [5] from essence, by continually being in transition, and so they are secondary evil.

But soul in itself is not evil nor, again, is all soul evil. What is the evil soul? It is the sort of thing Plato is referring to when he says: "those who have enslaved the part of the soul that naturally brings evils to it,"[14] because the nonrational form of the soul is receptive of evil, that is, of

---

[13] See Plato *Phd.* 65A10.
[14] See Plato *Phdr.* 256B2-3.

absence of measure and excess and defect, from which [10] also come wickedness and cowardice and the other evils of the soul: involuntary states, false beliefs that make it believe that evils and goods are what it is actually fleeing and pursuing.

But what is it that produces this evil, and how will you connect it to that principle and cause [primary evil]? In fact, first, [15] this type of soul [the evil one] does not transcend matter, nor does it exist in itself. It has, then, been mixed with absence of measure and is without a share in the form that orders it and connects it to measure, for it is mixed up with a body that has matter. But, then, the reasoning part of the soul, if it is harmed, is prevented from seeing by its states and by being darkened by matter and inclined to matter and, generally, by looking not towards [20] essence but towards becoming, whose principle is in this way the nature of matter which, being evil, fills with its own evil that which is in no way in it but is only looking at it. For since it is absolutely without a share of good and a deprivation or unmixed lack of this, it makes like itself everything that comes into contact with it [25] in any way.

The soul, then, that is perfect and inclines towards Intellect is always pure and turns away from matter and all that is indeterminate and without measure and neither sees evil nor approaches it. It, then, remains pure when it is completely determined by Intellect. That which does not remain like this but proceeds from itself by not being perfect or primary is in a way a [30] reflection of that [pure] soul, owing to its deficiency, just to the extent that it is deficient, and is filled up with indeterminateness and sees darkness and at that moment acquires matter and looks at that which it does not see, which is what we mean when we say it sees, that is, it sees darkness.

§5. But if the lack of that which is good is the explanation of seeing and consorting with darkness, evil would consist in the deficiency that is in the soul and would be primarily there—let the darkness be secondary—and the nature of evil will no longer be in matter but in that which is prior [5] to matter. In fact, evil consists not in any particular type of deficiency but in absolute deficiency. Indeed, that which is slightly deficient with respect to that which is good is not evil, for it is still able to be perfect according to its own nature. But when something is absolutely deficient—which is what matter is—this is really evil, having no share of good.[15] [10] For matter does not even have being, which would have allowed it to partake of good to this extent; rather, we say that it has being in name only, so that the true way to speak of it is as nonbeing.

[15] See Plato *Phil.* 20D1; 54C10; 60B4.

Deficiency, then, is not being good, but evil is absolute deficiency. Great deficiency consists in being able to fall into evil and is thereby already evil.[16] Accordingly, it is necessary to think of evil not as a [15] particular evil, such as injustice or some other kind of vice, but as that which yet is none of these, since these are in a way forms of that made by their own additions. For example, wickedness in the soul and its forms are specified either by the matter with which they are concerned or by the parts of the soul or by one being a sort of seeing and one a sort of impulse or experience.

But if [20] someone were to suppose the evils like sickness or poverty to be external to the soul, how will he connect it to the nature of matter? In fact, sickness is defect and excess in bodily systems that do not maintain order and measure. Ugliness is matter not conquered by form, and poverty is a lack or privation of that which we need owing to [25] the matter to which we are joined, a nature that has neediness.

If this is rightly stated, the principle of evils should not be supposed to be in the evils that are within ourselves but to be prior to us. Whatever evils take hold of human beings, they take hold of us unwillingly;[17] and while there is a "flight from evils in the soul"[18] for those [30] who are able, not all are able. Though matter is present to the perceptible gods, evil is not present, I mean the vice which human beings have, because that is not even present to all human beings. For they master matter—though the gods in whom matter is not present are better—by that in them which is not enmattered.

III 8 (30) ON NATURE AND CONTEMPLATION AND ON THE ONE (COMPLETE)

Since the activity of Intellect is contemplation, and since Intellect is eternally identical with all that is intelligible, whatever partakes in intelligibility must also partake in contemplation. In particular, nature, the lowest expression of embodied soul, contemplates. The products of its contemplation are the things that exist in nature. The goal of anything that contemplates in any way is return to the first principle of all.

---

[16] Following the punctuation of H-S₁ with a full stop before τῷ.
[17] See Plato *Gorg.* 488A3; *Protag.* 345D8, 358C7, 358E2–359A1; *Rep.* 589C6; *Tim.* 85D2, E1; *Lg.* 731C2.
[18] See Plato *Phd.* 107D1.

§1. What if we begin by speaking playfully, before trying to be serious, and say that everything desires to contemplate and looks towards this goal? This is so not only for rational living beings but also for nonrational ones as well and even for nature as it exists in plants and the earth that generates these. [5] Indeed, all things attain it insofar as it is possible for them according to their nature, though different things contemplate in different ways, and some attain it in a genuine way, some by having an imitation and image of this—could one maintain this counterintuitive line of reasoning? In fact, since this matter has arisen among ourselves, there is no harm in entertaining the consequences that should arise [10] from such play.

Are we, therefore, contemplating while we are, at the present moment, playing? In fact, we and all who are playing do this or at least desire this when we are playing. And, as a matter of fact, when either a child plays or a man is being serious, it is on account of contemplation that the one is playing and the other being serious, and [15] every action has the serious aim of contemplation; forced action drags contemplation even more towards externals, while what is called "voluntary" action less so, though it itself nevertheless comes about by a desire for contemplation. But we will discuss these matters later.[1]

For now let us talk about the earth itself and trees and, generally, [20] what the contemplation of plants themselves is, and how we shall connect up the things made or generated by the earth to the activity of contemplation, and how nature, which they [the Stoics] say does not consciously represent and is nonrational, both has contemplation in itself and makes what it makes by means of contemplation, which it does not have [according to them].[2]

§2. That there are no hands or feet here nor any instrument either added or innate, but a necessity for matter, on which it can operate and produce a form in it, should, I suppose, be clear to all. But one should exclude brute force from nature's making. [5] For what sort of manipulating or brute force makes the variegated colors and multifarious shapes? Not even the wax modelers, to whose manipulating people looked and thought that the workings of nature were like that, are able to make the colors if they do not bring the colors from elsewhere for the things they are making.

But [10] those who are making this comparison ought to have thought that even for those involved in these sorts of crafts there should

---

[1] See *infra* III 8. 6, 1 ff.
[2] See *SVF* II 1016 = Sextus *M* 9, 111–15. Also, *SVF* II 458.

be something static in them, and that it is according to what is static that they will produce their works with their hands. They should similarly apply their thinking to nature and realize that here as well all the power that produces, though not with hands, [15] is static. For it [power] does not need some things that are static and some that are in motion—for matter is in motion, while none of nature is in motion—otherwise, that [power] will not be that which moves primarily, nor will nature be this, but that which is immobile in the whole universe.

Someone, however, might say that the expressed principle[3] is immobile, whereas nature itself is [20] different from the principle and is in motion. But if they are saying that all nature is in motion, then the expressed principle [will be in motion, too]. But if they say that some part of it is immobile, the expressed principle will be this part, for nature should be a form and not a composite of matter and form.[4] For why would it need either hot or cold matter? In fact, the underlying and worked-upon matter comes to form bearing these [hot or cold], [25] or becomes such when the expressed principle, though it itself does not have the property, works on it; for it is not necessary for fire to be added in order for matter to become fire, but rather an expressed principle [to be added], which is not an inconsiderable sign of both the fact that in living beings and in plants the expressed principles are the producers, and the fact that nature is an expressed principle, which makes another expressed principle, a product of it, [30] giving something to the underlying subject, while it is itself static. This expressed principle that is in the ultimate visible shape is at the same time a corpse and is no longer able to make another, whereas that which has life is the brother of that which produces the shape and, having itself the identical power, produces in that which comes to be.

§3. How, then, by producing, that is, producing in just this way, would nature attain to contemplation? In fact, if it produces while being static, that is, being both static in itself and an expressed principle, it would itself be contemplation. For the [natural] action would occur according to an expressed principle, since it is clearly different from the expressed principle. [5] However, the expressed principle itself, which accompanies the action and directs it, would not be the

---

[3] Here Plotinus uses the word λόγος in the semitechnical sense, referring to the image of the higher as it is found in the lower. Thus the expressed principle in nature refers to the rules or laws in the soul of the universe that are manifested in nature's "body."

[4] See Aristotle *Phys.* B 1, 193b12, 18.

action. If, then, it is not an action but an expressed principle, it is contemplation. And in every expressed principle the ultimate [expression] of it comes from contemplation and so is in this way contemplation—in the sense that it is the result of contemplation—whereas the expressed principle prior to this is all contemplation, though one part is this in a different way, the one which is not as nature is but as soul is, and the other which is in nature, that is, is [10] nature.

Therefore, indeed, does nature itself also come from contemplation? Yes, it comes entirely from contemplation. But what if [it is produced] by itself having contemplated itself? In fact, how else [could it be produced]? For it is the completion of contemplation, that is, of something having contemplated. How, then, does nature have contemplation? Well, on the one hand, it does not have it as a result of reasoning,[5] I mean, as a result of the reasoning which is an examining of what is contained in nature. Why is this the case, then, [15] since it has life and an expressed principle and power that produces? Is it because examining implies not yet having? But it does have [what it examines], and because of the fact that it has it, it also produces.

For [nature] to be what it is is for it to produce, and insofar as it is what it is, it produces. But it is contemplation and the result of contemplation, for it is an expressed principle. Then, by being both contemplation and [20] the result of contemplation, in this way it is also an expressed principle and it produces insofar as it is these things. The producing, therefore, has shown itself to us to be contemplation, for it is in the completion of contemplation that, while remaining contemplation, it does not do some other thing, but by being contemplation, it produces.

§4. And if someone should ask nature if it produces on account of something, assuming it wishes to listen to the one speaking and to speak itself, it would say, "You ought not ask but understand it and be silent, just as I am silent and am not accustomed to speak." "What is it, then, that one is supposed to understand?" [5] "That which comes to be is my vision, my act of silence, a thing contemplated that comes to be by nature, and since I come to be by contemplation that is like this, it is the case that I have the nature of a lover of contemplation. And my contemplating makes the product of contemplation, just as geometricians draw what they are thinking. But with me, I do not draw; rather, I contemplate, and the outlines [10] of bodies materialize as if they resulted from my contemplation. And there exists in me my mother's state and

---

[5] "Reasoning" translates the same word, λόγος, used previously throughout the treatise and translated as "expressed principle."

the beings that generated me.[6] Those, too, come from contemplation, and my becoming was through no action of theirs; rather, those greater expressed principles contemplated themselves, and I came to be."

[15] What, then, does this mean? That what is called "nature" is in fact soul, generated from a prior soul having a more powerful life, having in itself contemplation in silence, not in regard to the upper region nor even in regard to the lower, but staying in that in which it is, in its own stable position,[7] and in its understanding or [20] sort of awareness, it knows what comes after it as much as is possible for it, and it seeks no longer but has achieved a brilliant and delightful contemplation.

And if someone wants to attribute to nature some sort of comprehension or awareness, it is not the sort of awareness or comprehension that we say is attributable to other beings, but rather it is as if one were comparing the awareness of one asleep [25] to one awake. For contemplating its product of contemplation, it pauses, and that product comes to it from what is in it and remains with it, a product of contemplation. And its contemplation is without a sound, but murkier.

For there is another type of contemplation, clearer in its vision, and nature is the reflection of this other contemplation. So for this reason, that which is generated from it is [30] altogether weak, because a weak contemplation makes a weak product of contemplation. Indeed, human beings, too, whenever they are weakened for contemplation, engage in action, a shadow of contemplation and of reasoning. This is because contemplation is not enough for them, owing to the weakness of their soul not being able to grasp sufficiently the vision and, owing to this, [35] not being filled up but desiring to see it, they are impelled to action in order that they might see [with their eyes] what they were not able to see with their intellect. At any rate, whenever they make something, they themselves want to see it and others to contemplate and be aware of it [especially] when the action maximally realizes their intention.

We shall discover that it is everywhere the case that making [40] and acting are either a weakened form of contemplation or a consequence of it. It is a weakening if the one who does it has nothing beyond that which is done; it is a consequence if he has something other prior to this, better to contemplate beside that which is done. For why would

---

[6] "Mother" refers to the soul of the universe, and "the beings that generated me" refers to the principles in soul derived from the Forms that are in Intellect, according to which nature is constituted.

[7] Deleting the words οἷον συναισθήσει in line 19 with H-S₂ according to their *addenda ad textum* and adding <οἷον> to συναισθήσει in line 20.

someone, being able to contemplate that which is true, intentionally go after the reflection of that which is true? [45] The stupider children are also a witness of this, for those who are incapacitated for studies and contemplation are driven to crafts and manual labor.

§5. But having said, in regard to nature, the way in which generation is contemplation, let us speak of the soul, which is prior to this, and say how its contemplation, its love of learning, its inquiring nature, its labor pains arising from the things its recognizes, and its fullness [5] have made it, when it became completely a product of contemplation, produce another product of contemplation. In a way, art produces like this. Whenever each is full, it makes another sort of small art in a plaything that has a reflection of everything in it. But in other respects, these reflections are murky and are visions and products of contemplation that are not able to help themselves.

The first part of [10] [the rational part of the soul],[8] then, always being filled up and illuminated by that which is above, remains in the intelligible world oriented towards what is above it, whereas the other part of [the rational part of the soul], that which participates by the primary participation of that which is participating, goes forth.[9] For life always goes forth from life, for by its activity it reaches everywhere, and nowhere does it leave off. But in going forth it allows the prior part, that which is a part of [15] itself from before, but which it has left, to remain. For abandoning that which it was previously, it will no longer be everywhere, but only where it ends up.[10] But still, that which goes forth is not equivalent to that which remains.

If, then, it must come to be everywhere, and there is nowhere where its activity is not, there must always be the prior, which is different from the posterior, and while the activity arises [20] from contemplation or action, action that did not exist previously—for it was not possible for it to be before contemplation—it is necessary for one to be weaker than the other, though all of it is contemplation. So the action that arises ac-

---

[8] Accepting Kirchhoff's deletion of τὸ λογιστικόν, and understanding τὸ πρῶτον ... αὐτῆς as indicated in the translation. The reference is apparently to intellect, the first part of the rational part of the soul.

[9] Adding "goes forth" <πρόεισι> at the end of the sentence, in accord with H-S$_2$ addenda ad textum. Plotinus is here distinguishing the part of the rational soul that does not descend from the part that does.

[10] The sense of this difficult line is that the soul that descends leaves a part of itself above, that is, there remains a part of itself above, for if it had abandoned that part, it would no longer be everywhere.

cording to contemplation seems to be a weaker form of contemplation. For that which comes to be must always be of the same kind [as that which produces it], [25] though it be weaker, owing to the fact of its diminution while it goes down. Everything happens without a sound, for there is no need for any obvious external contemplation or action, and the soul that is contemplating also makes that which contemplates in this way: that which comes after it and is not like that which is before it inasmuch as it is more external; in other words, contemplation [30] makes contemplation. For neither contemplation nor the product of contemplation has a limit.

This is why [soul contemplates], in fact, why [soul] is everywhere. For where is it not? Indeed, it is the same in every soul. For it is not circumscribed by a magnitude. Contemplation is certainly not present in the same way in every soul, since it is not even present in the same way in every part of the soul. For this reason, the charioteer is said to give to the horses part [35] of what they saw, whereas it is clear that the horses in receiving this would have desired to possess that which they saw, for they did not receive all of it.[11] And if they act, it is because they desire, that is, they desire that for the sake of which they act. But that was the product of contemplation and contemplation itself.

§6. Action, therefore, is on account of contemplation and the product of contemplation, so that for those who act, contemplation is the goal, and such things that they are not able to get directly, these they seek to acquire by indirect means, for again, whenever they hit upon that which they wish for, what [5] they wanted to happen, it is not so that they should not know it, but rather so that they should know it and they should see it as present in the soul; in this case, it is clear that it is something that is situated as an object of contemplation. And this is so since they act for the sake of a good. But this is not in order that the good should be outside of them, nor in order that they should not have it, but in order that they should have the good resulting from action.

But where do they have the good? In the soul. [10] Action, then, has again turned back to contemplation. For as to what one receives in the soul, which is an expressed principle, what else could it be but a silent expressed principle? And the more [silent is the reception], the more [is the reception that of an expressed principle]. For then the soul is tranquil and seeks nothing, since it has been filled up, and the contemplation that occurs in this sort of thing, owing to the confidence it has,

---

[11] An allusion to Plato *Phdr.* 247E5–6, the allegory of the soul as a charioteer driving two horses.

remains internal. And the clearer is the confidence, the more tranquil is [15] the contemplation, too, insofar as it proceeds further to unity, and that which knows to the extent that it knows—for at this point we should be serious—comes into unity with that which is known.

For if they are two, the knower will be one thing, and the known another, so that they are in a way set alongside each other, and the soul has not yet joined together this duality, as is the case whenever expressed principles in the soul do nothing. For this reason, the expressed principle must not be [20] external but rather must be united with the soul of one who is learning, until it discovers what is its own.[12]

The soul, then, whenever it is joined with an expressed principle and disposed to it, still expresses it or uses it—for it did not have it at first—and learns about it and, by using it, becomes in a way different from it and, thinking about it, looks at it as one thing looks at [25] another. And yet soul was an expressed principle and a sort of intellect, but one that is looking at another. For it is not full but is deficient in respect to that which is before it. Still, it sees and is tranquilly what it expresses. For what it has expressed well,[13] it expresses no longer whereas what it expresses owing to a deficiency, it expresses for the sake of an investigation in order to learn what it has.

But in [30] active persons, the soul harmonizes what it has with the things that are external to it. And by having more [of what it possesses than does nature], it is more tranquil than nature, and by having it to a greater degree, it is more contemplative, whereas by not having these things perfectly, it desires to learn that which it has contemplated and the contemplation that comes from investigation. And when it abandons itself and comes to be among [35] others and then returns again, it contemplates by that part of itself that it has left behind. The soul that is at rest in itself does this less. For this reason, the virtuous person has already concluded reasoning at the moment when he announces to another that which is in himself. But in relation to himself, he is vision, for he is already this way in relation to the One and to the tranquility not only of things external, [40] but also to himself, and to everything internal.

§7. That all things, then, arise from contemplation and are contemplation—both the things that truly are and the things that come to be from those when they are contemplated and are themselves objects of contemplation, some by sense-perception, some by knowledge or belief; and that the actions that have a conclusion in [5] knowledge and the

---

[12] That is, when it has joined itself to or identified with the object known.

[13] Reading εὖ as in H-S₁ instead of οὐ as in H-S₂.

desire for knowledge and the products of contemplation, directed to the completing of a form, that is, of another object of contemplation; and, generally, that each of the things that produce, being an imitation, produces objects of contemplation or forms; and that the realities that come to be, being imitations of real things, show that their producers have, as an end in the things produced, not [10] products or actions, but the thing completed in order that it should be contemplated; this is what acts of discursive thinking want to see and, even before that, acts of sense-perception, the goal of which is knowledge; and, even before these, nature produces the object of contemplation in itself, and the expressed principle, completing another expressed principle, is more or less clear. Some of these claims are immediately [15] understandable, and some, the argument has brought to mind.

Then this, too, is clear, namely, that it was necessary that, since the primary things were contemplating, all the others desired this as well, given that the [first] principle[14] is the goal of everything. Also, whenever living things generate, the expressed principles that reside in them move them, and this is the activity of contemplation and the birth pangs of [20] producing many forms and many objects of contemplation and filling all things with expressed principles and, in a way, always contemplating, for to produce is to make some form to be, and this is to fill up everything with contemplation. And errors, too, both those that arise in things that come to be and those that arise in things done, result from a distraction from the object of contemplation by the contemplators. [25] And, indeed, the bad craftsman seems to be one who makes ugly forms. And lovers, too, are looking at and striving towards form.

§8. Let us take this as given. But as contemplation ascends from nature to soul and from soul to Intellect, the acts of contemplation become ever more personal and produce unity within the contemplators. In the soul of the virtuous person, the objects known are verging towards [5] identity with the subject, since they are hastening towards Intellect. In Intellect it is clear already that both are already one, not by assimilation, as in the case of the best soul, but by essence and owing to the fact that "being is the same as thinking,"[15] for here there is no longer one thing different from another. If there is, there will be another thing again which is [10] no more the one or the other. It is necessary, then, that Intellect comprises both as really one.

---

[14] Here "the principle" (ἀρχή) is the One.
[15] See Parmenides Fr. B3 D–K (= I 4. 10, 6; V 1. 8, 17).

But this is living contemplation, not an object of contemplation of the sort that is in another. That other, whatever it is, which is living in another, is not living independently. If, then, some object of contemplation or thought is to live, it must have an independent life that is not that of a growth faculty or sense faculty or some other psychic faculty, [15] for the other kinds of life are somehow acts of thinking, though one is "growth-faculty thinking"; one, "sense-faculty thinking"; one, "psychic-faculty thinking." How, then, are they thinking? Because they are expressed principles. And all life is a kind of thinking, though one kind is murkier than another, as is the case with life itself.

But the clearer life is itself also primary life and primary Intellect, and these are one. Thinking, then, is the primary life,[16] and [20] secondary thinking is secondary life, and the most remote form of thinking is the most remote form of life. All life, then, belongs to this kind and is thinking. But perhaps human beings would speak of different types of life, though they are not speaking of different types of thinking; they rather say that some are types of thinking while some altogether are not, because they completely fail to investigate what kind of thing life is. [25] But at least this must be indicated, namely, that the argument again shows that all things are a by-product of contemplation. If, then, the truest life is a life of thinking, and it itself is identical with the truest thinking, then the truest thinking lives, and this is contemplation and the object contemplated, living and life, and the two are together one.

[30] If, then, the two are one, how again will this one be many? In fact, it is because it does not contemplate one thing, for whenever it contemplates the One, it does not contemplate it as one.[17] If this were not so, it would not become Intellect. But having begun as one, it did not remain as it had begun, but without itself noticing it, it became many, in a way, "weighted down"[18] and unrolled itself wishing to have everything—[35] it would have been better for it not to have wished this, for it thereby became second—for in a way it became like a circle unrolling itself, and shape and surface and circumference and center and radii and some parts above and some below. But where it came from is better, and where it went is worse. For where it went was not like where it came plus where it went, [40] nor is where it came from plus where it went like where it came from alone.

---

[16] See Aristotle *Met.* Λ 7, 1072b26–30.
[17] See V 3. 11; VI 7. 15.
[18] See Plato *Symp.* 203B7.

Stated otherwise, Intellect is not the intellect of some one thing, but rather it is universal. But being universal, it is the Intellect of all. It must, then, be all things and of all things and the part of it must have all things and everything. If this is not so, some part will not have intellect, and Intellect will be composed from nonintellects and will be some heap [45] thrown together from all things, waiting to become Intellect. For this reason, it is also in this way limitless, and if something comes from it, it is not diminished, neither in the fact of something coming from it (since it is itself all things, too), nor in itself (since it is not a combination of parts).

§9. This, then, is the sort of thing Intellect is. For this reason, it is not first, but rather it is necessary that there be something "transcending it,"[19] [that *is* first] for the sake of which the previous arguments were offered; first, because a plurality is posterior to one. And Intellect is number, whereas the principle of number, that is, the principle of this sort of number, is really one.[20] [5] And this Intellect is at the same time intelligible,[21] so that it is at the same time two. If, then, it is two, one must grasp what is prior to the two. What, then, is this? Intellect alone? But to every intellect is joined that which is intelligible. If, then, it were necessary for that which is intelligible not to be joined to it, it will not be Intellect. If, then, it is not Intellect and is to escape being two, that which is prior to these transcends [10] Intellect.

What, then, prevents it [what is beyond Intellect] from being that which is intelligible? In fact, the reason is that that which is intelligible is joined to Intellect. If, then, it were to be neither Intellect nor intelligible, what would it be? We shall say that it is that from which comes Intellect and the intelligible, which is with it. What, then, is this, and what sort of thing shall we imagine it to be? For, again, it will either be thinking or something nonintelligible.[22] [15] If it is thinking, it is Intellect, but if it is nonintelligible it will also be ignorant of itself.[23] In that case, what is there majestic in it?[24] For even if we were to say that it is the Good and the simplest thing, we shall not be saying anything clear

---

[19] See Plato *Rep.* 509B9.

[20] For the sense in which Intellect is number, see V 1. 5, 5–18; V 4. 2, 7–8; VI 6. 8–9.

[21] See Aristotle *De An.* Γ 4, 430a2–3.

[22] That is, since thinking and the intelligible are necessarily joined, if it is not one, it will not be the other.

[23] That is, if it is nonintelligible, it cannot be known.

[24] See Plato *Soph.* 249A1–2; Aristotle *Met.* Λ 9, 1074b17–18.

and transparent in thus speaking the truth so long as we did not have something on which to focus our thought when speaking.

For, again, since knowledge of [20] other things comes through intellect, and we are able to know Intellect, owing to intellect, by what concentrated intuition would one be able to grasp that which transcends the nature of Intellect? To him to whom we must indicate how this is possible, we shall say that it is by the likeness in us, for there is something of it in us as well. Or else there is nowhere where it is not, in those things that are able to partake of it. [25] For by bringing to the fore whatever in yourself is able to have that which is everywhere, you have what is there. It is just as if a voice were filling an empty space, and in the empty space there were other human beings, too; in whatever part of the empty space you stand, you will receive the whole voice and, again, not all of it.

What is it, then, which we shall receive when we bring our intellect to the fore? In fact, [30] intellect must in a way retreat backwards and in a way release itself to that which is behind it, since it is facing both ways, and there,[25] if it wishes to see that, not to be intellect altogether. For it is itself primary life, being an activity amidst the procession of everything. But it is in the procession not by processing but by its having processed. [35] If, then, it is life and it is processive and has all things exactly and not in a vague manner—for in that case it would have them imperfectly and inarticulately—it comes from something else, which is not at all in the procession, but is rather the principle of the procession and the principle of life and the principle of Intellect and of everything. For the [40] totality of things does not constitute a principle; rather, all things come from a principle, whereas the principle itself is not at all the totality nor some one of the totality in order that it should be able to generate the totality and in order that it not be a plurality but the principle of plurality. For that which generates is everywhere simpler than that which is generated.

If, then, the One generated Intellect, it must be simpler than Intellect. But if someone [45] should think that the One is itself also all things, then either it will be each one of the things or it will be all of them together. If, then, it is all of them together, it will be posterior to the totality. But if it is prior to the totality, the totality is one thing, and it will be other than the totality. But if it is simultaneously itself and the totality, it will not be [50] a principle. But it must be a principle and prior to the totality in order that the totality be after it. But if it is each one of

---

[25] Reading κἀκεῖ with Kirchhoff.

the totality, first, any one will be the same as any other, and second, it will be all of them together, and nothing will be distinguished [from anything else]. And so it is not one of the totality, but prior to the totality.

§10. What is it, then? It is the totality virtually.[26] And if it were not, the totality would not be, nor would Intellect, the primary and universal life. But that which is above life is the cause of life, for the activity of life, being all things, is not primary, but flows forth in a way just as [5] from a spring. Think of a spring not having another source, giving itself to all the rivers, and not being used up in the rivers but remaining tranquil by itself, whereas those rivers proceeding from it, prior to flowing out to different places, stay together for a while, at the same time each one knowing where it will release its [10] waters. Or think of the life of a great plant that courses through the whole of it while its principle remains undispersed in all of it, since it is in a way seated in its root. So it gives the complexity of the whole life to the plant, while it remains itself not complex but the principle of complexity. And this is no wonder.

In fact, it is a wonder, too, how [15] the plurality of life comes from what is not a plurality, and the plurality would not exist if there were not prior to the plurality that which is not a plurality. For the principle is not partitioned among the all. For if it were partitioned, it would destroy the all, too, and it would no longer come to be if there did not remain the principle in itself, being something different from it. [20] For this reason, the return is everywhere to one. And in each case, there is some one into which you will link it, that is, this all is linked to one prior to it, but not simply one, until you would arrive at that which is simply one. But this can no longer be linked to something else.

But if one should consider the one of the plant—this is, its stable principle—the one of the living being and the one of the soul [25] and the one of the all, one is considering in every case that which is most powerful and valuable in it. But if one should consider the one of the things that are truly real, "the principle and spring"[27] and their virtual source, shall we lose confidence and think of it as nothing? In fact, it is none of these of which it is the principle, but it is of such a sort that nothing can be predicated [30] of it, neither being nor essence nor life, since it is above all of these. But if you should consider it by removing its being, you will be in a state of wonder. And hurling yourself towards it, and coming to rest in its interior, your understanding of it will be magnified, perceiving its greatness by means of the things that are after it and because of it.

---

[26] See IV 8. 6, 11; V 1. 7, 9; V 4. 1, 23–6, 36; V 3. 15, 33; V 4. 2, 38; VI 9. 5, 36.
[27] See Plato *Phdr.* 245C9.

§11. Further, there is this. Since Intellect is a certain vision, that is, a vision that sees, it will be a potency that has come into actuality. So there will be, on the one hand, matter and, on the other hand, its form—as in the case of actual seeing—but the matter will be intelligible matter.[28] Since also seeing [5] in actuality implies two things, it was certainly one prior to seeing. That which was one, therefore, became two, and that which was two, one. The fulfillment, then, for seeing is from sense-perception and is a sort of perfecting of it, whereas the Good is that which fulfills the vision of Intellect. For if it was itself the Good, what did it have to see or, in general, why did it have to act?

For while the other things are [10] around the Good and have their activity because of the Good, the Good is in need of nothing. For this reason, there is nothing in it other than itself. Having said "the Good," then, there is nothing further to which to turn one's thought. For if you add something, you will make it deficient, owing to whatever you have added. For this reason, do not add even thinking, in order that you do not add something else and make it two, Intellect and [15] Good. For Intellect needs the Good, but the Good does not need Intellect. So achieving the Good, it becomes Good-like and is perfected by the Good, its form comes to it from the Good making it Good-like.[29] In a way, a trace of the Good is seen in it, [20] and it is appropriate to form a concept of Intellect's true archetype like this, having formulated it from the trace occurring in Intellect.

The Good, then, has given a trace of itself to Intellect to have by seeing, so that whereas in Intellect desire and desiring are eternal and eternally achieving, that[30] [the Good], desires nothing—for what would it desire?—nor does it [25] achieve anything. For it desired [to achieve] nothing. So it is not even Intellect, for there is desire in Intellect and an inclination towards its form.

Intellect is indeed beautiful, or rather the most beautiful of all, situated in a pure light and pure radiance,[31] encompassing the nature of real things, of which this beautiful universe is a shadow and [30] image, and situated in complete glory, since there is nothing unintelligible nor dark nor unmeasured in it, living a blessed life, amazement would possess the one who saw this and, as he must, he would fall into it and become one with it. As one who looks up at the heavens and, [35] seeing the light of the stars, considers the one who makes them and seeks that

---

[28] See II 4. 3–5 for Plotinus' account of intelligible matter.

[29] See Plato *Rep.* 509A3.

[30] Reading ἐκεῖ <νος> with H-S₂ *addenda ad textum*.

[31] See Plato *Phdr.* 250C4.

one, so must one who has contemplated the intelligible world and seen into it and wondered at it seek, therefore, either the identity of the maker who brought such a thing into existence or how the maker produced such an offspring as Intellect, a beautiful boy filled up from itself.[32]

The One is absolutely [40] neither Intellect nor fullness, but prior to Intellect and fullness. For after it comes Intellect and fullness, having needed to be filled and to have been made intelligible. They [Intellect and the intelligibles] are near to that which needs nothing and is in no need of thinking, but is true fullness and true thinking, because it has them primarily. That which comes before these things is in need of nothing nor [45] has it anything. It would not be the Good if it did.

IV 7 (2) On the Immortality of the Soul (§§ 1, 9–15)

This treatise is a defense of the Platonic conception of the soul against Stoic, Epicurean, and Peripatetic alternatives. This selection omits the refutations of Plato's opponents. Plotinus argues for the immortality and incorporeality of the soul and identifies soul with the person, or true self. The soul's purification is here associated with coming to know intelligible reality.

§1. Examining the matter in a way that follows nature, one could learn whether each of us is immortal, whether the whole of each of us is destroyed, or whether some parts of each of us disperse and are destroyed while some parts remain forever, these parts being the self.

Now the human being is not simple, [5] but there is in it a soul, and it also has a body, whether this be, then, an instrument for us or whether it is attached to us in some other way.[1] In any event, let us make this kind of distinction and consider the nature of each [part] and its essence. Of course, the body is itself also composite, and it stands to reason that it is not able [10] to endure; and sense-perception observes it to be something that falls apart and wastes away and is also susceptible to destruction in all sorts of ways, with each of its parts dispersing to its own place,[2] each corrupting and changing the other into something else and

---

[32] A pun on the word κόρος which means both "boy" and "filled up."

[1] See Plato [?] *Alc.* I 129D–E; Aristotle *EE* H 9, 1241b18; *PA* A 1, 641b9–12.

[2] That is, its own natural place, as Aristotle specifies in *Phys.* Δ 4, 211a4–6.

destroying it, especially whenever soul, which serves to reconcile the parts, is not present in the masses [of materials out of which the human being is made].

[15] And even if each part is isolated when it comes to be one, it is not one,[3] being susceptible to dissolution into shape and matter, from which even the simple bodies necessarily have their composition. And further, since they are bodies, they have magnitude, so they are divisible and can be broken up into small pieces and in this way undergo corruption. [20] So if this body is a part of us, we are not entirely immortal, but if it is an instrument that was given to us for a certain period of time, its nature surely had to be like that [temporally limited]. But the other part is the most important and is the human being himself, and if it is indeed this, it stands to the body as form to matter or user to instrument.[4] In either way, the soul is [25] the self.[5]

§9. But the other nature,[6] which has its being by itself, is all that is really real, that which neither comes to be nor is destroyed. Or else all the other things would have disappeared, and they would not come to be later if that had been destroyed which preserves them, that is, the other things [5] and, indeed, the whole universe, which is preserved and kept in order by means of soul,[7] for soul is the "principle of motion,"[8] which directs the motion in other things and is itself moved by itself, giving life to the ensouled body, whereas it has life by itself, a life that is never destroyed, since it has it from itself.

For it is not the case that all things [10] avail themselves of a life that is added from outside them; otherwise, this would go to infinity. Rather, there must be some nature that is primarily living, which must necessarily be "indestructible and immortal,"[9] since it is also the principle of life for other things. Here, indeed, everything that is divine and blessed must be situated, living by itself and being by itself, [15] being primarily and living primarily,[10] having no part in essential change, neither be-

---

[3] Reading γενόμενον ἕν, <ἓν> οὐκ ἔστι with Igal and H-S₂ *addenda ad textum*. Plotinus means that the unity of a part is only a qualified unity.

[4] See Aristotle *Met.* Z 10, 1035b14–16 and H 3, 1043b3–4. See also *De An.* B 1, 412a6–22.

[5] See Plato [?] *Alc.I* 129E5; 130C3.

[6] That is, other than the body. See 8, 45.

[7] See Plato *Phdr.* 245D–E which is here paraphrased.

[8] Ibid. 245C9.

[9] See Plato *Phd.* 88B5–6; 95C1.

[10] See Plato *Symp.* 211A1.

coming nor being destroyed, for where would it come from, or into what would it be destroyed?[11]

And if we must truly attribute the name "being" to it, it must not be at one time and not be at another as whiteness, the color itself, is not at one time [20] white and another time not white. But if whiteness were a being as well as being whiteness, it would always be. But in fact it has only whiteness,[12] for that in which being would be present from itself and primarily will always be a being. Then this has being primarily, and it is always being, never a dead thing like a rock or piece of wood, but it must be living and [25] availing itself of a pure life insofar as it remains alone. But whatever is mixed together with that which is inferior, though it has an "impediment"[13] in regard to [a return to] the best—at least it cannot lose its own nature—it can yet regain its "ancient nature"[14] on the way back to what belongs to itself.

§10. Our demonstration that the soul is not a body also makes clear that the soul is akin to a "more divine and everlasting nature"[15] and, indeed, that it has neither shape nor color and that it is intangible.[16] Nevertheless, this can also be shown in the following way.

Since we have agreed [5] that all that is divine and really real avails itself of a good and intelligent life,[17] it is necessary to examine what comes next, starting from our soul, that is, what sort of thing its nature is. Let us consider not the soul that has acquired nonrational appetites and passions, owing to being in a body, and has allowed other states into itself, but the one [10] which has divested itself of these and which, insofar as possible, has no association with the body.[18] This soul also makes it evident that evils that accrue to the soul come from elsewhere, whereas the best things are present in it, owing to its having been purified, and wisdom and the rest of virtue are its own.[19] If, then, the soul is such whenever it goes back into itself, how does it not have [15] the kind of nature that we say everything that is divine and everlasting has? For wisdom and true virtue, being divine, do not come to be in a low and mortal thing, but that

---

[11] See Parmenides Fr. B 8, 19 D-K.
[12] That is, it does not have being itself.
[13] See Plato *Phd.* 65A10.
[14] See Plato *Rep.* 547B6–7.
[15] See §§2-3 for the demonstration, and Plato *Rep.* 611E2–3.
[16] See Plato *Phdr.* 247C6–7.
[17] See Plato *Rep.* 521A4.
[18] See Plato *Phd.* 80E3–4.
[19] See Plato *Symp.* 209A3–4.

which has these is necessarily divine, since it shares in divine things owing to its kinship or essential likeness to the divine.

For this reason, whoever of us [20] is like this would differ very little from the things above in his soul, diminished only in this respect; inasmuch as his soul is in a body. For this reason, too, if every human being were like this, or if there were a plurality possessed of such souls, no one would lack the confidence to trust in the complete immortality of his soul. But as it is now, [25] most people, frequently seeing the soul in a wounded state,[20] do not think of it as a divine or immortal thing. But it is necessary to examine the nature of each thing starting with its purified state, since that which has been added to it is always an impediment to knowing that to which the addition has been made.[21]

[30] So examine it by removing what has been added to it,[22] or rather let the one who is doing the removing look at himself, and he will have confidence that he is immortal, when he contemplates himself as one who has come to be in the intelligible, that is, in the pure world, for he will see an intellect seeing no sensible thing nor any mortal thing, but the everlasting grasping it by its everlasting [nature], and all the things in the [35] intelligible world, a universe become intelligible and bright, illuminated by the truth, which is from the Good,[23] which shines truth on all the intelligibles. His experience will be such that he will often think to himself that this has been well said: "Hail, I am for you an immortal god,"[24] having returned to the divine and [40] having concentrated on his likeness to it.

But if purification produces in us understanding of the best,[25] then the types of knowledge being inside us will appear, those which are indeed types of knowledge, for it is not by running around somewhere outside that "the soul sees Temperance and Justice,"[26] but rather itself, by itself, in its grasp [45] of itself, that is, of that which it previously was, seeing them situated just like "statues"[27] in itself, statues that are covered with rust by the passage of time and which it [the soul] has now re-

---

[20] See Plato *Rep.* 611B10–C1.
[21] See Plato *Phd.* 65A10.
[22] See Plato *Rep.* 534B9.
[23] Ibid. 508D5.
[24] See Empedocles Fr. B 112, 4 D-K.
[25] See *supra* 9, 26–7.
[26] See Plato *Phdr.* 247D6.
[27] See Plato *Symp.* 216E6.

stored.[28] It is as if gold were ensouled and knocked off all that was dirty in it,[29] being ignorant of its previous self,[30] because it did not see the gold, but then seeing itself alone, [50] it at once marveled at its value and realized, therefore, that there was nothing beautiful that needed to be added to it from outside, but that it itself was the best, provided that one let it be by itself.

§11. Who in his right mind would dispute that something of such value is immortal? For that whose life comes from itself cannot possibly be destroyed. How, indeed, could soul be destroyed, since life is not added to it from outside, nor does it have it in the way heat is present to fire? [5] I mean not that the heat is added to the fire from outside, but that, even if the heat is not added to fire from outside, it is added to the matter that underlies the fire, for in this way fire is extinguished.[31] But soul does not have life in this way, as if there were matter that underlies, and the life that comes to be in it renders it a soul.

In fact, [10] life is a substance, and the soul is the sort of substance that lives by itself—which is what we are seeking, the soul—and this, they will agree, is immortal. Or else, they will agree that it is like a composite, and they will continue to analyze it until they arrive at something immortal, moved by itself,[32] for which it is forbidden to receive "death as its lot."[33] But if they say that life is a state added from outside [15] to matter, from whatever source this state has come into matter, they will be forced to agree that that itself is immortal, being nonreceptive of the contrary [death] of that which it brings [life].[34] But as a matter of fact, there is but one nature whose life is in actuality.

§12. Further, if they will say that every soul is destructible, all things should have long ago been destroyed.[35] But if they say that some souls are destroyed, and some are not— for example, the soul of the universe [is immortal], whereas our souls are not— they should explain why, for soul is the principle of motion for each of these,[36] [5] and each one lives

---

[28] See Plato *Rep*. 611C–D.

[29] Ibid. 612A1.

[30] See Plato *Symp*. 228D10.

[31] That is, by removing heat from it.

[32] See Plato *Phdr*. 245C–D for the definition of soul as "self-mover."

[33] See Plato *Tim*. 41B4.

[34] See Plato *Phd*. 72D2–3 and 105D10–11 for the argument that the soul is not able to receive the contrary of the property "life."

[35] Plotinus is referring to the Stoics. See SVF II 774; 809; 821.

[36] See Plato *Phdr*. 245C9.

on its own, and each of them grasps the same things by the same means, thinking the things in heaven and the things beyond heaven, seeking to understand everything in its essence, until they ascend to the first principle. And the understanding of each thing itself by itself from the sights of each thing in itself [10] comes about from recollection, endows it [the soul] with an existence prior to the body, an everlasting existence in virtue of its having been furnished with everlasting types of knowledge.[37]

And everything which is dissolvable, owing to its having come into existence as a composite, is naturally dissolved in the way in which is was composed. But the soul is one and simple, having a nature whose actuality is living. In that case, it will not be destroyed in this way. [15] But [one might say] that if it were chopped up and therefore divided into parts, it would be destroyed. But the soul is not some mass or quantity, as was shown.[38] And [one might say] that if it is altered, it will be destroyed. But the alteration that destroys something removes the form while leaving the matter. This is the state of a composite. If, then, it is not possible for it to be destroyed in any of these ways, [20] it must necessarily be indestructible.

§13. How, then, since the intelligible world is separate, does the soul come to be in a body? Like this: the part of the soul that is just intellect alone is unaffected and, having only an intellectual life among the intelligibles, remains there always, for there is no impulse or desire in it but that which, [5] being right next to intellect, acquires desire and, owing to the addition of desire, in a way, immediately goes further forth and desires to arrange things according to what it saw in Intellect, just as if it were pregnant by these and laboring to give birth, is eager to make something, and it does produce. And by this zeal impelled towards sensibles, with the soul of the universe [10] standing over all things and transcending that which is ordered and sharing in the care for the whole while wanting to direct a part, it becomes isolated in that in which it is, belonging neither wholly nor completely to the body, but with some part of it also transcending the body.

And so not even the intellect of this soul is affected along with the body. But this part of the soul is sometimes in [15] a body and sometimes transcends it, on the one hand, starting from primary realities, and on the other, proceeding to tertiary realities,[39] the things here

---

[37] See Plato *Phd.* 72E3–73A3; 78C1–2.
[38] See 5, 24–51.
[39] See Plato [?] *2nd Ep.*312E1–4.

below,[40] owing to the activity of Intellect, which remains in the same and which, by means of the soul, fills up and orders all things with beauties, immortal employing immortal, and which, since it is always itself, will be engaged [20] in unceasing activity.

§14. Regarding the soul of other living things: as for those that falter and come into animal bodies, it is also necessary that these be immortal.[41] But if there is another form of soul, it must come from nowhere else but from the living nature, and [5] this must exist and be the explanation of life for living things as well as that for the life in plants,[42] for all of these started from the same principle and have their own lives, and they are bodiless and partless and are substances. But if it is said that the soul of a human being, since it is tripartite,[43] will be dissolved, owing to its being a composite, [10] we will also say that purified souls will abandon that which was stuck onto them when they were born[44] but that others will be connected with these for a long time. But when the worst part is removed, it will not be destroyed so long as that exists from which it has its origin,[45] for nothing that comes from real being is destroyed.

§15. What, then, it was necessary to say to those who require a demonstration has been said. But what it is necessary to say to those who require conviction that has been fortified by sense-perception, should be drawn from the many narratives of such things, for example, from the cases of the gods [5] responding to the oracles calling on them to appease the anger of souls who have been wronged[46] and to distribute honors to those who have died, as if they were conscious, just as all human beings do to those who have died. And many souls who were previously in human beings do not cease from benefiting human beings when they have transcended their own bodies.[47] They have also benefited us by [10] setting up oracles and using them in other ways as well, and they show by their own examples that other souls are not destroyed.

---

[40] Eliminating νοῦ in line 16 and reading ἐνεργείᾳ with Harder instead of ἐνέργεια with H-S₂.

[41] See also III 4. 2; VI 4. 16; IV 3. 24, 27; II 9. 9; VI 7. 6; III 2. 13, 15, 17; II 3. 8. Proclus, following Plato in *Tim.* 90E–92C, recognizes the transmigration of souls into animal bodies.

[42] See Plato *Tim.* 76E–77B.

[43] See Plato *Rep.* 439D–E; 441A.

[44] Ibid. 611B–C.

[45] See Plato *Tht.* 176A5.

[46] See Plato *H. Ma.* 282A7.

[47] See Plato *Lg.* 927A1–3.

IV 8 (6) On the Descent of the Soul Into Bodies (complete)

In this treatise, Plotinus addresses the question why incorporeal souls find themselves in an embodied state. He considers the moral and psychological consequences of embodiment. In addition, he argues that the highest part of the soul, intellect, does not descend but rather remains in the intelligible world.

§1. I have many times awakened into myself from the body when I exited the things other than myself, and entered into myself, and, seeing a marvelous and great beauty, I was then especially confident that I belonged to the better part and that I was engaging in the best life, [5] and that I had come to that activity having identified myself with the divine and having situated myself in it, that is, having situated myself above all else in the intelligible world. After this repose in the divine, descending from Intellect into discursive reasoning, I am puzzled how I have now descended and how my soul has come to be in [10] the body when it is the way it appeared to itself even while it was in the body.

Heraclitus, who exhorted us to examine this, in supposing "necessary changes from opposites"[1] and saying "the road up and down"[2] and "while changing, it is at rest"[3] and "it is weary to toil at and be ruled by [15] the same things,"[4] seemed to leave it to us to imagine what he meant, since he did not care to make clear to us his argument, perhaps on the grounds that it is necessary for one to seek by oneself, just as he found by seeking. And Empedocles, when he said that it was a law that sinful souls enter here and that he himself, "fleeing from the home of the gods," [20] "trusting in mad strife"[5] gave us a peek, I think, as much as did Pythagoras and his followers, who offered riddles about this and about many other things. But it was also possible that Heraclitus did not make himself clear, because he was writing poetry. We are left with the divine Plato, who said many and beautiful things about soul and [25] spoke in many places in his writings about its arrival here [the sensible

---

[1] See Heraclitus Fr. B 90 D–K.
[2] See Heraclitus Fr. B 60 D–K.
[3] See Heraclitus Fr. B 84a D–K.
[4] See Heraclitus Fr. B 84b D–K.
[5] See Empedocles Fr. B 115, 13–14 D–K.

world], so that we hope to grasp something clear from him. What then does this philosopher say?

He appears not to say the same thing everywhere, so that one could easily know his intention, but everywhere disdaining the whole sensible world and [30] blaming the soul for its association with the body,[6] he says the soul is "in its bonds" and "buried in it"[7] and that great is the saying among the mysteries that claims that the soul is "under detention."[8] And his cave, like the grotto of Empedocles, stands, I think, for this world when he actually says that the "journey"[9] to the intelligible world is a [35] "release from our bonds" and an "ascent from the cave" for the soul.[10] And in *Phaedrus*, "the shedding of wings" is the cause of our arriving here.[11] And according to him, the cycles bring here again the soul that has ascended,[12] and "judgments"[13] send others down here as well as "lots and fortunes,"[14] [40] or forces.

In addition, though blaming the soul for its arrival in the body in all these places, in *Timaeus*, when speaking about this universe, he praises it and says that it is a "happy god"[15] and that the soul was given by a good craftsman in order that this universe might be intelligent,[16] [45] since it had to be intelligent, and without soul it was not possible for it to become so.[17] The soul of the universe, then, was sent into it by the god for the sake of this, and the soul of each of us was sent for the universe's perfection. This occurred since it was necessary that there exist in the sensible world the same kinds of living things that there are in the intelligible world.[18]

§2. For us, the result of seeking to learn from Plato about our soul is that we find ourselves also compelled to focus on and to seek out a

---

[6] See Plato *Gorg.* 493A3.
[7] See Plato *Phd.* 67D1.
[8] Ibid. 62B2–5.
[9] See Plato *Rep.* 532E3.
[10] Ibid. 515C4–5; 517B4–5.
[11] See Plato *Phdr.* 246C2; 248C9.
[12] Ibid. 247D5 where Plato uses the term περιφορά instead of περίοδοι used here.
[13] See Plato *Phdr.* 249A6.
[14] See Plato *Rep.* 619D7; *Phdr.* 249B2.
[15] See Plato *Tim.* 34B8.
[16] Ibid. 29A3.
[17] Ibid. 30B2–3.
[18] Ibid. 39E7–9.

general account of the soul, investigating how by its nature it can ever be in association with the body, and in regard to the nature of the universe, what sort of thing we should suppose it is in which the soul resides: [5] whether it does so willingly, or under compulsion, or in some other manner; and about its producer: whether it has done its job correctly or, perhaps like our souls, which, since they had to direct inferior bodies, had to sink far below, owing to them, if, that is, they were going to rule over them at all; otherwise, each part of the body would be scattered and borne [10] to its own place[19]—though in the universe everything is in its own place by nature—whereas our bodies are in need of a lot of onerous providential care, since there are many alien things that befall them, and since they are always constrained by want, they need every type of assistance for the great difficulty that they are in.[20]

But since the body of the universe is [15] perfect and sufficient, that is, self-sufficient and having nothing in itself beyond what its nature requires, it is in need of little direction.[21] And as its soul is always as it naturally wanted to be, it has no appetite, nor is it affected. For "there is nothing that goes out of it and nothing that goes into it."[22] For this reason, Plato says that our soul, too, if [20] it should come to be with that perfect soul, is itself perfected and "travels on the heights and directs the universe."[23] When it departs for a state where it neither is within any body nor belongs to any one of them, then it will be like the soul of the universe effortlessly directing the universe with it, since it is not evil in any way for the soul to provide the body [25] with the power of doing well and of existing. This is because not every form of providence for what is inferior removes the superior status for that which is provident.

For there are two types of care for everything: the universal, by the inactive command of the one providing the order with royal oversight, and the particular, which consists in some immediate self-involved doing and, by contact with that which is done, [30] the doer is contaminated with the nature of what is done.[24] Since the divine soul is said al-

---

[19] Plotinus is here alluding to *Tim.* 32B5–6 where Plato discusses the elements that make up ensouled bodies.

[20] Ibid. 43B8–C1.

[21] Ibid. 34B2, 8–9 on these attributes of the body of the universe.

[22] Ibid. 33C6–7.

[23] See Plato *Phdr.* 246C1–2.

[24] The first type of "care" refers to that which the soul of the universe provides for the body of the universe, and the second type of "care" refers to that which the soul of an individual provides for his or her body.

ways to direct the heavens in the first way, with its higher part transcendent while sending its last [lowest] power into [the body of the universe], god could still not be said to be responsible for having made [35] the soul of the universe be in something worse, and the soul would not be deprived of what belongs to it according to nature, which it has from eternity and will have forever, which cannot possibly be counter to its nature, and which continuously belongs to it forever, without having ever begun.

And when Plato says that the souls of the stars stand to their bodies in the same manner as [40] does the soul of the universe in regard to its body—for he inserts the stars' bodies into the circles of the soul[25]—he preserves the appropriate state of happiness for them, for there are two things, owing to which the association of the soul with the body is made difficult to endure: first, because the association produces an impediment to thought[26] and second, because pleasures and [45] appetites and pains fill it up.[27] Neither of these could happen to a soul that did not descend into the interior of a body that does not belong to anyone nor is the body's possession, but rather the body belongs to it, and it is such as neither to need anything nor to be deficient in some respect, so that the soul is not filled up with appetites or [50] fears, for neither will it expect anything fearful from a body of this kind, nor will any occupation make it incline downward and lead it away from the better and blessed vision, but it is always directed to those [intelligible realities], governing this universe with an effortless power.

§3. Regarding the human soul which, when it is in the body, is said [by Plato] to suffer all forms of evil and to "experience distress,"[28] because it comes to be amidst inanities and appetites and fears and other evils—insofar as the body is a chain and a tomb, and the universe is for it a cave [5] or a cavern—let us now express how [Plato] understands its descent; here, he does not contradict what he says about the causes [of the descent of the soul of the universe], which are not, in its case, the same.

Now since universal Intellect is as a whole and universally in the world of thinking, which we suppose to be an intelligible universe, and since there are also intellectual powers and individual intellects contained in this—[10] for the intelligible world is not only one but also

---

[25] See Plato *Tim.* 38C7–8.
[26] See Plato *Phd.* 65A10.
[27] Ibid. 66C2–3.
[28] Ibid. 95D3.

one and many[29] — it had to be the case that there be both many souls and one Soul, with the many differing souls coming from the one,[30] just as from one genus come many species, some better and some worse, some more intellectually active, some less actualized; for in the intelligible world, in Intellect, there is Intellect encompassing virtually [15] the others [individual intellects] as a sort of great living being,[31] and there are the individual intellects in actuality, each of which the other encompasses virtually.[32] For example, if a city were ensouled, encompassing other ensouled beings, the [soul of the] city would be more complete and would be more powerful though nothing in its nature prevented other souls from existing. Or arising from a universal fire, there comes a large and [20] a small fire.[33] But it is the universal essence that is the essence of the universal fire, or rather that from which the universal fire also comes.

The function of the more rational Soul is thinking, but it is not just thinking.[34] For if it were, how would it differ from Intellect? For it added to the intellectual something else such that it did not remain Intellect. And it has [25] its own function, if it is the case that every part of intelligible reality has a function. But looking at that which is prior to it, it thinks,[35] while when looking to itself it arranges that which comes after it and manages and rules it, because it was not possible for everything to stay in the intelligible world, when it was possible for something else that is inferior to it to come to be, something that necessarily came to be if [30] that which was prior to it was also necessary.

---

[29] See V 1. 8, 23–7. Intellect is here said to be a "one-many" while Soul is a "one and many." Plotinus is alluding to an interpretation of Plato's *Parm.* 155E5. Also, see *Soph.* 248E–249B, which Plotinus interprets as indicating the presence of (the highest part of the) soul in that which is really real, that is, in the intelligible world. See VI 2. 7, 1–6.

[30] This "one Soul" is that which the soul of the universe, the soul of the stars, and individual souls have in common. It is like their "genus" understanding "genus" as ontologically prior to species. See IV 3. 2, 55–6.

[31] See Plato *Tim.* 39E8.

[32] See V 9. 6, 9–15 on the manner in which Intellect is virtually all that it contains.

[33] See Plato *Phil.* 29B9–C9.

[34] The "more rational soul" is universal Soul — the "hypostasis" Soul — not the soul of the universe.

[35] The verb νοεῖν here is paradigmatically used for what Intellect (νοῦς) does, but is also used for the higher cognitive functions of soul.

§4. The individual souls, not only exercise an intellectual desire for their return to that from which they came, but also have a power directed to here below, like a light dependent on the sun above, which does not begrudge [5] its bounty to what comes after it. But they are without pain if they remain with universal Soul in the intelligible world, governing the heaven with that whole Soul, like those living with the king of all, sharing in his rule but not themselves alighting from the royal thrones. For these are all together in the same place.[36]

[10] But they move away from the whole [Soul] into being a part, and being by themselves and, in a way, tiring of being with another, each withdraws into itself. And whenever a soul does this for a time, fleeing the all and standing apart in separateness and not looking in the direction of that which is intelligible, it has become a part isolated [15] and weak and consumed with its own affairs and looks to the part, and by a separation from the whole, it enters some one thing[37] and flees all the rest. And coming to and turning towards that one thing that is beaten up by the totality of things in every way, setting itself apart from the whole, it manages the individual [body] with complications [20] as soon as it has attached itself to it and, caring for externals and being present [to the body], it sinks far into its interior.

It is here that the so-called "molting"[38] occurs, and it comes to be in the "chains"[39] of the body, since it has failed to achieve the immunity that pertains to the more exalted management that belonged to it when it was with universal Soul. [25] It was in every way better for it before, when it was traveling on the upward path. It has, then, been captured and it is falling in the direction of its chains and acting by sense-perception, owing to its being prevented from acting with intellect in its new state. And it is said to be "buried" and "in a cave,"[40] but when it is turning in the direction of thinking, it is loosed from its chains and ascends, [30] whenever it might get a start, owing to recollection, to view reality.[41] For it always has, still, something that is transcendent.

Souls, then, in a way become amphibious,[42] necessarily living a part of their life in the intelligible world and a part here, those which are

---

[36] Plotinus here seems to consider universal Soul and the soul of the universe as one, the latter being the governor of heaven.

[37] That is, the body.

[38] See Plato *Phdr.* 246C2.

[39] See Plato *Phd.* 67D1.

[40] See Plato *Rep.* 514A5.

[41] See Plato *Phdr.* 249E5–250A1.

[42] That is, capable of living in two different worlds.

able to consort with Intellect living more of their life there while those who are governed in the opposite way by nature [35] or by chance, live more of their life here. Plato gently shows this when he divides again that which[43] comes from the second mixing, that is, he divides [the mixture] into parts.[44] It is then that he says that they must enter into the world of becoming, since they have become such parts.[45] But if he says that god "sowed"[46] them, this must be taken in the same way as when he says that god is speaking [40] and in a way making a public speech. As for the things that are in nature, these the hypothesis generates and makes as a demonstration, adducing in order things that are always becoming and always being.[47]

§5. There is, then, no discordance between "the sowing in becoming" and "the descent of the all into completion," and the judgment and the cave, and the necessary and the voluntary, since the necessary includes the voluntary and the being in an evil state that is being in a body.[48] [5] There is discordance in neither Empedocles' flight from god and the wandering, nor the error upon which judgment follows, nor the halting of Heraclitus in flight,[49] nor, in general, the voluntariness of the descent and, again, its involuntariness. For while everything that gravitates to the worse does so involuntarily, still, since it does so in fact by its own impetus, when it suffers the worse it is said to receive punishment [10] for the things it did. But it suffers these things and does what it does necessarily by an eternal law of nature, and this occurs when it meets up with the needs of another [the body] in its procession from that which is above it [above the human being]. So if someone were to say that a god had sent it down, he would not be out of tune either with the truth or with himself. For each thing, [15] including the ultimate things, must be referred to the principle from which it comes, even if there are many intermediaries.

---

[43] Reading αὖ τὰ with Igal and H-S₂ *addenda ad textum*.

[44] See Plato *Tim.* 41D4–7. As Plato says, these "parts" are the individual souls that are "sown" each into a different star.

[45] Ibid. 42A3–5.

[46] Ibid. 41A7–D4.

[47] Plotinus means that the "sowing" and "speaking" of the Demiurge, like the generation of the universe, must not be taken literally, where "literally" implies temporality. See *Tim.* 29D2 for the claim that the work is a "likely story." Plotinus thus accounts for the narrative quality of the work.

[48] See IV 8. 1, 29–48 for Plotinus' explanation of the expressions reintroduced here.

[49] See the references in §1.

But since the error of the soul is twofold, one being the explanation for its descent and one being the evils it does when it has come here,[50] <the punishment> for the first is the fact that it experiences the descent and for the second, that it enters [20] other [inferior] bodies; this occurs quickly, based on the judgment of what it deserves—the word "judgment" shows that it happens by divine decree—whereas the limitless kind of evil deserves a more severe judgment, rendered by the oversight of punishing spirits.[51]

In this way, then, even though the soul is divine and comes to be in a body from divine regions [25] above, since it is a god of a lesser rank, it comes here by a self-determining inclination, and by reason of its power, and to order what comes after it. And if soul flees quickly, there is no harm in its acquiring a knowledge of evil, and knowing the nature of vice, and rendering its own powers [30] manifest, and displaying its works and deeds, which, if they were to have stayed in the bodiless world, would have remained quiet in vain being eternally unactualized. And the soul itself would not have been aware of what it had if these had neither been made manifest nor proceeded forth. This is so, because everywhere it is the case that actuality shows potentiality totally hidden, and in a way [35] nonapparent, and not ever being really real. As it is now, each of its interior properties is an object of wonder, owing to the external variety [of their manifestations] such that it is from this interior that someone achieves these splendid manifestations.[52]

§6. If, then, it had to be the case that there was not one thing only—for if there had been, all things would have been hidden in that one thing, which did not have any shape, and there would not have existed any of the beings had the One remained in itself, neither the multiplicity of these beings generated from the One[53] [5] nor those things which assumed the order of souls, which proceeded after these—in the same way, it had to be that souls not be alone without there being the things that are made apparent through them, if indeed it is the case that each nature makes what comes after it and unfolds itself like a seed from some partless source, proceeding to its perceptible conclusion.

[10] On the one hand, that which is prior remains in its own position; on the other, that which comes after is in a way produced from un-

---

[50] See Plato *Phdr.* 248C3–D2 and 248E5–7, which describe the two forms of punishment.

[51] See Plato *Phd.* 113D1–114C6.

[52] The exterior refers to the body, and the interior, to the soul.

[53] Plotinus is referring to Intellect and to the Forms.

speakably great power,[54] consisting of all that was in those [higher powers]. It had not to remain in itself in a way circumscribed in grudging,[55] but it had to go forward eternally, until all things should arrive at the ultimate limit of power, owing to its enormous power, which, [15] in sending forth itself in every way, does not fail to permit anything to share in its own power. For there was nothing that prevented anything from having a share in the nature of good insofar as it was possible for each thing to share in it.

Either, then, the nature of matter is eternal and it is not possible for it, since it is existing,[56] not to participate in that which provides that which is good to each thing [20] insofar as it is able, or else the generation of it followed from necessity upon the causes that came before it, though even so it was not the case that it had to be separate [from all existing things], owing to the fact that before it came into being, there was an immobilization of activity because of a lack of power in that which gave it existence as a sort of grace.

The most beautiful part of the sensible world, then, is a manifestation of the best among the intelligibles, of their [25] power and of their goodness; and all things, both sensible and intelligible, are eternally connected, the intelligibles existing by themselves, the things that partake always receiving their existence from them, imitating the intelligible nature insofar as they are able.

§7. Even if the nature of the soul is twofold, being both intelligible and sensible and, though it would be better for the soul to be in the intelligible world, still it is necessary for something having such a nature to be able to share in the sensible world, and it should not be irritated with itself, because [5] even if all things are not in the best way, it occupies a middle rank among things. Though it has a "divine portion,"[57] it is at the outer limit of intelligibility such that it has a common boundary with the sensible nature, giving something of itself to this while receiving in return something from it,[58] unless it governs the universe in a detached manner [10] rather than, possessed of a greater zeal, entering into the interior, not remaining wholly with the whole Soul.[59] At any

---

[54] See II 5. 3, 19–22.

[55] See Plato *Tim.* 29E1–3.

[56] But see I 8. 3, 4–5 and II 5. 5, 9 where Plotinus says that matter does not have being.

[57] See Plato *Phdr.* 230A5–6.

[58] What soul gives to the sensible world is λόγος, an expressed principle; what it gets in return is evil.

[59] That is, universal Soul.

rate, it is possible for it to surface again and acquire the narrative of the things it saw and experienced here, and then for it to learn what it is like to be in the intelligible world, and then to learn more clearly which is better by making a comparison of what are, in a way, contrary states.

[15] For the experience of evil is a clearer understanding of the Good for those with a capacity too weak to know evil before experiencing it. And just as the intellectual procession is a descent into the limits of that which is worst—for it is not in it to ascend to that which transcends it,[60] but it necessarily acts from itself and, [20] not being able to remain in its own nature, it must by necessity and law arrive at soul, for this is its goal, and it must hand over that which comes next[61] to soul and return again—so the activity of soul operates in the same way: one part is that which comes after it, namely, the things here, and the other part is the contemplation of the beings that are prior to it.

For some particular souls, such an experience comes [25] with time, when they are in a bad state and they make a return to the better, whereas for the one called the soul of the universe, it has not been involved in inferior work, and, since it is unaffected by evils, it reflects contemplatively on the things below here and remains forever dependent on the things prior to it. In fact, it is able to do both at once; [30] it receives from there, and at the same time provides here, since, being soul, it was unrealistic for it not to be attached to these things.

§8. But if one must, contrary to the opinions of others, dare to say more clearly what appears to be the case, it is not our entire soul that has descended, but rather there is some part of it always in the intelligible world. But if the part that is in the sensible world should rule, rather if it should be ruled and confused,[62] [5] it does not allow us awareness of the things that the upper part of the soul contemplates. In that case, that which is thought comes to us, but only when it comes into our awareness in its descent. For we do not know everything that occurs in every part of our souls before it reaches the whole soul. For example, appetite, while remaining in the appetitive part of the soul, [10] is cognized by us, but only when we grasp it by the internal perceptual power, or by the discursive power, or by both. For every soul has something of that which is below, which is connected to the body, and something of that which is above, which is connected to Intellect.

---

[60] A reference to the Good. See Plato *Rep.* 509B9.
[61] That is, the governance of bodies.
[62] See I 4. 10, 12–15.

And universal Soul or the soul of the universe,[63] by means of the part of it that is connected to the body, governs the whole while remaining effortlessly apart, because it does [15] not do this by calculation, as do we, but by intellect, just as "art does not deliberate"[64] that part of the whole governing its [the universe's] inferior part [the body]. But particular souls that occupy part of the universe have a part that stands apart, though they are busy with sense-perception and with the apprehension, apprehending many things that are, contrary to nature, painful and [20] terrifying, since that which gets their attention is a part that is defective, having many alien things around it, many that it desires. And it is pleased, and pleasure deceives it. But there is that part that, being immune to pleasure, the momentary pleasures do not please, and its way of life is like that in the upper region.[65]

V 1. (10) On the Three Principal Hypostases (complete)

This treatise contains a complete exposition of the three fundamental principles of Plotinus' metaphysics: the One, Intellect, and Soul. Against this metaphysical background, Plotinus discusses the means available to embodied persons for ascent or return to their source. Plotinus also shows how the three principles are found within the individual.

§1. What can it be, then, that has made the souls[1] forget the god who is their father[2] and be ignorant both of themselves and him even though they are parts of the intelligible world and are completely derived from it?

The starting point for their evil is audacity, that is, generation or primary difference, [5] or wanting to belong to themselves.[3] Since they

---

[63] Here Plotinus seems not to be distinguishing the two. The soul of the universe is perhaps the part of universal soul that is connected to the body of the universe.

[64] See Aristotle *Phys.* B 8, 199b28.

[65] See Aristotle *Met.* Λ 7, 1072b14–15.

[1] Meaning individual souls.

[2] This is probably a reference to Intellect, not to the One. Intellect is the immediate superior of Soul.

[3] See IV 4. 3, 1–3; IV 8. 5, 28; VI 9. 8, 31–2; Plato *Phdr.* 248D1–2; *Tim.* 41E3.

then appeared to be pleased with their self-determination[4] and to have made much use of their self-motion, running as far away as possible and producing the maximum distance, they were also ignorant that they themselves came from the intelligible world. They were like children who at birth are separated [10] from their fathers and, being raised for a long time far away, are ignorant both of themselves and of their fathers. Since they no longer can see their father or themselves, they dishonor themselves, owing to ignorance of their lineage, honoring instead other things, in fact, everything more than themselves; marveling at and being awestruck and loving and being dependent on these, and they [15] severed themselves as much as possible from those things from which they turned away with their dishonor.

So it follows that it is honor of these things and dishonor of themselves that is the cause of their complete ignorance of god. For one to pursue and marvel at something is at the same time to accept that one is inferior to that which one is pursuing and marveling at. If one supposes oneself inferior to things that come to be [20] and perish and assuming oneself to be the most dishonored and mortal of the things one does honor, neither the nature nor the power of god would ever be impressed in one's heart.

For this reason, the way of arguing with those so disposed should be twofold—that is, if one is going to turn them in the opposite direction and towards the things that are primary and lead them up to that which is [25] highest or first, that is, the One. What, then, are the two ways?

First, one shows how the things now honored by the soul are in fact dishonorable, which we will discuss further elsewhere.[5] Second, one teaches the soul to remember the sort of lineage it has and its worth, a line of reasoning that is, in fact, prior to the other and, once having been set forth, makes that other evident, too. This is the one that needs to be spoken of now. [30] It is close to that which we are seeking and provides the groundwork for that. For that which is doing the seeking is the soul, and it should know that which is doing the seeking so that it can learn, first about itself and next whether it has the ability for seeking such things, whether it has the sort of "eye" that is able to see,[6] and whether it is fitting for it to seek these things, for if the things sought are

---

[4] See VI 8 on "self-determination."

[5] It is difficult to know exactly what texts, if any, Plotinus is alluding to. II 4., III 4., III 6., and VI 4. have all been suggested.

[6] On the "eye" of the soul, see Plato [?] *Alc*.I 133B–C; *Rep.* 533D2; *Soph.* 254A10.

alien to it, why should it seek them? But if they are of the [35] same lineage, it is fitting for it to seek them, and it is possible to find that which it is seeking.[7]

§2. Let every soul, then, first consider that soul itself made all living things by breathing life into them, those that are nourished by the earth, the sea, and the air, and the divine stars in heaven.[8] Soul itself made the sun and this great [5] heaven, and it ordered it, and it drives it in a regular arrangement, being a nature different from that which it orders, from that which it moves, and from that which it makes to be alive.[9] And it is necessary that it be more honorable than these, since while these are generated and destroyed whenever soul departs from them or supplies them with life, soul itself exists forever by "not departing from itself."[10]

[10] As for the manner in which it supplies life to the whole[11] and to each individual, this is how soul should reason about the matter: let it consider the great soul, being itself another soul[12] of no small stature, worthy of consideration once it has been released from deception and from the things that have enchanted the other souls by being in a state of tranquility. Let [15] not only its encompassing body and its surging waves be tranquil, but all that surrounds it;[13] let the earth be tranquil, the sea and the air be tranquil, and heaven, the better part.[14] Let soul, then, think of itself as, in a way, flowing or pouring everywhere into im-

---

[7] See Plato *Tim.* 35A ff., where soul is composed of the same material as that with which it is to interact, based on the principle, Presocratic in origin, that "like knows like." See also *Phd.* 79D3; *Rep.* 409B4; 611E1 ff.; *Lg.* 899D7.

[8] See IV 8. 3 for the distinction between the soul of the universe and universal Soul. Here Plotinus is referring to the former. The fourfold division of the living things in the universe comes from Plato *Tim.* 39E10–40A2.

[9] See Plato *Phdr.* 246B6–7; *Lg.* 896E8–9.

[10] See *Phdr.* 245C7–8. This passage contains Plato's argument that since soul is self-moving, it is immortal.

[11] In this paragraph and elsewhere, Plotinus uses the terms "the whole" (τὸ πᾶν, τὸ σύμπαν), "the universe" (ὁ κόσμος), and "heaven" (ὁ οὐρανός) interchangeably. See *Tim.* 30B5; 31B2–3. See Aristotle *De Ca.* A 9, 278b9 ff. for technical uses of "heaven" and 10, 280a21 for "heaven" and "universe" as synonyms.

[12] The "great soul" is the soul of the universe, and "another soul" refers to the human soul. See *infra* 2, 44 and II 1. 8, 4 ff.

[13] Perhaps an allusion to *Tim.* 43B5.

[14] Reading ἀμείνων in line 17 with some manuscripts. The meaning of the phrase αὐτὸς οὐρανὸς ἀμείνων here is doubtful.

mobile[15] heaven from "outside,"[16] inhabiting and completely illuminating it. [20] Just as rays from the sun light up a dark cloud, make it shine, and give it a golden appearance, so soul entered into the body of heaven and gave it life, gave it immortality, and wakened the sleeping. And heaven, moved with an everlasting motion by the "wise guidance"[17] of soul, became "a happy living being,"[18] and acquired its [25] value from soul's dwelling within it, before which it was a dead body, mere earth and water, or rather the darkness of matter and of nonbeing and "what the gods hate," as the poet says.[19]

The power and nature of soul would be more apparent, or clearer, if one would reflect here on how soul encompasses and directs heaven with its [30] own acts of will. For soul has given itself to the entire extent of heaven, such as that is, and every interval both great and small is ensouled, even as one body lies apart from another, one here and one there, some separated by the contraries of which they are composed, and some separated in other ways, though they be mutually interdependent.

[35] The soul is, however, not like that, and it does not make something alive by a part of it being broken up and put in each one, but all things live by the whole of it, and all soul is present everywhere by its being like the father who begat it, according to its unity and its universality.[20] And though heaven is multiple and diverse, it is one [40] by the power of soul, and this universe is a god owing to this.[21] The sun is also a god—because it is ensouled—and the other stars: and we, if we are divine in some way, are so for just this reason, "for corpses are more apt for disposal than dung."[22]

---

[15] The text has ἑστῶσα which, as H-S₂ recognize in the *addenda ad textum*, is a typographical error for ἑστῶτα.

[16] See *Tim.* 36E3.

[17] Ibid. 36E4.

[18] Ibid. 34B8.

[19] Homer *Il.* XX 65, said of Hades.

[20] The "father" refers to the second hypostasis "Intellect." See *Tim.* 37C7, where the "father" is the Demiurge. Plotinus' Intellect represents his interpretation of Plato's Demiurge. See *infra* 8, 5; II 1. 5, 5; II 3. 18, 15; V 9. 3, 26. Soul is like Intellect, because it is an image of it. See *infra* 3, 7. It images the unity and universality, that is, omnipresence, of Intellect. See VI 4 and VI 5 on the latter.

[21] See Plato *Tim.* 92C6–7. Heaven is "multiple" in the sense that it has many parts.

[22] Heraclitus Fr. B 96 D-K.

But the explanation for gods being gods must necessarily be a god older than they. Our soul is of the same kind, and when you examine it without the [45] accretions, taking it in its "purified condition,"[23] you will find that it is the same honorable thing that soul was found to be, more honorable than everything that is bodily. For all bodily things are earth, but even if they were fire, what would be the cause of its burning?[24] And so, too, for everything composed of these, even if you add water and air. But if the body is worth pursuing just because it is ensouled, [50] why would one ignore oneself to pursue another? If you loved the soul in another, then love yourself.

§3. Since the soul is so honorable and divine a thing—trusting at once that such a thing is able to approach god[25] with [the help of] such a cause—ascend to him. Certainly, you will not have to cast far, "nor are the intermediary steps many."[26] Understand, then, the soul's higher neighboring region, [5] more divine than the divine soul, after which and from which the soul comes. For even though the argument has shown the kind of thing soul is [honorable and divine], it is an image of Intellect.[27] Just as spoken words are an expression of thinking, so, too, Soul is an expression of Intellect,[28] and its whole [external] activity,[29] that which Intellect sends forth as life for the existence of something else.[30] [10] It is just like fire that has both internal heat and radiant heat.[31] But in the intelligible world, one should understand that the internal activity does not flow out of it, but rather one activity remains in it, and the other is the independent reality.

---

[23] See Plato *Rep.* 611C3–4.

[24] That is, just as soul provides life to inert matter ("earth"), so, even if things were made of fire, they would need an animating principle.

[25] That is, Intellect.

[26] See Homer *Il.* I 156.

[27] See *infra* 7, 1; also, II 9. 4, 25; V 3. 4, 20 ff.; V 3. 8, 46 ff. It is the higher (i.e., cognitive) part of the soul that is an image of Intellect. See V 3. 4, 20–1; V 3. 8, 45–7. The lower soul is an image of the higher. See V 9. 6, 15–20.

[28] See *infra* 6, 44–5; IV 3. 5, 8. Soul is an expression of Intellect as Intellect is, in some way, an expression of the One. See V 3. 16, 16–7; VI 4. 11, 16; VI 7. 17, 41–2. The forms in souls are images of and an expression of the Forms in Intellect. See V 9. 3, 30–7. The intelligible structure of the sensible world is ultimately derived from Intellect via the instrumentality of Soul.

[29] See *infra* 6, 30–48; V 4. 2, 27–30; VI 2. 22, 26–8 on the distinction between an "internal" and an "external" activity.

[30] The soul's role is to give life, i.e., existence, to bodies.

[31] For this example, see Aristotle *Met.* α 1, 993b25.

Since, then, Soul is derived from Intellect, it is intellectual, and its own intellect[32] is found in its acts of discursive reasoning, and its perfection comes from Intellect, again like a father raising a child whom he begat as imperfect [15] in relation to himself. Then both its independent reality is from Intellect and the actuality of it as an expression of Intellect occurs when Intellect is seen in it. For whenever it [Soul] looks into Intellect, it has inside of itself objects of thought and activity that belong to it. And these alone should be called activities of Soul, namely, those that are intellectual and belong to it. The inferior activities come from elsewhere, and are states of [20] an inferior soul.[33]

Intellect, then, makes Soul even more divine by being its father and by being present to it. For there is nothing in between them but the fact of their being different, soul as next in order and as receptive, and Intellect as form.[34] Even the matter of Intellect is beautiful,[35] since it is both in the form of Intellect and simple. What Intellect is like, then, is clear from the above, namely, that it is superior [25] to Soul thus described.

§4. One might also see this from the following: if one starts by marveling at this sensible universe, looking at its expanse and its beauty and its everlasting motion and the gods in it, both the visible[36] and the invisible ones,[37] [5] and the spirits,[38] and all the animals and plants, let him then ascend to the archetype of this universe and the truer reality, and there let him see all that is intelligible and eternal in it with its own understanding and life,[39] and "pure Intellect" presiding over these, and

---

[32] A clear distinction between Intellect and individual intellects, though not so clear a distinction between Soul and individual souls. The emphasis here, however, seems to be on the hypostasis Soul, which includes both the soul of the universe and individual souls. See Aristotle *De An.* Γ 9, 423b26, where Aristotle notes one sense of "intellect" as "rational faculty" (τὸ λογιστικόν), that which is responsible for "acts of discursive reasoning." See Plato *Rep.* 440E8–9 for "rational faculty." There are no acts of reasoning in Intellect. See VI 7. 1, 29. On the distinction between Intellect and the intellects of individual souls, see I 8. 2, 7; 10, 12; V 3. 2, 22; 3, 21.

[33] See Aristotle *De An.* A 1, 403a3–8 for the distinction between thinking and those other psychic functions that require a body.

[34] See V 9. 3, 20–4.

[35] This is intelligible matter. See II 4. 2–5; V 3. 8, 48.

[36] The visible gods are the stars. See Plato *Tim.* 40D4.

[37] These are the Forms, or "intelligible gods." See III 5. 6, 21–4.

[38] On spirits, see III 5. 6, 24 ff. and Plato *Symp.* 202D13 ff.

[39] See Plato *Tim.* 37D1, 39E1 on the "life" of the "eternal paradigm." Also, *Soph.* 248E6–249A2.

indescribable wisdom, and the life that is truly that of Kronos, a god [10] of "fullness" and intellect.[40] For it encompasses every immortal within itself, that is, every intellect, every god, every soul, always at rest. For why should it seek to alter itself from its happy condition?[41] Where should it go to, having all things within itself? It does not even seek to enlarge itself, since it is most perfect.

For this reason, in addition, all the things in it are perfect so as to be [15] perfect in every way, having nothing which is not like this, nothing in it that it does not think, though it thinks not by seeking but by having.[42] Its blessedness is not acquired; rather, everything is in it eternally, and it is true eternity, which time imitates,[43] moving around along with Soul,[44] dropping some things and picking up others. For different things occur at the level of Soul; [20] one time there is a Socrates, one time there is a horse—always some particular reality—whereas Intellect just is everything. So it has all things at rest in it in eternity, and it alone is, and the "is" is always,[45] and the future is nothing to it (for it "is" then, too), nor is there a past for it (for nothing in the intelligible world has passed away), but all things are set in it always, and [25] since they are the same, they are in a way pleased with the condition they are in.[46]

Each of them is Intellect and Being,[47] that is, the totality consists of all Intellect and all Being—Intellect, insofar as it thinks, making Being exist, and Being, by its being thought, giving to Intellect its thinking, which is its Being. But the cause of thinking is something else, something that is also the cause of Being. So the cause of thinking, then, which is also the cause of Being, is something else. Both of these, then, have at [30] the same time a cause other than themselves. For those coexist simultaneously and do not abandon each other, but this one thing

---

[40] The fanciful etymology of Κρόνος, κόρος ("fullness") plus νοῦς ("intellect"), comes from Plato *Crat.* 396B6–7.

[41] See Aristotle *Met.* Λ 7, 1072b22–4; Λ 9, 1074b25–7.

[42] Ibid. Λ 7, 1072b23.

[43] See Plato *Tim.* 37D5–7 and the entire treatise III 7.

[44] Reading παραθεών with Atkinson instead of H-S$_2$ περιθέων.

[45] See *Tim.* 37E6.

[46] Reading in lines 21–2: ἐν [τῷ] αὐτῷ . . . ἐν τῷ <αἰῶνι>. The whole line is then: ἔχει οὖν ἐν αὐτῷ πάντα ἑστῶτα ἐν τῷ αἰῶνι.

[47] Referring to the γένος Being in Plato *Soph.* 254B–D. Each individual intellect is in a way identical with Intellect and with being, that is, the entirety of Intellect's intellectual contents. Cf. V 3. 5, 26 ff.; V 5. 3, 1; V 9. 5, 13; V 9. 8, 2–4; VI 7. 41, 12. See also Parmenides Fr. B 3 D-K.

is nevertheless two: Intellect and Being, thinking and being thought—
Intellect, insofar as it is thinking, Being insofar as it is being thought.
For thinking could not occur if there was not Difference as well as
Sameness. The first things that occur, [35] then, are Intellect, Being,
Difference, and Sameness. And one should include Motion and Rest—
Motion if Intellect is thinking, and Rest, so that it thinks the same
thing.[48] There must be Difference, so that there can be both thinking
and being thought; if you were to remove Difference, it would be made
silent, having become one. It also must be that things that are thought
are different from each other. [40] There must also be Sameness, since
Intellect is one with itself, that is, there is a certain commonality in[49] all
its objects, but "differentiation is Difference."[50] And their having become many produces number and quantity, and quality is the unique
character of each of these, and from these as principles all the other
things arise.

§5. The god, then, who is above the soul is complex,[51] and soul exists
within this complex, connected to it, so long as it does not wish to be
"separated" from it.[52] Then, when it approaches near to Intellect and in
a way becomes one with it, it seeks to know who it is that produced it.[53]
It is he who is simple and who is prior to this multiplicity, [5] who is the
explanation for the being and the complexity of this god;[54] it is he who
is the maker of number.

For number is not primary. Before the Dyad is the One; the Dyad is
second and, having come from the One, it has that as limit imposed on
it, whereas it is itself unlimited. When it is limited, it is henceforth a
number, a number in the sense of a substance.[55] The soul, too, is a

---

[48] See Plato Soph. 254B–255D for the deduction of "the greatest Kinds" (τὰ
μέγιστα γένη), Being, Sameness, Difference, Motion, and Rest. Also, see
Parm. 145E. On Plotinus' understanding of "the greatest Kinds" see especially
VI 2. 7–8.

[49] Reading ἐν in line 40 with Kirchhoff, not ἕν with H-S₂.

[50] See Aristotle Met. Γ 2, 1004a21.

[51] The "complexity" of Intellect consists in the totality of Forms. See V 3. 10, 10;
VI 7. 13, 1–2.

[52] See Plato Parm. 144B2.

[53] Reading ζητεῖ in line 3 with the mss. followed by a comma instead of H-S₂'s
ζῇ ἀεί.

[54] See V 3. 12, 9–10; V 3. 15, 28; VI 7. 15, 20; VI 7. 16, 22–3.

[55] On the difference between "substantial" numbers (i.e., Form-Numbers) and
quantitative numbers, see V 5. 4, 16–17. For Form-Numbers see V 4. 2, 7–8. For
the evidence Plotinus is relying on for his view that this is Plato's doctrine, see

number.⁵⁶ [10] The first things are neither masses nor magnitudes. The things that have thickness come later, those things that sense-perception takes to be real. Nor is it the moist part in seeds that is valuable, but the part that is not seen. This is number and an expressed principle. So, what are called number and the Dyad in the intelligible world are expressed principles and Intellect. But whereas the Dyad, [15] understood in a way as a substrate, is unlimited,⁵⁷ each number that comes from it and the One is a Form, [Intellect] in a way having been shaped by the Forms that come to be in it. In one manner, it is shaped by the One, and in another by itself, as in the way the faculty of sight is actualized.⁵⁸ For thinking is [as] sight's seeing, and both are one.⁵⁹

§6. How, then, does it [Intellect] see, and what does it see, and how in general did it get realized and come to be from the One so that it can even see? For the soul now grasps that these things [the Forms] must of necessity be, but in addition it longs to grasp the answer to the question much discussed among the ancient wise men, too, of how from a unity, such as we say the One [5] is, anything acquired existence, whether plurality or duality or number.⁶⁰ Why did it not remain by itself, but instead such a plurality flowed from it, which [plurality], though seen among existing things, we think right to lead back to it.

Let us speak of this matter, then, in the following manner, calling to god himself,⁶¹ not with spoken words, [10] but by extending ourselves with our soul in prayer to him, in this way being able to pray alone to him who is alone.⁶² Since god is by himself, as if inside a temple, remaining tranquil while transcending everything, the contemplator

---

Aristotle *Met.* A 6, 987b14; **M** 7, 1081a14 and Alexander of Aphrodisias' citation of Aristotle's *On the Good* in his *In Met.* 55, 20–56, 35.

⁵⁶ See VI 6. 16, 45 ff. Xenocrates, successor to Plato after Speusippus, held this view, basing it in part on Plato *Tim.* 36E6–7.

⁵⁷ See V 4. 2, 7–8 and Aristotle *Met.* **M** 7, 1081a14–15.

⁵⁸ See III 8. 11, 1–8; VI 7. 15, 21–2; 16, 10–13; Aristotle *De An.* Γ 2, 426a13–14; 3, 428a6–7.

⁵⁹ That is, Intellect is the same as the activity of intellection, or thinking. See V 3. 6, 7; Aristotle *Met.* Λ 9, 1074b29-1075a10 for the argument that the intellect of the unmoved mover is identical with its thinking.

⁶⁰ See III 8. 10, 14–15; III 9. 4; V 2. 1, 3–4; V 3. 15.

⁶¹ Plotinus is now referring to the One, the first principle of all.

⁶² On the expression "alone with the alone" see I 6. 7, 9; VI 7. 34, 7–8; VI 9. 11, 51.

should contemplate the fixed statues which are in a way outside the temple already, or rather the [15] first statue which appeared in the following manner.

It must be that for everything in motion there is something towards which it moves.[63] Since the One has nothing towards which it moves, let us not suppose that it is moving, but if something comes to be after it, it has necessarily come to be by being eternally turned towards the One.[64] Let the sort of coming to be that is [20] in time not get in our way, since our discussion is concerned with things that are eternal. When in our discussion we attribute "coming to be" to them, we are doing so in order to give their causal order.[65] We should say, then, that that which comes to be from the intelligible world does so without the One being moved. For if something came to be as a result of its having moved, then that which came to be from it [25] would be third after the motion and not second. It must be, then, that if something came second after it, that came to exist while the One was unmoved, neither inclining, nor having willed anything, nor moving in any way.[66]

How, then, does this happen, and what should we think about what is near to the One while it reposes? A radiation of light comes from it, but from it while it reposes, like the light from the sun, in a way [30] encircling it, eternally coming from it while it reposes. And all things that exist, so long as they continue to exist, necessarily, in virtue of their present power, produce from their own essence a dependent reality around them at their exterior, a sort of image of the archetypes from which it was generated.[67] Fire produces the heat that comes from it. [35] And snow does not only hold its coldness inside itself. Perfumes especially witness to this, for so long as they exist, something flows from them around them, the reality of which a bystander enjoys. Further, all things, as soon as they are perfected, generate.[68] That which is eternally perfect generates eternally an everlasting reality, and it generates something inferior to itself.

---

[63] See Aristotle *Phys.* Δ 11, 219a10–11; E 1, 224b1–10.

[64] Reading αὐτό with Atkinson, instead of αὑτό with H-S₂ The point is that Intellect is turned towards the One, not that the One is turned towards itself.

[65] Reading αἰτίας <τι> τάξεως αὐτοῖς ἀποδώσειν with Atkinson thus enabling us to understand αἰτίας as genitive singular.

[66] See V 5. 12, 43–9.

[67] See IV 8. 6, 8–12; V 3. 7, 23–4; V 4. 2, 27–33; VI 7. 18, 5–6; VI 7. 21, 4–6; VI 7. 40, 21–4.

[68] "Perfected"' in the sense of having come to maturity. See V 4. 1, 26; V 2. 1, 7–9; Aristotle *De An.* B 4, 415a26–8.

What, then, must we say about [40] that which is most perfect? Nothing can come from it except that which is greatest after it. The greatest after it is Intellect, that which is second. For Intellect sees that and is in need of it alone. But the One has no need of Intellect. And that which is generated from something greater than Intellect is Intellect, which is greater than other things, because other things come after it. [45] For example, Soul is an expression of Intellect and a certain activity, just as Intellect is an activity of the One. But Soul's reason is murky, for it is a reflection of Intellect, and, owing to this, it must look to Intellect. Similarly, Intellect has to look to the One, so that it can be Intellect. It sees it not as having been separated from it, but because it is after it and there is nothing in between, as there is nothing in between Soul and Intellect. Everything [50] longs for that which produced it and loves this, especially whenever there is just producer and produced. And "whenever the producer is the best,"[69] the produced is necessarily together with it, since they are only separated by difference.

§7. Since we really should speak more clearly, let's say that Intellect is an image of the One. We must say first that that which is produced must somehow be the One[70] and preserve many of its properties, that is, be a likeness in relation to it, just like the light that comes from the sun. But [5] the One is not Intellect. How, then, does it generate Intellect? In fact, by Intellect's reversion to it, Intellect saw the One, and this seeing is Intellect.[71] For that which grasps anything else is either sense-perception or intellect. Sense-perception is a line, etc.[72] But the circle is the sort of thing that can be divided, though intellect is not like that. There is unity here, but the One has the power to produce [10] all things.[73] Thinking observes those things that the One is virtually, in a way cutting itself off from that virtuality.[74] Otherwise, it would not have

---

[69] See Aristotle *Met.* N 4, 1091b10, quoting Pherecydes (6th c. B.C.E.), one of the "sages" of the early cosmological tradition.

[70] On Intellect's being "One-like" see III 8. 11, 16; V 3. 16, 18–19; VI 7. 15, 23; VI 9. 5, 26.

[71] See VI 8. 16, 19–21.

[72] That is, sense-perception is comparable to a line, Intellect to a circle, and the One to the center of the circle. The text of this line, αἴσθησιν γραμμὴν καὶ τὰ ἄλλα is taken by H-S₂ as corrupt.

[73] See V 3. 15, 31; V 4. 2, 38; VI 9. 5, 36–7.

[74] See III 8. 10, 1; IV 8. 6, 11; V 4. 1, 23–6, 36; V 4. 2, 38; VI 9. 5, 36; VI 7. 32, 31. The term is δύναμις, which needs to be translated sometimes as "power," sometimes as "potentiality." It is always used in the former sense of the One, and

become Intellect, since it already has by itself a sort of awareness of the One's power to produce essence.[75]

At any rate, Intellect, by means of itself, also defines its own being by the power that comes from the One and, because it is a sort of [15] unitary part of what belongs to the One and is the substance coming from it, it is strengthened by it and brought to perfection as substance by it, and comes from it. It sees what is there by seeing itself, a sort of division of the indivisible, life and thinking and all things, none of which the One is.

For in this way all things come from it, because it is not constrained by [20] some shape, for it is one alone. If it were all things, it would be among the things that are. For this reason, the One is none of the things in Intellect, but from it all things come. For this reason, these are essences, for each has already been defined, and each has a sort of shape. Being should not be suspended, so to speak, in the indefinite, [25] but fixed by definition and stability. Stability in the intelligible world is definition and shape, by means of which it [essence] acquires reality.

"This is the lineage"[76] of this Intellect, worthy of the purest Intellect, born from nowhere else than from the first principle, and, having been generated, at once generating all things together with itself,[77] both all the beauty [30] of the Ideas and all the intelligible gods. And it is full of the beings it has generated and, so to speak, swallowing them again by having them in itself and neither letting them fall into matter nor be reared by Rhea (as the mysteries and myths about the gods enigmatically say that Kronos, the wisest god, before the birth of Zeus, [35] holds back in himself what he generates, so that he is full and is like Intellect in satiety).[78]

After this, so they say, being already sated, he generates Zeus, for Intellect generates Soul, being perfect as Intellect. For since it is perfect, it

---

there means something like "virtually" as in "white light is virtually all the colors of the rainbow."

[75] The word οὐσία is sometimes appropriately translated as "substance" indicating the complex being of Intellect, and sometimes as "essence" (as here and at line 23) indicating the intelligible natures or Forms with which Intellect is cognitively identical.

[76] See Plato *Rep.* 547A4–5, quoting Homer *Il.* VI 211.

[77] Intellect is generated as that which is cognitively identical with all Forms. See V 2. 1, 11–13; VI 7. 17, 33–4.

[78] Rhea is the wife of Kronos.

had to generate and since it was such a great power, it could not be barren. That which was generated by it could, in this case as well, not be superior to it [40] but had to be an inferior reflection of it, first similarly undefined and then defined by that which generated it, in a way made to be a reflection. The offspring of Intellect is an expressed principle and a reality, that which thinks discursively [Soul].[79] This is what moves around Intellect and is a light and trace of Intellect, dependent on it,[80] on one side [45] attached to Intellect and filled up with it and enjoying it and sharing in it and thinking, and on the other side, attached to the things that came after it, or rather itself generating what is necessarily inferior to Soul. These matters should be discussed later.[81] This is as far as the divine realities go.

§8. And it is for this reason that Plato says that the principles are three: "around the king of all," meaning the primary things, "second around the secondary things," and "third around the tertiary things."[82] And he says "father of the cause"[83] [5] meaning by "cause," Intellect.[84] For the Intellect is his Demiurge.[85] And he says that the Demiurge makes the Soul in that "mixing bowl."[86] And since the Intellect is cause, he means by "father" the Good, or that which is beyond Intellect and "beyond essence."[87] Often he calls Being and the Intellect "Idea," which shows that Plato understood that [10] the Intellect comes from the Good, and the Soul comes from the Intellect.[88] So these statements

---

[79] See IV 3. 5, 9–11 where the same point is made and applied to both Soul and individual souls. The latter are said to come from the former.

[80] See V 3. 9, 15–17.

[81] No particular treatise is clearly indicated here.

[82] See Plato [?] *2nd Ep.* 312E1–4. Plotinus' meaning is: Plato's reference to the "king of all" is a reference to the One; his reference to a second principle is a reference to Intellect and its contents; and his reference to a third principle is a reference to Soul. This letter is generally thought by contemporary scholars to be spurious, though Plotinus and others in antiquity supposed that it was genuine.

[83] See Plato [?] *6th Ep.* 323D4, also probably spurious.

[84] See Plato *Phd.* 97C1–2, quoting Anaxagoras Fr. B 12 D-K.

[85] See II 1. 1, 5; II 3. 18, 15; V 9. 3, 26.

[86] See *Tim.* 34B–35B; 41D4–5.

[87] See *Rep.* 509B9; Aristotle, in Simplicius *In Ca.* 485, 22, is quoted as identifying god as "Intellect" or "something greater than Intellect."

[88] The identification of Forms with reality is made at *Rep.* 507B5–7; 597B4. The identification of Intellect (i.e., Demiurge) with Forms is based on Plotinus' interpretation of such passages in *Tim.* as 29E1–3; 30C2–D1; 39E7–9.

of ours are not recent or new, but rather were made a long time ago, though not explicitly. The things we are saying now are interpretations of those, relying on the writings of Plato himself as evidence that these are ancient views.

[15] Parmenides previously touched on this doctrine to the extent that he amalgamated Being and Intellect, that is, he did not place Being among sensibles, saying "for thinking and being are the same."[89] And he says that Being is "immobile,"[90] though he does attach thinking to it, eliminating all bodily motion [20] from it so that it would remain as it is, likening it to a "spherical mass,"[91] because it encompasses all things and because thinking is not external to it, but rather in it itself. Saying that it was "one" in his own writings,[92] he got blamed for saying that this one thing was in fact found to be many.[93]

Plato's Parmenides, speaking more accurately, distinguishes [25] from among other ones the primary One, which is one in a more proper sense, calling the second one "one many" and the third one "one *and* many."[94] In this way, too, he is in harmony with [the doctrine of] the three natures.[95]

§9. Anaxagoras himself, too, in saying that "intellect is pure and unmixed," is positing the first principle as simple and the One as separate, although he neglects to give an accurate account owing to his antiquity.[96] In addition, Heraclitus knew the One to be everlasting and intelligible, since bodies are always coming into being [5] and are "in flux."[97]

---

[89] See Parmenides Fr. B 3 D-K. Plotinus frequently alludes to this line. See I 4. 10, 6; III 8. 8, 8; V 9. 5, 29–30.

[90] See Parmenides Fr. B 8, 26 D-K.

[91] Parmenides Fr. B 8, 43 D-K.

[92] Parmenides Fr. B 8, 6 D-K.

[93] See Plato *Soph.* 245A5–B1.

[94] See *Parm.* 137C–142A; 144E5; 155E5. The passage 137C–142A was taken by Plotinus and later Neoplatonists as a fundamental expression of the three basic metaphysical principles of Platonism.

[95] That is, the character Parmenides in the dialogue argues on behalf of the three principles, or hypostases: the One, Intellect, and Soul.

[96] See Anaxagoras Fr. B 12 D-K, which Plotinus is quoting inexactly. Cf. Aristotle *Met.* A 8, 989a30 ff.; *De An.* A 2, 405a13 ff.

[97] See Heraclitus Fr. A 1 D-K; Aristotle *Met.* A 6, 987a33–4; M 4, 1078b14–15; *De Ca.* Γ 1, 298b29–33.

And for Empedocles, "Strife" divides and "Love" is the One—this itself is incorporeal—and the elements are posited as matter.[98]

Aristotle later said that the first principle was "separate"[99] and "intelligible,"[100] but when he says that "it thinks itself,"[101] he no longer makes it the first principle.[102] Further, he [10] makes many other things intelligible (as many as there are spheres in the heavens, so that each intelligible moves each sphere),[103] but by doing so he describes intelligibles in a way different from Plato, supposing an argument from plausibility, since he did not have an argument from necessity.[104] One might pause to consider whether it is even plausible, for it is more plausible that all the spheres, contributing to one system, should look to one thing that is the first principle.

[15] And one might inquire if the many intelligibles are, according to him, derived from one first principle, or whether he holds that there are many principles among the intelligibles. And if they are derived from one, it will be clear that, analogous to the way it is among sensibles, where one sphere encompasses another, until you reach the outermost one that is dominant, so the first there will also encompass everything, that is, [20] there will be an intelligible world. And just as here the spheres are not empty, but the first is full of stars, and the others also have stars, so, too, in the intelligible world the movers will have many things within themselves, and the truer realities will be there. But if each one is a principle, the principles will be an arbitrary collection. And what will be the explanation for their working together[105] and their agreement on a single task, [25] the harmony of the entire universe? How can there be equality [in number] of the sensibles [spheres] in the

---

[98] See Empedocles Fr. B 17, 7–8 D-K (=B 26, 5–6); IV 4. 40, 5–6; VI 7. 14, 19–20. Aristotle also says that Empedocles identified Love as "the One," that is, as the first principle. See *Met*. B 4, 1001a12–15.

[99] See Aristotle *De An*. Γ 5, 430a17; *Met*. Λ 7, 1073a4.

[100] Ibid. Λ 7, 1072a26.

[101] Ibid. Λ 7, 1072b20.

[102] That is, because self-thinking is a complex activity, and the first principle must be absolutely simple. Supplying the negative οὐ, which is missing from H-S$_2$.

[103] On the plurality of movers of the spheres, see *Met*. Λ 8.

[104] Plotinus is alluding to the argument in *Met*. Λ 8, 1074a14–16 that it is plausible to suppose that the number of unmoved movers or principles is equal to the number of heavenly spheres, that is, fifty five. Aristotle declines to say whether this is in fact necessary.

[105] Reading συνεργήσει in line 24 with Harder instead of συνέσονται as in the manuscripts and in H-S$_2$.

universe in relation to the intelligibles or movers? How can these incorporeals be thus many, without matter to separate them?[106]

So, among the ancients, those who adhered most closely to the doctrines of Pythagoras and to those who came after him, and to those of Pherecydes, held to this account of this nature [the One]. But some among them worked out this view among themselves in their own writings, while some did not do so in writings but demonstrated it in unwritten discussions[107] or, altogether left it alone.

§10. It has already been shown that it is necessary to believe that things are this way: that there is the One beyond Being, that it is such as the argument strove to show to the extent that it is possible to demonstrate anything about these matters; that next, there is Being and Intellect; and third, there is the nature of the Soul.[108]

[5] And just as in nature[109] these aforementioned three are found, so it is necessary to believe as well that these are in us. I do not mean that they are among sensibles—for these three are separate from sensibles—but that they are in things that transcend the sensible order, using the term "transcend" in the same manner in which it is used to refer to those things that transcend the whole universe. In the same way, in saying that they belong to a human being, [10] I mean what Plato means by "the inner human being."[110]

Our soul is, then, something divine and of another nature, like the nature of all soul. But the soul that has intellect is perfect, and one part of intellect is that which reasons and one part is that which makes reasoning possible.[111] The reasoning part of soul is in need of no [15] bodily organ for its reasoning,[112] having its own activity in purity in order that it also be possible for it to reason purely; someone who supposed it to be separate and not mixed with body and in the primary intelligible

---

[106] See Aristotle *Met.* Λ 8, 1074a31.

[107] Probably a reference to Plato's "unwritten teachings." See Aristotle *Phys.* Δ 2, 209b11–17, the only explicit reference to such teachings, though Aristotle does frequently attribute views to Plato that are not easily or obviously mirrored in the dialogues.

[108] See *supra* 2–9.

[109] Plotinus means to contrast intelligible external reality with the personal or subjective.

[110] See *Rep.* 589A7–B1.

[111] See *supra* 3, 13. The distinction is between intellect in us and Intellect.

[112] See Aristotle *De An.* Γ 4, 429a24–7, where Aristotle argues that intellect is "unmixed" with the bodily.

world would not be mistaken. For we should not search for a place in which to situate it, but we should make it transcend all place. For this is how it is for that which is [20] by itself, transcendent and immaterial, which it is whenever it is alone, retaining nothing from the nature of the body. For this reason, Plato says that the Demiurge "in addition" encircled the soul of the universe from "outside," pointing to the part of the soul that abides in the intelligible world.[113] As for us, hiding his meaning, he said that it is "at the top of our head."[114]

And his exhortation [25] "to be separate"[115] is not meant spatially— for this is by nature separated—but is an exhortation not to incline to the body, even by acts of imagination, and to alienate ourselves from the body, if somehow someone could lead upward the remaining part of the soul and even bear upward that which is situated here below, that part that alone is [30] craftsman of the body and has the job of shaping it and caring for it.[116]

§11. Since, then, there is soul that reasons about just and beautiful things and reasoning that seeks to know if this is just or if this is beautiful, it is necessary that there exist permanently something that is just, from which the reasoning in the soul arises.[117] How else could it reason? And [5] if soul sometimes reasons about these things and sometimes does not, there must be in us Intellect that does not reason but always possesses Justice, and there must be also the principle of Intellect and its cause and god [the One].[118] And it must be indivisible and remain so, and while not remaining in [any one] place, it is still seen in many things, each one [10] able to receive it [the One] in a way as other than it,[119] just as the center of the circle exists by itself, but each of the points on it has a mark of the center in themselves, that is, the radii bring to the center that which is in each case unique. For it is by something like this in ourselves that we are in contact with god and are with him and depend on him. And if we converge on him, [15] we would be settled in the intelligible world.

---

[113] See *Tim.* 34B4. See also 36D9–E1. On Plotinus' interpretation of Plato according to which a part the soul is "undescended," see IV 8. 8, 2–3.

[114] See *Tim.* 90A5.

[115] See *Phd.* 67C6.

[116] See Plato [?] *Epin.* 981B7–8.

[117] See V 3. 3. See Plato *Parm.* 132A1–4 for the argument that Forms are required to account for predication.

[118] See Aristotle *De An.* Γ 5, 430a22.

[119] See III 8. 9, 23–6.

§12. How, then, given that we have such great things in us, do we not grasp them, but rather are mostly inactive with respect to these activities; indeed, some are altogether inactive?

Those are always involved with their own activities—I mean, Intellect and that which is prior to Intellect, eternally in itself, and [5] Soul as well, which is thus "always moving."[120] For not everything in soul is immediately perceptible, but it comes to us whenever it comes to our sense-perception. But whenever there is perceptual activity that is not being transmitted to the perceptual faculty, it has not yet come to the entire soul.[121] We do not yet know it, then, since we are the whole soul, including the perceptual faculty, not just a part [10] of it. Further, each of the parts of the soul is always acting always by itself with its own object, but cognizing occurs whenever transmission, that is, apprehension, occurs.

If, then, there is going to be apprehension of things present in this way, then that which is to apprehend must revert inward, and focus [15] attention there. Just as if someone were waiting to hear a voice that he wanted to hear, and, distancing himself from other voices, were to prick up his ears to hear the preferred one, waiting for the time when it would arrive—so, too, in this case one must let go of perceptible sounds, except insofar as they are necessary, and guard the soul's pure power of apprehension and be ready to listen to the sounds from above.

V 2 (11) On the Generation and Order of the Things That Come after the First (complete)

This treatise consists of a concise statement of the three fundamental principles of Plotinus' metaphysics—the One, Intellect, and Soul—and includes consideration of nature, the lowest part of soul.

§1. The One is all things and not one thing.[1] For it is a principle of all things,[2] but not those things, though all things are like it, for they do,

---

[120] See Plato *Phdr.* 245C5.
[121] See IV 8. 8, 3–9.

[1] See Plato *Parm.* 160B2–3.
[2] See III 8. 9, 19–32; III 8. 11, 8–11; V 4. 1, 5–15; VI 8. 8, 8–9 for arguments that there must be a first, absolutely simple, principle of all.

in a way, find their way back to the intelligible world, or rather they are not there yet but will be.

How, then, do they arise out of a simple One, which is self-identical and has neither apparent complexity in it nor any doubleness [5] whatsoever?[3] In fact, it is because there was nothing in it that all things come from it, and, in order that Being should exist, it is not Being but the generator of it.[4] This is, in a way, the first generation. Since it is perfect,[5] owing to its neither seeking anything nor having anything nor needing anything, it in a way overflows and its superabundance has made something other than it. That which was generated [10] reverted to it and was filled up and became what it is by looking at it, and this is Intellect.[6] The positioning of it in relation to the One produced Being; the gazing upon the One produced Intellect. Since, then, it positions itself in relation to the One in order that it may see, it becomes Intellect and Being at the same time. So Intellect, being in a way the One[7] and pouring forth abundant power, makes things like it—[15] Intellect is, after all, a figure of the One—just as that which is prior to it [the One] in turn pours forth.[8]

And this activity, arising from the substance of Intellect, is Soul's, which comes from Intellect while Intellect remains in itself. For Intellect also came to be while that which was before it remained. But Soul does not remain when *it* produces; rather, being moved, it generated a reflection of itself. It looked to the intelligible world from where it came, [20] it was filled up, and it proceeded to another and contrary motion, generating a reflection of itself, namely, sense-perception and the principle of growth in plants [nature].[9] Nothing of that which is before it is separated or cut off. For this reason, the Soul from above also seems to extend down to plants, for Soul does, after all, extend down in a definite manner, since there is life in plants. Of course, not all of Soul

---

[3] See V 1. 6, 4–8.

[4] That is, it is the generator of the sort of being that implies any complexity. See V 1. 7, 18–22.

[5] See V 1. 6, 38; V 6, 2, 13.

[6] See III 8. 9, 29–32; III 8. 11, 1–8; V 1. 5, 18–19.

[7] See VI 7, 3; also, VI 4. 11, 16; VI 7. 17, 41–2. Intellect is the first product of the One and so in some way resembles its producer. It resembles the One as an "expressed principle" of it, as an "image" of it, and as the One's "external activity."

[8] The idea is that Intellect can produce things similar to itself, because it has acquired this power from the One.

[9] Sense-perception for animals and a principle of growth for plants.

is [25] in plants, but it comes to be in them in just this way, in that it advanced downward, having made another reality by that procession and by the desire for that which is inferior to it.[10] And since the part [of Soul] prior to this was dependent on Intellect, it permits Intellect to remain by itself.

§2. They [the principles] proceed, then, from the beginning to the end, leaving behind each one eternally in its own place, with that which is generated taking another and inferior rank.[11] And yet each one is the same as that upon which it follows, so long as it connects itself with that. Whenever, then, [5] Soul comes to be in a plant, it is another sort of part of it, that which is the most daring and non-intelligent part and one that has proceeded up to just this point. And then, whenever Soul comes to be in a nonrational animal, the power of sense-perception, having been dominant, brought it there. And whenever Soul comes to be in a human being, Soul's motion is either entirely in the rational part, or it comes from Intellect, since [an individual] soul has its own intellect and [10] a will of its own to think or, generally, to be in motion.

Let us return to what was said before. Whenever someone cuts off the shoots or the tops of plants, where has the soul of the plant gone? Where did it come from? For it has not separated itself spatially. So it is in its principle. But if you were to cut off or burn the root, where would the soul in the root go? [15] In the soul, for it has not gone to another place. It could be in the same place or in another, if it ran back [to its source]. If not, it is in another plant, for it is not constrained [as to where it can go]. If it were to go back to its source, it would go back to the power preceding it. But where is that power? In the power preceding *it*. That takes us back to Intellect, not to a place, for Soul was not in place. And Intellect is even [20] more not in place [than Soul], so neither is this [Soul]. It is then nowhere but in that which is nowhere, and at the same time it is also everywhere. If it proceeded in this way to the upper region, it would pause in the middle before coming to be completely in the highest, and it has a life in a middle position and has rested in that part of itself.

All these things are the One and not the One; [25] they are the One, because they are from it; they are not the One, because it endowed them with what they have while remaining by itself. It is then in a way

---

[10] Intellect generates Soul, and Soul generates its nonrational reflections, i.e., all types of psychic functions other than the higher cognitive one of discursive reasoning. See III 4. 1, 1–3. On desire as a property of Soul see I 7. 1, 13; III 5. 9, 40–1; IV 4. 16, 26–7.

[11] See IV 8. 6, 10; Plato *Tim.* 42E5–6.

like a long life stretched out in length, each of the parts other than those that come next, all continuous with itself, but one being different from the other, the first not being destroyed with the [appearance of] the second. What, then, is the soul that comes to be in [30] plants? Does it generate nothing? In fact, it generates in that in which it is. We should examine how by taking another starting-point.[12]

V 3 (49) On the Knowing Hypostases and on That Which Is Transcendent (§§ 1–9; 13–17)

This treatise is Plotinus' most sustained analysis of the nature of thinking and of the relation of the individual intellect to the principle, Intellect. The first principle, the One, is, owing to its simplicity, beyond thinking and beyond intelligibility.

§1. Must that which thinks itself be complex in order that, with some one part of itself contemplating the others, it could in this way be said to think itself, on the grounds that were it altogether simple, it would not be able to revert to itself, that is, there could not be the grasping of itself?[1] Or is it possible for that which is [5] not composite also to think itself? In fact, that which is said to think itself for the reason that it is a composite, just because some one part of itself thinks the others, as if we were to grasp in sense-perception our own shape and the rest of our bodily nature, would not be able truly to think itself. For in this case, it will not be the whole that [10] is known, since that part which thinks the other parts which are with it has also not been thinking itself. And then this will not be the sought for case of "self [thinking] itself,"[2] but a case of one thing thinking another.

One should, then, suppose that the grasping of itself is by something that is also simple and seek to discover, if one possibly can, how this oc-

---

[12] See III 4. 1–2; IV 4. 22.

[1] See Sextus Empiricus M. VII 283–7; 310–13, who recounts the skeptical argument against the possibility of "self-thinking." Sextus, like Plotinus, assumes that self-thinking is a property of knowing. "Self-thinking" is roughly equivalent to "knowing that one knows," although the supposition that this knowing is propositional should be resisted. See also Aristotle *De An.* Γ 4, 429b9; 6, 430b25–6 for the necessary self-thinking of intellect.

[2] See Aristotle *Met.* Λ 9, 1074b21–3.

curs, or else relinquish the belief in something [15] truly thinking itself. But relinquishing this belief is completely impossible given that so many absurdities would follow. For even if we should refuse to allow self-thinking to the soul on the grounds that that would be quite absurd,[3] still it would be completely absurd not to give it to the nature of intellect and to claim that though it has knowledge of other things it will not be counted as having knowledge, that is, understanding, of itself.[4]

[20] Now it is sense-perception and, if you like, discursive thinking and belief that apprehend externals, but not intellect, though whether intellect has knowledge of them or not should be examined. Clearly, though, intellect will know all intelligibles.[5] Therefore, will that which knows these know only these, or itself as well? Or will it then know itself in this way: [25] because it knows only these, it will not know who it is, I mean that it will know that it knows that which is its own [the intelligibles], but it will have no further knowledge of who it is? Or rather will it know both that which is its own and itself? In what manner this occurs and to what extent is something that must be investigated.

§2. But first we must examine whether we ought to give the soul knowledge of itself and what is that in it that knows and how it does it. We should start by saying that its power of perception is only of externals, for even if there were some awareness of what occurs inside the body, [5] the apprehension would still be of what is external to itself [the power of perception], for it perceives states in the body by itself.

As for the part of the soul that reasons, it makes judgments about the sensory images presented to it by sense-perception, organizing and distinguishing these. In fact, in regard to what comes from Intellect, it also even considers [10] something like impressions [of these],[6] and has the same power [of discrimination] in relation to these.[7] And it acquires

---

[3] That is, one might suppose that it would be absurd for the entire soul to be capable of self-thinking.

[4] Here Plotinus seems to make a distinction between the general term "knowledge" (γνῶσις) and the specific term "understanding" (ἐπιστήμη). Elsewhere and throughout this treatise, when Plotinus is talking about intellect, he uses forms of the verb γιγνώσκειν, from which γνῶσις is derived, for the highest type of cognition, namely, understanding.

[5] That is, it will know what is *internal* to it.

[6] Or "representations." See V 5. 1, 24 ff., where the contents of Intellect itself are specifically said not to be impressions. See Sextus Empiricus M. VII 227 ff., where Sextus focuses on the Stoic idea of impressions, or representations, and argues that knowledge cannot be the "having" of these.

[7] See I 4. 10, 6 ff.

further understanding as if by recognizing and matching up those impressions that have been in it from before with new ones recently arrived. And we would call these acts the soul's "recollections."[8]

And does the intellect, which is a part of the soul[9] [15] stop at this point in its power, or does it turn to and know itself? Or is this to be attributed [only] to Intellect? For by giving self-knowledge to this part of the soul—we shall now call it "intellect"—we shall find ourselves investigating in what way it differs from the higher [Intellect], but if we do not give self-knowledge to this part, we shall, by proceeding with the argument, arrive at [self-knowledge] in [Intellect] [20] and we shall [here] have to investigate what "it [thinks] itself" means.

Further, if we should give it to the intellect here below, we shall have to investigate the difference between its "thinking itself" and [Intellect's], for if there is none, this intellect will straightaway be the "unmixed" [Intellect].[10] Does, then, this discursive thinking part of the soul itself revert to itself? It does not. Rather it acquires comprehension from the impressions it receives from [25] each of its sources [sense-perception and Intellect]. And how it acquires comprehension is the matter that should be first investigated.

§3. So, then, sense-perception saw a human being and gave the impression to discursive thinking. What does discursive thinking say? In fact, it says nothing yet, but rather just became aware and stopped at that. Unless, that is, it were to converse with itself and say, "Who is this?" assuming it had met this human being before and would then say, relying [5] on its memory, that this is Socrates. And if it analyzes the shape, it is dividing up what the imagination has given it. And if it should say whether he is good [or not], it has said this based on what it has become aware of through sense-perception, but what it has said about these things it would already have in itself, having a rule about the Good in itself. How does it have the Good in itself? [10] In fact, it is Good-like,[11] and is fortified for the sense-perception of this sort of thing by Intellect illuminating it. For this is the purified part of the soul, and it receives the traces of Intellect that have been impressed on it.

---

[8] See II 9. 16, 45–7. See Plato *Phd.* 72E5; *Men.* 81E4 for the doctrine that all learning is recollection.

[9] That is, embodied or descended intellect, involved in discursive reasoning. See V 1. 3.

[10] See Anaxagoras Fr. A 15 D-K; Aristotle *De An.* A 2, 405a16–17.

[11] See Plato *Rep.* 509A3 on the Form of the Good. The word ἀγαθοειδής here, indicates that the soul shares in that Form (εἶδος) in some way. See I 8. 11, 16; III 8. 11, 16; VI 7. 15, 9.

Why, then, is this not what Intellect is, and all the other powers, starting with the perceptual, are what the soul is? Is it not because soul has to be involved in acts of reasoning? For all of these acts are the works of [15] a reasoning power. But then why should we not just put an end to the matter by endowing this part with self-thinking? Is it not because we already endowed it with the job of examining and busying itself with externals, whereas we think it belongs to Intellect to examine and busy itself with its own affairs, that is, the things that are internal to it? But if someone will say, "What then prevents this [discursive thinking] from examining [20] things internal to it by another power?" he is not asking about the discursive or reasoning power; rather, he has in view pure Intellect.

What, then, prevents pure Intellect from being in soul? We will say, "Nothing." But should we say in addition that Intellect belongs to soul? What we will say is that it does not belong to soul, though we will say that it is our intellect; and though it is other than the discursive power, [25] having gone upward, nevertheless it is ours even if we were not to count it among the parts of the soul. In fact, it is ours and not ours. For this reason we use it and do not use it, though we always make use of discursive reasoning. It is ours when we use it and not ours when we do not.[12]

What then does "using it" mean? [30] Is it when we ourselves become it or speak as Intellect does? Or is it rather when we do so in accord with Intellect? For we are not Intellect. We are, then, in accord with it by the primary reasoning power that is receptive of Intellect. For we perceive by means of sense-perception even if we are <not> perceivers.[13] Is it, then, that we reason discursively in this way, that is, we think by means <of Intellect> in this way? [35] In fact, we ourselves are the discursive reasoners, and we ourselves think the thoughts in the faculty of discursive thinking. For this is what we are.[14]

The activities of Intellect are from above just as the activities arising from sense-perception are from below. We are this—the principal part of the soul,[15] in the middle between two powers, a worse and a better one, the worse being the power of sense-perception and [40] the better being the power of Intellect. But it has been conceded that sense-perception seems to be always ours, for we are always perceiving; whereas Intellect

---

[12] The word προσχρώμεθα ("we use it") indicates use in addition to the use of the other psychic powers.

[13] That is, we perceive with our senses even though we are not identical with those senses.

[14] See I 1. 7, 9–17.

[15] See Aristotle *EN* K 7, 1178a2.

is disputed, because we do not always use it, and because it is separate.[16] And it is separate owing to its not inclining towards us, whereas we rather are looking upward to it. Sense-perception is our messenger, but Intellect "is our king."[17]

§4. But *we* are kings, too, whenever we are in accord with Intellect. We can be in accord with it in two ways: either by having, in a way, its writings written in us like laws[18] or by being, in a way, filled up with it and then being able to see it or perceive it as being present. And we, owing to this vision,[19] know [5] ourselves by learning about other [powers], either learning according to the power of knowing such a thing by that power itself or else by becoming that, so that one who knows himself is double, one part knowing the nature of the psychic power of discursive thinking, the other knowing that which is above this, [10] knowing himself according to that Intellect that he has become.[20]

Further, in thinking himself again, owing to Intellect, it is not as a human being that he does so, but as having become something else completely and dragging himself into the higher region, drawing up only the better part of the soul, which alone can acquire the wings for thinking,[21] in order that someone could be entrusted with what he saw in the intelligible world.

[15] Is it, then, that the discursive part does not know that it is the discursive part, and that it acquires comprehension of externals, and that it discerns what it discerns, and that it does so by the rules that are in itself which it has from Intellect, and that there is something better than it that seeks nothing but rather no doubt has everything? But after all, does it not know what it itself is just when it understands [20] the sort of thing it is and what its functions are? If, then, it were to say that it comes from Intellect and is second after Intellect and an image of Intellect,[22] having in itself all its sort of writings, since the one who writes and has written is in the intelligible world, will one who knows himself in this way halt at these?

---

[16] See V 1. 9, 7 and Aristotle *De An.* Γ 5, 430a17.

[17] See Plato *Phil.* 28C7.

[18] See Aristotle *De An.* Γ 4, 430a1.

[19] Eliminating H-S$_2$'s <τῷ>.

[20] Plotinus is not here contradicting 3, 31. We "become Intellect" when we recognize that Intellect constitutes our ideal identity. We become it when we acknowledge our patrimony.

[21] See Plato *Phdr.* 246B7–C2.

[22] See V 1. 3, 7 with n.20 on soul as an image of Intellect.

Shall we, using a power other than [intellect], [25] observe again Intellect knowing itself, or sharing in Intellect,[23] since that is ours and we are also its; shall we in this way know Intellect and ourselves? In fact, it is necessary that we know it in this way, if we are going to know what this "self [thinking] itself" Intellect is. Someone has, indeed, himself become Intellect when, letting go of the other things that are his, [30] he looks at Intellect with Intellect; he then looks at himself with himself. Then it is indeed as Intellect that he sees himself.

§5. Does it then with one part of itself observe another part of itself?[24] But in that case, one part will be seeing, and one part will be seen, though this is not "self [thinking] itself." What if then the whole is comprised of parts that are in a way of the same kind, so that the part that sees does not differ at all from the part that is seen? [5] For, in this way, the part of itself that is seeing that which is the same as it, sees itself. For then there is no difference between that which sees compared to that which is seen.

In fact, first of all, the division of itself is silly, for how does it divide? Surely, it does not do so by chance. And what is it that is doing the dividing anyway? Is it the part that undertakes for itself the task of seeing or the part that belongs to what is seen? [10] Then how will that which is seeing know itself in that which is seen when it is undertaking for *itself* the task of seeing? For the seeing was not in that which is seen. In fact, knowing itself in this way, it will think itself as that which is being seen and not as that which sees, so that it will neither know all of itself nor wholly know itself. For what it saw was what was seen; it did not see the seeing. [15] And in this way it will be another, not itself, that it is seeing.

Or perhaps it will add from itself that which has seen, too, in order that it would be thinking of itself perfectly.[25] But if it adds that which has seen, at the same time it also adds the things seen. If, then, the things that have been seen exist in the seeing, and if they are impressions of them, it does not have them. But if it has them, it does not [20] [think] itself by the seeing that is a result of a division, but it was prior to dividing itself that it saw and had them. If this is so, the seeing must be the same as the seen, that is, Intellect must be the same as the intelligible,[26] because if they are not the same, there will not be truth, for that

---

[23] See Aristotle *Met.* Λ 7, 1072b20.

[24] The subject now shifts from the individual to Intellect. See V 6. 1; V 9. 5 on the unity, that is, simplicity and complexity of Intellect.

[25] That is, it adds seer to what is seen.

[26] See Aristotle *Met.* Λ 7, 1072b21; *De An.* Γ 4, 429b9; 6, 430b25–6.

which possesses things different from the things that are, will have an impression, which is not [25] truth.[27] The truth, therefore, should not be about something different from itself; rather what it says, this is what it is.[28] Therefore, in this way, Intellect and that which is intelligible are one; and this is the primary Being and primary Intellect which has the things that are, or rather which is the same as the things that are.

But if thinking and that which is intelligible are one, how will this be the explanation for the fact that that which thinks, thinks itself? [30] For though thinking will, in a way, encompass that which is intelligible, or will be the same as that which is intelligible, it is not yet clear how Intellect will be thinking itself. But if thinking and that which is intelligible are the same[29] (for the intelligible is a certain kind of actuality, and it is neither a potency nor something unintelligible, nor is it separated from life,[30] nor are life and thinking added by something that is other than it [35] in the way that they might be added to a stone or to something inanimate),[31] then the intelligible is the primary substance. If, then, it is actuality, that is, the primary actuality and the most beautiful, it would be thinking, that is, substantial thinking.[32] For it is most true. And such thinking, being primary and primarily Intellect, would be the primary Intellect, for neither is this Intellect in potency nor is [40] it one thing and its thinking another.[33] For if it were, again, the substantial part of it would be in potency [to thinking].

If, then, it is actuality, that is, the substance of it is actuality, it would be one and the same with its actuality. But Being, or that which is intelligible, is also one with that actuality. All will be simultaneously one: Intellect, thinking, and that which is intelligible. If, then, its thinking is that which is intelligible, and the intelligible is it, [45] it will, therefore, be thinking itself, for it will think by its thinking, which it is, and it will think that which is intelligible, which it is. In both ways, therefore, it will think itself: because it is thinking and because it is that which is intelligible — that which it thinks by the thinking — which is what it itself is.

---

[27] See V 5. 1, 18–25, where primary thinking is contrasted with the imagistic thinking of sense-perception.

[28] See V 5. 2, 18–20.

[29] See Aristotle *De An.* Γ 4, 430a2–9.

[30] See Aristotle *Met.* Λ 7, 1072b27.

[31] See IV 7. 3, 23–9.

[32] Plotinus is referring to the paradigmatic type of thinking, what he elsewhere calls "primary thinking." See V 6. 1.

[33] See Aristotle *Met.* Λ 9, 1074b34.

§6. The argument has demonstrated that "self [thinking] itself" in the proper sense exists. Thinking, then, does occur in the soul, though it more properly occurs in Intellect. The soul thought itself because it belongs to something else,[34] whereas Intellect thought because it is itself, that is, because it is the sort of thing it is or who it is, [5] starting from its own nature and then reverting upon itself. For seeing reality, it saw itself; and in seeing, it was in actuality, and the actuality was it. For Intellect and thinking are one. And the whole thinks by means of the whole, not one part by means of another.

Has this argument then shown itself also to have, in some way, persuasive force? In fact, it has the force of necessity, [10] though it does not persuade. For necessity is in Intellect, but persuasion is in soul. But it does seem as if we are seeking more to persuade ourselves than to see the truth by means of pure Intellect, for while we were up in the nature of Intellect, we were content, and we were thinking, and, gathering all things into one, we saw. For it was Intellect doing the thinking and speaking about itself, [15] whereas the soul was tranquil and ceded to the working of Intellect. But since we have come to be here again in soul, we are seeking for some kind of persuasion to arise, wanting to see the archetype in a sort of image. Perhaps then we ought to teach this soul of ours how Intellect sees itself, and to teach this part [20] of soul that is somehow intellectual, supposing it to be a "discursive power,"[35] by which name we are signaling that it is some sort of intellect or that it has this power owing to Intellect and from Intellect.

It belongs, then, to the discursive power to know that it knows the things which it sees by itself and that it knows what it is speaking about. And if it were that about which it is speaking, it would know itself [25] in this way. But since the things it is speaking about are above or come to it from there [the intelligible world], where even it itself came from, it might also occur that by its being an expressed principle and receiving things that are akin to it and fitting them to the traces in itself, it would in this way know itself.

Let us then transfer the image to the true Intellect, which was identified with the truths being thought, [30] those that are really real and primary, both because it is not possible that something like this could be outside of itself—so that if it is in itself and with itself and that which it is, it is Intellect (for a nonintelligible Intellect could not exist), and it is

---

[34] That is, the soul's thinking is derived from Intellect's thinking, as an image of it.

[35] The soul is "discursive" (διανοητικόν) "owing to Intellect" (= διὰ νοῦ).

necessary that the knowledge of itself accompanies it—and because it is in itself and has no other function [35] and no other essence than to be Intellect alone. For it is, of course, not practical intellect which looks to externals and does not remain in itself, and has a kind of knowledge of externals. If it [Intellect] were entirely practical, it would not be necessary for it to know itself. But in that in which there is no action—for pure Intellect has no desire for that which [40] is absent from it[36]—the reversion to itself demonstrates not only that it is reasonable but also that it is necessary that it should have knowledge of itself. For if action is removed from it, what else would the life of that which is in Intellect be?[37]

§7. Let us say that it contemplates god. But if someone will agree that it knows god, he will be compelled to concede that in this respect it also knows itself. For it will know all such things as it has from god, that is, what he has given and what he has the power to do.[38] [5] Learning these and knowing them, it will in this respect know itself. Indeed, it is itself one of the things that has been given, or rather it is all the things that have been given. If, then, it will know god by learning about his powers,[39] it will also know itself, since it is come from there and has been provided from there with what it has the power to do. But if it is powerless to see god [10] clearly, since seeing is perhaps the same as what is seen, in this way especially it would be left to it to see and know itself, if this seeing is the same as that which is seen.

What else should we give to it? Tranquility, by Zeus. But for Intellect, tranquility is not a self-transcending experience; rather, the tranquility [15] of Intellect is an activity free from occupation with other things. For other things, too, in which there is tranquility apart from the things that are other than them, their own proper activity remains and especially for things whose being is not potential but actual.[40] The being [of Intellect] is activity, and there is nothing else to which the activity is directed. Therefore it is directed to itself. Therefore, in thinking itself, it is in this way directed to [20] itself and has its activity within itself. Indeed, if something comes from it, this will be owing to its being

---

[36] See IV 7. 13, 3–4.

[37] See Aristotle *EN* K 8, 1178b20–1.

[38] God, or the One, has the power to produce everything. See V 1. 7, 9; V 4. 2, 38; VI 9. 5, 36–7. Thus, Intellect, in knowing all the Forms, that is, all possible intelligible objects, knows all that the One is virtually.

[39] Reading αὐτοῦ, according to H-S$_1$.

[40] We translate the same word ἐνέργεια as "actuality" when in explicit contrast with δύναμις ("potentiality") and as "activity" when used alone.

in itself and directed towards itself. For it first had to be in itself and next directed towards something else, or something else must have come from it, having been made like it. Similarly, fire, which is first in itself fire and, having the activity of fire, is able to produce a trace [25] of itself in another.[41]

Indeed, again, Intellect is an activity in itself, whereas for soul, as much of it as is directed to Intellect is in a way internal, and as much as is external to Intellect is directed to what is external to it. One part of soul is likened to that from which it comes, whereas the other, being unlike, is nevertheless likened to that [from which it comes] even while it is here, whether it be acting [30] or doing,[42] for when it does something it is nevertheless contemplating, and in doing something it makes forms, which are, in a way, detached thoughts,[43] so that all things are traces of thinking and of Intellect proceeding according to the archetype and imitating it, the ones closer are doing it more so while the ones furthest away are preserving a murky image.

§8. What sort of thing is Intellect that sees that which is intelligible and what sort of thing is it that sees itself?[44] In fact, one should not seek that which is intelligible as if it were a color or a shape of a body, for before these existed, the intelligibles exist. And the expressed principle in the seeds that produce these colors or shapes is [5] not the same as them. For by nature these are invisible, and the intelligibles, even more so. And the nature of those intelligibles and those things that have them is the same, as is the expressed principle in the seeds and the soul that has these.

The soul, however, does not see what it has, for it did not generate them but is itself a reflection, as are the expressed principles, whereas that from which it [the soul] came is [10] that which is clear and true and primary and belongs to itself and is for itself. But this reflection, if it did not come to be from another thing and exist in another thing, does not even last, "for it belongs to an image, coming from something else, to be in something else,"[45] unless it is dependent on that from which it

---

[41] See IV 8. 6, 8–12; V 1. 6, 30–4; V 4. 2, 27–33; VI 7. 18, 5–6; VI 7. 21, 4–6; VI 7. 40, 21–4.

[42] That is, acting or doing, insofar as these have an intelligible structure, produce a likeness to Intellect.

[43] Reading ἀπηρτημένας with Theiler instead of H-S₂'s ἀπηρτισμένας. See III 8. 1–7 on action as contemplation.

[44] See V 5. 12, 1–5 on the "seeing" of Intellect.

[45] See Plato *Tim.* 52C2–4, partially quoted.

came.[46] For this reason, soul does not see, since it does not have enough light, and even if it does see, [15] having realized itself in something else, it does not see itself.[47]

But there is, then, nothing of these things in the intelligible world; rather, seeing and the object of sight are the same in it, and the object of sight is the same sort of thing as the seeing, and the seeing is the same sort of thing as the object of sight. Who, then, will say what it is like? The one who sees. And Intellect is that which sees. Even here, seeing, since it is light or, rather, united [20] with light, sees light, for it sees colors. But in the intelligible world, seeing is not by means of something different; rather it is by means of itself, because it is not of externals. Intellect thus sees one light with another, not by means of another. Therefore, light sees another light; therefore, it sees itself.

And this light shined in the soul and illuminated it, that is, made it intellectual. That is, it made it like itself [25] by means of the upper light. So, then, this is, in a way, the trace of light that came to be in the soul, and if you believe that it is like this and even more beautiful and greater and clearer, you would come closer to the nature of Intellect and of that which is intelligible. And again, having illuminated this, it gave the soul a clearer life, but not a productive one. [30] On the contrary, it made the soul revert to itself and did not allow it to be scattered; rather, it made it love the splendor in itself. It is surely not a life of sense-perception, for sense-perception looks to externals and perceives, whereas that which acquires the light of true realities sees visible things better but in [35] the opposite sense of "visible."[48]

What remains then is for it to have acquired an intellectual life, a trace of the life of Intellect. For in the intelligible world is where the true realities are. But the life and activity in Intellect[49] is the primary light, being an illuminating primarily for itself and gleaming for itself, illuminating and being illuminated together, that which is truly intelligible, that is, thinker and thing thought, [40] seeing by itself and in need of nothing else in order to see, sufficient to itself for seeing—for

---

[46] Plotinus is here alluding to the status of an image in Platonic metaphysics that, if it does not exist in an independent "receptacle," must cling to existence by its dependence on its original. The latter condition applies to the soul.

[47] That is, soul finds its perfection in the objects of its desires, which are outside of it.

[48] Eliminating the οὐ of H-S$_2$. The sense is that the intelligibles are the "truly visible" things. See VI 7. 7, 30.

[49] See Aristotle *Met.* Λ 7, 1072b27.

what it sees is itself—known by us owing to that light, since the knowledge of it has come to us by means of that. How else could we speak about it? Intellect is such that while, in a way, [45] it apprehends itself more clearly, we apprehend it by means of it.

By means of these arguments, our soul goes back up to it, supposing itself to be an image of it, so its life is a reflection and likeness of that, and so whenever it thinks, it becomes god-like, that is, "intellect-like,"[50] and if one were to ask the soul, "What sort of thing [50] is that Intellect that is perfect and complete and that knows itself primarily?" it is at that point that it first came to be in Intellect, or allowed for the activity that is in Intellect, and showed that it in fact possessed those things of which it has the memory in itself, so that, being an image, it is in some way able to see Intellect, through an image [55] that has been made more accurately like that to the extent that a part of the soul is able to achieve likeness to Intellect.

§9. It appears then that one who intends to know what Intellect is should observe soul, especially the most divine part of it. This would probably occur in the following way: if you first separated in thought the body from the human being, I mean, from yourself, and next [5] the [lower] soul that shapes it and, of course, all sense-perception, appetites, and passions and other such nonsense,[51] since these all tend towards the mortal. What remains of soul is this: that which we called an image of Intellect,[52] preserving something of the light of that—in a way, like the light of the sun, surrounding the spherical mass—which shines [10] out of it.

Now no one would allow that the light of the sun exists on its own around the sun, emitted and then remaining around it, one ray of light always proceeding from the one before it until it reaches us on earth. Rather one would suppose everything that is around the sun is in another so as not to allow a space [15] empty of body between the sun [and the light]. But the soul, having arisen from Intellect as a light around it, is dependent on it and is neither in another, but rather is around that, nor in place, for Intellect is not. That is why the sun's light is in air, whereas such a soul is pure, so that it is able to see itself [20] by itself and by any other soul of the same kind.

And soul ought to draw conclusions about Intellect, starting its investigation from itself, though Intellect itself [knows] itself without drawing

---

[50] See Plato *Phd.* 95C5, where the soul is spoken of as "god-like"; and *Tht.* 176B on "assimilation to god." Plotinus coins the expression "intellect-like" and takes the former to be equivalent to the latter.

[51] See Plato *Phd.* 66C3. See V 9. 6, 15–20 on the "lower" soul.

[52] See *supra* 4, 20–4; 8, 46; II 9. 4, 25; V 1. 3, 7; V 1. 7, 1.

conclusions about itself, for it is always present to itself, whereas we are only so whenever we are directed towards it. For our life has been divided, and we have many lives, whereas Intellect has no need of another life or of other lives, [25] since what it provides it provides to others, not to itself. For it neither has need of what is inferior to it, nor does it provide to itself that which is less when it has everything, nor does it have traces of primary realities, since it has the originals; more precisely, it does not have them, but *is* them itself.

If, however, someone is unable to grasp a soul such as this, one that thinks purely, [30] let him take soul in its opinionative power, and then let him ascend from this.[53] But if he cannot do even this, let him take sense-perception, which provides the forms in the broader sense, sense-perception in itself with its powers and already immersed in the forms.[54] But if someone wishes, let him descend to the generative power of soul and keep going until he arrives at the things it produces. Then when he is there, let him ascend from [35] the forms that are at one extreme to the Forms that are at the other extreme or rather to the primary ones.

§13. For this reason, the One is, in truth, ineffable, for whatever you might say about it, you will be saying something.[55] But to say "transcending all things and transcending the majesty of Intellect"[56] is, among all other ways of speaking of it, the only true one, since neither is that its name; rather, it indicates that it is not "something" among all the things there are, nor is that its name because [5] there is nothing to say about it.[57] But, insofar as possible, we try to give ourselves indications about it.[58]

But whenever we raise the following problem: "then it has no perception of itself and is not conscious of itself and does not know itself,"

---

[53] That is, let him start with the cognitive power of "opinion" (δόξα) instead of the higher power of intellect. The latter is separate from the other psychic powers, because it does not require involvement of the body. On different "kinds," i.e., powers, of soul—e.g., cognitive, generative, sentient, nutritive, etc.—see Aristotle *De An.* B 4, 415a15 ff.

[54] The words "in itself" refer to the power of the faculty of sense-perception to be aware that sense-perception is occurring. Sense-perception is "already immersed in the forms," because, in order for one to be aware that one is having a perception, a sensible form must already be present in the perceiver.

[55] Plotinus has been arguing in the previous chapter that the One is absolutely simple.

[56] See Plato *Rep.* 509B9.

[57] See Plato *Parm.* 142A3.

[58] See V 5. 6, 25; VI 9. 5, 39.

we ought to consider that in saying this we are turning ourselves around to the opposite claim,[59] for we are making it many when we make it [10] knowable and knowledge itself, and, endowing it with thinking, we make it to be in need of thinking. Even if thinking were to belong to it, it will be superfluous for it to think. And this is because, in general, thinking seems to be an awareness of the whole when many [parts] come together in the same thing, that is, whenever something thinks itself, which is thinking in the principal sense. [15] Each is itself some one thing[60] and seeks nothing, whereas if thought is to be of externals, it will be deficient and will not be thinking in the principal sense.

Now that which is completely simple and self-sufficient is really in need of nothing.[61] That which is self-sufficient in a secondary sense, needing itself, needs this for thinking itself. And that which is deficient in regard to itself has produced [20] self-sufficiency in the whole with an adequacy arising from all the [parts], being present to itself and inclining towards itself, for awareness is a perception of something that is many; even the name witnesses to this.[62] And thought, being prior, reverts inward to it [the object of thinking, i.e., that which is intelligible], which is clearly multiple. For even if it says only this, "I am real," it says it as [25] one discovering something and says it plausibly, for that which is real is multiple. This is so, since if it were to focus on itself as something simple and say "I am real," it would hit upon neither itself nor something real. For it is not saying it is real in the way a stone is real, when it speaks the truth, but it says many things in one word. For this real thing—which is really real and not said to have [merely] a trace of [30] what is real (for if this were the case, it could not be said to be real, being just like an image in relation to its archetype)—has many things.

What then? Will then not each of these things be thought? Now if you want to grasp the "isolated and alone,"[63] you will not be thinking. On the contrary, being itself is multiple in itself, and if you should say something else, being includes that. But if this is so, then if there is something that is [35] of all the things that are the simplest, it will not

---

[59] The objection is raised at VI 7. 38, 10.

[60] That is, each thinking unity.

[61] See V 4. 1, 12–14; VI 9. 6, 16–26.

[62] Literally, "awareness" (συναίσθησις) is so-called because it is "sense-perception" (αἴσθησις).

[63] See VI 7. 40, 28; Plato *Phil.* 63B7–8, taken somewhat out of context.

have thought of itself. For if it will have it, it will have it by being multiple. Then neither is the One thinking, nor is there thought about it.[64]

§14. How then do we speak about it? In fact, we do say something about it, but we neither say it nor have knowledge or thought of it. How, then, do we speak about it if we do not have knowledge or thought of it? In fact, if we do not have knowledge of it, does it follow as well that [5] we do not have it completely? But we have it in such a way that we can speak about it, though we cannot say it. For we say what it is not; what it is, we do not say, so that we are speaking about it on the basis of things that come after it.[65] We are not prevented from having it, even if we do not say it.

But just as those who are inspired and possessed have knowledge to the extent that [10] they know that there is something greater than themselves in themselves[66]—even if they do not know what it is, and from the things by which they are moved and speak they acquire a certain perception of that which moved them although their movements are different from what moved them—in this way we, too, are related to the One, whenever we have a purified intellect.[67] We thereby have it revealed to us not only that this is the [15] inner intellect,[68] which gives essence and whatever else belongs to this principle,[69] but also that the One is such as not to be those things; it is something more powerful than that which we call "Being," but it is also more and greater than what can be said about it, because it is more powerful than speech and intellect and sense-perception, and because it provides these, not being them itself.

§15. But how does it provide these? Either by having them or by not having them.[70] But how can it provide what it does not have? If, on the one hand, it has them, it is not simple; if, on the other, it does not have them, how can the multiplicity of things come from it? Someone might

---

[64] To think of the One would entail, falsely, that it have some finite essence (οὐσία), for that is the object of thinking.

[65] Cf. V 5. 6, 20.

[66] See Plato *Ion* 533E6–7.

[67] See Anaxagoras Fr. B 12 D-K.

[68] That is, intellect's activity is internal. See V 9. 7, 8.

[69] That is, we become aware of both intellect in us and its power.

[70] The manuscripts have τῷ ἔχειν ("either by having"), while H-S$_2$ add the words <ἢ τῷ μὴ ἔχειν> ("or by not having"). The reason for the conjectured change is that without the addition, Plotinus seems to contradict his claim that the One does not have any of the things that it gives.

perhaps grant that one simple thing came from it—though even then [5] one should inquire into how this could come from what is absolutely one. But nevertheless, even if it is possible to speak about how it comes from the One in something like the way that radiance comes from light—still, how do many things come from it?

In fact, that which was to come from the One is not the same as it. If, then, it is not the same, it is certainly not better. For what could be better than the One or transcend it entirely? Therefore, it is worse. And this means that it is more in need. [10] What, then, is more in need than the One? In fact, it is that which is not one. Therefore it is many, though all the same desirous of the One. It is therefore a "one-many."[71] For everything that is not one is preserved by that which is one and is whatever it is by this. For if it has not become one, even if it is composed out of many [parts], it is not yet that which one speaks of as "itself."[72] And even if one is able to say what each [part] is, [15] one would be saying this in virtue of the fact that each is one, that is, in virtue of its being itself.

But that which, not having many [parts] in itself, is thereby not one by participation in that which is one but is itself that which is one, is not one owing to something else but because it is one, that from which somehow other things also come, some by being near and some by being far. For that itself which comes after it makes clear that it comes after it in virtue of its multiplicity, [20] being a "one-everywhere." For though it is a multiplicity, nevertheless it is self-identical and you could not divide it because "all things are together."[73] Since each of the things that come from it, so long as it partakes of life, is a "one-many," each cannot show itself to be a "one-everything." But Intellect is a "one-everything," because it comes after the principle.[74] For that principle really is one, and truly is one. That which comes after the [25] principle is, somehow, by the influence of the One, all things partaking of the One, and any part of it is all things besides being also one.

What, then, are "all things?" In fact, they are those things of which the One is the principle. But how is the One the principle of all things? Is it because by making each of them to be one it preserves them? In

---

[71] See V 1. 8, 26; VI 2. 15, 14–15; VI 4. 11, 15–16; Plato *Parm.* 137C–142A; 144E5; 155E5.

[72] Following de Strycker's suggestion and reading ὃ ἂν εἴποι instead of H-S₂ ὅ τι εἴποι, now accepted by the latter in the *addenda ad textum*.

[73] See Anaxagoras Fr. B 1 D-K.

[74] Reading μετὰ τὴν ἀρχήν with Igal and also H-S₂ in their *addenda ad textum* instead of μεγάλην ἀρχήν as in H-S₂.

fact, it is also because it made them exist. But how did it do this? In fact, it was by [30] having them prior [to their existence]. But has it not been said that in this way it will be a multiplicity?[75] So, therefore, we must say that it had them, in a way, so as not to be distinct, whereas the things in the second principle are distinguished by reason, for this is at once actuality,[76] whereas the One is virtually the totality.[77]

But what manner of power is this? For it is not what is meant when matter is said to be potentially, because it is receptive. This is because matter is passive. [35] And this type of potentiality is the opposite of producing. How, then, does it produce what it does not have? Indeed, it does so neither by chance nor having reflected on what it will produce; yet it produces nevertheless. It has been said then that if there is something that comes from the One, it should be something other than it; being other, it is not one. For if this were one, it would be the One. But if it is not one, but two, it is at once necessary that it also be a multitude, [40] for it is at once different and the same and of some kind, etc.[78]

It has been shown that that which comes from the One is not one. But it is worth pondering that this is a multitude and the sort of multitude that has been observed to be in that which comes after the One. And the necessity of there being something that comes after the One is yet to be examined.

§16. That there must be something after the first has been said elsewhere and, generally, that the first is power, that is, incredible power—this, too, has been said, that this claim should be trusted on the basis of all other things, because there is nothing, not even among the most remote, that does not have the power [5] to generate.[79]

But as for those things, this point should now be made, namely, that since among things that are generated it is not possible to go upward, but only to proceed downward, that is, in the direction of multiplicity,

---

[75] See *supra* ll. 2–3.

[76] That is, the act of thinking by Intellect consists in distinguishing all Forms, and thinking is actuality.

[77] See III 8. 10, 1; IV 8. 6, 11; V 1. 7, 9; V 4. 1, 23–6, 36; V 4. 2, 38; VI 9. 5, 36; VI 7. 32, 31. The term is δύναμις which needs to be translated sometimes as "power," sometimes as "potency." It is always used in the former sense of the One, and there means something like "virtually," as in "white light is virtually all the colors of the rainbow."

[78] See Plato *Soph.* 254E5–255A1.

[79] See IV 8. 6; V 4. 1, 37; V 2. 1 on the necessity of generation; V 4. 1, 36; VI 7. 32, 31 and *supra* 15, 33 on the One as power; and V 1. 6, 30 ff. on the ability of everything to generate.

the principle of each of them is simpler than they are, for that which makes the universe sensible, then, cannot itself be sensible but is rather an intellect and an intelligible universe. [10] And that which is before this, then, that which generates it, could not be an intellect or an intelligible universe; rather, it must be simpler than intellect and simpler than an intelligible universe. For a many does not come from many, but that which is many comes from that which is not many. For if it [the intelligible universe] is many, this is not a principle; the principle is that which is before this. If, then, this is to be really simple, there must be a coalescing into what is really one, [15] transcending any plurality and any qualified simplicity.

But how can that which is generated from it [the really simple, i.e., the One] be a complex expressed principle and universal, while that from which it came is clearly not an expressed principle?[80] And if it is not this, how then can an expressed principle come from what is not an expressed principle? And how does that which is Good-like come from the Good? What indeed does it have in itself in virtue of which it is said to be Good-like?[81] [20] Is it, then, because it has what it has always and always in the same way? And what does this mean in relation to the Good? For we seek out that which is always the same, just because it is one of the things that is good. In fact, we seek that which is prior to it, which we should not leave, because it is good. If it were not, it would be better to be separated from it.

Is, then, living like this and willingly remaining with this [the Good] what we are seeking? If, then, [25] living like this is what it loves, it is clear that it seeks nothing.[82] It would seem, then, that it lives like this for this reason, namely, because its present life is sufficient for it. But it loves its life because all things are at once present to it, that is, present but not as other than it. And if its entire life is a life of clarity and perfection, then every soul and every intellect is in it, [30] and nothing of life or of intellect is absent from it. It is, then, self-sufficient and seeks nothing. And if it seeks nothing, it has in itself what it would have sought, had that not been present to it. It has, then, in itself that which is good, whether we say life and intellect are just that or something else that is accidental to these.

But if this is the Good, there [35] would be nothing beyond these [life and intellect]. But if that [the Good] *is* beyond them, it is clear that

---

[80] See VI 4. 11, 16; VI 7. 17, 41–2.
[81] See *supra* 3, 10; III 8. 11, 16; VI 7. 15, 9; VI 7. 18, 1.
[82] That is, for Intellect living as Good-like.

Intellect's life is directed to that and dependent on that and has its existence from that and lives directed to that. For that is its principle. The Good, then, must be better than life and intellect, for in this way, Intellect will revert to that, both the life that is in itself, being [40] a kind of imitation of what is in that, insofar as this [the Good] lives, and the intellect in it,[83] a kind of imitation of what is in that, whatever this is.

§17. What, then, is better than the wisest life, without a fault, unerring, that is, the life of Intellect, which has all things and all life and is all Intellect? If we say, then, "that which makes these" [we should also say] "How did it make these?" And, unless there should appear something better, [5] our reasoning will not go off in another direction but will stop at Intellect. But, still, one should go upward for many other reasons, especially because the self-sufficiency of Intellect, since it arises from [its being composed of] all things, is external to it, for each of these is clearly lacking. And because each of these has participated in and participates in the One itself, it is not the One itself. What, then, is that in which [10] it participates, which makes it exist and be all things together? If it makes each exist, and it is by the presence of the One that the multitude of Intellect and Intellect itself are self-sufficient, it is clear that that which is productive of being and of self-sufficiency is itself not being but "transcends this" and transcends self-sufficiency.[84]

[15] Is it enough, then, having said these things, to leave off? In fact, the soul is still in labor and even more so than before. Perhaps, then, she must now give birth, having both longed for the One and been consumed with labor.[85] But we must sing another charm if we are to find someone to relieve her labor. Perhaps it would come about as a result of what has already been said, [20] if someone were to sing it over and over, it would happen. What other fresh charm, then, is there? For since she has run through all the truths, truths in which we participate, and still flees them, if someone wants to speak and think through them, discursive thinking must go from one thing to the other, so that something should be said. For it is, in this way, successive. But what sort of succession is there [25] for that which is completely simple?

But it is sufficient if one grasps it intellectually. But having grasped it, so long as one does, it is quite impossible nor is there time to speak; later one can reason about it. But at that moment, it is necessary to be confident that one has seen, whenever the soul suddenly makes contact with

---

[83] That is, the activity within Intellect.
[84] See Plato *Rep.* 509B8–9.
[85] Ibid. 490B; *2nd Ep.* 313A4–5.

light,[86] for this comes [30] from the One and is it. And at that moment, it is necessary to believe that the One is present, just as when another god, called to someone's house, comes bringing light. If the god had not come, he would not have brought the light. Thus, the unilluminated soul, bereft of god, is without light. When she is illuminated, she has what she sought, and this is the soul's true goal: to make contact [35] with that light and to see it by itself, not by another light, but that light by means of which it also sees. For this is that through which it is illuminated, which it should see, for we do not see the sun through another light. How, then, would it happen? Eliminate everything.

V 5 (32) THAT THE INTELLIGIBLES ARE NOT OUTSIDE THE INTELLECT, AND ON THE GOOD (§§1–2)

This treatise argues for the identity of Intellect and intelligibles. Plotinus is here relying both on his interpretation of Plato, especially Timaeus, *and on his understanding of Aristotle's account of cognition in* De Anima.

§1. Could, then,[1] anyone say that Intellect, the true and real Intellect, will ever be in error, and not think about the things that are?[2] Not at all, for how could it continue to be Intellect if it were nonintellectual? It must, therefore, always know and never forget, and its knowledge [5] must not be made into an image or ambiguous or the way it would be if it were like something heard from someone else. Moreover, its knowledge is not acquired by means of demonstration, for even if someone were to say that some of what it knows it knows by means of a demonstration, in that case there would still be something self-evident to it.

---

[86] See Plato *Symp.* 210E4; *7th Ep.* 341C7–D1.

[1] The theme of this treatise is continuous with V 8 (31). Grammatically, the beginning here responds to the end of that treatise: "So, is what has been said sufficient to lead to a clear understanding of the intelligible region, or should we go back and take another path like this one?"

[2] The word translated as "think about" (δοξάζειν) usually means "believe" or "opine," but it would be misleading to say that Intellect has beliefs or opinions as opposed to knowledge. We translate the word assuming that it is being used loosely and is synonymous with νοεῖν.

Actually, our argument maintains that everything it knows is self-evident to it, for how could one distinguish the things that are self-evident to it from the things that are not?

But as for those things that they concede are self-evident [10] to it—from where will they say the self-evidence arises?[3] From where will it derive the conviction that things are self-evident to it? For even the things [known] on the basis of sense-perception, though they seem to bring with them the most self-evident conviction, do not, in fact, convince us that their apparent existence is in underlying subjects rather than in our experiences [15] and not in need of intellect or discursive reasoning to make judgments about them, for even if they are conceded to be in the subjects underlying that which is sensed, of which sense-perception will be made the apprehension, that which is known by means of sense-perception is a reflected representation of the thing, and it is not the thing itself that sense-perception receives, for that remains external.

[20] So when Intellect knows, it knows intelligibles. If it knew things that were different, how would it connect with them? For it is possible that it is not connected, so that it is possible that it not know them or that it know them only at the time when it knows them, and it will not always have the knowledge. But if they will say that they are linked, what does the term "linked" mean?[4] In that case, acts of thinking will be impressions.[5] [25] But if that is so, they act externally, that is, they are impacts. But how will these impressions be made, or what is the shape of such things? And in that case, thinking will be of externals, just like sense-perception. And how will it differ [from sense-perception] unless by its grasping smaller objects? And how will it know that it has really apprehended them? And how will it know that this is good, or that it is noble or [30] just? For each of these is other than it, and the principles of the judgment, by which it will attain conviction, are not in it but are external, and that [on this hypothesis] is where the truth is.

Then, either those [the good, the noble, the just, i.e., intelligibles] are without perception and without any portion of life and intellect, or

---

[3] This appears to be a criticism of Epicureans. See Sextus Empiricus M. VIII 9 and VII 203.

[4] It is not clear to whom Plotinus is referring. But Sextus Empiricus M. VIII 152 uses the term (συνεζεῦχθαι) to describe the position of those who take "commemorative signs" to indicate what is presently nonevident but has in the past been seen to accompany the sign.

[5] See V 3. 5, 19.

they have intellect.[6] And if they have intellect, both are simultaneously there—this truth and this primary Intellect—[35] and we shall investigate the truth there and the intelligible and Intellect, and if they are simultaneously in the same thing, are they still two and different, or how are they related? But if the intelligibles are nonintelligible and without life, what sort of realities are they?[7] For they are not "premises"[8] or "axioms" or "sayables,"[9] for one would at once refer them to other things, and [40] they would not be the things themselves; for example, [if they said] "that which is just is beautiful" when, in fact, that which is just and that which is beautiful are other than these [premises, axioms, and sayables].

But if they will say that they [intelligibles] are "simples,"[10] Justice and Beauty being separate from each other, then, first of all, that which is intelligible will not be some one thing[11] or in one thing, but each will be dispersed. Further, where and in what places will they be dispersed? And how will Intellect hit upon them, [45] meandering through these places? And how will it remain [in its own place], or how will it remain in the same place? In general, what sort of form or impression will it have if they are not just like images erected of gold or of some other material made by some sculptor or engraver? But if they are like this, the Intellect that is contemplating them will be sense-perception. And why should one of these be [50] the Form of Justice and one, something else?

---

[6] An allusion to Plato *Soph.* 248E6–249A2, where it is insisted that "that which is completely" has intellect, life, and soul. This does not necessarily mean that Forms, insofar as they can be identified as "things that are completely," think and have life and soul apart from or over and above that which thinks them. Plato may well mean that "that which is completely" includes intelligibles and intellect as inseparable aspects of eternal reality, and Plotinus may well be following him.

[7] See V 1. 9, 8 and Aristotle *Met.* Λ 7, 1072a26; *De An.* Γ 4, 430a2–3. Plotinus means that those things which are primarily intelligible cannot exist apart from an intellect thinking them. The words "intelligible" (νοητά) and "nonintelligible" (ἀνόητα) can equally be translated without the "-able" ending, indicating "object of intellection" and "non-object of intellection," respectively.

[8] A critical reference to Aristotle *APr.* A 1, 24a16.

[9] A critical reference to the Stoics. See Sextus Empiricus *M.* VII 38 and VIII 12.

[10] Perhaps a criticism of certain contemporary Platonists who held that Forms were external to Intellect and therefore unconnected with each other.

[11] It will not be some one thing because it will be a composite of whatever it is, owing to which it is one and whatever it is, owing to which it is the kind of thing it is.

But the greatest objection of all is this. If, indeed, someone were to grant that these intelligibles are totally external to Intellect and Intellect is to contemplate them thus, it is necessary that it will not have the truth of these things and that it will be mistaken in all the things it contemplates, for those intelligibles would be the true realities. It will contemplate [55] them when it does not have them, instead receiving representations of them in this [putative] type of knowledge. Since it does not then have true reality but is receiving representations of the truth in itself, it will have falsities and nothing true. If, then, it will know that it has falsities, it will agree that it has no share of truth. But if it will be ignorant of this and [60] will think that it has the truth when it does not, the falsity that will be in it will be double and will separate it far from the truth.

This is the reason, I think, that there is no truth in the senses but only opinion, because opinion is receptive, and for this reason, being opinion, it receives something other than that reality from which [65] it has that which it receives. If, then, there is no truth in Intellect, this is the sort of intellect in which there will neither be truth nor truly Intellect nor Intellect altogether. But there is nowhere else for the truth to be.

§2. One, then, should neither seek the intelligibles external to the Intellect nor assert that they are impressions of realities in it nor, depriving it of truth, make it ignorant of the intelligibles, make them nonexistent, and even eliminate Intellect. But since one should bring in [5] knowledge and truth and be heedful of reality and knowledge of what each thing is (not, however, of the quality of each thing,[12] since if we had that, we would have only a reflection and a trace of reality and not real things themselves, living and merging with them), we ought to endow true Intellect with all these, for in this way it would know and [10] truly know and would neither forget nor run around seeking them, and truth will be in it, and it will be a foundation for real things, and it will live and think.

All of this must exist in the most blessed nature. Where else will its honor and dignity be? Indeed, again, being this way, it will have need neither of demonstration nor of conviction that it is this way—[15] for it itself is just this way, and it is self-evident to itself that it is this way—so if there is something prior to it, it is self-evident to it that it comes from it, and if there is something after the One, it is self-evident to it that it is itself that—and no one can be more convinced of this than it—and that what is truly real is in the intelligible world.

---

[12] That is, as opposed to the substance of each.

Thus, the real truth is not in harmony with something else, but with itself, and says nothing else besides itself, <but [20] what it says,> it is, and what it is, this it says. Who would then refute it, and from where would he bring the refutation? For the refutation that is adduced would come to the same thing as what was previously said and even if it were to provide something else, it is brought in line with that which was originally said, that is, it is one with it, for you could not find something else that was truer than truth.

VI 4 (22) On the Presence of Being, One and the Same Simultaneously Existing Everywhere as a Whole[1] — Part One (§§ 1–11)

This treatise considers how intelligible reality, including Soul, can be present to the corporeal or sensible world. It turns on its head the assumption that the intelligible is an abstraction from the sensible. It focuses on the derived nature of the images of intelligible reality.

§1. So[2] is the soul present everywhere in the universe, because the whole body of the universe is of a certain size, having a nature that is divisible into [particular] bodies?[3] Or is it everywhere by itself, not brought forth anywhere by a body? In that case, does body find [5] that soul exists everywhere prior to body, so that wherever body happens to be situated, there it finds soul existing already prior to body's being situated in a part of the universe, and the whole body of the universe is situated in soul which already exists. But if it exists to such an extent that, prior to coming to a body of a certain size, it filled up all the interval of space, how will it not have a magnitude? [10] Or in what manner would it exist in the universe prior to the universe coming to be, when the universe did not exist? How would someone accept that what is said to be without parts and without magnitude is everywhere, if it does not have magnitude?[4]

---

[1] See Plato *Parm.* 131B1–2.

[2] The beginning of this work suggests that Plotinus is repeating a question to which he is about to give the answer.

[3] See *Tim.* 35A2–3, where Plato addresses the question of the composition of the soul of the universe and its relation to immaterial and material reality.

[4] For arguments that soul has no magnitude, see IV 7. 8, 1–3.

And if it were said to be extended along with a body, though it is not a body, one does not thus [15] avoid the problem by giving it accidental magnitude.[5] Similarly, someone would reasonably inquire here how it acquired magnitude accidentally, for the soul does not, like a quality such as sweetness or color, belong to the whole body,[6] for these are affections of bodies, so that the whole of [20] that which is affected has the affection, and the affection is nothing in itself, belonging to a body and known at the time when the body is affected. For this reason, the affection necessarily has the magnitude of the body, and the white of a part of the body is not affected along with the white of another part. Further, in the case of white, the white in the one part and the white in another are the same in form though not in number, whereas in the case [25] of the soul, that which exists in the foot is the same in number as that which exists in the hand, as our acts of apprehension make clear.

And generally, among qualities, the same quality is understood to be divided into parts, whereas, in the case of the soul, the same soul is not divided into parts, but is divided in the sense that it is everywhere. Let us, then, speak from the beginning about these matters, [30] to see if there is something clear and satisfying for us to say regarding how the soul can be incorporeal or without magnitude and yet reach the greatest extent, either as prior to bodies or in bodies. Perhaps if it were also to appear to be able to do this prior to entering bodies, it would be easier also to accept that this happens in bodies.

§2. Now both the true universe exists and the imitation of the universe, which is the nature of the visible universe.[7] That which is the real universe is then in nothing, for there is nothing prior to it. Whatever exists after this is at once necessarily existing in the universe, if it [5] is to exist at all, and is especially dependent on that, not being able to be at a standstill or to be in motion without that. And, indeed, even if someone were not to suppose such a thing to be in place, thinking that place is "the limit of a surrounding body" insofar as it surrounds, or an interval that was prior to the nature of the void and still is;[8] [10] if he were rather to suppose

---

[5] Meaning that if soul is coincident with a body, and a body has magnitude, then one might try to argue that the soul has magnitude incidentally or indirectly. Plotinus is probably referring to the Stoic position that the soul is a body. See *SVF* I 518; II 790, 836.

[6] See IV 2. 1, 47–8.

[7] See Plato *Tim.* 48E6–49A1.

[8] See Aristotle *Phys.* Δ 4, 212a6 for the definition of place as a limit and Δ 4, 212a11 for the definition of place as an interval.

it to be in the universe, as if it were propped up and resting against the universe, which is everywhere and continuous; let him, putting aside the application of a name, grasp the meaning of that which is said.

This was said for the sake of something else, because that universe, first and real, neither seeks out place nor is altogether in something. And the universe, being everything, [15] is not such that it falls short of itself; rather, it is both self-complete and self-identical.[9] And where the universe is, it is there, for it is the universe. Generally, if something that is other than the universe is seated in it, it partakes of it and comes together with it and gets its strength from it, not by dividing it [20] but finding it in itself as it approaches it, without the universe being external to itself. For it is not possible for being to exist in nonbeing, but rather, if anything, for nonbeing to exist in being.[10] It [something in the universe] encounters being, then, as a whole. For it was not possible for it to be severed from itself, and to state that it is everywhere clearly means that [25] it is in being, so that it is in itself.

And there is nothing amazing if that which is everywhere is in being and in itself, for when it comes to be, that which is everywhere is at once in one,[11] for in supposing that there is being in the sensible world, we suppose that that which is everywhere is there, and believing that the sensible world is vast, we are puzzled how that nature extends into the vastness to such an extent. [30] But that which is said to be vast is, in fact, small, whereas that which is believed to be small is vast, at least if it extends entirely into every part of the sensible world; rather, this, proceeding from everywhere with its parts to that, finds it everywhere a universe and greater than itself. As a result, since nothing more would be obtained in its extension — [35] for in that case, it would come to be outside the universe — it wanted to circle around it, and having been able neither to encompass it nor again to be inside it, it was satisfied to have a place and order where it would be preserved, bordering on that which is present and again, not present. For that universe is in itself, even if something should want to be present to it.

And wherever [40] the body of the universe meets with it, it finds the universe, so that it no longer has a need to go further, but it turns in the same place,[12] since it is this perceptible universe, where every part of it

---

[9] That is, it lacks nothing, nor is there anything in it, like an accidental attribute, with which it is not identical.

[10] See Plato *Soph.* 256D.

[11] That is, it is a unity, and so is in itself.

[12] See Plato *Tim.* 34A3–4.

enjoys the entirety of that universe. If that universe were in place, it must have approached it there and proceeded in a straight line, [45] in some other part of it, to touch another part of that and to be both far and near. But if it is neither far nor near, it must be entirely present, if it is present at all. And it is entirely present to each of those [perceptibles] to which it is neither far nor near. And it is present to things that are able to receive it.

§3. Will we, then, say that it[13] is itself present or that while it is by itself, the powers that come from it extend to everything, and, in this way, it can be said to be everywhere? For it is in this way that they[14] say that the souls are like rays, so that while true reality stays seated [5] in itself, the rays that are sent out produce one living being or another. In fact, in things in which that which is one is, because it cannot preserve all the nature that is present in the intelligible, [only] a power of the intelligible is present to that in which it is present. Not that it is entirely present, since [true reality] is not cut off from its power, [10] which it gave to that which received it. But the receiver was able to receive just so much, though it was wholly present.

But where all the powers are present, it itself is clearly present, though it is nevertheless separate. For if it had become the form of this one thing, it would be removed from being everything and from being in itself everywhere, and it would be the form of something else accidentally. [15] Since it belongs to nothing that wishes it to belong to it, it approaches, insofar as it is able, to whatever it might wish,[15] not coming to belong to that, but to that which desires it, not something else.

There is, then, nothing amazing in its thus being in all things, because, again, it is in no one of them as belonging to them. For this reason, it is perhaps not absurd to claim that, in this way, the soul [20] goes together with the body accidentally, if the soul were said to be on its own, not belonging to matter or body, and the whole body is in a way illuminated by it over the entirety of itself. One should not be amazed if the [true] universe, while not being in place, is present to everything that is in place. On the contrary, it would be amazing, and on top of

---

[13] The reference is to the "true universe" in 2, 1. This includes the hypostasis Soul and the soul of the universe.

[14] A reference to a Gnostic view. See Plutarch *De Fac. Orb.* 28, 943D8, where the word for "ray" is ἀκτίς, not βολή as here.

[15] The text is uncertain here. We follow Igal's ᾧ ἂν αὐτὸ ἐθέλῃ ὡς δύναται instead of H-S₂'s ὃ ἂν αὐτῷ ἐθέλῃ ὡς δύναται and translate accordingly.

amazing, [25] impossible if, having its own place, it was present to something else that was in place, or was present wholly and was also present in the way we say it is. But now the argument says that it is necessary for it, since it has not been assigned a place, to be wholly present to that to which it is present, and present to all so that it is also wholly present to each. [30] If this is not so, a part of it will belong to this here and another part to something else there, in which case it will be divisible and a body.

How, in this case, will you divide it? Will you, in that case divide its life? But if the whole of it is life, the part of it will not be life. What about the Intellect, so that one part would be in one thing and another part in another? But neither one of these parts will be Intellect. What about its Being? [35] But the part will not have being, if the whole was being. What if someone were to say, then, that the body is divided, and it has parts that are bodies? In fact, the dividing was not of body but of a certain quantity of body, and each body is called a body in virtue of its form. But this form did not have "a quantity of a certain amount," since it did not have [40] any kind of quantity.

§4. How, then, are there being and beings and many intellects and many souls, if Being is everywhere one and not just in kind and Intellect is one and Soul is one? Well, there is the soul of the universe, and there are other souls.[16] This seems to be evidence that contradicts [5] what was said, which, even if it has a certain necessity, does not have persuasive force at all, since the soul believes that it is unconvincing that that which is one is thus everywhere the same.

Perhaps it would be better for the whole to be divided so that there not be a diminution of that from which the division has come about or else, having come to be from it (to put it in better terms) thus allow one thing to come [10] from it and the rest to come from it, as it were, like parts, namely, souls, thereby at once inhabiting all the things [that have souls]. But if that being remains in itself, because it seems paradoxical that that which is a whole is at the same time present everywhere, the same argument will apply to souls. For they will not be wholes in the whole bodies they are said to be in, but either they will [15] be divided or, while remaining wholes, they will give their powers to someplace in the body. And the same problem of how the whole can be everywhere will arise for them and their powers.

---

[16] Cf. Plato *Tim.* 41D5–8. In this passage, the "other" souls are the souls of the stars.

Further, some part of the body will have soul and some part only a power. But how can there be many souls and many intellects and Being and beings? Moreover, proceeding [20] from what is prior as numbers but not as magnitudes, they will provide a similar problem about how they fill the universe. For us, then, there is nothing proceeding from a plurality in this way that has been discovered to lead to a solution, since we will concede that being is many, owing to difference, not place, for being is all together, even if it is thus many; "being [25] borders on being"[17] and "everything is together."[18] And intellect is many, owing to difference, not place, and all together.

Are souls then, too, [the same way]? In fact, souls are, since "that which is divided among bodies"[19] is said to have a nature that is partless, but since the bodies have magnitude, and the nature of soul is present to them (more to the point, [30] the bodies come to be present to *it*), to the extent that they are divided, and this nature is being imagined to be present to every part, it was believed to be divided in this way among bodies. Since it is the case that it was not divided along with the parts but is everywhere whole, it makes clear that it is one and really undivided in its nature.

The fact, then, that the Soul is one [35] does not eliminate the many souls, just as Being does not eliminate beings, nor does the multiplicity in the intelligible world fight with the One, nor must we fill bodies up with life by means of multiplicity, nor must we believe that, because of the magnitude of body, the multiplicity of souls arises; rather, souls were many and one prior to bodies.

For [40] the many souls are already in the whole, not in potency but each one in actuality, for the unity and wholeness does not prevent there being many souls in it, nor do the many prevent the unity. They stand apart by not standing apart and are present to each other by not being alienated from each other, for they are not divided by limits, just as the many types of knowledge in the soul are not [divided], and [45] are one such that it [knowledge] has in it all of the types.[20] In this way, such a nature is limitless.

---

[17] See Parmenides Frs. B 8, 5 and B 8, 25 D-K.
[18] See Anaxagoras Fr. B 1 D-K.
[19] Plato *Tim.* 35A2–3.
[20] See Plato *Phil.* 13E9 ff., where Plato uses the example of "types of knowledge," which are nevertheless one insofar as they are types of the same thing.

§5. And its greatness should be understood in this way, not in terms of bulk. For this is a small thing, proceeding into nothingness, if one removes it [in thought, part by part]. But in the intelligible world, it is not possible to remove anything, nor, if you could remove anything, would it afterwards be found wanting. And if it will not be found wanting, why should one be afraid that it will be absent?[21] [5] For how could it be absent when it is not found wanting but is a nature that eternally rises and does not flow away? For if it did flow away, it would go to a certain point, as far as it would be able to flow. But it does not flow away, for were it to flow away, there is nowhere to which it could flow, for it has gotten hold of the universe; rather, it *is* the [true] universe. And, being something greater than the nature of body, [10] it would reasonably be believed to give little of itself to the universe of bodily nature, just as much of it as this is able to bear.

One should neither say that it is less nor, supposing it as less in bulk, thereby at once lose one's conviction, since it is not possible for the less to proceed to that which is greater than itself, for "less" should not be predicated of it, nor should bulk be compared to what is without bulk [15] in measurement—this would be as if someone were to say that the physician's art is less that the body of the physician. Nor should one believe that the universe is, in this way, greater in quantity of measurement, since this does not apply to the soul. Rather, the great and the small belong to body in this way. There is evidence of the greatness of soul in the fact that when the bulk of a body increases, [20] the soul itself, having been in the lesser bulk, anticipates this and extends to the entirety of that, for it would be ridiculous in many ways if someone were also to add bulk to the soul.

§6. Why, then, does the soul not go into another body? In fact, the body must come to it, if it is able, whereas the one that has come to it and received it has it. What then? Does the other body have the same soul when it has the soul that it has? What would the difference be? In fact, [5] it consists in the additions.

Further, how is it that there is the same soul in the foot and the hand, whereas that soul which is in this part of the universe is not the same as that soul in another part? But if the acts of sense-perceptions differ, the states that go along with these should be said to differ as well. But then it is not that which judges that differs but the things judged. The one who judges is the same judge who comes to be [10] in different states.

---

[21] See Plato *Parm.* 144B3-4.

Yet it is not the case that the judge is the same as that which is experiencing these states; it is the nature of a body [part] that is in a state of this sort. It is as if the same judge judges the pleasure in our finger and the pain in our head.[22]

Why, then, is the judgment of one not perceived by another? In fact, it is because it is a judgment, not [15] a state. Further, that soul that says, "I have judged" is not the same as that soul that judges, but only judges.[23] Not even within ourselves is it the case that sight says "I have judged" to hearing, though both have judged, but reasoning judges both. And this is different from both. Frequently, reasoning also knows the judgment made in another and has comprehension of the state that the other is in. We have spoken about [20] these matters elsewhere.[24]

§7. But let us say again how it is the same thing that is present to all. This is the same question as to how each of the many perceptibles is not without a share in the same thing, even though they are situated in many different places,[25] for on the basis of what has been said, it is not correct to divide the same thing into [5] the many, but rather to conduct the divided many into the one, and that one has not come to these many, but these, because they are scattered, give us the belief that also one and the same thing has been divided among them, as if one were to divide that which controls or holds together into parts equal to what is controlled.

Still, a hand might control [10] the whole body and a piece of wood many cubits in length and something else, and, while controlling all of these, it is not divided into parts equal to what is controlled by the hand. It seems that the power extends as far as what is grasped, but nevertheless, the hand is limited by its own quantity, not by that of the body [15] that it lifts and controls. And if you were to add to the body that is controlled another length and if the hand had the power to hold it, that power would control it and would not be divided into the number of parts that the body has. What, then, if someone supposed the corporeal bulk of the hand removed, but leaving the [20] same power that previously held up that which was in the hand? Would it not, in that case, be the same undivided power in all the parts as much as it is in each one?

---

[22] The soul judges that different parts of its body are in different states. Plotinus is here distinguishing the act of judgment from being the subject of the state.

[23] Plotinus is distinguishing between one who judges that he is in a state and another who, without being in that state, judges that the first is in the state.

[24] Possibly a reference to IV 7. 6–7 or IV 9. 2–3.

[25] See Plato *Parm.* 131A–C.

And what if one were to make the center of a small bulk luminous with a greater transparent spherical body surrounding it, so that the light [25] from the inside shone in all the surrounding parts and no ray of light came from anywhere outside to the bulk. In that case, will we not say that the inside is not affected but that it has extended to every part of the exterior of the bulk while remaining itself and that light that was seen in the small bulk got hold of the exterior? Now since that light does not come from [30] the small corporeal bulk—for it is not insofar as it is a body that it has the light but insofar as it is a luminous body, luminous owing to a power other than a corporeal one—come now, if someone were to remove the bulk of the body but preserve the power of the light, would you, in that case, still say that the light was somewhere, or [would you rather say] that it was equally present [35] in the whole sphere up to the exterior? You would no longer remain stuck on your previous thought, and you would not say anymore where it came from and where it is going, but, having been puzzled, you would be in a state of amazement, when, simultaneously staring at the spherical body in this and that place, you would yourself see the light.

This is also the case with the sun, [40] since you are able to say where the light that shines on all the air comes from when you look at the sun's body, though it is the same light everywhere that you see, and this is undivided. And, in addition, the things that cut off light make this clear, since neither do they allow the light to pass through to the side opposite to that from which the light comes nor do they divide it. And then if the sun only were a power [45] separated from a body and [only] provided light, the light would not begin from the sun, and you would not be able to say where it came from, but that light would be everywhere one and the same, not having begun nor having a beginning anywhere.

§8. Then, given that light comes from a body, you are able to say where it came from, since you can say what body it came from. But if there is something immaterial and in need of no body, since it is prior in nature to every body and self-situated, or rather needing [5] no seat of this sort, this has the sort of nature having neither a source from which it originated nor a place from which it came nor a body to which it belongs. How in this case will you say that some of it is here and some there? For, in this case, you would already be able to say both where it originated and to what it belonged. It remains then to say [10] that if something shares in it, it shares in the power of the whole of it, and neither is it affected in any way, then, nor has it been divided.

For that which has a body, if it is affected, would be so by accident and, owing to this, it could be said to be subject to affection and divisible, since it is some sort of affection or form of a body. [15] That which belongs to no body but to which a body wishes to belong, must necessarily in no way experience any other affection of the body and cannot possibly be divided. For this [division] is an affection of a body, namely, the primary affection, and a property of a body as such.[26] If, then, that which is divisible is so, insofar as it is a body, insofar as something is indivisible, it is not a body. For how [20] will you divide that which does not have magnitude? If, then, that which has magnitude in any way shares in that which does not have magnitude, it would not share in it by that being divided. Otherwise, it will again have magnitude.

Whenever, then, you say that it is in many things, you do not mean that it has become many but rather you apply the affection of the many to that one in [25] the many, seeing it simultaneously in the many. But the words "in them [the many]" should be taken to indicate that it belongs to neither each of the many nor all of them but that it belongs to itself and is itself and that it does not leave off from itself. Nor, again, is it of the same size as the perceptible universe, nor is it some part of the universe. For, generally, it does not have [30] a quantity. How, then, could it have a size? For "size" belongs to a body, whereas one should in no way attribute "size" to that which is not a body but is of a different nature. Nor should a term such as "wherever" be used of it, for indeed it is not anywhere. Nor, then, should "here" and "there" be used of it, for in that case it would be in many "wheres."

If, then, [35] division is into places, whenever something belongs to something here or there, how could you divide that which exists in nothing "here" or "there?" It therefore must be undivided and with itself, even if the many should happen to desire it. If, then, the many do desire it, it is clear that they desire it as a whole, so that if they are able to share in it, [40] they would share in the whole of it, insofar as they are able. It must be, then, that the things that share in it, share in it as if they did not share in it, since it is not a personal possession of theirs, for in this way it would remain itself whole in itself, that is, whole in the things in which it is seen. For if it is not whole, it is not itself, nor will there be sharing in that which was desired [45] but in something else, which was not the object of desire.

§9. For, indeed, if the part that has come to be in each were a whole, and each one was like the first, each one always being cut off, then the first things would be many, and each would be first.[27] Further, what

---

[26] Quantity is the primary accidental attribute of any body. It is that upon which all other attribution depends.

[27] See Plato *Parm.* 142D–E for the deductions following from the hypothesis that "a one exists."

would be that which kept these many firsts separate, so that they were not [5] all together one? It would certainly not be their bodies, since it would not be possible for them to be forms of the bodies, if these are to be like that first from which they came. If the parts that are in the many are said to be its powers, in the first place, each is no longer a whole. Next, how did they come to the many, having been cut off and having abandoned the first? [10] For if they did abandon it, it is clear that they abandoned it to go somewhere.

Further, are the powers that have come to be here in the perceptible universe still in the first or not? If they are not, it is absurd for that to be diminished and to become powerless by being deprived of the powers that it previously had. And how would it be possible for the [15] powers to be separated from their substances or to be cut off? But if they are in it and elsewhere, too, either the wholes or parts of them will be here. If it is parts, the rest of the parts will be there. If it is wholes, either what is both there and here is not divided, and again the same thing will be everywhere not [20] divided, or the powers will each be one whole that has become many, and they will be like each other, so that the power will be with each substance. Or else there will only be one power that goes with the substance, and the others will be powers only. But just as it is not possible to have a substance without power, so it is not possible to have a power without a substance, for the power [25] in the intelligible world is reality and substance, or greater than substance.[28]

But if the powers that come from there are different, since they are diminished and faint, like the light that is faint when it comes from a brighter light—and so, too, with the substances that go along with these powers, in order that a power does not come to be without a substance—then, first, in the case of all such powers, it is necessary—[30] since they are completely of the same form as each other—either to agree that they are the same everywhere or else, if they are not the same everywhere, but then extensively the same whole at the same time, that whole is not divided, as if it was in one and the same body. But if this is the case, why is it not like this in the whole universe? And if this is the case, each power is divided indefinitely and [35] would no longer be a whole in itself, but powerlessness, owing to division, will occur.

Next, if one power is here and another there, that will not allow awareness. And, further, just as a reflection of something, like the weaker light that it is, no longer exists when it has been cut off from that

---

[28] Here, "intelligible world" includes both Intellect and the One.

from which it is, generally, it is not possible to make something exist that [40] has its existence from another and is a reflection of that, once it is cut off. Nor could these powers that come from there exist, if they were to be cut off from that. But if this is so, then that from which they originate will be in the intelligible world at the same time [as they are elsewhere], so that again the same whole will be everywhere undivided.

§10. But if someone should say that it is not necessary for a reflection to be dependent on its archetype, since it is possible for an image to exist when the archetype of which it is an image is not there, just as what has been heated by fire can be hot when the fire is removed, [5] first, in the case of the archetype and image, if one is speaking about the image made by the painter, we will say that it was not the archetype that made the image, but the painter, since even if he paints himself, it is not an image of him; for neither was that which was painted the body of the painter, nor was it his shape that was reproduced. [10] It is not the painter but the arrangement of these colors that should be said to make [constitute] this image.

Nor is this the making of the image or reflection in the principal sense, such as occurs in water and mirrors or in shadows.[29] For in these cases, the images exist principally as derived from that which was prior to them, and they come to be from it, and it is not [15] possible for them to exist when they are cut off from that itself. But they will acknowledge that this is the manner in which the weaker powers come from the prior powers. In the case of the fire, the heat should not be said to be an image of the fire, unless someone were to say that the fire is in the heat. But if this is so, [20] it [the fire in the heat] will make heat apart from [the original] fire. Further, even if not immediately, that which was heated, having been cut off from the [original] fire, will stop being heated, and the body will cool down.

But if these people are going to snuff out these powers, in the first place they will say that there is only one thing that is indestructible, since they will be making souls and Intellect destructible. Next [25] they will make flow away things that come from a substance that does not flow away. And, indeed, if the sun were to remain, being situated somewhere, it would provide the same light to the same places. But if someone were to say that it is not the same, he would, in saying this, show his conviction that the body of the sun flows away. But that the things that come from there [the intelligible world] are not destructible,

---

[29] Cf. Plato *Soph.* 239D6–7; *Rep.* 510E2–3.

rather, that the souls and [30] every intellect are immortal, has been shown elsewhere by means of many arguments.[30]

§11. But why, if the intelligible world is a whole everywhere, does not everything share in the intelligible as a whole? And how is it that the first is there and then the second and all the others that come after that? In fact, one should believe that that which is present is so according to the fitness of the receiver, and being is everywhere not cut off from its own reality, but that which is able to be present to it is present to it and is so to the extent that it is able, though it is not present spatially. It is just as the transparent is present to the light, in contrast to the sharing in it by air that is clouded. And these "firsts" and "seconds" and "thirds" [are determined] by rank and [10] power and difference, not by place,[31] for nothing prevents things that are different from being all together, such as soul and intellect and all types of knowledge, both major and derivative. For the eye sees the color, and the nose smells the scent, and the other senses sense their different objects that all come from the same thing, being all together and not being separate from each other.

[15] Does this, then, make the intelligible world varied and multiple? In fact, the varied is simple, too, and the many are one,[32] for an expressed principle is one and many, and all Being is one. For Being is self-differentiating, that is, difference belongs to it, since it could not belong to nonbeing.[33] And Being belongs to that which is one, which is not separated from Being, and wherever being would be, the oneness of it is present to it, [20] and the one Being is again in itself,[34] for it is possible to be present while being separate.

But the way that certain sensibles are present to certain intelligibles is different from the way that intelligibles are present to themselves. And the way that body is present to soul is different from the way that understanding is present to the soul and understanding is present to understanding, when each one is in the same intellect. And body is present [25] to body in a way different from these.

---

[30] See IV 7. Also, V 1. 6, 27–39; VI 9. 9, 3–7.
[31] See VI 7. 42; Plato [?] 2nd Ep. 312E.
[32] See V 1. 8, 26; V 3. 15, 10, 22; VI 2. 15, 14–15.
[33] See Plato Soph. 255C–D.
[34] See Plato Parm. 144E1–2.

VI 7 (38) How the Multitude of Ideas Came to Exist, and On the One (§§ 1–23; 37–42)

This treatise is a wide-ranging discussion of the nature of the intelligible world and its relation to individual persons. It also explains the relationship between Intellect and the One and the justification for identifying the first principle of all as the Good, the object of all striving.

§1. When god or some god[1] sent souls into the world of becoming, he placed "light-bearing eyes"[2] in their faces, and he providentially gave them other organs for each of their senses, realizing that this is the way that they would be preserved; that is, if someone first saw or heard or [5] touched something, he could then flee or pursue it.

But how did he [god or some god] see this ahead of time? For it was not the case that first, other things having come to be and having been destroyed because of an absence of senses, he then afterward intended for human beings and other living beings to have that which would protect them from suffering. In fact, one might say that he knew that [10] the living beings would be among hot and cold things and have other bodily affections.[3] And, knowing these things, in order that the bodies of the living beings would not be easily destroyed, he gave them sense-perception and sense organs through which the senses would work.

Now either he gave the sense organs to those who had the perceptual powers, or he gave both the instruments and the powers at once. But if he also gave the perceptual powers, the souls, though they were souls, did not previously have [15] the perceptual powers. If they did, when souls came to be, they came to be in order to enter the world of becoming, it being in their nature to enter the world of becoming. Therefore, it was against nature for them to be apart from the world of becoming and in the intelligible world and, indeed, to have been made in order that they would belong to another world and in order that they should be in the midst of evil. And in that case, [god's] providence was directed to their being preserved in [20] the midst of evil, and this would be the calculative reasoning of god, and it would be comprehensive calculative reasoning.[4]

---

[1] See Plato *Tim*. 42D on the "assistant gods" who make the human body.
[2] Ibid. 45B3.
[3] Ibid. 33A3.
[4] Ibid. 34A8. Plotinus is here being ironic.

But what are the principles of acts of calculative reasoning? For even if they come from other acts of calculative reasoning, it is, at any rate, necessary that they are directed towards some thing or things prior to calculative reasoning. What sort of thing, then, are the principles? Either they are sense-perception or intellect. But there is no sense-perception yet [prior to the world of becoming], so it is, therefore, intellect. But if the premises are intellect, the [25] conclusion is knowledge. Therefore, calculative reasoning is not about any sensible object. But if the starting point of it is in the intelligible world, and the reasoning arrives at an end in the intelligible world, how, given that it is disposed in this way, is discursive thinking to arrive at a conclusion about sensibles? So, providence about a living being or about this universe in general did not arise from calculative reasoning, since there is altogether no calculative reasoning in the intelligible world. But [30] it is called "calculative reasoning"[5] to indicate that everything is the way it is as if it came about from the calculative reasoning that would occur later, and it is called "foresight," because it is as some wise person would have foreseen it.

For in things that did not come about before calculative reasoning, the calculative reasoning was useful in solving the problem of the power that was before calculative reasoning, and the foresight, because there [35] was not a power for the one having foresight, insofar as there was not a need for foresight. For foresight [is concerned] that "this not be" rather than "that be," and it fears, lest "some such thing turn out to be like this." But where there is only the "this," there is no foresight. But calculative reasoning [is concerned with things like] "this rather than that." For if either of these ["this" or "that"] alone were the case, what calculation would there be? How, then, can that which is alone and one[6] [40] and simple have explicitly the "this in order that that not be" and "this had to be if not that" and "this appeared useful and this served to preserve that when it came to be"? Therefore, did he have foresight and precalculate and—as was said at the beginning—give the senses for the above reason, even [45] if the giving, I mean the "how" of his giving, is especially puzzling?[7]

But still, if it is necessary that each [divine] activity not be incomplete, and it is sacrilegious to believe that anything belonging to a god be other than whole and complete, it is necessary that everything exist

---

[5] Ibid. 34A8.

[6] Referring here to Intellect.

[7] Omitting H-S₂'s brackets and reading καὶ πῶς and adding a question mark at the end of the last line with Hadot.

among the things that belong to him. It is necessary, then, that the future already be present, for the future is not something that comes later for [50] that, but what is already present there comes later in something else. If, then, the future is already present, it is necessary that it be present in this way: so that what comes later was preconceived. This is to say that there is no need of anything then, and it is missing nothing. Therefore, all things exist already and always and in such a way that [55] later one can say "this after this," for that which is stretched out and in a way simplified can reveal "this after this," whereas, in the case of being altogether, the all is the "this." That is what having the explanation in itself means.

§2. Accordingly, on this basis,[8] someone would be in a position to attain a grasp of the nature of Intellect, which we see more [clearly] than others [principles]. It is not that in this way we see the true measure of Intellect, for the "that" which we attribute to it is not the "why," but even if we should give the "why" of it, that is separate [from the "that"].[9] And we see [5] a human being, or an eye, as the case may be, just as an image, or belonging to an image. But in the intelligible world there is the human being[10] and the "why" of human being, provided that it is necessary that there be an intellectual human being there, and an [intelligible] eye and the "why" of an eye. In fact, they would not be there altogether if the "why" were not in the intelligible world. But here, just as it is the case that each of the parts is separate, so also is the "why" separate. But [10] in the intelligible world everything is in one, so that the "thing" [the "that"] and "why" of the thing are the same.[11]

But often here the "thing" and the "why" are the same, too, as in the case of an eclipse.[12] What, then, prevents each of the others [sensibles] from being its own "why" as well, and this [the "why"] from being the essence of each thing? This is actually necessary. And when we [15] attempt thus to grasp the essence correctly, this [the identity of the "thing" and the "why"] follows, for what each thing is, is "why" this is. I mean

---

[8] That is, on the basis of what is said in the preceding section.

[9] See Aristotle *APo*. A 13, 78a22 ff. on the distinction between knowing the "why" and the "that." The latter is the fact, and the former is the explanation for the fact. Knowing the fact generally means more than merely perceiving it; it includes being able to describe what it is.

[10] Plotinus is perhaps referring here to the Form of Human Being as well as to the individual human being, "the human being within the human being" that does not descend from the intelligible world. This is also said by Plotinus to be a Form. See V 7.

[11] Thus, the structure of the intelligible world is *self*-explanatory.

[12] See Aristotle *Met*. H 4, 1044b14; *APo*. B 2, 90a15.

not that the Form for each thing is the explanation of its being—though this is indeed true—but that, if you were to make explicit each Form itself by itself, you would find in it the "why," for that which is inactive—that is, does [20] not have life—does not have the "why" at all, while as for that which is a Form and belongs to Intellect, where would it get its "why" from? If someone should say, "from Intellect," it is not separate from that, since it is indeed the same thing as Intellect. If, then, it is necessary to have those things that are deprived of nothing, it must not be missing the "why."

Intellect has the "why" for each of the things in it in this way. [25] It is itself each of the things [the Forms] in it,[13] so that in no one of them is the "why" something that needs to be added. Rather, they have come to be altogether, and Intellect has in itself the explanation for their existence [the "why"]. But not having come to be randomly, no one of these would have its "why" omitted; rather, having everything, it also at the same time, as it has the explanation [the "why"] of its being, has [the explanation] of its being beautiful.[14] And, therefore, [30] in this way they give to the things that partake of them their "why."

And, indeed, just as in this universe, which has been constructed from many things, all things are connected with each other, and the "why" for each is in the being of the universe, every one of its parts is seen in relation to the whole—it is not the case that this has come to be, then this after [35] this, but together they establish explanation and are explained in relation to each other—so, in the intelligible world, it is much more necessary that all things be in relation to the whole and each with itself.

If, then, there is a coexistence of all things together and no one of them is randomly there and it is necessary that these not be separated, those things which are explained would have the explanations in themselves, and [40] each is such that, in a way, it has the explanation by not having an explanation [other than itself]. If, then, they [Forms or intelligibles] do not have an explanation of their being, but are self-sufficient and exempt from [ulterior] explanation, in having the explanation in themselves, they would have it among themselves.

For, again, if there is nothing in the intelligible world that is pointless,[15] and if in each there are many things, you would have to say that

---

[13] That is, by being eternally cognitively identical with it.

[14] All the Forms are an expression of the One or the Good or the source of all beauty. The explanation (the "why") for any Form thus includes the explanation for why it is beautiful. See I 6. 6.

[15] See Aristotle *De Ca.* A 4, 271a33.

each has the "why" for all the things being as they are. [45] Then the "why" was prior and coexisted in the intelligible world, not as "why" but as "that." More correctly, both are one. For what would [an intelligible] have beyond Intellect, as if the thought of Intellect were not just that, not a sort of perfect product? If it is, then, perfect, it is not possible to say in what way it is deficient nor why [the supposed missing part] is not present. If, then, it *is* present, you [50] would be able to say why it is present. Then, the "why" is in its existence [the "that"]. In each thought of Intellect, then, and in each actualization, all of the human being, so to speak, appeared, the human being bringing himself with it [the thought] and everything such as he has from the beginning, he has all together, and is available as a whole. Then, if he [the human being] is not all there, but there is something else that is necessary to add to him, that will be among the things [55] generated. But he [the human being] exists eternally. So, he [the human being] is all there, whereas it is the human being who belongs to the world of becoming who is generated.

§3. What, then, prevents there being deliberation about him [the human being in the world of becoming] beforehand? In fact, he exists in accord with that [the Form], so that it is necessary not to remove or add anything, but the deliberation and calculative reasoning are hypothetical. For [Plato] hypothesized the things that came to be. And this is the way that deliberation and [5] calculative reasoning are, with the words "always becoming" indicating that calculative reasoning has been eliminated.[16] For it is not possible for there to be calculative reasoning in the eternal; that would belong to someone who had forgotten how things were previously. Accordingly, if things are better afterwards, they would not have been suitable before. But if they *were* suitable, then they are such as to remain the same.

Things are beautiful when they include their explanation. [10] Also, even now [in the world of becoming] something is beautiful because it is complete—for form is this, that is, everything—and because it controls the matter.[17] Now, it controls the matter if it leaves nothing of it unshaped. But it leaves it unshaped if some shape is missing, such as an eye or some other part, so that when you give the explanation, you say

---

[16] See Plato *Tim.* 27D6–28A1, where Plato hypothesizes the distinction between "that which is always being" and "that which is always becoming, but is never being." Plotinus draws the conclusion that this entails the elimination of calculative reasoning by Intellect.

[17] Cf. I 6. 2, 16 for the definition of "beauty" in the sensible world as matter dominated by form.

everything. Why does it have eyes? In order that it be complete. And [15] why does it have eyebrows? In order that it be complete. For even if you say that it has these for the sake of preserving itself,[18] you are saying that what is protective of the substance exists in it. But this is to say that it contributes to its existence. In this way, therefore, the essence existed prior to this [what is protective of the substance], and the explanation, therefore, is part of the essence. But, of course, though this [what is protective of the substance] is distinct from [the essence], what it is belongs to the essence. All things, then, are with each other, [20] and the whole is perfect and everything and exists suitably with the explanation and in the explanation, and the substance and the essence and the "why" are one.

If, moreover, having perceptual powers, that is, having them in this way,[19] is contained in the Form by everlasting necessity and if it is perfect because Intellect is perfect and has in itself the [25] explanations, so that we can later see that thus and so is therefore the correct way for things to be—for in the intelligible world the explanation is one and perfective and the human being there was not only Intellect, with the perceptual powers being added when he was sent into the world of becoming—how would that Intellect not incline to the things here?[20] For what would perceptual powers be other than [30] the ability to grasp sensibles? Would it not be absurd if it [the human being] had perceptual powers eternally in the intelligible world, but sense-perception here, that is, for the actuality of the potency there to be fulfilled here, just at the time when the soul becomes worse?

§4. So, with a view to solving this puzzle, we have to again try to understand who that human being is [in the intelligible world]. Perhaps it is necessary first to say who the human being is here [in the world of becoming], lest not knowing this one accurately, [5] we seek *that* one as if we did know *this* one. Perhaps it would appear to some that this human being and that human being are the same.[21]

Let this be the starting point of the investigation. So is the human being here [expressed in the] account of a soul different from that of the

---

[18] See Aristotle *PA* B 15, 658b14–15.

[19] That is, having them paradigmatically or intelligibly as opposed to having them physically.

[20] The point is that since the perceptual powers eternally belong to the intelligible human being, and since a perceptual power is only of use in regard to sensibles, the "descent" of the intelligible human being into particular human souls was inevitable.

[21] Plotinus perhaps means Peripatetics, Stoics, and Epicureans.

soul that provides the human being with life and the ability to reason? Or is this kind of soul the human being?[22] Or is it the soul that uses [10] the body of a certain kind?[23] But if a human being is a rational living being,[24] and a living being is composed of soul and body, the account of this composite would not be the same as the account of the soul. But if the account of the human being is of that which is composed of rational soul and body, how could it have everlasting existence, since the account is of [15] the human being when soul and body were conjoined? For this account will be indicative of what is to be not the sort of thing we say the human being is but rather more like a definition of the sort that is not indicative of the essence, for it is not even [20] indicative of the form that is in the matter but rather of the composite, which exists already.[25]

But if this is the case, the human being has not yet been found, for he was to be that which was [constructed] according to this expressed principle. Now if someone were to say, "it is necessary for the expressed principle of these things to be the expressed principle of some composite, "a this in this,"[26] he would not be judging it important to state what each thing is. But it is also necessary, even if it is necessary to give the [25] expressed principles—especially of the forms in matter with the matter—to understand the expressed principle itself, which has made, for example, the human being; this is especially so for those who judge it important to define the essence in each case, whenever they are giving a definition in the primary sense.[27]

What, then, is it to be a human being? What is it that, having made this human being, exists in him and is not separate from him? [30] Is, then, the expressed principle just "rational living being"? Or is "rational living being" the composite and the expressed principle just that which makes the rational living being? In that case, what is the expressed principle itself? Is it that, in the expressed principle, "living being" should be substituted for "rational life"? Then the human being would be the rational life. But, then, is there life without soul? For either soul will provide the rational life, [35] and the human being will be the actuality

---

[22] See Plato [?] *Alc.* I 130C.

[23] Ibid. 129E–130A.

[24] See Aristotle Fr. 192 Rose$_3$ (= Ross, p. 132). See Iamblichus *V. Pythag.* 6, 31.

[25] That is, such a definition does not explain the form that is in the matter apart from the matter. It starts with the composite.

[26] See Aristotle *Met.* **Z** 5, 1030b18.

[27] Plotinus is here alluding to Aristotle *Met.* **Z** 4, 1030b4–6; **Z** 5, 1031a1.

of soul and not a substance, or the soul will be the human being. But if the rational soul will be the human being, whenever the soul should enter another living being, how will that not be the human being?

§5. It must be, then, that the account of the human being is [an account] of something other than the soul. What prevents the human being from being some kind of composite: a soul consisting of a certain kind of expressed principle,[28] that expressed principle being both some sort of activity and, since that activity is not able to be without an agent, [5] the agent as well? For this is the way that the expressed principles are in the seeds; they are neither without soul nor simply souls, for the expressed principles that make them are not soulless, and there is nothing to marvel at in such essences being expressed principles.

The expressed principles, then, that make the human being are the activities of what kind of soul? Are they, [10] therefore, those of the soul responsible for growth?[29] In fact, they are those of the soul that makes a living being, clearer[30] and, just because of this, more alive. The soul that is of the kind that comes to be in this kind of matter, insofar as it is such that it is disposed in this way even without the body, is a human being. But in a body, it shapes it according to itself and makes the body a different representation of [15] human being insofar as the body is able to receive this, just as the painter will make a representation of *this*, a kind of lesser human being. This kind of soul has the shape and the principles or habits, the dispositions, the powers—all in a murky way—because this kind is not first. It also has the other senses, which [20] seem to be clear but are, in fact, murkier compared with those before them and are images of them.

But the human being above this one is already [the product] of a more divine soul, which has a better human being and clearer senses. And this would be the one Plato was defining, and, by adding the phrase "using a body,"[31] he indicated that it supervenes on the one that [25] primarily uses a body, and since it uses it secondarily, it is more divine. For as soon as the human being with senses had been generated, this soul followed after and gave it a clearer life. More correctly, it did not

---

[28] The word λόγος here refers to what the "account" is of, namely, the expressed principle. The expressed principle of a soul or of that with soul is a reflection of or derivation from a principle higher than Soul, namely, Intellect.

[29] That is, the kind of psychic power.

[30] "Clearer" means higher in the intelligible hierarchy. See III 8. 8, 18; VI 3. 7, 22; VI 6. 18, 16.

[31] See Plato [?] *Alc.* I 129E11.

follow after but in a way attached it to itself.[32] For it does not exit from the intelligible world, but, being in touch with it, it has the lower soul, in a way, suspended from it, mixing itself by means of its expressed principle with that one's expressed principle. As a result, that human being who was murky came to be clear by the illumination.

§6. How, then, does perceptual power exist in the better soul? In fact, it is the power of perception of sensibles in the intelligible world as *they* exist there. And so, in this way, it perceives the sensible harmony,[33] whereas a human being in the sensible world has a receptive perceptual power and [5] harmonizes to the last degree what he senses with the harmony in the intelligible world, for example, fire being harmonized with the fire in the intelligible world, the perception of which was to that soul in the intelligible world corresponding <to> the nature of the fire in the intelligible world. For if there were bodies in the intelligible world, there would be perceptions and apprehensions of them by the soul. And the human being in the intelligible world, this kind of [10] soul, can apprehend these, as a result of which the subsequent man, the imitation, had the expressed principles in an imitative form. And the human being in Intellect is the human being prior to all human beings.

But this human being illuminates the second, and the second illuminates the third, and this lowest, somehow, has all, not becoming these, but [15] being set besides them. And one type of human being among us acts according to the lowest type, and another has something from the one before, and the activity of another is from the third from the lowest, and each one is according to how he acts, though each one has everything and, again, does not have everything. And when the third life and the third [20] human being are separated from the body, if the second[34] were to continue to be connected with the body, it would be connected while it is not separated from things above, to which that [the second] and it itself [the first] are said to belong.

But when [the second soul] takes on an animal body, one may wonder how the expressed principle of this is the expressed principle of a human being. In fact, the soul was all things, but sometimes it was acting in different ways. Then, in a purified state and prior to having been made into something worse, he wants to be a human being [25] and is a human being. For this is better, and it makes that which is better. Soul makes the preexistent spirits, which are similar in form to the soul

---

[32] Reading αὐτήν with H-S₁ instead of αὑτήν with H-S₂.

[33] That is, the mathematical proportion of elements in a sensible.

[34] Reading ἡ δευτέρα with the manuscripts instead of τῇ δευτέρᾳ with H-S₂.

<that> makes the human being. And that which exists prior to the soul is more of a spirit, more correctly a god. And a spirit is an imitation of a god, depending on a god just as a human being depends on a spirit, for that upon which a human being depends is not said to be [30] a god; a human being has the difference that the souls have to one another, even if they come from the same line. It is necessary to call spirits the kind of thing Plato calls "intelligences."[35] But whenever the soul that was connected to the spirit when it [35] was a human being follows the soul that has chosen an animal nature,[36] it gives to the animal the expressed principle of that living being that it has in itself, for the animal has it, but its activity is worse.

§7. But if at the time when the soul was degraded and became an inferior thing, it informed an animal nature, it was not originally that which made an ox or a horse and [the existence of] the expressed principle of horse and the horse would be contrary to nature. In fact, they *are* lesser things, though they are not contrary to nature, and what made them was somehow originally a horse [5] or a dog. And if the soul has the means, it makes something better; if not, it makes what it can, which at any rate was preordained as that which it should make. It is like craftsmen who know how to make many kinds of things and then make this: either what was preordained or what the matter allowed, owing to its suitability.

For what prevents the power of the soul of the universe from producing a sketch beforehand, [10] since the expressed principle of the soul of the universe is the expressed principle of everything, even prior to the psychic powers [types of souls] coming from it? And what prevents the sketch produced beforehand from being like illuminations anticipating the matter[37] and soul from executing these, following what are already traces of this kind and articulating the traces according to their parts, with [15] each soul making and becoming that to which it added itself as part of the arrangement, just as a dancer makes dance movements in accordance with the theme that has been given to him? Indeed, it was by following the argument step-by-step that we have come to this point.

---

[35] Plotinus is here likely alluding to Plato *Symp.* 202D13–E1 and *Tim.* 90A2–4, two passages dealing with spirits. In the etymologizing of *Crat.* 398B, Plato says that "spirits" (δαίμονες) are so called because they are "intelligences" (δαήμονες). Thus we follow Harder's emendation adopted by H-S$_1$ but rejected in H-S$_2$.

[36] See Plato *Tim.* 42C3.

[37] That is, the pattern for a kind of life to be followed by the matter that becomes this.

Our account concerned the way in which perceptual power belonged to the human being and how those [in the intelligible world] were not oriented towards generation. And [20] our argument appeared to show both that those things [sensibles] in the intelligible world were not oriented to these things [sensibles] in the sensible world, but rather these are dependent on those and imitate those and that this human being has his perceptual power from that human being and in relation to those things, and these sensibles are joined with this human being, and those [sensibles in the intelligible world] with that human being; for those *are* sensibles, which [25], though they are incorporeal, we so named because they are apprehended in a different way [from the way that ordinary sensibles are apprehended].

And the sense-perception in the sensible world, <because it is of bodies>, is murkier than what we called apprehension in the intelligible world, which, because it is sense-perception of incorporeals,[38] is clearer. And for this reason this man [in the sensible world] also has perceptual powers, since he has a lesser apprehension of lesser things, [30] images of those. So, these sense-perceptions are murky thoughts, and the thoughts in the intelligible world are clear sense-perceptions.

§8. So this is the way it is with perceptual power. But how are "horse" and each of the living beings in the intelligible world really there?[39] And how was it that [the divine maker][40] did not wish to look at things here below [in order to produce these animals]? But what if it were the case that [the divine maker] invented the thought of the horse in order that a horse or some other living being should come to be here below? But how would it be possible for it, [5] having wanted to make a horse, to think it up? For it is at once clear that the thought of the horse must have existed if it had wanted to make one. So, it is not possible that in order to make a horse it had to think it up first; rather, the horse that did not come to be, had to exist prior to the horse that will come to be after it.

If, then, horse existed prior to coming to be and it was not thought up in order that it should come to be, that which had the horse in the intelligible world [10] did not, looking to the things here below, thereby

---

[38] Reading αἴσθησιν ὅτι <ἀ>σωμάτων with Hadot, which follows the manuscripts, against H-S₂ with the change from σωμάτων to ἀσωμάτων.
[39] Reading ὅλως with the manuscripts instead of ὅμως with H-S₂ followed by a question mark and then a new sentence beginning <πῶς> with Hadot. Plotinus is here speaking about the Form of Horse.
[40] This is Intellect, or the Demiurge.

have its own version of it,[41] nor was it in order to make the things here below that it had both this and other [Forms of Living Beings], but rather they were there, and these things here followed necessarily from those, for [the production of things] was not to halt at the things in the intelligible world. For who could halt a power that can both remain in itself and go out of itself?

[15] But why are these living beings that are here [in the sensible world] in the intelligible world? Why are these in god [Intellect]? Let us grant [the appropriateness of there being] rational living beings. But where is the nobility in there being such a plethora of nonrational living beings? Why not the opposite? Now it is clear that this one has to be many, since it comes after that which is completely one,[42] for otherwise it would not be after that, but identical with it. But since it is after that, it could not be above [20] in the sense that it becomes more one than it, but it had to fall short of that. Since the best was one, it had to be more than one, for that which is a multiplicity is in a deficient condition.

What, then, prevents it from being a Dyad? In fact, it was not possible for each of the ones in the Dyad to be perfectly one, but again each had to be at least two, and each of those again [two], [25] and so on.[43] Next there was Motion in the primary Dyad, and Rest, and there was Intellect, and life was also in it, that is, there was perfect Intellect and perfect life.[44] As Intellect, then, it was not one but rather all and possessing all the particular intellects, as many as these are, and even more. And it lived not as one soul[45] but [30] as all, and, having a greater power in making each of the souls, it was a "complete living being,"[46] having not just Human Being in it. For [in that case] there would just be human being here.

§9. But let someone say, "[I concede the rationale for] the living beings that are valuable." How about the insignificant and nonrational ones? It is clear that their insignificance lies in their nonrationality, if value is owing to rationality. That is, if value is owing to an intellectual

---

[41] That is, Intellect did not get acquainted with horse by looking at sensible horses.

[42] The one-many is Intellect; the completely one is the One. See Plato *Parm.* 145A2.

[43] See Plato *Parm.* 142E3–143A1.

[44] See Plato *Soph.* 249A–C. These are "the Greatest Kinds" (τὰ μέγιστα γένη).

[45] Intellect is said to be soul, because soul is the principle of life, and Intellect is identical with the principle of life.

[46] Plato *Tim.* 31B1.

quality, then the opposite is owing to the lack of an intellectual quality. But how can anything be nonintellectual or [5] nonrational when it is [Intellect] in which each of them is or from which each of them comes?

Before we begin, then, to say what we have to say about these matters and against these claims, let us understand that just as the human being here is not like that one [in the intelligible world], so the other living beings here are not like those in the intelligible world; rather, it is necessary to understand those at a higher level. Nor is there reasoning in the intelligible world, for whereas here there is [10] perhaps a reasoning human being, in the intelligible world the human being exists prior to reasoning. Why then does this human being reason, whereas the other living beings do not? In fact, since thinking in a human being and thinking in the other living beings in the intelligible world are different, reasoning is also different.[47] For there are, somehow, in the other living beings many functions of discursive thinking. Why then are they not equally rational? And [15] why are human beings, among themselves, not equally rational?

One should consider that the many lives—being, in a way, motions—and the many thoughts did not have to be the same; rather, there are different lives and similarly different thoughts. And the differences are, in a way, the relative brightness and clarity of the first, second, and third [kinds of thought], according to proximity to the [20] first principles. And so, for this reason, some of the thoughts are gods, some belong to a second kind, in which what is here called "rational" [thinking] is included, and, next, the nonrational [kind] is named from these.[48]

But in the intelligible world, that which is nonrational is said to be an expressed principle, and that which is nonintellectual was Intellect, since it is Intellect that is thinking of horse, and the thinking of horse is Intellect. [25] But if it is just thinking, it would not be strange if that thinking, being just what it is, were thinking of what is nonintelligible. But now if thinking is the same as the thing thought, how can the thinking be one thing and the thing thought be nonintelligible?[49] For if this were the case, Intellect would make itself nonintelligible.

But in fact it is not nonintelligible but a certain kind of intellect, for it is a certain kind of life. For, as any kind of [30] life does not leave off being life, in this way intellect does not leave off being intellect. So, the intellect in any kind of living being, including the human being, does

---

[47] "Thinking" is broader than "reasoning," which connotes practical thinking.
[48] That which is "nonrational" (ἄλογον) is named from "rational" (λογικόν).
[49] See Aristotle *Met.* Λ 9, 1075a1–5.

not leave off being intellect in general, since each part, in whatever way you understand it, is everything, though perhaps differently in each case. In actuality it is that intellect, but it is virtually [35] all the others. But we understand the actuality in the particular. And that which is in actuality is the last, so that the last of this intellect is a horse, and insofar as it has stopped going forth always into a lesser life, it is a horse, but another will stop even lower.

For as the virtualities [of Intellect] unfold, they always leave something above. And as they proceed, they lose something, [40] and in losing different things, other [virtualities] discover and add other things for the needs of the living being that appeared, owing to the deficiencies. For example, when there is no longer [intellect] sufficient for life, nails appeared and claws or fangs or something in the nature of a horn, so that, to the extent that Intellect descended, from that point, by the [45] self-sufficiency of its nature, it rises and finds stored in itself the remedy for what it lacks.

§10. But how was it deficient within the intelligible world? Why, for example, were there horns in the intelligible world? Were they there for defense? In fact, they were there for the self-sufficiency and completion of the living being as [the kind of] living being it is. For insofar as it was a living being, it had to be complete; and insofar as it was Intellect, it had to be complete; and insofar as it was a life, it had to be complete; so that if it was not this, it was that.[50] And the [5] difference between one kind of living being and another consists in having one [property] instead of another, so that, on the one hand, the most complete living being and the perfect Intellect and the perfect life arise from all these, and, on the other, each living being is complete as the kind of being each is.

And, indeed, if it [the Form of Living Being][51] is composed of many [Forms], it has to be one as well. In fact, it is not possible for it to be composed of many, yet for the many to be all the same. In that case, it would be a self-sufficient one. It is necessary, then, that it be [10] eternally composed of specifically different things, just as is every composite, preserving the differences of each, as it is with [organic] shapes[52] and expressed principles. For the shapes, such as those of a human being, come from such differences, even though there be an overarching

---

[50] Meaning that a nature is by definition complete in itself, and calling the putative eternal nature deficient, as A, only means that it is complete, as B.

[51] See Plato *Tim.* 30C2–31A1.

[52] The "organic shapes" (μορφαί) present in the sensible world are here distinguished from the "Forms" (εἴδη) contained in the Form of Living Being.

unity. And they are better and worse than each other, an eye and a finger, but they belong to one being. And that the whole is like this is [15] better, not worse. And the account is of "living being" plus "something else,"[53] which is not the same as "living being." And "excellence" refers to what is common [the genus] and to what is unique [the specific difference], and what is noble is [an instance of] the genus in combination with the difference [to make the species], whereas the genus is indifferently [good or bad].[54]

§11. But it is said that heaven itself [the universe]—and there are many things that appear in it—does not dishonor the nature of all living beings, since the universe has all of them in it. From where, then, does it get them? Does the intelligible world have them all as they are here? In fact, it has all such things as are made with an expressed principle and according to form. [5] But when it has Fire, it has Water,[55] and it has a complete array of plants. How then are plants there? And how does Fire live? And how does Earth live? In fact, it lives, or it will be in the intelligible world, a sort of corpse, so that not everything in the intelligible world lives.

And, generally, how can these things here be in the intelligible world? Now plants could be fitted into the argument,[56] since the [10] plant here is an expressed principle situated in life. If the enmattered expressed principle, which belongs to the plant and according to which the plant exists, is a certain life and a soul, and if the expressed principle is some one thing, then either this expressed principle is the first plant or not, in which case, the plant before it [the Form of Plant] is the first plant, from which this plant is derived. For that first plant is one, and the particular plants are many and [15] necessarily come from one. If this is so, then that plant should be alive in a much more primary way and be the plant itself, from which these particular plants live in a secondary and tertiary way and as a trace of that.

And how does earth live? What is it for earth to exist? And what is it for Earth in the intelligible world to have life? In fact, a prior [question] is "What is earth itself?" This is the question "What is it for earth to be earth?" Now it is necessary for it to have some [20] [organic] shape here

---

[53] That is, the differentia, "rationality."

[54] The genus is "disposition" (ἕξις). Its species are excellence and vice. The species of excellence are moral and intellectual. A disposition in itself is neither good nor bad.

[55] Forms of Fire and Water are mentioned by Plato at *Parm.* 130C. The sense of "when" here is "if."

[56] See *supra* l. 4.

and an expressed principle. In the case of the plant, it was alive in the intelligible world, and its expressed principle was alive here. Is the expressed principle of earth here, then, alive? In fact, if we were to understand the particularly earthy things generated and molded in it, we would find the nature of the earth here. One must believe that the growths and moldings of stones, then, and the shaping of mountains as [25] they spring up are altogether owing to an ensouled expressed principle working in them and shaping their forms. And this is what is making the form of the earth, just like what in trees is called "nature," in which the wood of the tree is analogous to what is called "earth," and [30] a stone, having been cut off, is in the same state as if it had been cut off from the tree, where this is not affected. But if it is still connected, it is like that which has not been cut off of the living plant.

No doubt, once we have discovered the active nature situated in the earth to be a life in an expressed principle, we would have an easy confidence that the Earth in the intelligible world is living [35] in a far more fundamental way and that it is the rational life of earth, [the Form of] Earth itself and primary Earth, from which the earth here also arises.

But if fire is also a principle in matter and the rest of such things as well, and fire is not generated adventitiously, where does it come from? Not from friction, as someone might think,[57] for friction occurs when fire is already present in the universe, and [40] the bodies that are rubbed together have it. Further, matter is not in potency such that fire can come from it. If, then, what makes fire must do so by shaping it according to an expressed principle, what would it be other than soul that is able to make it? But this is life and an expressed principle, both one and the same. For this reason, Plato said that the soul of each of these [fire and earth, etc.] in it [45] is just like that which makes the perceptible fire.[58] There is here, then, a sort of fiery life, a truer Fire, a productive Fire. Therefore, the transcendent [Form of] Fire, being more fire, would be more of a life. Therefore, Fire itself lives.

And the same argument applies to the others, namely, water and air. But [50] why are these not ensouled just as is earth? Now it is, I suppose, clear that these are in the complete Living Being, that is, that they are parts of a Living Being. But there does not appear to be life in them, just as there does not appear to be life in earth. One could, however, reason

---

[57] See Aristotle *De Ca.* B 7, 289a20.

[58] Plotinus is perhaps here referring to the doctrine found in the work known as *Epin.* 981B–C and 984B–C, which was in antiquity assumed to be a sort of appendix to *Laws* by Plato but whose authorship has been questioned in contemporary scholarship.

to [the conclusion that there is life in earth] from the things that come to be in it. But that living beings also come to be in fire and in water is even clearer. And [55] in air there are collections of living beings. But the particular fire that has come to be and is quickly quenched passes by the soul in the whole and has not come to remain in the bulk, so that it could have displayed the soul in it. Air and water are like this, since if they were somehow fixed by nature, they would have displayed their soul. But since they had to be flowing, they were not [60] able to display it.

And it is likely similar in the case of the liquids in us, like blood. For flesh and whatever might come to be flesh seem to have soul from blood,[59] whereas blood itself, not having sense-perception,[60] does not seem to have soul, though it is necessary for soul to exist in it, since nothing violent [65] happens to it. But it is ready to be separated from the soul that exists in it, just as one should believe to be the case for the three elements [fire, air, and water]. Also, the sort of living beings that have a predominance of air in their constitution have the characteristic of not being perceivable by us.[61] For just as air itself passes through a beam of light that is rigid and stable so long as it is being emitted, in the same way [70] air moves past the soul of the air in a circular motion and yet does not move past it. And similarly with the other elements.

§12. But let us again say it this way: since we say[62] that this [sensible] universe is in relation to that one [the intelligible world], which is a sort of paradigm for it, it is also necessary that in the intelligible world priority be ascribed to a universe that is alive, and, if it is to be "complete,"[63] it has to have all living beings in it. And, of course, the sky in the intelligible world must be a living being and not, [5] then, be a sky bereft of the stars, which, it is said, comprise the sky here. I mean that this is what it is to be the sky. And it is obvious that in the intelligible world, it is not bereft of earth but much more full of life than ours, and all living beings are in it, all those that are here said to walk or to be terrestrial, obviously in addition to the plants that are rooted in life. And the seas [10] are in the intelligible world and all water fixed in flow and life[64] and all the things that live in the water, and the nature of air is part of the totality in

---

[59] See Plato *Tim.* 80D–81B; Aristotle *PA* B 3, 650a34.

[60] See Aristotle *PA* B 3, 650b5. The idea is that whereas we perceive our flesh being touched, we do not perceive our blood being touched.

[61] These are δαίμονες, "spirits," mentioned at III 5. 6, 31.

[62] See 3, 1–2; 8, 3–14.

[63] See Plato *Tim.* 31B1.

[64] That is, the paradigm of what is ever-changing is "fixed."

the intelligible world, and the things that live in the air are in it analogous to the air itself, for how could the things in the [Form of] Living Being not be alive, when they are so here?

How, then, is not every living being necessarily in the intelligible world? For as [15] each of the major parts of the universe are there, necessarily it has the nature of the living beings in them. So, then, in this way, the intelligible world has all the living beings in heaven, and they exist in the intelligible world as heaven does, and it is not possible that they do not exist there. Otherwise, those living beings will not exist. Whoever, then, is inquiring into where living beings come from is inquiring where heaven in the intelligible world comes from. [20] This is the same as inquiring where the Living Being comes from, which is the same as inquiring where life, that is, universal life, and universal Soul and universal Intellect come from, for in the intelligible world there is neither poverty nor insufficiency, but all things there are full of life and, in a way, boiling with life.[65] They are a sort of outflow from a single spring, not like from some single breath or [25] heat, but in a way as if there were some single quality holding all the other qualities in itself and preserving the qualities—of sweetness with fragrance, at once the qualities of wine and the powers of all tastes, the sights of colors, and all the objects of touch that the senses recognize. And all such sounds as are heard are fixed there and all tunes and rhythms.

§13. For neither Intellect nor the Soul that comes from it is simple, but rather all[66] are variegated just as much as they are simple, that is, to the extent that they are not composite and to the extent that they are principles and to the extent that they are activities, for whereas the activity of the last [of each of Intellect and Soul] has the simplicity of something that is petering out, the activity of the first [Intellect and Soul] are all the activities.[67] And Intellect [5] in motion is moved in this way, that is, always according to the same things and in the same way, though it is not selfsame in the way that one of its parts is, but is all of them, since the part is also not one but is indefinitely divisible.[68]

---

[65] Perhaps an allusion to Aristotle *De An.* A 2, 405b26–9, where Aristotle says that certain Pre-Socratics connected "to live" (ζῆν) etymologically with "to boil" (ζεῖν).

[66] Referring to Intellect, Soul, and all the intellects that partake of Intellect and all the souls that partake of Soul.

[67] See *supra* 9, 35–8. The activity of Intellect and the activity of Soul are virtually all the activities of that which partakes of them.

[68] See Plato *Soph.* 248A12, the passage to which Plotinus may be referring.

But from what do we say it would arise and, as a whole, to what does it move as an end? And is the entire extent of what is between [the beginning and the end] therefore like a line or just like some [10] different body that is uniform and unvariegated? But what nobility is there in that? For if it has no variation in it, and there is no difference that wakes it into life, it would not be activity,[69] for such a fixity would not differ from nonactivity. And if Intellect's motion were of this kind, its [15] life would be monotonous, not multifarious. But it is necessary for it to live in every way and everywhere and for nothing of it not to live. It must then move itself in every way or rather it must have moved itself. Of course, if it were to move itself in a simple way, it would then have that [the activity that belongs to just that motion] alone. And either it is itself and did not proceed into anything, or, if it did proceed, another [part of it] remained. So, then, it is two. But if this same thing is in that [part that remained], it remains one and has not gone forth, but if it is [20] different, it has gone forth with difference, and from something the same and different it has made a third one.[70]

Now, having come to be from sameness and difference, that which has come to be [Intellect] has the nature that is sameness and difference; it is not just something that is different, but it is universal difference, for its sameness is also universal. And being universal sameness and universal difference, there is no one of the others that it [25] leaves out. Intellect has therefore the nature of being different in every way. If, then, all the different things existed prior to it, it would already have been affected by them. But if they did not, then Intellect generated all things, or, rather, it was all things.

It is not possible, then, for real things to exist, if Intellect is not active, eternally actualizing one thing after another and, in a way, having wandered across every expanse and [30] having wandered in itself, as it is natural for true Intellect to wander in itself. And it is natural to wander among essences, while the essences run along with its wanderings. But it is itself everywhere. So, then, it has a wandering that is constant. And the wandering in itself is in "the plain of truth,"[71] [35] from which it does not exit. And, by understanding, it also has everything in itself, making a sort of place for motion, and the place is the same as that whose place it is.

[69] See Aristotle *Met.* Λ 9, 1074b17–18.

[70] See Plato *Tim.* 35A3–5 where the "third one" refers to the construction of the soul of the universe. Here it refers to the "self-construction" of Intellect, that is, to the actualization of all intelligibles or Forms.

[71] See Plato *Phdr.* 248B6.

But this plain is variegated, so that Intellect might pass through it. And if it is not eternally and universally variegated, to the extent that it is not, it stands still. But if it stands still, it does not think, so that if it stood still, it has not [40] thought. If this is so, it does not exist. It is, then, thinking. And it is all motion filling up all essence, and all essence is all thinking, encompassing all life, and one essence eternally follows another, and whatever of it is the same is also other, and, while dividing, the other eternally appears. And its entire passage is through life and through all [45] living beings, just as one passing across all the parts of the earth passes through earth, even if the earth has its differences.

And in the intelligible world, the life through which it passes is the same, but, because it is eternally different, it is not the same. But it is eternally in the same state, passing through things that are not the same, because it does not change but is present in the others in the same way with the same things, for if it were not present [50] in the others in the same way with the same things, it would be totally inactive, and its activity, that is, activity [itself] would be nowhere. But it is itself also the others, so that it is everything. And since it is everything, if it were not, it would not be itself. But if it is itself everything, and everything because it is all things, and there is nothing that does not contribute to all things, there is nothing [55] of it that is not other, so that, being other, it might contribute. For if it is not other, but the same as an other, it diminishes its own unique substance by not providing for the completion of its own nature.

§14. But by using intellectual paradigms it is also possible to understand the sort of thing that Intellect is, namely, it does not allow itself not to be other as if it were a unit. What expressed principle of a plant or a living being do you wish to grasp as an example? For if it was some one being and not [5] this one variegated being, there would not be an expressed principle, and that which comes to be would be matter, and the expressed principle would not come to be in all its parts, everywhere entering the matter and would not allow anything of it to be the same. For example, a face is not one mass, but nostrils and eyes. And the nose is not just one thing, but one part has to be different, and, [10] again, another different from it, if it is going to be a nose. For one simple being would be a uniform mass.

And the indefinite is this way in Intellect, because it is one in the sense of a "one-many,"[72] not like one mass, but like a complex expressed principle in itself, in the one figure of Intellect, having, in a way, in an

---

[72] See Plato *Parm.* 137C–142A; 144E5; 155E5. On Intellect as a "one-many," see IV 8. 3, 10; V 1. 8, 26; V 3. 15, 11, 22; VI 2. 15, 14–15, etc.

outline, outlines inside it and again figures inside it and powers and thoughts and [15] division, not in a linear direction but eternally inward, as the natures of living beings are encompassed by the complete Living Being. And, again, other natures are included, extending to the smaller of living beings and to the lesser powers, where it will stop at an indivisible form.[73]

But the division involved is not a jumble, although it is a division of things that are one; rather, it is [20] what is called the "love in the universe"[74] but not the love in *this* universe [in the sensible world]. For this love is an imitation, since it is love that arises from things that are separated. The true love is where everything is one and never separated. [Empedocles], however, says that what is in this [sensible world] is separated.[75]

§15. Who, then, seeing this multiple and universal and primary and single life, does not welcome the prospect of being in it, despising all others? For the others below are in darkness and small and murky and insignificant and impure, and [5] defile pure lives. And if you were to look into these lives, you would no longer be seeing nor living one of those lives that is all together and where there is no one that does not live purely, since there is no evil in it, for the evils are here, because here is a trace of life and a trace of Intellect. But in the intelligible world, Plato says, is the archetype, that which was "Good-like," because Intellect has the Good [10] in the Forms.[76]

For this is the Good, but Intellect is good by having its life in contemplation.[77] And it contemplates the things it contemplates as Good-like,[78] that is, as those things that it came to possess when it contemplated the nature of the Good.[79] But they came to it, not as they were there, but as

---

[73] See Aristotle *Phys.* E 4, 227b7; *Top.* Γ 6, 120a35 on the term "indivisible form."
[74] See Empedocles Frs. B 17, 7 and B 26, 5 D-K. The reference is intended to indicate the intimate relationship among Forms in Intellect.
[75] See Empedocles A 52 D-K = Simplicius *In de Ca.* 293, 22–3; *In Phys.* 31, 23.
[76] See Plato *Rep.* 509A3. Plotinus is here making a distinction between the Idea [or Form] of the Good, or simply the Good, and the way the Good is possessed by Intellect, that is, as the entire array of Forms. The Good itself, though called an "Idea" (508E3), is "beyond essence" (509B9) and so, according to Plotinus, beyond Forms. For Intellect as Good-like see I 8. 11, 16; III 8. 11, 16; V 3. 16, 19.
[77] That is, "the Good is good" is an identity statement whereas Intellect is good by partaking of the Good.
[78] See III 8. 11, 16–17.
[79] See Plato *Phil.* 60B10.

Intellect itself had them, for [15] the Good is the principle, and it is from that [that they came to be] in Intellect, and Intellect made these from that.[80] For it was not licit for Intellect, in looking at the Good, to think nothing nor, again, to think the things [as they existed] in it, for, in that case, Intellect itself would not have generated them.

It had, then, the power from the Good to generate and to be filled up with its own generated products, the Good having given what it itself did not [20] have. Rather, from what was itself one, many things came to be in Intellect, for being unable to retain the power that it received, it broke it up and made that which was one many, so that, in this way, it would be able to bear it as divided into parts. Whatever it then generated was from the power of the Good and was Good-like, and it itself is good, composed of the many Good-like things—a variegated good.

Accordingly, [25] if one compares it to a sphere with a variegated life,[81] or if one were to compare it to a shining visage comprising all living visages or to imagine it as the totality of purified souls concurrently alive—which are not deficient but have everything that belongs to them, and Intellect in its totality situated on their heights, so that the place is illuminated [30] by an intellectual light—if one were to imagine it in this way, one would be doing so in the way someone sees another thing external to it. On the contrary, it is necessary for one to become Intellect, thereby making oneself that which is seen.

§16. It is necessary not to pause forever in this multiple beauty but to advance further, rushing towards the higher region, leaving this beauty, Intellect, not this heaven [the intelligible world], wondering at what generated Intellect and how. So each thing there is a Form, [5] and each is a sort of unique type. Since each Form is Good-like, they all thereby have something in common that applies to all of them. They then also have Being in common, and each has the Living Being, since life is present to them in common. And probably there are other things as well, but to the extent that they are good, and as the reason why they are good, what explains this?

For this sort of inquiry, perhaps it would [10] be useful to begin here: when Intellect looked towards the Good, did it think that that One was many and, being one itself, think it to be many, dividing it in itself, owing to the fact that it was not able to think it as a whole altogether?[82]

---

[80] That is, Intellect made the Forms out of its relationship with the Good (as a result of desiring it).

[81] See Plato *Phd.* 110B7.

[82] See *supra* 15, 20–2.

But it was not yet Intellect when it looked at the Good, but it looked non-intellectually. In fact, it should be said that it saw nothing, [15] but rather lived facing it and was dependent on it and turned towards it, whereas its motion was filled up by moving in the intelligible world and around the Good, and it filled Intellect and was no longer only motion, but motion satisfied and full.

And it next became all things [all Forms] and knew this in its [20] awareness of itself and henceforth became Intellect, on the one hand having been filled up, so that it might have what it should see, and on the other hand, looking at these with light from that which gave these, and also providing the light. This is the reason why the Good is said [by Plato] to be the cause not only of essence, but also of essence being seen.[83] Just as the sun—since it is the cause of [25] sensibles being seen and of their coming to be, is somehow also the cause of sight—therefore is neither sight nor the things that come to be; in this way, the nature of the Good is the cause of essence and of Intellect's being and of light, and, according to the analogy, to the real things seen in the intelligible world by the one who sees, being itself neither those things nor Intellect but the cause [30] of these, providing, with its own light, thinking and being thought to real things and to Intellect. So Intellect, having been filled up [with Forms], came to be and was at that moment also perfected, and it saw. But its principle was [in one way] that which it was before it was filled up, but a different principle of it was that which filled it up and was outside it—that from which, having been filled up, it [35] was given its character.

§17. But how are the Forms in Intellect, and how are they the same as it, since they are neither there in what fills it [the One] nor again in that which is filled? For when it was not yet filled, it did not have them. In fact, it is not necessary for someone to have what he gives.[84] It is only necessary in these matters to believe that [5] the giver is superior and the recipient is inferior to the giver, for that is how generation occurs among real things. Thus it is necessary that first there be that which is in actuality, whereas the things that are posterior must be in potentiality the things that are prior to them. That is, the first transcends the second, and the giver transcends that which is given, for it is stronger.

So if there is something prior to an [10] actuality, it transcends actuality, so that it also transcends life. If, then, life is in Intellect, the giver gave life but is better and more worthy than life. Intellect, then, had life

---

[83] See Plato *Rep.* 509B2–8; 509A1, B2, B4.
[84] See *supra* 15, 19.

and was not in need of a variegated giver of life, and the life was some trace of the One, not *its* life. It, then, first [15] looked at the One when it was unlimited, and then, having looked there, it was limited by that which has no limit, for as soon as it looked at something that was one, it was limited by this, and it had in itself limit and finitude and form. And the form was in that which had been shaped, but that which shaped was without shape. But the limit was not outside it, as if surrounded by a magnitude, but was a limit of [20] that life, which was multiple and infinite, as befits a life shining forth from such a nature.

And it was not the life of this [or that]; for if it were, it would, as the life of an individual, at once be limited. But it was still limited. It was therefore limited as being some one-many—each of the many was also limited—and while it was limited as many, because of the multitude of its life, it was still one, [25] because of the limit. What, then, does "limited as one" refer to? Intellect, for Intellect is limited life. What, then, does "many" refer to? Many intellects. Then all are intellects, and the totality is Intellect and the individual intellects. But then does the totality of Intellect, encompassing each intellect, therefore encompass each by being the same as they? But in that case it would encompass them as one. If, then, it does so as many, it is [30] necessary that there be difference among them. But then, again, how did each one have difference? In fact, it had difference by becoming completely one, for the totality of Intellect does not have the identity of any one intellect.

The life of Intellect, then, was all-powerful, and the seeing that came from the One was the potentiality for being all [Forms], whereas the Intellect that came to be appeared as all [Forms] themselves.[85] But the One sits above [35] them, not in order that it might be situated, but in order that it might situate the "Form of Forms" of the first Forms,[86] being itself without form. And in this way Intellect comes to be, for soul, a light upon it, as the One is a light upon Intellect. And whenever Intellect limits the soul, it makes it rational by giving to it a trace of the things it has. Then Intellect, too, is a trace of the One, since Intellect is Form [40] and is [nonspatially] extended and multiple, whereas the One is without shape or form, for this is the way that it makes form. But if the One were form, Intellect would be an expressed principle of it. But it was necessary that the first not be in any way multiple,[87] for its

---

[85] Plotinus is here distinguishing the two "moments" of seeing the One, and then, as a result of the seeing, actualizing all Forms.

[86] See Aristotle *De An.* Γ 8, 432a2, where Aristotle identifies "Intellect" (νοῦς) as "form of forms."

[87] That is, since the One cannot be multiple, it cannot have form.

multiplicity would then be dependent on another which was again prior to it.

§18. But in what way are the things in Intellect Good-like? Is it that each is a Form, or that each is beautiful, or how? Indeed, if everything that comes from the Good has a trace or an impression of it, or else comes from it—just as that which comes from fire is a trace of fire, and that which comes from a sweet thing is a trace [5] of sweet, and also if life comes to Intellect from the Good (for it came to exist from its activity), and Intellect exists because of the Good, and the beauty of the Forms is from there—then everything, life, and Intellect, and Idea, would be Good-like.

But what is it that is common to them? For just the fact that they come from the Good is not sufficient for their being the same. [10] There should be something in these themselves that is common to them, for things not the same could come from the same thing, or the things that received the same thing could become different. Since that which is in the primary activity is one thing, and that which is given by the primary activity, another, that which results from these is at once, thereby, another. In fact, there is nothing that prevents each [life, Intellect, and Idea] from being Good-like, [15] but rather differently in each case.

What, therefore, is the particular explanation for their being the same [being Good-like]? But before answering that question, it is necessary to look at this: is life good insofar as it is bare life, considered in isolation and stripped? In fact, it is good insofar as it is life that comes from the Good. But do the words "from it" mean something other than that it is of this kind [good]? Then again, what is this kind of life? In fact, it is the life of the Good. But that does not mean that it is [20] the Good's life; rather, that it is life that comes from the Good. But if [the life of the Good] would have entered that life, and this is real life, and nothing unworthy comes from the Good, then insofar as it is life, it should be said to be good. And it is necessary to say of Intellect, which is true and the first thing coming from the Good, that it is good.

And it is clear that each [25] Form is good and Good-like insofar, then, as it has something good, whether in common with the others [life and Intellect], or, rather, with one having it more than the other, or with one of them having it primarily and another derivatively and secondarily.[88] For, since we have taken each [Form, Intellect, and life] as already having something good in its essence and being good because of this—for life was good not simply, but because it [30] was said to be

---

[88] Plotinus is here contrasting three ways in which the predicate "good" can apply to Forms, Intellect, and Intellect's life.

true, and because it was from the Good, and Intellect, because it was really Intellect — it is necessary to observe something of the same thing in themselves [Forms], for being different, whenever the same thing is predicated of them, there is nothing to prevent this [predicate] from being present in the essence of them, though at the same time it is possible to understand it separately in thought, as, for example, predicating animal of human being and horse, [35] and heat, of water and fire — in the first case as genus and, in the second, in the sense that one [fire] has it primarily, and the other [water] has it secondarily. Otherwise, each of these would be said to be [animal or fire] equivocally, or each [life, Intellect, and Forms] would be said to be good equivocally.

Does, therefore, the Good belong to the essence of them? In fact, each is good as a whole. But then the Good is not said of them univocally.[89] How, then, does each have it? Does each have a part of it? But [40] the Good is without parts. In fact, it is itself one, but one thing is good in one way, and another, in another way. For the primary activity [of Intellect] is good, and that which is defined as a result of it is good; that is, both are good. And the one is good because it is generated by the Good, and the other is good because the universe comes from it, and the third [these together — the life of Intellect] is good because it is the sum of these. They come from the Good, then, and are not the same, as if from the same [human being] [45] sound and walking and something else were to arise, all in the appropriate manner.

In fact, here [there is good], because there is order and rhythm. Why not in the intelligible world, too? One might say that here generally that which is noble always comes from the outside, with the difference among things coming from the order which they have, whereas in the intelligible world the things are the same. But why are these themselves good? For it is not that one should trust that they come from the Good and leave off, for one should [50] concede that all honorable things come from the Good, but the argument longs to grasp that according to which they are good.

§19. Shall we, then, turn over the judgment to desire, I mean, to the soul and, trusting to its experience, say that that which is good is that which is desirable to it, not seeking to know why it desires what it does? Are we going to provide demonstrations for each thing, but, in this case, just assign [5] that which is good to desire? But many absurdities

---

[89] That is, each is not Good-like in the same way. The words τὸ ἀγαθόν ("the Good") may also be understood here as "goodness" and below as "that which is good."

become apparent to us [if we say this]. The first is that that which is good will also be one of the relatives.⁹⁰ Next is that there are many things that desire, and they desire many different things. How, then, shall we decide, on the basis of the one that desires, whether one thing desired is better than another? But probably we will not know what is better, if we are ignorant of that which is good.

But, then, should we define [10] that which is good according to the excellence of each thing?⁹¹ Of course, if, in this way, we refer to Form and to the account of it, we shall be proceeding correctly. But when we come to the intelligible world, what shall we say when we seek to understand how each of these [Forms] in itself is good? For it seems that we might recognize this kind of nature [that which is good] in things that are inferior, even though they do not have it purely [15] (since they do not have it primarily), by comparison with things that are worse. But wherever there is nothing evil, where these themselves [the Forms] are the things that are better, we shall be puzzled.

Is the problem, then, that since reason is seeking the "why" for things that are in themselves, it is puzzled that, in this case, the "why" is the "that"?⁹² And even if we say that the explanation is other, namely, god, the problem is the same, since our argument has not attained that. But we should not leave off, if by proceeding along another path something should appear.

§20. Since we do not, for the moment,⁹³ trust our own desires for determining what [that which is good] is or what its qualities are, is it necessary then to make recourse to judgments and the oppositions of things, for example, order and disorder, symmetrical and asymmetrical, health and [5] sickness, form and shapelessness, substance and destruction, in general, constitution and dissolution? For who would want to argue that the first of each of these pairs is not in the class of the good?⁹⁴ But if this is so, it is necessary to place that which produces them in the category of good as well.⁹⁵ And, indeed, excellence and intellect and

---

⁹⁰ That is, if that which is good is just the object of desire, it will be relative to desire.

⁹¹ See Aristotle *EN* A 6, 1098a15–16.

⁹² See *supra* § 2.

⁹³ See *supra* 7, 24.

⁹⁴ "Class of the good" (εἴδει ἀγαθοῦ) is a play on words, recalling the term "Good-like" (ἀγαθοειδές).

⁹⁵ See Plato *Phil.* 54C10. Cf. 20D1 and 60B4.

life and soul (at least an [10] intelligent one) are in the class of the good[96]—and the things desired by an intelligent life, too.

Why, then, someone will say, should we not stop at Intellect and put this down as the Good? For soul and life are traces of Intellect, and soul desires this. And, indeed, it judges according to Intellect and then desires it, judging justice better than injustice and each [15] form of excellence [as better than] the form of vice, and it chooses the same things that it values. But if it only desires Intellect, perhaps it would require further reasoning to show that Intellect is not the ultimate—both that not all things desire Intellect and that all things desire the Good.[97]

And those things that do not have intellect do not all seek to possess it, whereas [20] the things that do have intellect do not stop at that point but go on to seek the Good; they seek Intellect on the basis of reasoning, whereas they seek the Good even prior to argument.[98] But if they desire life, that is, eternal existence and activity, that which is being desired is not so insofar as it is Intellect, but insofar as it is good and from the Good and directed to the Good, since this is also life.[99]

§21. What, then, being one in all these, makes each good? Let us dare to say this: Intellect and its life are Good-like and so, too, their desire, insofar as it is Good-like. By [saying that life is] "Good-like," I mean that it is the activity of the Good or, more properly, the [5] activity that comes from the Good, [and, by saying that Intellect is "Good-like,"] I mean that it is the already defined activity.[100] Both are themselves filled with glory and pursued by soul, since she came from there and is going back to those. In that case, does soul pursue them because it is related to them and not because they are good?[101] But still, since they are nevertheless Good-like, they are not to be rejected [as worthy of pursuit] for this reason [because soul is related to them].

For if that to which one is related is not good, it remains [10] that to which one is related, even though one avoids it. Otherwise, things being far away and below would move one [even though one is related to them]. An intense love for them [Intellect and its life] arises in the soul,

---

[96] See Plato *Rep.* 521A4.

[97] See Plato *Phil.* 20D8 and Aristotle *EN* A 1, 1094a3.

[98] See Plato *Symp.* 206A12.

[99] That is, life belongs to the Good as well as to Intellect.

[100] Plotinus makes a distinction between "the activity of a principle" and "the activity that comes from a principle." See IV 8. 6, 8–12; V 1. 6, 30–9; V 3. 7, 23–4; V 4. 2, 27–33; VI 7. 18, 5–6; VI 7. 21, 4–6; VI 7. 40, 21–4; etc.

[101] Reading the sentence as a question with Hadot.

not just because they are what they are but because, just in virtue of being what they are, something else is added to them. For just as with bodies, though light is mixed with them, nevertheless there is need of another light in order for [15] the light of the color in them to appear, so it is necessary for the things in the intelligible world, though having an abundance of light, to have a greater light in order that those things there should be seen by them and by another [the soul].

§22. Then, when someone sees this light, he is at that moment moved towards them [Intellect and its life] and, longing for the light that glimmers on them, he is delighted, just as, also, in the case of bodies here, love is not for their underlying substrata but for the [5] beauty shining on these. For each of these [Intellect and its life] is what it is in itself, but it becomes desirable when the Good itself colors it, as if giving graces to them, and, to those desiring it, the loves that they have for it. Then the soul, receiving into itself "the outflow from there"[102] [the Good], is moved and dances in a frenzy and is stung with longings and [10] becomes love.

Prior to this, it is not moved towards Intellect even though it is beautiful. The beauty of Intellect is inactive until it should receive the light of the Good, and the soul by itself "falls flat on its back"[103] and is inactive in regard to everything, and, though Intellect is present, it is indifferent to it. But when a sort of warmth comes to it [15] from the intelligible world, it is strengthened and awakens and is genuinely winged.[104] And though it is excited by that which is right next to it [Intellect], nevertheless it is lifted up by means of memory to something in a way greater.[105] And so long as there is something higher than what is present to it, it is raised upwards by nature, raised by the one who gives love. And it rises above Intellect, though it is not [20] able to run beyond the Good, because there is nothing placed over it. But if it remains in Intellect, it sees beautiful and venerable things, though it does not yet have everything it seeks.

It is as if it were in front of a face that is beautiful, but not yet able to appreciate the sight of it, owing to the fact that it does not have the grace glimmering on its beauty. For this reason, [25] we should say that here beauty is that which shines on that which is of good proportions, rather than the good proportion itself, and that this is what is loved, for why is

---

[102] See Plato *Phdr.* 251B2, D6.
[103] Ibid. 254B9.
[104] Ibid. 251B2–3.
[105] Ibid. 251D6.

the light of beauty rather on the face of someone living, while there is no longer a trace of it on one who has died, even if its flesh and its good proportions have not yet deteriorated? And are not [30] the more lifelike statues the more beautiful ones, even if the others were of better proportion? And why is a living person, even though he is ugly, more beautiful than a beautiful statue? In fact, this is because he is more desirable. And this is because he has a soul. And this is because the soul is more Good-like. And this is because the soul is, in some way, colored by the light of the Good, and, being colored, it wakes and [35] rises and carries up what belongs to it, and, insofar as it is possible for the Good, it makes the soul good and wakes it up.

§23. It is that intelligible world, indeed, that the soul is pursuing[106] and that which provides light to Intellect and, falling on the soul, moves the trace of itself [the soul]. And there is no need to wonder if it has the power to draw things to itself and call them back from all their wandering, in order that they should have repose in it,[107] for if all things come from [5] something, there is nothing greater than it; indeed, everything is lesser. How could the best of all things not be the Good?

Moreover, if it is necessary that the nature of the Good[108] be most self-sufficient and without need of anything else at all, what other nature would someone find that was [10] what it was before the others, when there were not yet evils? But if evils come later in the things that have not partaken in the Good in any one way — that is, in the ultimate things where there is nothing beyond evils in the direction of the worse — one would have evils in opposition to the Good without any mediation of the opposition.[109]

The Good, then, would be this: either there is altogether no [15] Good, or, if it is necessary that it exists, it would be this and not something else. But if someone were to say that it does not exist, then there would be no evil either. In that case, things would be indifferent, by nature, as a basis for choice. But this is impossible. All other things said to be good are said so in relation to this, but the Good is related to nothing.

What, then, does it make, if it is like this? In fact, it made Intellect, and it made life, and from Intellect it made souls and all [20] the other

---

[106] See Plato *Rep.* 505E1.

[107] See Plato *Phd.* 81A6; *Rep.* 532E3.

[108] See Plato *Phil.* 60B10.

[109] Plotinus means that if evils do not partake of the Good at all, then good and evil are contradictories, not contraries. Thus, the presence of one would entail the absence of the other.

things that partake of reason or intellect or life. As for that which is the "source and principle"[110] of these, who could say in what way and to what extent it is good? But what is it making now? In fact, it is now preserving those things in existence, that is, making thinking things think and living beings live, inspiring intellect, inspiring life, and, if something is not capable of living, then making it exist.

§37. Those, then, who, in their reasoning, endow the Good with thinking, did not endow it with thinking about the lesser things that come from it.[111] Even so, some say that it is absurd for it not to know other things.[112] But in any case, those [Peripatetics], not finding anything more honorable than [the Good], [5] endowed it with thinking of itself—as if by thinking it would be more venerable, that is, on the grounds that thinking is something better than what it is itself, and that it was not it that made thinking venerable.

For owing to what will it have its worth—to thinking or to itself?[113] If it is to thinking [rather than to itself], the worth is either not owing to itself or, to a lesser extent, [to itself]. But if it is to itself [rather than to thinking], the perfection is there prior to the thinking, and it is not by thinking that [10] it is perfected. But if it is necessary that it be thinking, because it is actuality,[114] not potentiality, if it is a substance always thinking[115]—and they say that its actuality means this—they are nevertheless saying that there are two things, the substance and the thinking, and they are saying that it is not simple, but rather they are adding something to it, just as the actuality of seeing is an addition to the eyes, even if they are always looking at something.

[15] But if they say that actuality means being in actuality,[116] that is, thinking, it would not *be* thinking since it *is thinking*, just as it is not motion that would be in motion.[117] What then? Will they not say, "Do you not yourselves say that [first principles] consist of substance and actuality?" We do, but what we agree on is both that these are many, and therefore different—whereas the first principle is simple, and we endow

---

[110] See Plato *Phdr.* 245C9, where, however, Plato is speaking about the soul.

[111] See Aristotle *Met.* Λ 9, 1074b17-35.

[112] This is perhaps a reference to the Stoics and their doctrine of divine providence.

[113] See Aristotle *Met.* Λ 9, 1074b21.

[114] Ibid. Λ 6, 1071b20; Cf. Λ 7, 1072b27; Λ 9, 1074b20.

[115] Ibid. Λ 7, 1073a4; Λ 9, 1074b20.

[116] Ibid. Λ 7, 1072b27.

[117] See VI 9. 6, 53.

that which comes from another with thinking and, in a way, [20] seeking its own substance and its self and that which made it—and that it reverted to [the Good] in its vision of it, and, recognizing [the Good], it immediately was rightly said to be Intellect.

But as for that which neither has come to be nor has anything prior to it but rather is always what it is, what reason would there be for it to have thinking? For this reason, Plato correctly says that it is beyond Intellect,[118] for Intellect, if it did not think, would be [25] nonintelligent; that whose nature it is to have thinking, if it does not do this, is nonintelligent. But as for that for whom there is no proper activity, if someone characterized it as not engaging in the activity, what would he be adding when he claims that it is deprived of this activity? It is as if one were to say that it [Intellect] does not possess the art of medicine. But there is no proper activity for it, because there is nothing additional for it to do, [30] for it is sufficient to itself and it is not necessary for it to seek anything besides itself, since it is above everything else. For it is sufficient to itself and to all others by being itself what it is.

§38. But even the term "is" [is not predicated] of it,[119] for it has no need of this, since "is good" is not predicated of it as well; rather, it is predicated of the same thing that "is" is predicated of. The "is" is not predicated as one thing of another but as indicating that which is.[120] But we use the words "the Good" [5] neither to name it nor to predicate "good" of it because that belongs to it, but because it is that.[121] So, then, since we do not regard it as proper to say "is good" nor even to put the article "the" in front of it [the Good] (we are not able to make ourselves clear if someone altogether removes it), in order that we do not make it one thing and then another so as not to need the further "is," we thus say "the Good."

---

[118] See Plato *Rep.* 509A7, B9. Plato does not say this exactly; rather, he says that the Good transcends being and knowability. But if the Good transcends knowability, then it cannot have or be an intellect; otherwise, it would be an intellect with nothing to know.

[119] See Plato *Parm.* 141C9–11.

[120] The point is that there is no complexity whatever in the first principle. If one says that "it is" or "it is good," one is implying that there is some sort of composition in the subject. See *supra* 17, 41–3.

[121] The point is that if "good" is a (descriptive) name of the first principle, so presumably is "being" or "real." Then an illicit complexity would be implied for it, namely, whatever accounts for its being one and whatever accounts for its existing or being real. See Plato *Soph.* 244B–C.

[10] But who will accept a nature not in a state of self-perception and knowledge? What, then, will it know? "I am"? But it does not. Why, then, will it not say, "I am the Good"? In fact, it would again be predicating "is" of itself. But it will only say "good" of itself by adding something, for one could think "good," without the "is" only [15] if one did not predicate it of something else. But that which thinks of itself that it is good will always think, "I am that which is good." If not, it will think "good," but the thought that it is this will not be present to it. It is necessary, then, that the thought be "I am good."

If, however, the thinking is the Good, its thinking will not be of itself, [20] but of the Good, and it will not be the Good, but it will be thinking. But if the thinking of the Good is different from the Good, the Good is already there, prior to the thinking of it. If the Good is self-sufficient prior to the thinking, then being self-sufficient to itself for being good, it would have no need of the thinking that is of itself. So, insofar as it is good, it does not [25] think itself.

§39. But insofar as it is [good], what then? In fact, there is nothing else present to it, but there will be a certain simple contact in it in relation to itself. But since there is nothing like a distance or difference in relation to itself, what could it be in contact with other than itself? For this reason, [Plato] correctly understands difference to be [5] wherever there is intellect and essence.[122] This is because it is always necessary that intellect receive both sameness and difference, if it is going to think. For without that, it would not be able to distinguish itself from the object of thinking by the relation of difference it has to itself, and it would not be able to contemplate all things if no difference arose among all [intelligible] things.[123] For if there were no difference, there could not even be two. Then, if the Good is going to think, it will never, [10] I suppose, only think itself, if it is going to think at all. For why would it not also think all [intelligible] things? Would it be incapable of doing so?

But, in general, in thinking itself, it [the Good] will become other than simple; rather, it is necessary that the thinking of itself be of something different from it, if it is to be able to think itself in general. But we said[124] that there is no thinking by the Good, not even if it wanted to see itself as other, for in thinking itself, it becomes [15] many, intelligible, intelligent, in motion, and all such other things that pertain to Intellect.

---

[122] See Plato *Soph.* 254E5–255A1; *Parm.* 146A–D.

[123] The relation that all intellect has to itself is the relation a subject has to itself when it is identified with a form and it is aware of that state of identification.

[124] See *supra* 38, 21–4.

But, in addition to these points, it is appropriate to observe that which was said previously:[125] that each thought, if it is going to be a thought, must be something variegated, whereas that which is simple and totally itself—in a way like a motion, if this is to be a sort of touch—has [20] nothing thought-like in it.[126]

What then? Will the Good know neither other things nor itself but "majestically abide in itself"?[127] The other things come after it, and it was prior to them, and the thought of them would be something additional, and in that case it would not be eternally the same and would be of things that are not stable. But even if it thinks the things that are stable, it will be many, [25] for it is surely not the case that the things that come after the Good will possess essence [content] with their thought, whereas the thoughts of the Good will only be empty speculations. And providence is sufficiently provided for in its being itself, that from which all things come.

But what is its relation to itself, if the Good does not [think] itself but merely majestically abides in itself? Plato did say,[128] then, in [30] speaking about essence, that it will think, but that it would not abide majestically as thinking essence, meaning that on the one hand, essence thinks, but on the other, that which does not think will abide majestically. The words "will abide" are used, because he could not explain himself in any other way, and because he believed that which is above thought to be more majestic or truly majestic.

§40. And those who have had contact with something of this sort would know that it is necessary that it not be thinking of itself. But we should provide some words of encouragement in addition to what has already been said, supposing that it is possible to make this clear with words, for it is necessary that persuasion be mixed with necessity.[129]

[5] It is necessary, then, that one who knows recognize that all thinking comes from something and is of something. One kind of thinking, which resides close to that from which it comes [the soul], has, as a sub-

---

[125] See VI 9. 2, 40–4. But also see in the present treatise, 13, 2 and 37; 14, 5; 15, 24; 17, 13; 32, 3; 33, 10; 35, 8.

[126] See V 3. 10, 42 on Intellect in the primary phase of its generation, prior to its seeing the Good.

[127] See Plato *Soph.* 249A1–2. Eliminating H-S$_2$'s bracketing of the quotation from Plato of the words ἀλλὰ σεμνὸν ἑστήξεται and including them within the question.

[128] See previous note.

[129] See I 2. 1, 52; V 3. 6, 9–10; VI 5. 11, 5–7. Persuasion is directed to the soul; necessity applies to the world of Intellect.

structure, that of which the thinking is, whereas it itself becomes a sort of superstructure, since it is the actuality of the substructure, and, since it fills up that which is in potentiality, itself generates nothing. [10] For it is only a sort of perfection of that from which it comes.

The other kind is the thinking [in Intellect] with essence, and, since it has made essence exist, it could not be in that from which it came to be, for it would not have generated anything, if it had been in that. But, being a power of generating, it generated from itself, and the actuality of it is [15] essence, and it is present in essence, and the thinking and the essence itself are not different, and, again, insofar as its nature thinks itself, it is not different other than in definition, the thinking and that which is thought being a multiplicity, as has been shown many times.[130] And this thinking is the first actuality that has generated existing essence; [20] if it is, in this way, a reflection of another, it is of something great, so that essence came to be.

But if that thinking belonged to the Good and was not from that, it would not be something other than that and would not be an existent on its own. And, indeed, being the first actuality and the first thinking, there would neither be an actuality nor thinking prior to it. [25] So, then, someone passing beyond this essence and thinking will arrive neither at essence nor at thinking, but he will arrive at something "beyond essence"[131] and thinking, "something marvelous,"[132] which has in itself neither essence nor thinking but is "alone by itself,"[133] having no need of the things that come from it, for it did not act [30] prior to generating activity; in that case, [activity] would already be there before it came to be. Nor did it generate thinking by thinking, for, in that case, it would have been thinking before thinking came to be.

For generally, thinking, if it is of the Good, is inferior to it [the Good], so that it [the Good] would not be the Good's thinking. I mean by "not be the Good's thinking" not that there is no thinking the Good—[35] let this be possible—but that there is no thinking in the Good itself. If this is so, then the Good and that which is less than it (its thinking) will together be one. But if thinking is inferior to the Good, thinking and essence will be together, while if thinking is superior to it, that which is thought will be inferior. Thinking, then, is not in the Good, but, being inferior and [40] being valued as such, owing to the

---

[130] See III 8. 9, 3–4; III 9. 1, 13; VI 7. 17, 39–40; VI 9. 5, 16.

[131] See Plato *Rep.* 509B9.

[132] See Plato *Symp.* 210E5.

[133] See Plato *Phil.* 63B8.

Good; it is located other than in it, leaving the Good exempt from thinking as from other things. Being exempt from thinking, it is purely what it is, and it is not prevented, by the presence of thinking, from being pure and one.

But if someone makes the Good simultaneously thinking and object of thinking, and essence and [45] thinking joined with essence, and in this way wishes to make it self-thinking, the Good will need another, and this will be prior to it, since activity in the sense of thinking is either the perfection of another subject, or, if it is coexistent with that subject, it also has another nature prior to it, insofar as it is to be genuine thinking. For it has something to think about, [50] because there is something else prior to it. And when it thinks itself, it, in a way, understands in itself what it had from the vision of another. But for that which has neither anything else prior to itself nor anything present with it coming from another, what will it think, or how will it think itself? For what did it seek, or what did it long for? Or did it seek to know the extent of its power, as if that were external to [55] it, insofar as it thought it? I mean if its power, which it sought to understand, were one thing, and the power by which it understood were another. But if they are one, what is it seeking?

§41. As it happens, thinking is an aid that has been given to the most divine natures, though they are inferior [to the Good] in the way that eyes are for those who are blind. But why would the eye, being itself light, have a need to see that which is?[134] That which does have a need to see is that which seeks light through the eye, [5] having darkness in itself. If, then, thinking is light, and the light does not seek light, that brightness, since it does not seek the light, neither seeks to think nor adds thinking to itself. For what will it do with it? And what will Intellect itself add when, out of need, it thinks?

The Good, then, does not have perception of itself—[10] for it does not need it—it is not two, indeed, <nor>[135] is it more than two: itself and its thinking—for it itself is certainly not its thinking[136]—whereas [if it were two], necessarily, [it would have to be three], the third being the object of thinking. But if Intellect, thinking, and object of thought are the same, in becoming totally one, they will disappear in themselves. But if they are distinguished by being other [than each other], then,

---

[134] See IV 5. 4; IV 5. 7; V 5. 7.

[135] H-S$_2$ suggests μᾶλλον δὲ <οὐδὲ> πλείω, correcting H-S$_1$'s μᾶλλον <οὐ> δὲ πλείω.

[136] See *supra* 38, 18–20,

again, they will not be the Good. Then, as for the best nature, we should leave aside [15] everything else, since it is in need of no assistance. Whatever you would add, it would, by addition, diminish that which has need of nothing.

Thinking is a noble thing—for us, because the soul needs to have intellect, and for Intellect, because its being is the same as its thinking,[137] and thinking has made it. It is, then, necessary for [20] Intellect to be united with thinking and always to acquire the comprehension of itself, because Intellect is this comprehension; the two are one. If it were only one, it would have been sufficient unto itself and would not have been in need of acquiring comprehension of itself. For the expression "know thyself" is spoken to those who, owing to their own multiplicity, have the task of counting themselves up and learning how many and what sorts of things they are, knowing neither all of them [25] nor none of them, nor what is ruling in them, nor what it is according to which they are what they are.

But if the Good is something for itself,[138] it is so in a way that is greater than with respect to knowing or thinking or self-awareness. But since it is nothing for itself, for it does not bring anything into itself, it suffices for itself. It is not, therefore, even good for itself, but [is good] for others. For these [other] things need [30] it, whereas it does not need itself. That would be ridiculous, for, if this were the case, it would be missing something of itself. Nor, indeed, does it look at itself, for there must be—that is, come to be—something for it from looking. For it has left all of these things for those coming after it, and, as it happens, no additions to the others are present to it, [35] just as essence is not. Therefore there is no thinking either, since essence is there where primary and principal thinking and being are both together. Accordingly, "there is neither discourse nor sense-perception nor understanding in it,"[139] because nothing can be predicated of it as present to it.

§42. But whenever, in an inquiry of this sort, you run into the problem of where one must situate these things—being drawn to their consideration by discursive reasoning—leave these things aside that you believe to be venerable, in the second position, and do not add the seconds to the first, nor the thirds [5] to the seconds, but place the seconds around the first and the thirds around the seconds.[140] For, in this way,

---

[137] See Parmenides Fr. B 3 D-K.

[138] Reading αὐτῷ with some manuscripts instead of αὐτό with other manuscripts and with H-S₂.

[139] See Plato *Parm.* 143E3–4.

[140] See Plato [?] *2nd Ep.* 312E3–4.

you will be allowing each thing to be itself, and you will be making posterior things, circling around prior things, depend on those things that are in themselves.

Accordingly, it is also rightly said in this regard "all things are around the king of all and are all [10] for his sake."[141] [Plato] is speaking of all *real* beings, and he adds the words "for its sake," since the Good is their cause, and, in a way, they desire that which is different from everything and has nothing of that which belongs to them. In fact, they would no longer be "all things" if anything of the other things that come after the Good were present to that. If, then, [15] Intellect is also among all things, intellect does not belong to the Good. But when [Plato] says that [the king] is "the cause of all beauties,"[142] he appears to be situating Beauty among the Forms, whereas the Good is above all this beauty.

Now in placing these [the Forms] second, he says that the thirds, the things that come to be after these, depend on them, and in positing the things around the thirds, it is clear that he means [20] the things that come to be from the thirds, namely, this cosmos, which depends on Soul [the third]. But Soul depends on Intellect and Intellect on the Good, and thus everything depends on the Good through intermediaries, some nearby, some neighbors of those nearby and, at the ultimate remove, sensibles dependent on Soul.[143]

VI 8 (39) On the Free Will and the Volition of the One (§§ 1–8; 12–16)

This treatise begins with a consideration of what it means for our actions to be "up to us." It then moves to consider in what sense the One can be said to have a will and therefore to exercise freedom. Human freedom is seen as an image of the freedom of the One. Freedom is viewed as the polar opposite of what happens by chance.

§1. Is it possible to seek to discover if there is anything concerning the gods that is "up to them"?[1] Or is it the case that though this question

---

[141] Ibid. 312E1–2.
[142] Ibid. 312E2–3.
[143] See V 4. 1, 1–4.

[1] The phrase ἐπ' αὐτοῖς ("up to them") or ἐφ' ἡμῖν ("up to us") is used by Plotinus as a technical term in contexts where, roughly, we would speak of "free will."

is appropriately pursued within the context of the incapacities of human beings or their disputed capacities, as for the gods, the power to do everything should be assigned to them; that is, not [5] only is something up to them, but everything is? Or, again, is it the case that we should assign every power to the One and say that "everything is up to it," whereas for some of the other gods, some things are in their power, for others they are not, depending on which of the gods it is? In fact, while we should seek to discover the answer to these questions, we should also do so in regard to the primary realities [Intellect] and, as for that which is high above all [the One], [10] even if we grant that it has the power to do all things,[2] we should seek to discover what it means for something to be "up to it." In addition, we should investigate the meaning of the phrase "the power to do," assuming we do not want to use the phrase to mean a potentiality distinct from an actuality, that is, a future actuality.

But these questions should be put aside for the present. We should first ask about [15] ourselves, as is our usual custom, whether there happens to be something "up to us." We should first ask for the meaning of the phrase "up to us." That is, what is the concept of this sort of thing? For if we can answer this question, we would perhaps be in a position to understand whether or not it is consistent to transfer it to the gods and, even more, so to god [the One]. [20] If it should be so transferred, we should investigate how the phrase "up to them" is to be applied both to the other gods and to the primary realities.

What then are we thinking of when we say "up to us," and why are we seeking to answer this question? I myself think that when we are moved by adverse fortune and constraints and the powerful impulses of feeling that fill up the soul, and when we believe that [25] all of these have authority over us and that we are enslaved to them and are borne away to where they lead, we wonder if we are nothing, and nothing is "up to us," assuming that if we were enslaved neither to fortune nor to constraints nor to powerful impulses, [30] we would act according to our will, and there being nothing opposed to our will, this would be "up to us."

If this is the concept of what is "up to us," then what is up to us is enslaved to the will and would occur or not depending on whether [or not] we willed it, for everything is voluntary that is done without force but with knowledge, whereas what is "up to us" is, in addition, what we are in charge of doing.[3] And both [the voluntary and what is "up to us"]

---

[2] See V 3. 15, 33.
[3] See Aristotle *EN* Γ 1, 1110a1; Γ 3, 1111a22–4. Cf. Alexander of Aphrodisias *Fat.* ch.14, 183, 27–30.

[35] may often come to the same thing even if their definition is different, though there are cases in which they are not extensionally equivalent. For example, if someone were responsible for killing someone else, it would not be a voluntary act for him to have done it if he did not know that it was his father that he was killing.[4] Perhaps for someone in this situation [the voluntary] is not extensionally equivalent to that act being "up to him." And for an act to be [40] voluntary, the knowledge must be not only of the particular, but also of the universal, for why, if someone is ignorant that it is one's relative, is it involuntary, but if someone is ignorant of the fact that he should not do it, it is not involuntary?[5] If this is so, is it because he should have learned? Not knowing that one should have learned is not voluntary, nor is that which diverts one from learning.

§2. But we should seek to discover the answer to this question: to what should we attribute that which is adduced for us as being "up to us"? Is it owing to impulse or some type of desire, for example, to what is done or not done, owing to passion or appetite or calculation about what is beneficial accompanied by desire?[6] [5] But if it is owing to passion or appetite, we shall be using the phrase "up to them" for children and animals and madmen and those who are in an ecstatic state and in the grip of drugs and adventitious fantasies, all of whom who are in states over which they are not in charge.[7] If it is owing to calculation with desire, what if the [10] calculation has gone astray? In fact, it should be attributed [if at all] to right calculation and to right desire.[8] But even here someone could ask whether the calculation moved the desire or the desire moved the calculation,[9] for even if the desires are natural, say, of an animal that is a composite [of body and soul], the soul followed natural necessity. If, then, the desires were of [15] soul alone, many of the things now said to be "up to us" would be out of the range of this [what is up to us]. Alternatively, what bare calculation precedes our [bodily and mental] states? Or when imagination is forcing us and

---

[4] See Aristotle *EN* E 10, 1135a28–30; *EE* B 6, 1223a28–30. Cf. Alexander of Aphrodisias *Fat.* ch.14, 183, 27–30; ch.15, 185, 13.

[5] See Aristotle *EN* Γ 2, 1110b30–3. Plotinus is here arguing against Aristotle's view.

[6] Understanding the line as a question. See Aristotle *EN* Γ 3, 1111a25–34.

[7] Ibid. Γ 4, 1111b8–9; Γ 7, 1114a32; H 7, 1149b35–1150a1. Cf. Alexander of Aphrodisias *Fat.* ch.14, 183, 30–184, 9.

[8] See Aristotle *EN* Γ 5, 1114b29.

[9] See Aristotle *De An.* Γ 10, 433a18–20.

desire is dragging us towards wherever they might lead, how does that make us in charge in these cases?[10]

How, generally, are we in charge in the cases where we are led? For that which is in need and [20] is desirous of a compulsive fulfillment is not in charge of that to which it is in every way led. How, generally, can something arise from itself that arises from something other, that is, has its origin in something other and has come to be what it is in that other? For it lives according to that, that is, it lives in the way that it has been shaped.[11] Or else, things without souls will be able to have something that is "up to them." [25] For example, fire acts according to what it is. But if it [being in charge] is because the living being or the soul knows what it is doing, if it [knows] by sense-perception, how does this help in regard to something being "up to us"? For the sense-perception has not made us in charge of the act, since it only observes. But if it is by knowledge, if it is knowledge of what is being done, here, too, it only knows, [30] whereas something else leads us on to the act. But even if reason does something contrary to desire, or if knowledge rules, on what basis it does this should be examined and, in general, where this occurs. And if reason makes another desire, how it does this needs to be understood. But if it arrested the desire and then stopped, and "up to us" is here, [35] then this will not be in action, but what is "up to us" will be inert in Intellect, for everything in action, even if reason should rule, is mixed and is not able to have that which is "up to us" purely.

§3. Accordingly, we should seek to discover the answer to these questions, for having done so, we will immediately be nearer to an account of what is up to the gods. Having, then, referred that which is "up to us" to will,[12] we next suppose that this is found in reason, and next we locate it in right reason.[13] Perhaps we should qualify this by saying that it is the right reason that belongs to [5] understanding, for if someone had a right belief and acted on it, he would perhaps not indisputably be said to be self-determining if he did not know why his belief was right but was led to doing what he ought by chance or imagination.[14]

Since we are saying that what those who act by imagination are doing is not "up to them," how could we place them among those who are [10] self-determining? But we do say this about imagination, which

---

[10] See SVF III 177 (= Plutarch *De stoic. rep.* 1057A).

[11] See III 3. 4, 31–4.

[12] See *supra* 1, 21–30.

[13] See *supra* 2, 10.

[14] See SVF II 975.

in the proper sense is the arousal arising from bodily states, for states of emptiness with respect to food and drink in a way shape the imagination, and someone who is filled with semen [15] imagines other things, as it is for all the qualities of bodily fluids. We do not place those who act according to these imaginings among those for whom the principle of acting is self-determining.

For this reason, we will not designate the actions of evil persons, who do many things according to these imaginings, as "up to them" or voluntary, whereas we will designate those as self-determining who, owing to the [20] activities of Intellect, are free from the affections of the body. Referring "up to us" to the most noble principle, the activity of Intellect, we will designate as really free the premises that come from there and claim that the desires that arise from thinking are not involuntary, and we will say that [self-determination] is found [25] among the gods who live in this manner.

§4. Still, one might seek to discover how that which comes about according to desire will be self-determining, since desire is directed to something outside us and indicates a lack, for that which desires is led, even if it is led to the Good.[15] In addition, there is a difficulty about Intellect [5] itself: since it acts by nature based on what it is by nature, should it be said to be free and for things to be "up to it" when it is not "up to it" not to act? In general, should "up to them" be said in the principal sense of those [the gods, Intellect] in whom there is no action present?

But for those in whom there is action, the necessity is external, too,[16] [10] for they do not act in vain. But, then, how can those be said to be free, when they are slaves to their own nature? In fact, unless one were forced to follow another, how could such a one be said to be enslaved? How could something borne towards the Good be forced, since its desire is voluntary, if, knowing that it is good, it goes towards it [15] as good? For that which is involuntary is a diversion from the Good and towards that which is forced, if something is borne towards that which is not good for it.[17] And that is enslaved which is not in charge of its going towards the Good, but since something else stronger than it is standing over it, it is led away from its own goods and enslaved to that. This is

---

[15] See III 8. 11, 22–4.

[16] See Aristotle *EN* Γ 1, 1110a2.

[17] Plotinus is here reflecting on the Platonic view that "no one does wrong voluntarily." See *Gorg.* 488A3; *Protag.* 345 D8, 358C7, 358E2–359A1; *Rep.* 589C6; *Tim.* 85D2, E1; *Lg.* 731C2. On forced behavior as nonvoluntary, see Aristotle *EN* Γ 1, 1110a1–b16.

why [20] slavery is blamed, not in the case of someone who does not have the power to go towards that which is evil, but in the case of someone who is led away from his own good towards that of another. But to speak of being a slave to one's own nature is to make [the person] two: that which is enslaved and that to which one is enslaved.

But how is a simple nature and single activity not free when it does [25] not have one part that is potential and another that is actual? For its acting by nature could not mean that one part is its essence and another, its activity, if being and acting in the intelligible world are the same thing. If, then, the activity is neither owing to another nor up to another, how could it not be free? And if it does not make sense to apply the term "up to it" to [30] Intellect,[18] but rather there is something greater than "up to it" here; its activity is still "up to it" just because neither is it up to another nor is another in charge of its activity. Nor is its essence in charge of it, if it is a principle. And if Intellect does have another principle, it is not external to it but in the Good. And if it is [active] according to that Good, [35] what it does is even more "up to it" and free, since someone seeks freedom and that which is "up to oneself" for the sake of the Good. If, then, it acts according to the Good, "up to it" applies to it even more, for it then immediately has an orientation towards that from which it arises and has in itself what is better for it to be in itself if it is oriented [40] towards the Good.

§5. Is it, then, only in Intellect when it is thinking—that is, pure Intellect[19]—where we find that which is self-determining and that which is "up to it," or is it also to be found in soul, when it is active according to Intellect or when it acts "according to virtue"?[20] If we attribute it to soul engaged in acting according to virtue, it is perhaps first of all necessary not to attribute it to what is [5] accomplished by acting, for we are not in charge of what occurs. But if it is attributed to what is done nobly and to all that is done from oneself, perhaps this would be rightly said.

But how is that "up to us"? For instance, there is the case in which, owing to a war, we were to act bravely. I mean, how is the activity at that time "up to us," since if the war were not [10] occurring, we would not be engaged in this activity? But it is the same with all other actions done according to virtue, since virtue is always forced to do this or that depending on what has happened, for even if someone were to give virtue itself the choice of whether it wants on the one hand, in order to be

---

[18] Because it does not make sense to deny this of Intellect.
[19] See Anaxagoras Fr. B 12 D-K.
[20] See Aristotle *EN* K 6, 1178b6.

active, that there be wars [15] so that it can be brave, and injustice so that it can formulate and erect laws, and poverty so that it can show its liberality, or on the other hand, it wants to be detached from action since all things are in a good state, it would choose to be detached, there being nothing in need of being taken care of by it, just as if some physician, like Hippocrates, wanted [20] no one to be in need of his skill.

If, then, being active in practical matters, virtue is forced to help, how could we say that it was purely "up to it"? Shall we then say that while actions are forced, the will that is prior to the actions and reason are not forced? But if this is so, [25] in placing them merely in what is prior to that which is done, we shall be placing what is self-determining and what is up to virtue itself outside of action. What about virtue itself, which is a habit or a disposition?[21] Will we therefore be saying that when a soul is in a bad state, virtue, as a moderating force, comes to reorient the passions [30] and the desires in it? In what way, then, are we saying that being good is "up to us," and that "virtue is without a master"?[22]

In fact, it is, at least for those who want it and choose it. Or because when it has come to be in us, it establishes freedom and what is "up to us" and no longer allows us to be slaves to that to which we were previously enslaved. If, then, virtue is, in a way, [35] another intellect and in a way a habit that makes the soul "intellectualized,"[23] what is "up to us" will again not come to be in action but in intellect detached from actions.

§6. How, then, did we refer this previously to will[24] saying "whatever would come to be in conformity with will"? In fact, it was there also said "or not come to be." If, then, things are now correctly expressed and those things are in harmony with these, we shall say that [5] virtue and intellect are in charge, and it is necessary to refer what is "up to us" and what is free to these.[25] And these have no master, since intellect is "up to itself," and virtue wants it to be "up to itself" to watch over the soul in order that it be good, and to this extent it is free, [10] and it makes the soul free. But when the force of passions and actions befell it, virtue was

---

[21] See Aristotle *Cat.* 8b25–9 on virtue as a habit (ἕξις) or disposition (διάθεσις) and the difference between these. At *EN* B 4, 1106a10–13 virtue is identified as belonging to the genus of habit.

[22] See Plato *Rep.* 617E3.

[23] See VI 7. 35, 4–6: "but when soul becomes intellect it contemplates, in a way being 'intellectualized' and coming to be in an 'intelligible place.'" See Plato *Rep.* 508C1; 517B5.

[24] See *supra* 1, 32–3.

[25] See Aristotle *EN* Γ 7, 1113b6 on the freedom of virtue.

watching over the soul, and it did not want these things to occur. Still, even in these conditions, it would preserve what is "up to it" in itself and keep it there, for it will not be led by circumstances—for example, [15] in saving the one who is in danger, if it thinks proper, it will sacrifice him or command him to sacrifice his life and property and children and even his fatherland, having as an aim its own nobility and not the being of things that are subordinate to it.

So, also in actions, that which is self-determining and [20] "up to us" is referred neither to the acting nor to what is external but to the activity of the interior, that is, thinking or the contemplation of virtue itself.[26] But it is necessary to say that this virtue is a kind of intellect, not including in it the passions that are subordinated to or moderated by reason,[27] for it seems that these, [Plato] says, "are [25] close to the body, since they are corrected by habits and practices."[28] For this reason, it is even clearer that that which is immaterial is that which is free, and the referral of what is "up to us" is to this, and this is the will which is in charge and is on its own, even if something can force it to be directed to externals by necessity. Such things, then, that arise from this and, owing to [30] this, are "up to us," both those that are external and those that are internal.[29] That which the will wants and acts upon without impediment is principally what is "up to us."

But the [activity of the] contemplative Intellect,[30] that is, the primary Intellect, is "up to it" in this way, because its function is in no way directed to another, but all of it reverts to itself,[31] and it is its own function, and it is situated [35] in the Good, being without need and full and, in a way, living according to its will. Its will is its thinking, but it was called "will" because [it was acting] according to Intellect. What is called "will" is that which imitates [the acting] according to Intellect, for the will wants the Good. But thinking is truly in the Good.[32] [40] Intellect, then, has what its will wants, the attainment of which is thinking. If, then, we place "that which is up to us" in the will for the Good, how could that which is already situated in that which its will wants not

---

[26] See Plato *Rep.* 443C10–D1.

[27] See Aristotle *EN* B 5, 1106b16–27.

[28] Plato *Rep.* 518D10–E2.

[29] That is, acts of will that do not result in action.

[30] See V 3. 6; Aristotle *De An.* Γ 9, 432b26–7.

[31] See V 1. 7; V 2. 1.

[32] That is, the Good is realized in thinking it.

have "that which is up to it"? In fact, it must be placed in something greater, if one does not want to refer "that which is up to itself" to this.

§7. The soul, then, becomes free when it hastens without impediment through Intellect to the Good. And what it does by means of this is what is "up to it." But Intellect is free by means of itself. And the nature of the Good is itself that which is desired and through which other things have what is "up to them," [5] either when they happen to attain it without impediment or when [Intellect] has it.

How, in the case of that which is itself in charge and more honorable than all the things after it and is in the primary position [the Good] — in relation to which the others want to ascend and depend[33] on it and have their powers from it, so that they are able to have that which is "up to them" — could someone put it [the Good] on a par with what is [10] "up to you and me"? For this is the place where Intellect was just barely, albeit violently, dragged. [One could not], unless someone were to express some daring line of argument brought in from elsewhere[34] to the effect that since the Good just happened to be the way it is, it is therefore not in charge of what it is and is what it is not from itself nor has it freedom nor is it "up to it" [15] to do or not to do what it is forced to do or not do.

This argument has it backwards and is a dead end and would eliminate altogether the nature of the voluntary and that which is self-determining and the concept of that which is "up to us," in arguing that these are said in vain and are mere words for things that do not exist. [20] For not only must one who argues thus say that there is nothing that is "up to anyone," but he must also hold that he is thinking and understanding nothing when he uses these words. But if he should concede that he understands what he is saying, he would at once be easily refuted, since the concept of what is "up to us" coheres with that with which he said it did not cohere,[35] for neither is the concept [of what is "up to us"] focused on [a kind of] substance nor does it bring [25] that into the discussion — for it is impossible to make oneself into some kind of thing or to bring oneself into existence[36] — but the idea regards what among

---

[33] See I 8. 2, 3; Aristotle *Met.* Λ 7, 1072b14.

[34] Perhaps a reference to Gnostic teachings, referred to in II 9. 15, 10.

[35] That is, with the idea of the Good as first principle.

[36] That is, the idea of self-determination is not about self-creation. The Good is above substance (οὐσία) and is uniquely self-creative. See *infra* 7, 53–4. So, if the objector thinks that self-determination is impossible because it is not up to something to be what it is, this fact does not apply to the Good.

things is subordinate to others and what has self-determination and what is not determined by others but is in charge of its own activity, which is purely the case for eternal beings insofar as they are [30] eternal as well as for those who are uninhibited in pursuing or in having the Good.

But since the Good is indeed above these, it is absurd to seek to discover besides this some other sort of good. And so it is also not correct to say that the Good exists by chance, for chance is in the things that come after it, that is, among things that are multiple. [35] We would say neither that the first existed by chance nor that it was not in charge of its own becoming, because it did not come to be.

The claim that it acts according to what it is is absurd, if someone thinks that it is free just whenever it should do something or act contrary to its nature. Nor does its solitude remove its power, if that solitude does not consist in its being prevented from having something from elsewhere but rather consists in [40] its being itself and, in a way, being sufficient to itself and not having something that is better than it. Otherwise, one will remove the self-determination of that which especially attains the Good.

If this is absurd, it would be more absurd to deprive the Good of self-determination, because it is good and because it [45] remains by itself, being in no need of being moved towards something else, since other things are moved towards it, and it has no need of anything. But since what is, in a way, its existence is, in a way, its activity—for these are not different in it if this is not even the case with Intellect, on the grounds that its activity follows its being more than [50] its being follows its activity—so that it does not have the ability to act according to its nature; neither will its activity and what is, in a way, its life be referred to what is, in a way, its essence, but that essence coexists with and, in a way, arises together from eternity with its activity, and it makes itself from both and by itself and from nothing.

§8. But we see the self-determination in the Good is not accidental to it but, rather, by removing the contraries[37] from the cases of self-determination in other things, we see it in itself. Owing to an inability [5] to attain what is appropriate to say about it, we might, by the transference of inferior attributes from inferior things, say this about it.[38] And still we would not only find nothing to attribute to it, we would also find nothing to say of it in the principal sense.[39] For all noble and venerable

---

[37] See V 3. 13, 1; 14, 1; V 5. 6, 12; VI 7. 36, 7.

[38] See *supra* 1, 19.

[39] That is, nonmetaphorically. See VI 7. 30, 27.

things are posterior to it. And it itself is the principle of these.[40] And yet it is not their principle in another way. [10] But for those [such as we] who have rejected all [attribution], that is, for those for whom that which is "up to it" and "self-determination" are posterior—for these at once indicate activity in another—so, too, must we reject the claim that the Good acts "without impediment" and "when other things exist, it is not prevented from acting on these." It is necessary to say that it is altogether related to nothing, for it is what it is prior to [all] other things, since we remove the "is" from it, so that we remove [15] any relation to the things that are.[41]

Nor do we use the phrase "as it is naturally" for this [its applicability] is posterior, and, if someone were to use it about posterior things, it would be used about things that come from another, so that it is primarily used for essence, because it was born from the Good.[42] But if nature is in the things that are in time, it does not apply to essence. Nor, indeed, should we say of it "not being from itself,"[43] [20] for we have removed "is" from it and the expression "not being from itself" should be used whenever something originated from another.

Did it, then, just happen to be this way? In fact, we should not employ the expression "happened," for nothing happened to it [in itself] nor in relation to another, for the expression "happened" is used of many things when, first, there are some things, and, then, something further happens. How, then, could that which is first happen? For it did not come on the scene, [25] so that one could inquire, "How, then, did it get here? Did luck bring it about or make it exist?" [Such questions make no sense] since there was no luck, nor did things just happen by chance, for what happens by chance is what comes from something else and exists in things that have come to be.[44]

§12. What, then? Is the Good not what it is? Is it at least in charge of its being what it is or of being beyond essence?[45] For, again, the soul, not being persuaded by what has been said, is puzzled. This then

---

[40] See V 2. 1, 1.

[41] Perhaps an allusion to Plato *Parm.* 141E9–10.

[42] Plotinus is employing the etymological connection between φύσις ("nature") and ἔφυ ("was born").

[43] See *supra* VI 8. 7, 13–14.

[44] On the distinction between "luck" and "chance," see Aristotle *Phys.* B 6, 197a36 ff. On "luck" as "what happened" (συμβῇ) "by accident" (κατὰ συμβεβηκός), see *Met.* K 8, 1065a28–b3.

[45] The One, that is, the Good, "provides 'being and essence' to other things and is 'beyond essence,'" as Plato says in *Rep.* 509b6–10.

should be said in addition, that each of us, insofar as we are identified with our [5] bodies, is far from our essence, but, insofar as we identify with our soul and what we are especially,[46] we partake of our essence, and we are a certain essence, that is, in a way, a composite of difference and essence.[47] We are, then, neither essence in the principal sense nor the essence itself.[48] That is why we are not in charge of our essence, for, in a way, our essence is one thing and we are another, and [10] we are not in charge of our essence, but the essence is in charge of us, provided that it adds the difference. But since we are, in a way, that which is in charge of us, in this way we would be said here [as embodied] to be no less in charge of ourselves.[49]

But that of which the essence itself is completely what it is—and it is not one thing [15] and its essence another—in that case, it is in charge of what it is, and it is no longer to another that it owes its being, that is, its being essence, for it is again left to be in charge of itself insofar as what it is is primarily essence.

That, then, which has made essence free—which clearly has the nature to make essence free and could thus be called "freedom-maker"—to what would it be subordinated, [20] if it is permitted even to utter this word? To its own essence? But essence gets its freedom from it and is posterior to it, and the Good does not have an essence. If, then, there is some activity in the Good[50] and we are going to place it in this activity, because of this it would not be something other than itself and would not itself be in charge of itself, that from which the activity arises, [25] because it is itself not different from its activity. But if we are going to completely deny activity to it but say that the others acting around it have their existence, we shall then even more deny that in the intelligible world there is one part that is in charge and another that is being ruled.

But we shall grant not even that it is "in charge of itself," not because another is in charge of it, but because [30] we have granted "in charge

---

[46] See I 4. 14, 1; IV 7. 1, 24–5.

[47] Plotinus means that we are ideally or primarily or really souls, but, insofar as we are embodied, our bodies are included in the definition of what we are. The difference here is "embodied" as opposed to "disembodied." See I 1. 10, 1–12; V 3. 3, 24; VI 4. 14, 16.

[48] That is, we are not identical with the Form of Humanity.

[49] See V 3. 4.

[50] See III 8. 11, 8–9; III 9. 9, 8 where Plotinus denies activity to the Good and locates primary activity in the thinking of Intellect. See also V 3. 12; V 5. 3, 23; VI 7. 37, 15–16; VI 8. 7, 46–54.

of itself" to essence, whereas we placed the Good in a more honorable position than that to which we applied this. What, then, is that which is in a more honorable position than being in charge of itself? In fact, it is because essence and activity in the intelligible world are somehow two, and the concept "being in charge of" was derived from the activity, though this was the same as essence—for this reason "being in charge of" came to be separate, [35] and it was said to be in charge of itself. But where there are not two, but one—either activity alone or completely not activity—the term "being in charge of" is not correctly applied.

§13. If, however, it is necessary to adduce these names for what is being sought, let it be said again that the names that are not correctly used are so because one should not make the Good two in our concepts, whereas the ones that are now being employed are being so employed for the sake of persuasion and must be so in our arguments somewhat counter to sense.

[5] For if we should grant activity to it—and its activities, in a way, are its will for it does not act unwillingly and its activities are, in a way, its essence—its will and its essence will be the same. But if this is so, then as it willed, thus it is. Therefore, no more does it will and act as it is natural for it [10] than is its essence as it wills and acts. Therefore, it is in every way in charge of itself, since it also has in itself its own being.

Observe this, too: each of the things that is real, desiring the Good,[51] wills to be that more than [it wills to be] what it is, and it thinks that it is especially that whenever it shares in the Good; and in this state [15] each will choose for itself the being it has to the extent that it has it from the Good. So, it is clear that the nature of the Good is more choiceworthy for itself if it is the case that what is most choiceworthy in another is to have whatever share of the Good it has, and, for the Good, essence is voluntary and comes to it by its volition, and its volition and what exists through its volition are one and the same. [20] And so long as each thing did not have the Good, it wanted something else, but insofar as it had it, it at once wants itself, and neither is this type of presence by luck nor is its essence external to its will, and it is by the Good that its essence is defined, and it belongs to itself by this.

If, then, it is by this that each thing [25] makes itself to be itself, it doubtless at once becomes clear that the Good would be such as it is primarily, owing to itself. It is that by which the other things are able to be owing to themselves, and in a way, its volition to be the sort of thing it is goes with what is, in a way, its essence, and it is not possible to grasp

---

[51] See I 6. 7, 1; VI 5. 1, 12; VI 7. 26, 6; Aristotle *EN* A 1, 1094a2–3.

it without its volition to be what it is, owing to itself, and that its wanting [30] to be itself, owing to itself, goes together with its being what it wants to be, and the volition and it are one and not less one, because it is not one thing, which happened to be, and that which it willed to be, another—for what would it have wanted to be, other than what it is? And even if we hypothesized that it chose for itself what it should want to be and that it was possible for it to exchange its [35] nature into another, neither would it will to become something other nor would it blame itself that it is by necessity that it is what it is, since this "being itself" is what it always wanted and wants, for the nature of the Good is really the volition of itself, having been neither bound nor impelled by its own nature but [40] choosing itself, because there was nothing else to which it could be drawn.

And one might also say this: that each of the other things does not include in its essence the principle of being self-satisfied, for something could even dislike itself. But in the existence of the Good[52] it is necessary for its choice and [45] volition of itself to be included; otherwise it would scarcely be possible for something to be satisfied with itself, since things are satisfied with themselves by partaking of or by imagining the Good. But it is necessary to make concessions to language, if someone, in speaking about the Good is, in order to show something, forced to make use of the sort of language that, strictly speaking, we do not allow to be used. One should understand the term [50] "in a way" as applying to each of them.

If, then, the Good has been established as existing, and choice and will together make it exist—for it will not be without these but it is necessary that the Good not be many— its will and its essence must be brought together into one. But if its wanting is from itself, it is necessary that its being also [55] be from itself, so that the argument has discovered that it has made itself,[53] for if the will is from itself—and, in a way, its function and its will is the same as its existence—it would, in this way, make itself exist so that it is not what happened to be by luck but what it itself willed.

§14. Further, one should look at it in this way: each of the things said to be is either identical with its being or different. For example, this human being is one thing, and the "being of a human being" is an-

---

[52] See *infra* 15, 28; VI 6. 3, 11; VI 8. 7, 47 on the Good, or One, as having "existence" (ὑπόστασις).

[53] See *infra* 15, 8–9; 16, 14–15, 29; 20, 2, 21.

other.[54] Of course, the human being partakes of the "being of a human being." But soul [5] and the "being of a soul" are identical, if soul is taken simply and not [dependent on] another,[55] and humanity itself and the "being of a human being" are identical as well.[56] And on the one hand, the individual human being could come to be by luck, since it is different from the "being of a human being," but on the other hand, the "being of a human being" could not come to be by luck. This means that Humanity itself comes from itself.

If, then, the [10] "being of a human being" comes from itself and does not come to be by luck or by accident, how could that which is above Humanity itself and generates Humanity itself and all the real things be said to come to be by luck, given that it is a nature simpler than "the being of a human being" and simpler than being in general? Further, as one moves towards the simple, it is not possible [15] to bring luck along, so that it is impossible to bring it up to the simplest of all.

Further, it is appropriate to recall that which was already said,[57] namely, that each of the things that truly are have come into existence from that [simple] nature and if something among sensibles is of a certain kind[58] it is a certain kind by coming from those [simple natures]. [20] I mean by "of a certain kind" their having, along with their essence, the explanation for their existence, so that a subsequent viewer of each thing is able to say why each of the [parts] exists in it—for example, why there is an eye and why the feet of these are such and such—and to say what the explanation is that goes with the generation of each part of each thing [25] and the interconnection of the parts with one another. Why are the feet of such a length? Because that is like this, and because the face is like this, the feet are like this.

And, generally, the harmony of all the [parts] in relation to each other is the explanation. And the explanation of why this [part] is like this is that this is "the being of a human being," so that "the being of a human being" and the explanation [of the parts] are one and identical.[59]

---

[54] The individual is a composite of its form or "being so and so" and its matter. See Aristotle *Met.* H 3, 1043b2–3.

[55] See I 1. 2, 1; IV 7. 1, 24–5.

[56] Plotinus means the Form of Humanity, which he identifies with the Aristotelian "being of a human being."

[57] See VI 7. 2.

[58] Retaining τοιοῦτον with H–S₁.

[59] See Aristotle *APo.* B 2, 90A15.

But these [parts] came to be this way [30] from a single source[60] that was not engaged in calculation but provided, all together as a whole, the explanation and the being.[61] The source, then, of being and of the explanation of being gave both together. But that from which these come, though it is like the things that have become, is so more archetypically and more truly and more than those, in regard to what is better.

[35] If, then, there is nothing that comes to be randomly or by luck or "it happened like this" among the things that have their explanations in themselves—and all things that come from the Good have [their explanations in themselves], [the Good] being "the father" of reason and "of explanation," that is, of explanatory essence,[62] which things exist far from luck—it would be the principle and, in a way, the paradigm[63] of such things as have no share in luck, that which is [40] truly and is first, unmixed with types of luck and with chance and coincidence and explanation of itself,[64] that is, by itself and through itself, for it is also primarily itself and is itself above being.[65]

§15. And the Good is object of love[66] and is itself love and love of itself, since it is not otherwise beautiful than from itself and in itself, for, in addition, its being present to itself would not otherwise occur if that which is present and that to which it is present were not one, that is, if these were not identical. But if [5] that which is present is one with that to which it is present, and that which is, in a way, desiring is one with that which is desired, and that which is desired is [understood] according to its existence and, in a way, as subject, again,[67] the desire and the essence would appear to us to be identical. But if this is so, again,[68] this itself is what makes itself and is in charge of itself and has not [10] come to be as something else wanted, but as it itself wants.

---

[60] See III 8. 10, 5; VI 7. 12, 24.

[61] See VI 7. 2, 10; VI 7. 19, 18.

[62] See Plato [?] *6th Ep.* 323D4.

[63] The Good is "in a way the paradigm," because the real paradigm is Intellect, containing the Forms.

[64] See *supra* 7, 54; 9, 13, 16, 38, 57; 15, 8; 16, 14, 21; 20, 1, 6, 21.

[65] See VI 8. 16, 33; VI 9. 6, 44–5. The word for "above being" (ὑπερόντως) appears uniquely here in Plotinus and indicates the status of the Good (the One) as absolutely transcendent and, in particular, as transcending Intellect and the Forms contained within, or Being.

[66] See I 6. 7, 3; V 5. 12, 7; Aristotle *Met.* Λ 7, 1072b13.

[67] See *supra* 13, 27.

[68] See *supra* 13, 55.

And further, when we say that neither does the Good receive anything in itself nor does anything else receive it, we would be in this way placing it outside the realm of luck, not only by making it alone and purified of everything, but because of this: if we ever see in ourselves some such nature [15] not having anything of the other things that are dependent on us, according to which whatever happens by luck occurs—for all the other things that are ours are subordinated and subject to acts of luck and in a way come to us by luck—this alone is in charge of itself and is self-determining by [20] the activity of the Good, which is light that is Good-like[69] and greater than the activity according to Intellect, having that which is above Intellect but not as something added to it.

Ascending to it and becoming this alone and leaving aside other things, what would we say of [that state] other than that we are more than free and more than self-determining? Who would, at that moment, connect us with acts of luck or with what is random or with what "just happened" when we have become the [25] true life itself or come to be in it, which has nothing else but is itself alone?

For the other things, when they are isolated, cannot be sufficient for their own being. But the Good is what it is, that is, isolated.[70] But as primary existence,[71] it is neither in that which is without soul nor in nonrational life, for nonrational life has a weakness in being and is itself a [30] dispersal of reason and unlimited. But to the extent that things progress to a rational life, they leave luck behind, for that which is according to reason is not by luck. But for we who ascend to the Good, it is not reason but something more beautiful than reason, so much is it removed from what happens by luck, for it is the root of reason coming from itself, and in this all things have their culmination. It [the Good] is like the principle and basis of the greatest tree, [35] living according to reason, for while remaining in itself, it [the Good] gives being to the tree according to the reason that it [the tree] has received.

§16. But since we say, and it seems, that the One is everywhere and, again, nowhere, we must reflect and think about what, from our perspective, we should claim about that which we are investigating, for if it is nowhere, it does not happen to be anywhere, and if it is [5] everywhere,

---

[69] See Plato *Rep.* 509A3.

[70] On the unique self-sufficiency of the Good, see V 3. 13, 18; V 5. 13, 6; VI 7. 23, 7; 33, 18.

[71] The word is ὑπόστασις. See *supra* 7, 47; III 9. 7, 5–6; IV 7. 8, 26; V 3. 12, 17; V 4. 2, 35; V 6. 3, 11; V 9. 5, 46. Depending on context, "being" and "reality" are suitable alternative translations.

such as it itself is, it is everywhere like that.[72] Thus, the "everywhere" and "in every way" are identical with it, not that it is in the "everywhere" but that it is the "everywhere" and gives to the others their being situated in the "everywhere." But it, which has the highest place, or rather does not have it but is itself the highest, has everything [10] subordinated to it. It does not happen [that is, it is not related] to them,[73] but others happen to it, or rather others happen around it, not with it looking at them but with them looking at it.

It is, in a way, borne to its interior, in a way, loving itself,[74] the "pure radiance,"[75] being itself that which it loved. This means that it causes [15] itself to exist,[76] if, in fact, it is an abiding activity and most loved, in a way, like Intellect. But Intellect is the product of activity, so that the One is, in a way, the product of activity, but not of the activity of anything else. It is therefore the product of its own activity. It is not therefore that it is as it happened, but as it acts.

Moreover, if it exists in the highest way, that is because it, in a way, adheres to itself and, in a way, [20] looks at itself and its being is, in a way, its looking at itself; in a way, it would make itself, and it would not therefore be as luck would have it but as it wants to be, and neither is its volition random nor did it just happen this way, for the volition of the best is not able to be random.

But that its inclination to itself[77] is, in a way, an [25] activity of itself and stability in itself that makes it what it is, is revealed by supposing the opposite, for if its inclination were external, it would cease being what it is. Therefore, its being what it is is its activity, which is directed to itself. But these [being and activity] are one or identical.

It, therefore, causes itself to exist, since its activity is [30] bound up with it. If, then, it did not come to be but its activity was always and, in a way, like being awake[78] with nothing else to wake it, and, being a waking state and a "hyper thinking,"[79] it is in this way always as in its waking

---

[72] See III 9. 4, 1–3; V 5. 8, 23; VI 4. 3, 18.
[73] See *supra* 8, 14.
[74] See VI 7. 27, 18.
[75] See Plato *Phdr.* 250C4.
[76] See *supra* 10, 35–8; 11, 1–5.
[77] See I 1. 12, 27; I 8. 4, 19; V 1. 6, 25–7.
[78] See Aristotle *Met.* Λ 7, 1072b17.
[79] The term "hyper-thinking" (ὑπερνόησις) appears uniquely here in Plotinus. For the related term κατανόησις see V 4. 2, 17; V 1. 7, 10ff.

state. But this waking state is "above essence"[80] and Intellect and intelligent life.[81] [35] But these are identical with it.[82] It is, therefore, activity above Intellect and wisdom and life. These come from it and not from another. Its being, therefore, is by itself and from itself. It is not, therefore, as it happened to be, but as it itself wanted to be.

---

[80] See Plato *Rep.* 509B9; 521A4.

[81] Simplicius, *In de Ca.* 485, 22 (= Fr. 49 Rose₃, p. 57 Ross), says that Aristotle held that the first principle of all is "above intellect" (ἐπέκεινα νοῦ).

[82] That is, the One is that which makes these. It is these virtually.

PORPHYRY

Launching Points to the Intelligible

Launching Points to the Intelligible (Ἀφορμαὶ πρὸς τὰ νοητά), more commonly known as the Sententiae, or Sentences, is a collection of passages, mostly derived from Plotinus' Enneads (of which, of course, Porphyry was the editor) and apparently designed to provide a kind of introduction to Platonic doctrine from a Plotinian perspective. It addresses most of the major issues in Platonism, though not in an obvious systematic order, but the overall theme is the freeing of the soul from a concern with bodily things and a redirection of attention to the intelligible world (hence the title).

§10.[1] All things are in all,[2] but in a mode proper to the essence of each: in the intellect, intellectually; in the soul, discursively;[3] in plants, seminally; in bodies, imagistically;[4] and in the transcendent, nonintellectually[5] and supraessentially.

§11.[6] Incorporeal realities,[7] in the process of descent, undergo fragmentation and multiplication to the point of forming individual things, by reason of diminution of power; while, on the other hand, in the

---

[1] Cf. Proclus ET Prop. 103; In Tim. I 335, 12–18.

[2] It should be noted that the reading of manuscripts U and N is such as to be rendered "We do not cognize alike in all cases," which gives a quite different sense to the whole. The text adopted is that of manuscript W and of Stobaeus.

[3] This is rather more technical than it sounds. It means "in the mode of λόγος," where a λόγος is a psychic projection of a form.

[4] Again, more technical than it sounds, εἴδωλα being the lowest level of the projection of forms. The word εἰδωλικῶς seems, actually, to be a coinage of Porphyry's.

[5] The adverb ἀνεννοήτως is first used by Porphyry and is not easy to render exactly. LSJ are wrong in translating it "without discursive thought, i.e., by intuition." At the level of the One, there is no kind of thought whatever.

[6] Cf. Plotinus V 3. 16, 5–16; V 8. 1, 26–31; VI 2. 22, 15–23.

[7] It seems best to render ὑπόστασις thus in this context, as we are not concerned with hypostases in the technical sense.

process of ascent they are brought to unity and converge towards togetherness by reason of superabundance of power.

§13.[8] Everything that generates in virtue of its essence generates something inferior to itself, and everything that is generated reverts by nature towards that which has generated it. Among beings that generate, however, some do not turn their attention[9] at all towards what they generate, while others both do and do not turn their attention there, and others, again, have their attention turned only towards what they generate and not towards themselves.

§16.[10] The soul[11] contains the reason-principles of all things, but it acts on them [only] either by being provoked to actualize them by some external stimulus or through directing itself towards them inwardly. And when it is provoked by an external influence, as it were, outwards, it produces sense-perceptions, while when it withdraws into itself in the direction of intellect, it finds itself in the process of thinking.[12] And neither sense-perception, generated, as it is, externally, nor thinking***;[13] but even as in the living being sense-perceptions do not occur without affection,[14] so, also, thinking does not occur without imaging;[15] so that

---

[8] Cf. Plotinus IV 8. 6, 8–12; V 1. 6, 37–50; V 3. 7, 21–4.

[9] This seems the best way to render the use of ἐπιστρέφειν of a higher principle towards a lower — certainly "revert" is no longer suitable.

[10] Cf. Plotinus III 6. 18, 24–9; IV 6. 2–3; V 3. 7, 26–34.

[11] We take this passage to be concerned with the individual soul; hence the use of the definite article.

[12] Literally, "it comes to be in intellections," a curious turn of phrase. It is not quite clear to us with what πρὸς τὸν νοῦν is intended to go, εἰσδῦσα or γίνεται, but we take it with the former.

[13] There seems to be serious corruption here. The general point that Porphyry seems to be making is that neither sense-perception nor intellection is unaccompanied by side effects, in the one case, πάθος, and in the other, φαντασία. We cannot find a satisfactory sense for the ἄλλη ποτὲ δὲ of Stobaeus, adopted by Lamberz, whereas something, at least, can be made of εἴ ποι τις of N (with an ἄν added, preferably). This would mean, then, "One might say . . ." Alternatively, one might excise the ποτὲ δὲ, and read ἀλλ' ὡς, preceded by a lacuna, which might be filled, perhaps, as <"coming about internally, takes place without some accompaniment">. We have adopted this latter course.

[14] This is an unsatisfactory translation of πάθος, but we can find no better. "Passion" is certainly less satisfactory. It means a reaction to an external stimulus in general.

[15] Again, an unsatisfactory rendering of φαντασία, but better than "imagination."

the analogy may be: as the [external] impression is an accompaniment to a living being experiencing a sense-perception, so is the image, in the case of the soul, a consequence of thinking.[16]

§22.[17] Intellectual essence is uniform through and through,[18] so that beings exist in the particular intellect in just the same way as they do in that Intellect that is the sum of all;[19] but in the universal Intellect even particular beings are found in a universal mode, whereas in the particular intellect even universals are found in a particular mode.

§25.[20] On the subject of that which is beyond Intellect, many statements are made on the basis of thinking, but it may be immediately cognized[21] only by means of a nonthinking superior to thinking; even as concerning sleep[22] many statements may be made in a waking state, but only through sleeping can one gain direct knowledge and comprehension;[23] for like is known by like, because all knowledge consists of assimilation to the object of knowledge.[24]

§26.[25] As for nonbeing, one type we engender when alienated from being, the other we acquire a preconception[26] of when cleaving close to being, for if we should by chance be alienated from being, we do not have a preconception of the nonbeing that is beyond being, but we engender nonbeing as a bogus experience,[27] which happens to someone

---

[16] The text of this clause is not without problems, but Lamberz's text (accepting Schwyzer's excision of ζῴου after ψυχῆς) gives an acceptable sense.

[17] Cf. Plotinus I 1. 8, 1–8; V 3. 5, 3–5; V 9. 8, 2–7.

[18] This seems to convey the sense of ὁμοιομερής; the only alternative is to transliterate as "homoeomerous."

[19] An attempt to render παντελείῳ.

[20] Cf. Plotinus V 4. 2, 18–9; V 6. 5, 4–5; VI 9. 4, 1–3.

[21] Or "contemplated" (θεωρεῖται), but we take this to be the sense of θεωρεῖν here.

[22] Taking τοῦ καθεύδοντος as meaning simply "sleep." Cf. Plato Phd. 72B9.

[23] That is, of what it is like to be asleep. Note that Porphyry is not talking of dreaming here, just of sleeping. We can "recall" dreams in a waking state and so have some notion of what it is like to dream, but we can never really, in a waking state, grasp what it is like to be asleep.

[24] Cf. Aristotle De An. A 2, 404b17–18; Met. B 4, 1000b5–8; Plotinus I 8. 1, 8.

[25] Cf. Plotinus III 9. 3, 7–14; VI 9. 2, 46–7; 11, 35–42.

[26] This is an inevitably inadequate rendering of a complex concept. It refers to having a supraintellectual intuition of what is above being.

[27] The phrase ψευδὲς πάθος seems to indicate an experience that is unreal, rather than (or in addition to?) an experience which is deceptive.

who has departed from his proper state,[28] for each human being, while remaining one and the same,[29] even as it were possible for him, truly and on his own initiative, to be elevated towards the nonbeing that is beyond being, may also be set astray towards that nonbeing that constitutes the collapse[30] of being.

§32.[31] The virtues of the human being at the "civic"[32] level are one thing, and those of the human being who is raising himself up towards the contemplative state and who is, for this reason, termed "contemplative," are another; and different again are those of the human being who is already a perfected contemplative and who already practices contemplation,[33] and different yet again are those of the intellect, insofar as it is intellect and transcends[34] soul.

The "civic" virtues, based as they are on moderation of the passions,[35] consist in following and going along with the process of reasoning relative to our duty in the field of practical action; for this reason, since they have regard to a community of action that avoids doing harm to one's neighbors, they are called "civic," by reason of their concern with public association[36] and community. They are as follows: practical wisdom,[37] relative to the reasoning element [in the soul]; courage, rela-

---

[28] More usually this verb would denote leaving one's normal state of consciousness behind to enter a higher state—to become "ecstatic" in the proper sense—but here Porphyry uses it to describe sinking into a lower, more "vulgar" state of consciousness.

[29] We prefer Schwyzer's emendation <ὁ> αὐτὸς for the manuscripts' αὐτὸς, to Lamberz's more radical suggestion αἴτιος, and translate accordingly.

[30] κατάπτωμα should mean something like "collapse" or "falling apart." LSJ's suggestion, "the lower limit of being," does not seem to convey the right sense.

[31] Cf. Plotinus I 2, the starting-point (after Plato) for Neoplatonic discussions of the virtues.

[32] That is, the virtues that are set out in Book IV of Plato's *Republic*.

[33] That is, a θεατής, "a viewer (of the Forms)."

[34] The word here is καθαρός ("purified") but seems to have the sense indicated in the translation.

[35] μετριοπάθεια is a technical term of later Greek ethical theory. It originally denoted an Aristotelian ideal, as opposed to the Stoic one, of ἀπάθεια, extirpation of the passions; in the Platonist tradition, they appear as two stages in moral progress. Cf. Plato *Phd.* 82A10–B8; Plotinus I 2. 1, 16–21.

[36] An attempt to render the rare word συναγελασμός, a term more proper to the herding of animals.

[37] Φρόνησις, as opposed to σοφία, "theoretical wisdom." "Prudence," the other favored rendering, seems in modern English to have too restrictive a connotation.

tive to the spirited element; moderation, which consists in the agreement and harmony of the affective element with the reason; and justice, consisting, for each of the elements in the soul, in its performance of its proper role with respect to ruling and being ruled.[38]

The virtues, on the other hand, of the human being who is making progress towards the state of contemplation[39] consist in detaching oneself from the things of this realm; for this reason, these are also termed "purifications," consisting in abstention from actions in concert with the body and from participating in the passions that affect it, for without doubt these virtues are those of a soul that is in the process of separating itself [from the body] in the direction of true being, whereas the civic virtues are concerned with the imposition of order on man in his mortal state—the civic virtues, we should specify, are precursors[40] of the purifications, for it is only after one has been set in order in accordance with them that one can abstract oneself from performing any act in concert primarily[41] with the body.

For this reason, at the purificatory level, practical wisdom[42] consists in the soul's not sharing any opinions with the body but acting on its own, and this is perfected by the pure exercise of the intellect; moderation is the result of taking care not to assent to any of the passions;[43] courage is not being afraid to depart from the body, as if one were falling into some void of not being;[44] and justice is the result of reason and intellect dominating the soul with nothing to oppose them. In brief, the disposition characteristic of the civic virtues is to be seen as the imposition of measure on the passions, since it has as its aim living a human

---

[38] All this, of course, reflects closely the tripartite division of the soul in *Republic* IV and the identifications of the virtues based on that. Cf. Plato *Rep.* 431C8; 434C8–9; 443B2.

[39] We are inclined to excise θεωρητικοῦ after προκόπτοντος, with manuscripts U and N. It can be translated, but it is redundant and sounds very like a gloss. Cf. Plato *Phd.* 69C1–3; Plotinus I 2. 3, 5–10.

[40] Not in the sense, of course, that practice of these will necessarily lead to acquisition of the purifications also, which is plainly not the case, but because one must master these first before attaining to the purifications.

[41] We take προηγουμένως as going with πράττειν, and as referring to physical activities performed *for their own sake* and not as "secondary" necessities (ἑπομένως), as is proper to a purified sage.

[42] Still τὸ φρονεῖν, and so "practical."

[43] This being, presumably, the force of μὴ ὁμοπαθεῖν. Cf. Plato *Phd.* 83D7; *Tht.* 176B1; Plotinus I 2. 3, 19–21; 4, 1–12.

[44] Taking the καί here as a hendiadys.

life in accordance with nature, while the disposition that results from the contemplative virtues is manifested in total detachment from the passions,[45] which has as its aim assimilation to god.[46]

But since "purification" can mean, as we know, in one sense, the process of purifying a soul and, in another, the state achieved by purified souls, the purificatory virtues can be viewed in accordance with either of these two meanings of "purification." In fact, they both serve to purify the soul and are an accompaniment to the purified soul—for the aim of the process of purification is the state of purification—but since the process of purification and the state of purity are, as is agreed, the suppression of all that is alien, the good will be distinct from the purifying agent,[47] for if, in fact, what is purified were good before its loss of purity, purification alone would be sufficient;[48] but if purification is going to be sufficient, what remains after it will be the good, not the purification. But the soul is not, as we know, by its nature good, but something that can participate in the good and is within the class of the good;[49] for otherwise it would not have come to be in an evil state. The good for it, then, consists in uniting itself with what has engendered it,[50] while evil lies in uniting itself to what is inferior to it. Evil, it should be specified, is of a double nature: first, to unite oneself with inferior entities, and secondly, to do so with an excess of passion. This is why the civic virtues, even though they deliver the soul from only one level of evil, are nonetheless judged to be virtues and are held in honor, while the purificatory virtues are accounted more worthy of honor, as delivering the soul also from the evil that is proper to it as soul.[51]

It is requisite, then, that, once purified, the soul unite itself with what has engendered it; and in consequence, the virtue that is proper to it after its conversion consists in the acquaintance and knowledge[52] of

---

[45] This seems to be the force of ἀπάθεια here.
[46] See Plato *Tht.* 176B; *Phd.* 69B-C; Plotinus I 2. 5, 2.
[47] If this is what is meant by τοῦ καθήραντος.
[48] Reading the (counterfactual) imperfect ἤρκει, with the manuscripts of Porphyry, in preference to the present ἀρκεῖ of those of Stobaeus and Plotinus.
[49] This seems to be the sense of ἀγαθοειδές here.
[50] That is, Intellect. Cf. Plotinus I 2. 4, 13–15.
[51] That is, consorting with what is inferior on any terms. Cf. Plato *Phdr.* 250B1–3.
[52] We can discern no real distinction here between γνῶσις and εἴδησις, and the fact that both are picked up in the next clause by the singular ταύτην would seem to indicate that there is none.

being, not because it does not possess it in itself,[53] but it is not capable of seeing what is within itself without the cooperation of what is superior to it.[54] There is, therefore, another class of virtues, a third one, after the purificatory and the civic, which is that of the soul as it is acting intellectually.[55] [At this level], wisdom, both theoretical and practical,[56] consists in the contemplation of the contents of intellect; justice is the fulfilling [by each of the parts of the soul] of the role proper to it in following upon intellect and directing its activity towards intellect; moderation is the internal conversion [of the soul] towards intellect; and courage is detachment from the passions through which the soul assimilates itself to that towards which it turns its gaze, which is itself free from passions. And, by the way, all these are reciprocally implicated as are the earlier ones, too. [57]

The fourth class of virtues is that of the paradigmatic, which are, as we agree, actually to be found in the intellect, seeing as they are superior to those of the soul and are the paradigms[58] of these, the virtues of the soul being their likenesses.[59] At this level, intellect is that in which the paradigms enjoy a simultaneous existence. What counts as practical wisdom[60] is understanding, while theoretical wisdom is the intellect in the act of knowing; moderation becomes self-concentration; perform-

---

[53] Preserving the παρ' αὐτῇ the manuscripts, as it makes adequate sense, though Lamberz's proposal παρ' αὐτῆς, "from itself," has much to commend it.

[54] Cf. Plotinus I 2. 4, 15–23; III 8. 6, 19–26.

[55] Cf. Plotinus I 2. 6, 12–13; 19–20; 23–6.

[56] Unlike the case of γνῶσις and εἴδησις, we take σοφία and φρόνησις as preserving their traditional meanings here, even though at this level they come to coincide.

[57] Cf. Plotinus I 2. 7, 1–6.

[58] It seemed best to keep the noun "paradigm," since we have used the adjectival form.

[59] There seems to be a syntactical oddity here, as ὧν cannot pick up τούτων, as one would expect it to, but depends directly on παραδείγματα. Otherwise, the virtues of the soul would come out as *likenesses* of themselves.

[60] We prefer to read φρόνησις here, with the manuscripts and Michael Psellus in his paraphrase. Plotinus I 2. 7, 3, admittedly, said ἡ νόησις ἐκεῖ ἐπιστήμη καὶ σοφία, but Porphyry here seems to want to make a distinction between archetypes of practical and theoretical wisdom at this level, and νόησις really makes very little sense. Even so, the definition of σοφία does not make much sense to us. We would prefer to have an object such as αὐτόν for γιγνώσκων, and read "intellect in the act of knowing *itself*."

[61] Cf. Plotinus I 2. 7, 5.

ance of its proper act is just "minding its own business";[61] courage is self-identity,[62] and remaining purely on its own owing to the superabundance of its power.

So then, it has become clear that there are four classes of virtues: those of the intellect, which act as paradigms and are intimately connected[63] with its essence; those of the soul that has already turned its gaze towards intellect and is filled with it; those of the human soul that is purifying itself and that has been purified from the body and its nonrational passions; and those of the human soul that is imposing order on the human being by assigning measures to the nonrational element and bringing about moderation of the passions.[64]

Whoever possesses the superior virtues, we may note,[65] also necessarily possesses the lower ones, but the converse is not the case. On the other hand, he who possesses the superior virtues will not, by reason of the fact that he possesses also the lower ones, conduct himself primarily in accordance with the lower ones but will only do so in response to the circumstances that confront him in the realm of generation,[66] for the objectives that they are aiming at are different, as has been said, and generically distinct.

That [objective] of the civic virtues is to impose measure on the passions in the direction of[67] activities that conform to nature; that of the purificatory virtues is to separate completely from the passion that which has just taken on measure;[68] that of the next level is to direct one's activity towards intellect without any longer giving thought to separating oneself from the passions;[69] while as for that of those virtues

---

[62] Here Porphyry has made an alteration from Plotinus where the mss. read αὐλότης, "immateriality," which seems a rather weak word in the circumstances. Henry Blumenthal suggested, *per litteris*, that the true Plotinian reading may have been the made up word αὐτότης, "self-ness," which Porphyry would then have "toned down" to ταυτότης.

[63] Σύνδρομος must have something like this meaning.

[64] Cf. Plotinus I 2. 2, 13–18.

[65] An attempt to do justice to the καί at the beginning of the sentence.

[66] Cf. Plotinus I 2. 7, 10–15; 19–21.

[67] We take this to be force of πρός.

[68] That is, the soul as acted on by the civic virtues. The text has come under suspicion here, but we see no reason to accept the emendations of Kroll, as the neuter phrase τὸ ... λαμβάνον as object of ἀποστῆσαι seems to make good sense.

[69] Preserving the ἀφικνουμένους of the manuscripts (or the ἐρχομένους of Stobaeus), rather than the genitive absolute proposed by Lamberz, but accepting Schwyzer's proposal to change ἀποστῆσαι to the intransitive ἀποστῆναι.

whose role is no longer to direct their activity *towards* intellect but that have actually come into confluence with its essence, <it is no longer possible to describe their activity>.[70] For this reason, then, he who acts in accordance with the practical virtues[71] is agreed to be a "good human being";[72] he who acts in accordance with the purificatory ones is a daemonic human being, or even a good daemon; one who acts only according to those that are directed towards intellect is a god, and one who practices the paradigmatic virtues, is a "father of gods."[73]

We should, therefore, direct our attention most of all to the purificatory virtues, basing ourselves on the reflection[74] that the attainment of these is possible in this life, and that it is through these that an ascent may be made to the more august levels. We must, therefore, consider up to what point and in what degree it is possible to receive purification;[75] for it involves, after all, separation from the body and from the nonrational motion provoked by the passions. We must state how this would come about and up to what point.

For a start, it is, as it were, the foundation and underpinning of purification to recognize that one is a soul bound down in an alien entity of a quite distinct nature. In the second place, taking start from this conviction,[76] one should gather oneself together from the body even, as it were,[77] in a local sense, but at any rate adopting an attitude of complete

---

[70] We accept the suggestion of Schwyzer for the filling of a lacuna that he discerns here. The sentence as it stands needs a main clause (the succession of genitives seems really too harsh otherwise), but we fear that there may be a worse corruption. At any rate, Porphyry is referring to the paradigmatic virtues, and this is the sort of thing he should be saying.

[71] Another term for the "civic" virtues.

[72] Σπουδαῖος being the (primarily) Stoic term for denoting the virtue of a human being.

[73] The precise significance of this is not clear, but certainly sounds Chaldean. Cf. Plotinus I 2. 6, 3–7.

[74] We take σκεψαμένοις to have this sense and to govern ὅτι.

[75] Cf. Plotinus I 2. 5, 1.

[76] We take πείσμα here as the noun deriving from πείθω, not the word for "ship's cable." One should hold fast to that, not launch oneself from it.

[77] Reading οἷον, with the manuscripts of Plotinus against the μὲν of the manuscripts, which is possible, but not very convincing. Even with οἷον, the expression is peculiar, but it is Plotinus' expression, not Porphyry's. We take it to mean that one should practice withdrawing one's consciousness from those parts of the body associated with the passions. The soul itself, of course, is not properly to be regarded as being *in* the body locally. Cf. Plotinus I 2. 5, 5–7.

disaffection with respect to the body, for, in fact, one who pursues a mode of activity constantly linked to sense-perception—even if he does this without the addition of passion, that is, without taking pleasure in it—nevertheless finds his attention dispersed about the body, because he is in contact with it by reason of sensation, but he subjects himself in addition to the pleasures and pains associated with sense-perceptions, if he abandons himself to them and assents to participation in them.[78] It is this attitude above all, then, from which one must purify oneself; and this should come about on condition that one confine oneself to taking on board those sensations of pleasure[79] that are necessary simply for purposes of healing or the relief of discomfort, in order that one's activity may not be interfered with.[80]

One should also strive to remove pains; but if that is not possible, then one should bear them mildly, rendering their effect less by declining to assent to the suffering associated with them. One should suppress anger, as far as one can, and not give rein to it;[81] if one cannot achieve that, at least one should not implicate one's will[82] with it, but the involuntary element should be related to another entity,[83] and that involuntary element should be weak and small. As for fear, one should suppress it completely, for such a human being will be fearful of nothing—although there is an element of the involuntary involved here too. One may, however, employ both anger and fear by way of admonition.[84] Desire for anything base must be eliminated altogether. Desire for food and drink, one will not have, insofar as concerns oneself in the strict sense;[85] while in the case of desire for

---

[78] We are inclined to take συμπαθεῖ as a verb governing προθυμίᾳ and ἐπινεύσει, since this provides an easier syntax.

[79] Excising the καὶ τὰς before αἰσθήσεις as a dittography.

[80] Cf. Plotinus I 2. 5, 7–24; 27–31.

[81] Lamberz has adopted a reading from the parallel passage of Plotinus I 2. 5, 12, καί, εἰ δυνατόν, πάντῃ, but the manuscripts of Porphyry (and Stobaeus) have a quite different text that makes reasonable sense, καὶ μὴ μελετητέον, so we translate that. The verb is used in the same sense in *Sent.* 29, p. 20, 2–3 Lamberz.

[82] Προαίρεσις, as used here, seems to come very close, at least, to the concept of will.

[83] That is, the body.

[84] This curious footnote, as it were, is taken from Plotinus. (One can see how anger might be used for purposes of νουθέτησις, but not so easily, fear.)

[85] That is, insofar as one is a soul.

natural[86] sexual intercourse, one should not even admit the involuntary element; but if it arises, it should extend only to the level of fleeting images, such as come about in dreams.[87]

In sum, this intellectualized[88] soul of the purified individual should be free from all these passions. It should also wish that the part that is set in motion towards the nonrational element in bodily experiences[89] should do so without sharing in any passion and without bestowing any attention upon such activity, in just such a way that these motions should be <small>[90] and straightway dissolved by the proximity of the reasoning element. Thus no conflict will manifest itself, in consequence of the progress of the process of purification, but from then on the mere presence of the reason will suffice, which gains the respect of the inferior element, so that the inferior element itself will actually come to feel indignation if it is set in motion at all, because it did not rest quiet in the presence of its master and will reproach itself for weakness.

These virtues, then, are still to be reckoned as instances of moderating the passions,[91] although they have adopted a tendency[92] towards freedom from passion. But when the element subject to the influence of passions has been completely purified, what is left coexisting with the purified individual is an element incapable of being affected, because even the "passionate" part now sets itself in motion at the bidding of the reason, which gives it its lead[93] on the basis of its own inclination.

---

[86] The specification φυσικά is somewhat obscure, but may be taken most naturally to refer to heterosexual, as opposed to homosexual (or other "unnatural"), intercourse.

[87] What counts as a φαντασία προπετής is a nice point. It cannot really be like a dream image, surely, since dream images are quite vivid and assented to *in the dream*. This is a case where Porphyry is expanding slightly on Plotinus and not very fortunately.

[88] This seems to be the sense of νοερά here. The purified soul is entirely turned towards νοῦς.

[89] We would take πάθη here in the broadest sense, since Porphyry is speaking of the ἄλογον aspect of them.

[90] The presence of τε after εὐθύς in W and Stobaeus would seem to indicate a small lacuna here, which may conveniently be filled with something like ὀλίγας, borrowed from the parallel passage of Plotinus I 2. 5, 23.

[91] Using the Peripatetic technical term μετριοπάθειαι.

[92] If this is not too mild a word to represent ἐπίτασις.

[93] We give this rendering of the musical term ἐνδόσιμον, "that which gives the key to the tune" (LSJ).

§41. That which has its being in another and has no essential existence on its own separate from another—if it turns to itself for the purpose of knowing itself without taking account of that to which it owes its essential existence, in withdrawing itself from that[94]—destroys itself through separating itself from its being, for that which is able to know itself without that which it is in—withdrawing itself from it and being able to do this without encompassing its own destruction—can in no way owe its essence to that from which it was able to turn itself to itself[95] without undergoing destruction and to know itself without that.

If it is the case with sight, and the sense faculties in general that none is perceptive of itself nor can it, if it separates itself from the body, have any consciousness of itself nor even survive—whereas intellect, when it separates itself from the body, then exercises its intellective function most of all and turns towards itself and does not perish—it is obvious that the sense faculties have acquired their activity through the medium of the body, while the intellect has acquired its activity and its essence in virtue of itself, and not in virtue of the body.[96]

§43.[97] Intellect is not the principle of all things, for Intellect is many, and prior to the many there must be the One.[98] That Intellect is many is obvious, for it is constantly thinking intelligibles, which are not one but many and not different from it. If, then, it is the same as they, and they are many, Intellect, too, would be many.

That it is the same as the intelligibles is demonstrated in the following manner: if there is something that it contemplates, it will contemplate this either as possessing it within itself or as situated elsewhere. And that it does contemplate is obvious, for it is, after all, in conjunction with thinking that it is Intellect, while if it is deprived of thinking, it is deprived of its essence. It is, therefore, through paying attention to the

---

[94] After ἐκείνου, the manuscript W has νοήσει γὰρ αὐτὸ καὶ, which makes no sense as it stands. It seems misguided to try to emend—e.g., νοήσει to νοοήσει (Creuzer) or νοσεῖ (Kroll). Far more probably it is a gloss (to which καί has been added by the scribe who included it in the text), explaining the nature of the fatal move that those entities that have only dependent being would be making—that is, they would be trying to intuit themselves. Cf. Proclus ET Prop. 83.

[95] After εἰς ἑαυτὸ the manuscript has ἀπ' ἐκείνου, which Lamberz seems right to excise.

[96] Cf. Aristotle De An. Γ 5, 430a18, 22–3.

[97] Cf. Plotinus V 3. 2–5; V 5. 1–2; V 9. 5.

[98] We take it that capitalization is justified here, by reason of the presence of the definite article, but Porphyry's point is quite general: prior to multiplicity, there must be unity.

various experiences attendant on the various modes of cognition that one must seek out the nature of its contemplation.

The cognitive powers in us are, in sum, sense-perception, imagination,[99] and intellect. In all cases that which employs sense-perception contemplates by apprehending what is external to it, not being united to what it contemplates, but only taking in an impression of those things by virtue of applying itself to them. When, therefore, the eye sees the object of vision, it is impossible for it come into identity with that object of vision, for it would not see it, if it were not at a distance from it. And similarly, the object of touch would suffer destruction if it were to come into identity.[100] All of this demonstrates that in all cases the sense faculty, and that which employs the sense faculty, must direct their activity outwards, if they are going to grasp the object of sense. And likewise, also, the imagination is, in all cases, directed outwards, and the image comes into being as the by-product of its attention[101] — the imagination actually generating from outside, by virtue of its very attention outward, the appearance of the image as being external.[102]

In the case of these faculties, then, their mode of apprehension is of such a nature as this: in no case would any of them, through reverting towards and being concentrated on itself, come to the cognition of any form, sensible or nonsensible.[103] In the case of intellect, on the other hand, apprehension does not take place in this way, but in virtue of its concentrating on itself and contemplating itself, for if it were to go beyond the contemplation of its own activities, and be the "eye" of its own activities, which constitute the object of its "vision," it would think nothing. Even as was the relation of sense-perception to the object of sense-perception, such is the relation of intellect to that which is intelligible.

---

[99] We use this as a convenient translation of φαντασία, properly, "image-making faculty."

[100] That is, with the sense of touch.

[101] An attempt to render τάσις, perhaps "outward striving."

[102] We are not at all confident of having reached the right solution here, but rather than postulate a lacuna before ἤτοι with Usener, W-H, and Lamberz, we would (adopting a number of suggestions from Kroll, Holstein, Creuzer, and Heeren) read: ἥτις καὶ παρασκευάζει ἔξωθεν αὐτῇ τῇ πρὸς τὸ ἔξω τάσει τὴν ὡς ἔξω ὄντος εἰκονίσματος ἔνδειξιν. This at least gives a sense of approximately what is required, but it does, admittedly, take a number of liberties with the received text.

[103] We are inclined to accept W-H's suggestion of ἤτοι..ἢ for the ἢ τῳ..ἢ τῳ of the manuscript. The use of the definite article is awkward.

But the former contemplates through being extended outside of itself, discovering the sensible lodged in matter, whereas intellect does so through being concentrated on itself. But if it is not extended outwards[104] — as indeed was the opinion of those[105] who regarded the difference between the status[106] of intellect and imagination to be one of name only;[107] for the imaginative faculty in a rational being was, in their view, thinking; but if it was logical for them — seeing as they made everything to depend on matter and the nature of body — to make intellect to depend on these also, in the case of intellect as we understand it,[108] being, as it is, the contemplator of incorporeal and more divine essences,[109] where, then, will those things grasped by it be situated? Since they are outside of matter, these things would be nowhere — obviously as being intellectual[110] — and they will be comprehended by thinking and so, if intellectual, will be united[111] to intellect and to that which is intelligible[112] —

---

[104] This phrase, beginning εἰ δὲ μὴ, and containing no main verb, is followed by a very extended and complex parenthesis, from 56, 1–10, and is only picked up at 56, 10 by καὶ ἑαυτὸν θεωρήσει . . . This has seemed too extreme to some scholars, such as Canter, Meineke, and Thomas Taylor, but substituting οὐδαμῇ, οὐδὲ μὴν, or οὐδὲ μὴ for εἰ δὲ μὴ does not seem to solve the syntactical problem. It seems simply to be a case of extremely sloppy and incoherent composition by Porphyry. The parenthesis is really a kind of footnote.

[105] This seems to refer to the Stoics.

[106] This seems to be the meaning of ὑπόστασις here. The point is that they were thought to differ only conceptually and not in reality.

[107] One could postulate a μόνον before ὀνόματος, as suggested by Meineke. In any case, it should be understood.

[108] This, we think, must be the sense of ὁ ἡμέτερος (νοῦς) here.

[109] We adopt the emendations of Usener, ἀσωμάτων καὶ θειοτέρων, for the σωμάτων καὶ ἑτέρων of the manuscript, which is meaningless in the context. For ἑτέρων one might alternatively read νοερῶν, as Kroll suggests, but, though nearer to the text, it is not so satisfactory in meaning. Obviously, whatever the νοῦς contemplates will be νοερόν, but on the Stoic theory that could also be corporeal.

[110] The syntax of this phrase is rather rough, certainly, but it is translatable. It does not seem necessary to prefix καὶ ταύτῃ to δῆλον as Lamberz proposes.

[111] Taking the εἰς here as dependent on συναχθήσεται which has already been rendered by "comprehended," and must now be repeated with a slightly different sense.

[112] W-H wished to excise καὶ τὸ νοητόν here, and indeed it is difficult to see to what it is referring. It is surely the objects that are being "united to intellect,"

then[113] it [intellect] will actually be contemplating itself in cognizing the intelligibles, and in proceeding towards itself it cognizes by virtue of its proceeding towards them. But if the intelligibles are many—for intellect cognizes many things and not one—it would necessarily be, itself, also many. But prior to the many lies the One, so that it follows necessarily that prior to Intellect there is the One.

§44.[114] Intellect and the intelligible are one thing, and sense-perception and the sensible are another;[115] and the intelligible is coordinate with intellect, while sense-perception is coordinate with the sensible. But neither sense-perception nor the sensible is capable of grasping itself by itself; the intelligible, on the other hand, being coordinate with intellect and intelligible by intellect,[116] is in no way subject to sense-perception, but intellect is intelligible by means of intellect. If, then, intellect were intelligible by means of intellect, intellect would be intelligible by itself. So, if intellect were intelligible and not sensible by the senses, then it would be an intelligible; but if it were intelligible by intellect and not by sense-perception, then it would be a thinking agent.[117] So, therefore, the same thing will be, as a whole, acting on a whole, a thinking agent and object of thinking,[118] and not in the manner of something that rubs and is rubbed.[119] So, it is not thought in respect of one part of itself and thinking with another, for it is partless and intelligible as a whole by the whole of itself and also intellect through and through, containing in itself no conception of lack of intellection.[120] For this reason, it is not the case that one part of it

---

after all, that will themselves be intelligibles. Cf. Plotinus I 4. 10, 20–1; IV 7. 8, 1–23; V 5. 1, 19–68.

[113] Picking up, at last, the protasis from the beginning of the sentence at 55, 19.

[114] Cf. Plotinus III 7. 2–4; 11; V 1. 4; V 3. 5–6; VI 5. 11; Proclus ET Props. 169–70.

[115] This sentence could also mean "Intellect is distinct from the intelligible, and sense-perception is distinct from the sensible," but this does not seem to fit the context so well.

[116] We omit here, following Holstenius, Creuzer, and all subsequent editors, a repetitive and incoherent passage, which seems to result from a scribe's eye straying from the αἰσθήσει in l. 6 back to the αἰσθήσει in l. 2.

[117] That is, because intellect is something which thinks *itself*.

[118] Nooύμενον here, not νοητόν.

[119] "Rubbing" (τρίβειν) being used as the paradigm of a physical activity performed by one part of an organism upon another.

[120] Cf. Plotinus V 3. 6, 7–8.

thinks,[121] and another part does not think, for in respect of any part that does not think, it will be devoid of thought.[122]

Nor does it turn its attention from one thing to go on to another, for in the case of that from which it has turned its attention and is therefore not thinking it, it would be devoid of thought in respect of that thing. But if one thing after another does not impose itself on its consciousness, it must entertain all the objects of its intellection simultaneously;[123] so since it thinks all simultaneously and not now one thing and now another, it thinks everything simultaneously and eternally. If, then, it is characterized by present time, and the past and the future are abolished in connection with it, it exists in a nonextended timeless moment,[124] which is the "now," so that it is "together" both in respect of multiplicity and in respect of temporal extension, for this reason, in its case all things are at one in unity and freedom from extension and timelessness. And if this is so, then it is subject neither to "whence" and "whither," nor, consequently, to motion, but it enjoys an activity at one in unity, exempt from increase and change and every sort of transition. But if its multiplicity is unitary and its activity simultaneous and timeless, then necessarily there arises, as consequential on[125] such an essence, the characteristic of being always in one state; but this is eternity; so, then, eternity is a by-product of intellect.

On the other hand, as a by-product of not thinking at one in unity, but transitively and in motion, and in the mode of leaving off one thing and picking up another and dividing one's attention and proceeding discursively, there came into being time, for as a by-product of such motion as this there arise futurity and pastness. The soul switches its attention from one thing to another through alternating its thoughts — not that the earlier ones have been expelled nor the later ones brought in from anywhere else, but the former pass out of view, as it were, while

---

[121] We have thought fit to switch, at this stage, from the jargon word "intelligize" to the simple "think," just to remind the reader that all that is in question is the simple verb νοεῖν. However, exigencies of consistency seem to demand the use of derivatives and cognates of "intellect" as a general practice, since there are no usable adjectival forms of "think" nor can one properly translate νοῦς as "thinking" rather than "intellect."

[122] Cf. Plotinus V 3. 6, 32; V 9. 5, 8.

[123] Cf. Plotinus III 7. 3, 16–38; VI 7. 1, 54–7.

[124] Translating παραστήμα, a most interesting ἅπαξ λεγόμενον in this sense.

[125] This expression, and "is a by-product" below, are attempts to capture the sense of παρυφίστασθαι.

remaining in it, while the latter give the impression of coming in from elsewhere but do not, in fact, arrive from elsewhere, arising as they do from itself and from its self-motion towards itself and from its directing its eye to one part or other of its contents, for it is like a spring that never flows outwards, but which causes its contents to well up and circulate within itself.

Time, then, is the by-product of this mobility of the soul, while eternity is the by-product of the stability of intellect within itself, not distinct from it, even as time is not[126] distinct from soul, because by-products are integrated[127] at that level also. But that which is subject to motion comes to be falsely identified <with the stability of>[128] eternity, the measurelessness of its motion being assimilated to the concept of eternity,[129] and likewise that which is stable comes to be falsely identified with the motion that is time, as though its eternal present extended and multiplied itself on the model of time. Hence, some people have come to view time as being at rest no less than as in motion, and eternity, as we have said, as infinite time, as if each were applying to the other the characteristics proper to itself, that which is constantly in motion, on the basis of the stable nature of its sameness, picturing its own constant succession[130] as eternity, and that which is stable in the sameness of its activity applying the concept of temporality to its stability on the basis of that sameness.[131]

Finally, at the level of sense-perception, divided time differs according to the various instruments of time, there being one, for example, proper to the sun; another, to the moon; another, to Venus; and another, to each of the others; and the year that comprises all these[132] finds its consummation in the motion of the soul. All these move in im-

---

[126] Accepting the addition of οὐδ' proposed by Levêque, on the basis of the parallel passage of Plotinus III 7. 11, 59–62.

[127] With their essences.

[128] If we accept Mommert's addition here, πρὸς τὸ μένον, designed to balance πρὸς τὸ κινούμενον of the next line. In general, this phrase is sadly corrupted. The manuscript just after this gives αἰὼν δὲ αὐτοῦ, which Lamberz has, reasonably, emended to αἰῶνα ἑαυτοῦ, on the model of χρόνον ἑαυτοῦ in the next line. Such rather mechanical balancing of *clausulae* is certainly characteristic of Porphyry in this work.

[129] That is, confusing true eternity with what we would term "sempiternity."

[130] Porphyry says simply "its own 'always'" (ἀεί).

[131] Cf. Plotinus I 5. 7, 14–30; III 7. 12, 20–55.

[132] That is, the Great Year.

itation of it, but since its motion is of a nature different from theirs, the time proper to it is also different from that which is characteristic of them. This latter is dimensional in respect to both local motions and transitions, . . .[133]

INQUIRIES INTO VARIOUS TOPICS[1]

Inquiries into Various Topics (Σύμμικτα ζητήματα), *a work preserved only in fragments in later writers, such as Proclus, Nemesius of Emesa, and Priscianus, seems to have comprised a variety of topics, as the name implies, but chiefly to have concerned the soul and the mode of relationship between soul and body.*

Fr. 259 Smith[2]

We must investigate how there might come about the union of soul and soulless body, for the problem is a baffling one. And if, in fact, the human being is made up not just of these components but of intellect as well, as some would have it, the problem is still more baffling, for all things that come together into the actuality of a single substance[3] are undeniably made a unity, and all things that are unified suffer alteration and do not remain what they previously were, as will be shown in the case of the elements, for when they are unified, they come to be something else.

How, then, could body, when united with soul, still remain body, or, conversely, how would soul, being as it is incorporeal and truly real of itself, be united with body and become a part of a living being while preserving its own essence uncontaminated and uncorrupted?[4] For

---

[133] Here the single manuscript, W, breaks off. Porphyry, is, presumably, going on to characterize the time proper to soul in terms antithetical to those that he has just employed for the times proper to the various instruments of time, but we cannot know how much more has been lost after that.

[1] This seems a reasonable rendering of the Greek ΣΥΜΜΙΚΤΑ ΖΗΤΗΜΑΤΑ.

[2] The Porphyrian provenance of this text, from Nemesius of Emesa's *De Nat. Hom.* 3, p. 38, 12–40, 20 Morani, is indicated by a number of virtually verbatim parallels with Priscian's *Solutiones ad Chosroen*, p. 50, 25–51, 25 Bywater, since there is no indication that Priscian knew Nemesius.

[3] An attempt to render the troublesome phrase εἰς μιᾶς οὐσίας ὑπόστασιν.

[4] Cf. Plotinus I 1. 3ff.

necessarily either the soul and the body will be unified and both suffer alteration and destruction together, like elements, or they will not be unified because of the aforementioned absurdities that will result, but will remain juxtaposed like dancers in a chorus, or pebbles beside one another, or else they will be mixed like wine and water.[5]

But that the soul cannot be simply juxtaposed with the body has been demonstrated in the discussion of the soul;[6] for in that case it would be only the actual part of the body contiguous with soul that would be ensouled, and that which was not in contact would remain soulless, in addition to the impossibility of characterizing as a unity things that are merely juxtaposed, like a heap of sticks, for instance, or of iron bars or something such.

As for the mixture of wine and water, it blends both components together,[7] for the mixture is neither pure water nor [pure] wine—although, in fact, this mixture is the result of mere juxtaposition. This eludes our senses by reason of the fineness of the constituents of the mixture, but its nature becomes obvious from the fact that these constituents can be separated from each other, for a sponge infused with olive oil, along with a papyrus reed, can draw off the water in a pure form, whereas it is impossible to separate out in any way perceptible to the senses things that are unified in the strict sense.

If, then, it is neither unified in the strict sense, nor juxtaposed, nor mixed, what is the formula on the basis of which a living being is said to be one? Certainly Plato, owing to this difficulty, does not wish to characterize the living being as [a compound] of body and soul, but rather as a soul *making use of* a body and, as it were, "clothing itself in" the body concerned.[8] Even this account, though, involves a difficulty, for how

---

[5] The mixture (μῖξις) of wine and water, while being much more unified than mere juxtaposition (παράθεσις) and leading to the contamination of one component by the other, nevertheless does not produce complete union (ἕνωσις) such as that of the elements that go to make up a body.

[6] This is a reference back to Nemesius *De Nat. Hom.* 2, p. 22, 10–13 Morani, which passage also may be derived from Porphyry.

[7] We take this to be the meaning of συνδιαφθείρει; "corrupt" would give a wrong connotation.

[8] Platonic passages supporting the former characterization ("using"), as suggested by Smith (*ad loc.*) would be *Phd.* 79C3 and, probably more significantly, *Alc.* I, 129E3–5; while for the latter, one might refer to *Phd.* 82A1 (ἐνδύεσθαι) and *Rep.* 620C3 (ἐνδυομένην)—though in both these cases the reference is to human souls entering a nonhuman body. Aristotle also uses the term at *De An.*

can the soul be one with its "garment"? A cloak, after all, is not one with its wearer.

Ammonius, the teacher of Plotinus, sought to resolve the problem in the following way:[9] he used to maintain that intelligibles have such a nature as both to be united with those things able to receive them, in the manner of things that are blended together and, when united, to remain unmixed and unblended, just like things juxtaposed. In the case of bodies, union always produces alteration of the elements that combine, seeing as they change into other bodies, as in the case of elements into compound bodies, and various types of food into blood, and blood into flesh and other bodily parts. In the case of intelligibles, on the other hand, union comes about, but change does not follow, for intelligibles are of not of such a nature as to change, but they either withdraw or perish into nonexistence;[10] at all events, they do not admit of change. But they do not perish into nonexistence, for in that case they would not be immortal. And the soul, being life, if it changed in the process of mixture, would have been altered and thus would no longer be life. But what then would it contribute to the body, if it did not provide it with life?[11] So, then, the soul does not change in the process of union.

Once this has been demonstrated, then—that intelligibles are unchanging in their essence—it necessarily follows also that when they are united with something else, they do not experience blending with that to which they are united. The soul, then, is united, but united without contamination with the body.

That it is united is shown by the fact of unity of sensibility,[12] for the living being as a whole enjoys a unified sensibility with itself as one single being. That it remains uncontaminated, on the other hand, is plain from the fact that the soul is, in a certain way, separated from the body in sleep and leaves it to lie there like a corpse, merely infusing it with the breath of life, in order that it may not perish completely, while it activates itself on its own in dreams, prophesying the future and consorting with intelligible reality. The same is the case when, on its own, it

---

A 3, 407b21–3, with reference to the Pythagorean doctrine of transmigration of souls.

[9] This would presumably be orally transmitted from Plotinus to Porphyry.

[10] This seems to be a reference to the last argument of the *Phaedo*, in particular 102D–E.

[11] That is, soul is both life and the provider of life to the body.

[12] An adequate translation of συμπάθεια is a difficult problem; simple transliteration ("sympathy"), though a common option, is not really good enough.

considers some aspect of true being, for at such time, so far as in it lies, it separates itself from the body and comes to be on its own, in order that it may cognize true being, for, incorporeal as it is, it pervades the whole (composite) like things that are blended, while remaining uncontaminated and unmixed. (= Nemesius *De Nat. Hom.* 3, p. 38, 12–40, 20)

Fr. 261 Smith[13]

For just as the sun changes the air into light, making it lightlike, and the light is united with the air both in an unmixed manner and yet being mixed with it, even so the soul too, in being united to the body, remains in all cases unmixed, with only this difference: that the sun, being a body and circumscribed spatially, is not everywhere that its light is, even as fire is not, for it also remains confined in the logs or in the wick, as in a place. The soul, on the other hand, being incorporeal and not spatially circumscribed, completely and wholly penetrates both its light and its body, and there is not a part that is lit by it in which it is not present as a whole, for neither is it controlled by the body, but rather it controls the body, nor is it in the body as in a container or a bag, but rather the body is in it.[14]

For since intelligibles are not hindered by bodies but, rather, control and penetrate and traverse them, they cannot be contained in a corporeal space, for being intelligible, they are in intelligible locations, either in themselves or in intelligibles superior to them; and so the soul is sometimes in itself and sometimes in intellect, that is, whenever it is thinking. So, when it is said to be "in the body," it is not said to be in the body as in a place but as being in relation to it and as being present to it, even as god is said to be "in us;" for, indeed, it is by reason of relationship and inclination and attitude towards an object that we say that the soul is "ensnared" by the body, even as we say that the lover is "ensnared" by the beloved, neither corporeally nor spatially[15] but by relationship; being something without size or bulk or parts, it [soul] is superior to any

---

[13] Cf. Plotinus IV 3. 4, 19–21; 22, 1–12; 8. 4, 3–4.

[14] Cf. Plato *Tim.* 36D9–E1; Plotinus IV 3. 22, 8–9.

[15] It has seemed necessary to translate the adjective τοπικός and the adverb τοπικῶς, formed from the noun τόπος, as "spatial" and "spatially," respectively, while retaining the more accurate translation "place" for τόπος itself. We trust that this will not prove too misleading.

spatial circumscription of part by part, for by what sort of spatial circumscription could something that does not possess parts be contained? Place, after all, is ontologically coordinate with bulk, for place is the limit of the containing element,[16] in accordance with which the contained is contained.

If someone were to say, "So, then, my soul is in Alexandria and Rome and everywhere," he would fail to see that he is speaking in spatial terms, for being "in Alexandria" and in general "in such and such a place" is a spatial concept. But soul is absolutely not in place but, rather, in relation, for it has been demonstrated that it cannot be contained in a place. So, then, when an intelligible comes to be in relation to some place or to some object that is in a place, we improperly describe it as being there because of its exercising its activity there, talking of place instead of relation and activity, for whereas we should have said, "It is exercising its activity there" we say, "It *is* there." (Nemesius *De Nat. Hom.* p. 40, 22–42, 9)

ON THE RETURN OF THE SOUL

On the Return of the Soul *(De regressu animae) is known only from numerous references in Augustine's* City of God—*hence, it is only known by its Latin title. It, too, concerned the immortality of the soul, its relations with the body, and its fate after death.*

Fr. 284 Smith[1]

Porphyry also says that, according to the response of the divine oracles, we cannot be purified by the initiatory rites of the sun and moon, the purport of this response being that a man cannot be purified by the rites of any gods, for where is the god whose rites can purify us, if those of the sun and moon do not do so, seeing as they are the chief among the heavenly gods? His main point is that it is made clear in the same oracle

---

[16] Cf. Aristotle *Phys.* Δ 4, 212a20–1.

[1] These passages quoted by Augustine from Porphyry's treatise *De Regressu Animae* indicate that, despite his skeptical-sounding *Letter to Anebo*, Porphyry was by no means dismissive of the importance of theurgy. What he may be criticizing in the *Letter* is what he regards as misuses of theurgy, or incorrect presuppositions about its nature.

that it is the first principles that are capable of purification, lest one should suppose, when it is said that the rites of the sun and moon are not effective for purgation, that the rites of some other divinity from the crowd should be deemed effective.

Now we know what Porphyry, as a Platonist, thinks are " first principles." He declares them to be God the Father and God the Son,[2] the latter of whom he calls in Greek "the paternal intellect" or "paternal mind."[3] About the Holy Spirit he says nothing, or at least nothing clear; although I do not understand what other being he refers to as holding the middle position between these two.[4] If, like Plotinus, in his treatise on the three principal hypostases,[5] he had intended it to be inferred that this third entity is the natural substance of the soul, he would certainly not have said that this held "the middle place"—that is, median between the Father and the Son. Plotinus certainly regards the nature of the soul as inferior to the paternal intellect; but Porphyry, when he calls it "median," places it between, not below, the two others. (*De Regr. An.* Fr. 284 Smith = Augustine, *CD* X 23)

Fr. 285 Smith

In some way, it seems to me, Porphyry exhibits a certain embarrassment in his attitude to his friends, the theurgists, for he believed more or less what we do, but he did not defend his opinions straightforwardly against the worship of a multiplicity of gods. He claimed, in fact, that there are two classes of angels: one sort descends from above to reveal divine truths to men who practice theurgy, while another are those who, on earth, make known the truth about the Father—his height and his depth.

Is it to be believed that those angels whose role it is to declare the will of the Father wish us to be in subjection to any being other than he

---

[2] Augustine is being somewhat tendentious here in making this identification, but in the process he lets slip that Porphyry's metaphysical scheme—according to which the One, as first principle, is also "father of the noetic triad" (Being or Essence, Life, Intellect)—happens to provide an excellent model for the Christian Trinity.

[3] The Latin *paternus intellectus, paterna mens* = πατρικὸς νοῦς.

[4] Here Augustine is surely being disingenuous. It must have been plain to him that Porphyry was referring to the median element in the Chaldean triad, the "Power of the Father," which indeed, as a life principle, and the processive element within the triad, can be regarded as a sort of archetype of Soul, while not being Soul. It does, in fact, provide a good model for the Holy Spirit.

[5] See V 1.

whose will they announce to us? Thus our Platonist himself very rightly advises us that they are to be imitated rather than invoked. . . .[6] Why then are you afraid, my dear philosopher, to raise your voice freely against the powers who are envious of genuine virtues and the gifts of the true god? You have already distinguished the angels who announce the will of the Father from those who come down to the theurgists, attracted by magical art of some kind or other. (= Augustine CD X 26)

Fr. 287 Smith

You did not learn this from Plato, but from your Chaldean masters, that you should elevate human vices into the ethereal or empyrean[7] heights of the universe in order that your gods might be able to give divine revelations to the theurgists—to which divine revelations, however, you consider yourself superior, by reason of your intellectual life, so that you, of course, feel that, as a philosopher, you have not the slightest need of the purifications of the theurgic art.[8] Yet to others you prescribe such purgations as a kind of repayment of your debt to those masters of yours, which [payment] consists of inveigling those who are not capable of becoming philosophers to indulge in practices that are avowedly of no use to you, who are capable of higher things. So, then, all those who are remote from philosophic virtue—which is a very lofty ideal, and attained by only a few—are authorized by you to resort to theurgists, that they may receive from them the purgation, not of the *intellectual* soul, but merely of the *spiritual* one.[9] And so naturally, since the number of those who have no taste for philosophy is incomparably the greater, you collect far more clients for those secret and illegal masters of yours than for the Platonic schools. (= Augustine CD X 27, 8–25)

---

[6] Smith rightly omits here a passage of purely Christian rhetoric by Augustine.

[7] Αἰθέριος and ἐμπύριος are favored Chaldean epithets of the heavenly realm; cf. *Or. Chald.* Fr. 61 (αἰθέριος δρόμος), 76, 184; 2 (ἐμπύριοι ὀχετοί), 130.

[8] Such a view on the part of Porphyry would be quite in accord with that of Plotinus (cf. IV 4. 40), who, while accepting the reality of magic, felt that it had no power over the higher soul.

[9] This contrast between the "intellectual" (νοερά) and "spiritual" (πνευματική) soul occurs also in Augustine CD X 9, 20ff. (= Porphyry Fr. 290 Smith) and elsewhere and represents the contrast between the rational soul and the "pneumatic vehicle" (ὄχημα), which for Porphyry was the seat of the imagination (φαντασία).

Fr. 300 Smith

If it is considered improper to introduce any subsequent correction into the teachings of Plato, why then did Porphyry himself propose a number of not insignificant corrections? For it is beyond doubt that Plato wrote that the souls of men return after death and even enter into the bodies of beasts. This was also the view of Plotinus, the teacher of Porphyry. Nevertheless, Porphyry rejected it—and rightly so.[10] He considered that human souls return not into the bodies that they left but into other new bodies. Presumably, he was ashamed to hold that [traditional Platonist] theory, lest perhaps a mother come back as a mule and be ridden by her son! And yet he was not ashamed to hold a belief that would allow a mother's returning as a girl and marrying her own son. . . .[11] However, as I have said, Porphyry is very largely correct in his opinion, in that at least he held that it is only into men that human souls can be inserted: he had no doubt at all about abolishing their animal prisons. (= Augustine CD X 30, 1–10)

THE HISTORY OF PHILOSOPHY

The History of Philosophy (Φιλόσοφος ἱστορία) was a work in four books, that began with Thales, though with some prefatory material, and went down only as far as the death of Plato. It survives only in fragments, some of which we quote from the fourth book, concerning Plato's doctrines.

Fr. 220 Smith[1]

Porphyry states in the fourth book of his *History of Philosophy* that Plato held, and indeed explicitly states, the opinion about the One [who is]

---

[10] This would indeed be an important innovation by Porphyry, but there is some evidence that he was not entirely original here. We learn from the Nemesius *De Nat. Hom.* 2, p. 35, 4–5 Morani, that Cronius, the companion of Numenius, had maintained this position back in the second century C.E. in his treatise *On Reincarnation*.

[11] Following Smith, we omit a passage of Christian rhetoric by Augustine.

[1] This and the following passages present, as do a number of passages in the *Sentences* §§ 25–26, an apparently unequivocal account of a One, above Intellect and Being (or Essence), of an orthodox Plotinian type. The problem is how to

God, that no name is fitting to him nor can human understanding grasp him,[2] but that the titles bestowed upon him are improper usages borrowed from entities posterior to him. He says: "If we are to venture to say anything at all about him[3] relying on names familiar to us, it is particularly the titles 'the One' and 'the Good' that are to be attributed to him. The former emphasizes his simplicity, and hence his self-sufficiency, for he is in need of nothing—neither parts, nor substance, nor potencies, nor activities, but he is the cause of all these things [to others]. The epithet 'the Good,' on the other hand, establishes that it is from him that everything that is good comes, since other things imitate, so far as possible, this 'characteristic'[4] of it, if we may use the term, and are preserved in being through it." (= Cyril of Alexandria *Against Julian* I 31a–b)

Fr. 221 Smith

So Porphyry writes in the fourth book of his *History of Philosophy*: "Plato declared that the substance of the divine extends over three levels of reality.[5] The highest god is the Good, and after him and second there is the Demiurge, and third is the Soul of the Universe;[6] for the divine realm proceeds as far as Soul.[7] After that, what is bereft of divinity[8] takes its start from the realm of corporeal diversity."[9] But the aforementioned

---

reconcile these with Damascius' evidence to the contrary (see *Anonymous Commentary on Parmenides* [Frs. IV–VI *infra*]). Briefly, it is necessary to suppose that Porphyry made a distinction between the One "in itself" and the One as first principle of all things, the One in its latter aspect being the "father of the noetic triad."

[2] Probably a reference to the final section of the first hypothesis of the *Parmenides* 142A3–4.

[3] Or perhaps "it," referring to the first principle of Platonism—it is not clear whether Porphyry is using a neuter or a masculine pronoun in this passage.

[4] The Greek term is ἰδιότης.

[5] Or "principles." The Greek term is ὑποστάσεις. Cf. Plotinus V 1. 8, 1 ff.

[6] The first of these entities is, of course, the Good of *Republic*; the second and third are derived from *Timaeus*—the Demiurge, or creator god, being identified with Intellect in the Plotinian system, and the Soul of the Universe being identified with Soul.

[7] Cf. Plotinus V 1. 7, 48–9.

[8] In the context, this is what must be the meaning of τὸ ἄθεον.

[9] If that is the meaning of σωματικὴ διάφορα. The characterization of the realm of the corporeal and of matter as ἄθεος seems to betoken a more dualis-

authorities[10] oppose this scenario, asserting that one should not count in the One with what follows it, for it transcends all communion with anything else through being absolutely simple and not receptive of any association; the triad owes its preservation to Intellect—for it is the true first principle. (= Cyril C. *Iul.* VIII 271a, 916B3–15)

Fr. 222 Smith[11]

And again the same Porphyry about Plato: "Wherefore, hinting in riddles about these things, he says,[12] 'Around the king[13] are all things, and all are for his sake, and he is the cause of all that is fine, and around the second are the secondary things, and around the third the third.' [He says this] to establish that all things are related to these three gods, but primarily to the king of all, while secondarily to the god who proceeds from him and, on a tertiary level, to he who proceeds from him.[14] He[15] has clearly indicated here their existence apart from each other,[16] beginning from the king, and the stages of descent and declination of those after the first by the use of the terms 'firstly,' 'secondarily,' and 'thirdly' and that all things come from one [source], and are preserved in being by it."[17] (= Cyril C. *Iul.* I 34c, 553C9–D8)

---

tic system than one would expect from a follower of Plotinus, but perhaps this should not be taken too literally.

[10] This is a mysterious reference, since there is nothing in the previous text of Cyril to explain it. It may be, in fact, that Cyril is continuing to quote from, or at least summarize, Porphyry, in which case Porphyry must be referring to predecessors who disagree with him. This would be most significant, since the disagreement concerns how far the One is to be linked with what follows it, Porphyry wishing to assert a link with "the triad"—presumably Being (or Essence), Life, and Intellect.

[11] Cf. Plotinus I 8. 2, 28–32; V 1. 8, 1 ff.

[12] A quotation here of the notable passage of Plato [?] *2nd Ep.* 312E.

[13] The original has "king *of all*," and πάντων may well have dropped out here, since it is included in the resumptive passage just below.

[14] That is to say, Intellect, or the Demiurge, and the Soul of the Universe respectively (though this latter entity is here referred to, in the masculine, as a *god*).

[15] This is either Porphyry referring to Plato or Cyril referring to Porphyry—it is not at all clear which, but it matters little for our purpose.

[16] The Greek words are τὴν ἐξ ἀλλήλων ὑπόστασιν.

[17] Cf. Plotinus V 3. 15, 28; VI 7. 23, 22.

Fr. 223 Smith

Porphyry says in the fourth book of his *History of Philosophy* that Plato speaks about the Good as follows: "From this, in a manner incomprehensible to humans, there derives Intellect as a whole and self-substantiated, in which are to be found true beings and the whole substance of beings. It is this that is the primarily beautiful and the Beautiful Itself, having the Form of Beauty derived from itself, and it has proceeded preeternally[18] taking its start from god as a cause, being self-generated and father of itself;[19] for it was not by reason of the former's [that is, the One's] motion towards the generation of the latter that the procession came about,[20] but through this latter's coming forth self-generatively from god, though coming forth not at any point in time (for time did not yet exist) but even when time did come into existence, it was still of no relevance to it, for Intellect is always timeless and uniquely eternal. And even as the first god remains one and alone always, even if all things derive from him, by neither being counted with them nor allowing their value to be ranked with his mode of existence,[21] so also Intellect, which is solely eternal and came to exist nontemporally, is itself the time of all things that have their being in time while remaining in the identity of its own eternal existence." (= Cyril, *C. Iul.* I 32cd, 552B1–C8)

COMMENTARY ON PARMENIDES

The attribution of this work, which is found only (and in a fragmentary state) in a palimpsest in Milan that was subsequently destroyed in a fire in the library, is still disputed, but we accept the attribution to Porphyry, proposed originally by Pierre Hadot, as at least extremely probable. The doctrine on the One, in particular, propounded here accords well with what we know of Porphyry's finely nuanced position.

---

[18] Reading προαιωνίως as suggested by Pierre Hadot, rather than the adjectival form, προαιώνιος.

[19] The Greek is αὐτογέννητος καὶ αὐτοπάτωρ, a rather colorful way of expressing the Plotinian doctrine of the self-substantiation of Intellect from the One.

[20] Cf. Plotinus III 4. 1, 1.

[21] The Greek word is ὕπαρξις.

Fr. IV[1]

... brings them[2] to birth in himself, from previous nonexistence. But those who declare[3] that he "has snatched himself away" from all that belongs to him, grant him both Power and Intellect as unified in his simplicity, and also another Intellect, and, although they have not removed him from the triad, they think it proper to eliminate number in his regard, so that they absolutely refuse to say that he is the One.

All this may be, in a way, a correct and true account, especially if it is the case that, as those say who have handed down this tradition, it is gods that have proclaimed these things, but it does surpass all human understanding; indeed, it is as if one were to speak to people blind from birth about the differences between colors, introducing concepts expressed in speech relating to things that transcend all speech as regards their presentation, with the result that the hearers receive on the one hand true statements concerning colors but yet have no idea what color is, since they do not possess the faculty by which color is naturally apprehended. Even so, we lack any faculty for the apprehension of god (even if those who produce any sort of representation of him try to explain to us through reasoning how it is possible to attain an understanding of him), since he remains superior to any reasoning and any conception, in view of the ignorance of him in which we are placed.

If this is indeed so,[4] then those who, in the quest for knowledge of him, give precedence to what he is not are better advised than those who inquire into what he is, even if what the latter say is true, since we are incapable of understanding what is being said, for even if we understand something about him with respect to what they declare to be his attributes and rise to some conception of him by grasping or otherwise

---

[1] This passage seems to come from a commentary on the end of the first hypothesis of *Parm.* 141E–142A. We seem to have here an important statement of Porphyry's rather subtle doctrine of the One, according to which it is both completely simple, when regarded *in itself,* and at the same time "father of the noetic triad" and so triadic when viewed in its relation to what is below it.

[2] What these (feminine) entities might be is quite uncertain, but they could be "powers" (δυνάμεις), such as Power and Intellect, discussed just below.

[3] Porphyry seems here to be indulging in some irony at the expense of the authors of the *Chaldean Oracles.*

[4] Porphyry now embarks on an interesting discourse on negative theology, accompanied by some shrewd comments on "analogical" language about the supreme principle.

taking on board examples taken from this world, these same people then turn around and give it as their view that we should not understand what they have said in a literal sense but should distance ourselves from these characterizations and, in general, from an understanding of god based on such concepts; and so this comes to be the end result of the teaching of these things that were just previously presented as his attributes. It would no doubt serve remarkably well for the purification of our concept [of god] if, after learning of his supposed attributes, one were to abandon these also, seeing as this would be abandonment of the greatest things and of those that would have been conceived as immediately following from god himself!

Now the Stoics do not give up the notion that apprehension of reality might come about on the basis of some reasoning, but they do maintain that it is impossible to apprehend the god who is above all things,[5] never mind by reasoning, but not even through intuition,[6] for the situation is hopeless, they say, if, when the soul is seeking to know not *of what kind* something is [its quality] but *what it is* [its essence] and to gain knowledge of the essential nature of its being and of its substance, all the cognitive powers, which report on the quality of something, do not report on that which we are looking for according to [our] desire but on what we are not looking for. But god is not a being of a certain quality, but his being prior to being[7] has even removed him from both being and the "it is"; it [the soul] does not have a criterion for the knowledge of him, but sufficient for it is the image of the ignorance of him, which refuses any form that is present in a knowing subject. So, one can know neither him himself nor the mode of the procession of secondary entities from him and through him or by him. But they actually do try to expound him, those who have ventured to intimate his characteristic qualities, and they try also, by getting a grasp on the things around him, [to expound their nature too].

---

[5] This expression for the supreme deity is found also in Porphyry's *De Abst.* I 57; II 49, and *VP.* 23, 16, as well as at I 4 of the present work. It seems to be a favored term of Porphyry's.

[6] The Greek word is νόησις.

[7] This seems to be the first use of the term προούσιον in extant Greek literature.

Fr. V[8]

... in the case of the second [One], though he [Plato] has passed on to treat of being, not of what participates in being, he produces a different argument, as though he were talking about what participates in being.[9]

So if, having hypothesized being, he had said that it participated in being, the reasoning would have been paradoxical; but if, as he says, having put forward the One [as his principle], it participates in being, we must realize that, because it is no longer the One in its pure form, but the property of being [one] has changed with it [that is, with the change of reference to the second One], it is for this reason that he says that it participates in being. It is as if one were to say, having chosen "animal," as a definition of "human being," that it participated in "rational," although in fact "human being" is "rational animal" as a single entity, and "animal" has changed along with "rational" as well as "rational" with "animal," for in this case as well One has both changed along with being and being with One, and there is not simply a juxtaposition of One and being.

Nor is the One a subject and being [considered] as an accident of it. But there is a particular nature of the entity,[10] on the one hand imitating the simplicity of the One, while on the other hand not remaining in the pure form of it but bringing it [oneness] around with it to being, for since it was not the first One, and the second is not owing to anything other than the first, it follows that it is not the same as the first, since in that case neither would it be different nor would it be derived from that

---

[8] This passage concerns the beginning of the second hypothesis, *Parm.* 142B. Porphyry's position here seems to be that while both the first and second hypotheses concern the One, the first presents it in its "pure" form, in relation to itself, whereas the second presents it as in relation to Being and so somehow "contaminated" by Being. This is significantly different from the position of both his master Plotinus and of his successors, who took the second hypothesis as concerning, rather, Intellect. Proclus, admittedly, in his *In Parm.* 1053, 38 ff., declares that Porphyry took as the subject of the first hypothesis "the primal god," and as the subject of the second the intelligible realm, but we must take him to be oversimplifying somewhat. In fact, as "father of the noetic triad," the supreme god can be regarded as already part of the intelligible realm.

[9] The words τὸ ὄν ("being") μετέχει ("participates") in being (οὐσίας) rest on Porphyry's understanding that while the primary One transcends being, it is false that it does not exist. Hence, it has being in some sense, though not in the sense implied by participating in οὐσία. The οὐσία participated in is finite or limited being or essence.

[10] The Greek word is ὑπόστασις.

nor would it have gone out of and away from that, having the cause of its procession from another.

But since it is from that, it is on the one hand certainly One, too; but because it is not that, this whole thing is One Being, whereas that is One alone, for how could One change into One unless the one were pure One, and the other not pure? For this reason, this latter both is and is not that [the first One] at the same time, because that which comes after something and is derived from something is, in a way, that from which and after which it is and is also something else, which is not only not that from which it is, but may also be perceived as possessing the contrary attributes. And so, in this case, that is One alone, but this is One-All; and that is One without Being, but this is One endowed with Being;[11] and being endowed with Being and being "essentialized"[12] are what Plato means by saying that it "participates in Being";[13] not, we may note, postulating Being and saying that *Being* participates in Being, but postulating One, but a One that is essentialized—he says that *that* participates in Being.

But one might perhaps argue that it is because the second derives from the first that the second is said to be "one" by participation in the first—the whole, which is One Being, having come about by participation in the One; and since it has not first come into existence and then participated in the One but came into existence by declination[14] from the One, it was not described as participating in the One but rather as a One participating in Being, not because the First was a Being, but because difference from the One has led it around to this whole being one, for in a sense it is because of its having become One in a secondary mode that it has taken on the status of One Being.

But consider whether Plato may not seem to be talking in riddles here, since the One that is beyond Being and beyond existing [finitely],[15] is, on the one hand, neither the existent nor Being nor actuality but is rather,

---

[11] The only other place where these two adjectives, ἀνούσιον and ἐνούσιον, are found in conjunction is Marius Victorinus, *Adversus Arium* (I 50, 24–5), a work which is imbued with Porphyrian metaphysics.

[12] The rare term οὐσιῶσθαι is also found at *Sent.* §39, p. 47, 3 and §41, p. 52, 8, 9, 14 Lamberz as well as Porphyry's *In Cat.* p. 99, 7 Busse.

[13] *Parm.* 142B6.

[14] The Greek word is ὑφείμενον.

[15] The words ἐπέκεινα οὐσίας καὶ ὄντος refer to Plato *Rep.* 509B6–10 where the Good (= the One, for Porphyry) is the cause of τὸ εἶναί τε καὶ τὴν οὐσίαν, while not itself either.

on the other hand, *actualizing itself,* and is, indeed, pure *act,* even as it is essential "is-ness,"[16] which is prior to Being, by participation in which the [second] One comes to possess an "is-ness" that has declined from it, and this is what it means to participate in Being. So, then, there are two levels of "is-ness":[17] one exists prior to Being, the other is produced by the One that is beyond that which is and that is absolutely [Being] and, as it were, the Idea of Being, by participating in which another One has come into being, to which is linked the "is-ness" that is produced by it. It is as though you were to form the concept of a "white being" . . . [18]

Fr. VI[19]

. . . not being able to enter into itself, for by what means will it be able to see itself, this entity that cannot enter into itself, other than by virtue of the One? And how will it be able to see itself as that into which it cannot enter? And what is this faculty that, in the mode of identity, will be able to lay hold of either of these two aspects in their partitioned state? What is it that is in a position to say that that which thinks and that which is thought are different? Or to see both when that which thinks unites itself with that which is thought and when it cannot?

It is clear, then, that this is a level of activity that is over and above those, transcending all of them and making use of them all as instruments, laying hold of them all while at the same time not being *in* any of them. Each of the others is fixed in relation to something and assigned to it totally, in respect of both its form and of its name, but this is related to nothing; therefore, it has neither form nor name nor substance, for it is not controlled in any respect, but it is not even given

---

[16] The Greek is αὐτὸ τὸ εἶναι.

[17] The Greek is διττὸν τὸ εἶναι.

[18] This concept of the mutual "contamination" of One and Being, which results in their combining to form something that is distinct from either of them, is a subtle and distinctive notion.

[19] This passage appears to be a comment on *Parm.* 143A. The problem that Porphyry is addressing here seems related to that which Plotinus raises at the beginning of V 3: "Must that which thinks itself be complex in order that, with some one part of itself contemplating the others, it could in this way be said to think itself, on the grounds that were it altogether simple, it would not be able to revert to itself, that is, there could not be the grasping of itself? Or is it possible for that which is not composite also to think itself?"

form by anything, being essentially incapable of being affected and essentially inseparable from itself, being neither intelligence, nor object of intelligence, nor substance, but beyond everything and the unconnected[20] cause of everything.

So, just as sight is not capable of grasping the audible; or hearing, the visible; or either of them, the tasteable; and as each does not even know that it is different from the other and that the audible is different from the visible, still, there is another power transcending these,[21] which distinguishes between them and knows their identity and difference and substance and condition and can grasp them all and employ them as instruments by reason of its being superior to and transcending them; even so, the power, too—according to which that intellect sees that is unable to enter itself—must be other, differing from the thought process[22] that distinguishes thinking and the intelligible, and being beyond those in seniority and power.

And so, though being One and simple, "this itself"[23] nevertheless differs from itself in act and existence, and it is thus One and simple in one aspect but differs from itself in another, for that which differs from the One is not One, and that which differs from the simple is not simple. Thus it is One and simple according to its first Idea, that is, according to the Idea of "this itself," taken in relation to itself—Idea or power or whatever we are to call it merely for the sake of identification, ineffable and inapprehensible as it is—but not One and not simple on the level of existence and life and intelligence.[24]

Both the element that thinks and that which is thought enjoy existence, but the thinking element, if the mind passes from existence to the thinking element in order to return to the intelligible and to see itself, is in life. For this reason, on the level of life, intellect is undetermined. And whereas all are activities, an activity on the level of existence is an activity at rest, an activity on the level of thinking is an

---

[20] The metaphor ἀσύζυγος probably indicates here an absence of reciprocal relatedness. Thus, things can be related to the One, but it is not related to anything else. Cf. Plotinus VI 7. 23, 17–18.

[21] A creative use, here, of Aristotle's doctrine of the "common sense" (κοινὴ αἴσθησις) at De An. Γ 2, 426b8 ff.

[22] The Greek word is ἐπίνοια.

[23] Plato Parm. 143A9.

[24] Note the use here of the three "moments" of the noetic triad, Being (or Essence), Life, and Intellect.

activity turning towards itself, and one on the level of life is an activity descending from existence.

And in this aspect, it is at rest and is in motion at the same time, is in itself and in another, is a whole and has parts, and is the same and is different, but in that aspect of it that is purely and simply One, and, as it were, first and really One, it is neither at rest nor in motion, neither the same nor different, neither in itself nor in another. And that it is neither an object of thought nor acting, neither in relation to itself nor another, . . .

COMMENTARY ON TIMAEUS

This work, which seems to have covered the whole dialogue, is known only from references in Proclus' commentary on the same dialogue, and from Macrobius' commentary on Cicero's Dream of Scipio. It is criticized by Proclus (and apparently by Iamblichus before him) for inadequate attention to metaphysical subtleties, but it was probably, for them, the chief source of knowledge for Middle Platonic and earlier interpretations of the dialogue.

Fr. LXXIX Sodano[1]

The commentators from the school of Plato,[2] on the other hand, in their investigation of the cause of this, have related the origin of the equality and inequality of the circuits to the vital principles[3] of the planets concerned, as indeed Porphyry and Theodorus declare. According to them, the equality or inequality of speed is a function of the direct or

---

[1] This forms part of the discussion of a problem arising from the exegesis of *Tim.* 38D—which concerns the circuits of the heavenly bodies—as to why the speeds of the circuits of the Sun, Venus, and Mercury are, overall, the same, while those of the other planets vary. Proclus has given the opinion of "the mathematicians" just before this.

[2] As emerges just below, these are, in fact, Porphyry and Theodorus of Asine. How much of the present formulation may be due to Theodorus is not clear, but the basic scheme, at least, must go back to Porphyry. This passage is of interest because it shows Porphyry making creative use in his exegesis of the intelligible or noetic triad: Being (or Essence), Life, Intellect (cf. *supra* Fr. 284 Smith).

[3] The Greek word is ζωαί.

mediated relation of the intellects [of these planets] to the essence and whether they tend towards the same goal, even if through different intermediaries, or towards different ones in each case. Thus, the Sun, *qua* Essence, proceeds towards Intellect via Life; Venus is Intellect, certainly, but proceeds towards Intellect via Life; Mercury is Life, but proceeds via Essence to Intellect; and even if Intellect is the goal of the reversion of all three, yet, in the one case, it is of the essential order; in another, of the intellectual; and in another, of the vital. And that is why these planets, though moving at different speeds and giving the appearance of alternately passing each other and leaving each other behind, yet all finish at the same point.

As for Saturn and Jupiter and Mars, it is possible that they belong to different divisions [of Intellect], and, for that reason, that they are not of the same speed. If, however, they belong to the same, they will be of unequal speed, either because they do not return to the same goal or because they do not do that through an equal number of intermediaries. For example, if Saturn, being Essence, proceeds to Essence without any intermediary, if Jupiter proceeds to it via Intellect alone, and if Mars does so via Intellect and Life, one will rest in Essence immediately, the second via one intermediary, and the third via two, and so they will not be equal in speed. In fact, among the planets, the first triad is directed towards Essence, the second towards Intellect, and the Moon towards Life, because it [Life] comprehends within itself the whole of generation and proceeds as far as the ultimate recesses of the earth.

This, then, is the view of Porphyry and Theodorus, pursuing their own distinctive hypotheses, declaring that all—Being (or Essence) and Life and Intellect—are everywhere. They postulate that each of the gods participates in all three fathers,[4] but that a different property predominates in each; that the activity of each is different in each one of them; and that their ascent to their goal is through different intermediaries. (= Proclus *In Tim.* III 64, 8–65, 7 Diehl)

---

[4] Using a Chaldean term for the three "moments" of the intelligible realm.

Commentary on Categories[1]

This is Porphyry's short commentary, in the form of questions and answers, on Aristotle's Categories, which has survived intact. His big commentary, dedicated to his pupil Gedalios, is known to us from Simplicius' commentary on the same work, which actually preserves large portions of it, as does also the commentary of Iamblichus.

Q: On the basis of this one, is there another objection that follows?

A: I would say that there are those who object that, according to his [Aristotle's] own view, it is actually intelligible entities that are said most strictly and above all and primarily to be substances in the primary sense—to wit, the intelligible god and intellect[2] and the Forms, if there are Forms, but he ignores these and claims that it is individuals in the sensible realm that are primary substances.

Q: And so how would you solve this difficulty for him?

A: I shall say that since the subject of the work is significant expressions, and expressions are applied primarily to sensibles—for men assign names first of all to what they know and perceive, and only secondarily to those things that are primary by nature but secondary with respect to perception—it is reasonable for him to have called the things that are primarily signified by expressions, that is, sensibles and individuals, primary substances. Thus with respect to significant expressions, sensible individuals are primary substances, but from the perspective of nature, intelligible substances are primary. However, his intention is to distinguish the genera of being according to the expressions that signify them, and these primarily signify individual sensible substances.[3]

Q: But, granted that "species" and "genus" are used homonymously, which species and which genera is he speaking about?

---

[1] This passage will serve as a good example of Porphyry's defense and appropriation of Aristotle. He is able to do this by putting forward the position that Plato and Aristotle are really talking about different things and so are not in conflict. For this passage we have benefited from consulting the excellent translation of Steven Strange, in *Porphyry, On Aristotle Categories*, Duckworth: London, 1992, pp. 81–4.

[2] It is not quite clear whether these two appellations are intended to refer to Aristotle's Unmoved Mover or, rather, to the Neoplatonic One and Intellect, respectively.

[3] Porphyry is here able to treat the secondary substances, species and genera, not as Platonic Forms but rather as "universals" abstractable from the contemplation of particulars, in the Aristotelian manner.

A: Those he calls secondary substances.

Q: And how has he indicated this?

A: I reply that he did so when he says, in effect, "Do not think that I am speaking of the genera of any other species—that is, the species of any other individuals, such as individual accidents—but rather of those species to which individual substances belong, as well as the genera of those species." He himself explains what he means when he says, "the particular man belongs in man as a species, and animal is the genus of this species." (Aristotle *Cat.* 2a16–7)

Q: You have sufficiently indicated, then, why it is individuals that are the primary substances. Now you need to teach us why the genera and species of individual substances are secondary substances.

A: I claim that it is reasonable to call the genera and species of primary substances secondary substances, for they are the only predicates that reveal primary substance. If someone states what Socrates is, he will do so properly if he gives his species and genus, and he will be more informative if he says "man" or "animal" than if he gives any of the other nine categories, for if he gives any of those others, he will not strictly have answered the question—for example, if he says "white" or "three cubits tall" or "moist" or "running" or any thing like that, for such predications are accidental and do not belong to the nature of the subject, not indicating *what it is*, but predications of the species and genus are proper to its nature. Therefore, it is reasonable that of the other items besides primary substances, only the species and genera of substances are said to be secondary substances.

Q: Could you give yet another reason why the species and genera of primary substances are said to be secondary substances?

A: I would say that this is because species and genera possess the greatest degree of similarity to primary substances, for those are said to be substances in the strictest sense, because they are subjects for all other items, but the species and genera stand in the same sort of relation to all the others, for the remaining items, that is to say the accidents, are predicated of them, for just as it is possible to say, speaking paronymously, that a particular man is educated in grammar and is three cubits tall and has other accidents, so one can also say that a man and an animal are educated in grammar and three cubits tall. For this reason, secondary substances are predicated synonymously of primary substances, since in general everything that is predicated of something as a subject is synonymously predicated of that subject; for since man is predicated of particular man as a subject, man in this case will be predicated synonymously, since Socrates is both a man and a mortal rational animal. The other items, the accidents, do not correspond in account to substances, though in some cases they will be predicated of substances in name, as white is predicated of body—for one can say that a body is white—but not in other cases, for "whiteness" cannot be said of body. However, the account of white can never be said of a body, for a body is not "a color that pierces the eyes."[4]

Q: Next, since you have stated that the secondary substances are the species and genera, are we to take it that both of these have an equal status in relation to primary substances?

A: Not at all. The species is more a substance than the genus.

Q: Why is that?

A: The species is nearer to the individual substance than is the genus, for if one is giving a definition of a primary substance, it will be nearer the mark for him to give the species than the genus; for example, to say that the item in question is a man rather than that it is an animal. But a thing nearer to something that is more a substance will itself be more a substance, for one of them, that is, "man," is closer and more proper to the particular man, while "animal" is of more general application.

Q: Could you give another reason that you might use to show that the species is more a substance than the genus?

A: Primary substances are said to be substances most of all because they are the subjects for everything else, and everything else is said of them, either predicated of them as a subject or being in them as a subject. But the case of the species is similar, for primary substances bear the same sort of relation to their species and genus that the species bears to the genus, and the primary substances bear the same relation to the accidents that the species does. The species is a subject for the genus, which is predicated of it as a subject, for that is how the genera are predicated of the species. Similarly, the species is a subject for the accidents, and they are in it as a subject. So, the species is more a substance for these reasons as well. But none of the species and genera that do not fall under one another is more a substance than any other, even though one may be of more value than another, for it is no more proper to say of the particular man that he is a man than to say of the particular horse that it is a horse. And the same is true in the case of primary substances: for even though Socrates is more valuable than the horse Bucephalos, he would not, for that reason, be said to be more a substance than Bucephalos. (Pp. 91, 12–93, 24 Busse)

---

[4] The standard Platonist definition of the color "white," χρῶμα διακριτικὸν ὄψεως. Cf. Plato Tim. 67E.

ON PRINCIPLES

It is known from the Suda *that* On Principles *(Περὶ ἀρχῶν) was a work in two books, presumably discussing such topics as the One, Intellect, Soul, and matter, but all we have of it is this one fragment, preserved by Proclus.*

Fr. 232 Smith[1]

Porphyry, in turn, following on him [Plotinus],[2] in his treatise *On Principles*, demonstrates, through a large number of excellent arguments, that Intellect is eternal but that nonetheless it possesses within itself an element that is preeternal[3] and that the preeternal element of Intellect is linked with the One (for that is beyond all eternity) and the eternal holds a second rank, or rather a tertiary rank, within it, for, I presume,[4] eternity is established in the middle between the preeternal and the eternal. (= Proclus *Platonic Theology* I 11, p. 51, 4–11 S–W)

FROM DAMASCIUS *On Principles (De Principiis)*

Fr. 367 Smith[1]

After this let us bring up the following point for consideration, whether the first principles before the first intelligible triad are two in number — the completely ineffable and that which is unconnected to the triad — as is the view of the great Iamblichus in the twenty-eighth book of his work on *The Most Perfect Theology of the Chaldeans* — or, as the great major-

---

[1] Cf. Proclus *ET* Props. 87–8.
[2] Proclus has just been referring to Plotinus' treatise *On Numbers* (VI 6. 9 and 16), but one could think also of Plotinus' VI 7. 35 and its distinction between "Intellect in its right mind," and "Intellect drunk on nectar" — the latter aspect being that with which Intellect unites with the One.
[3] The Greek is προαιώνιον τι.
[4] This is Proclus inserting himself into the discussion, but he is presumably basing himself on Porphyry's own doctrine.

[1] This passage concerns Iamblichus and Porphyry equally, but it seems best to place it here.

ity of those after him preferred to hold, whether the first triad of the intelligible realm follows directly after the ineffable single first cause; or shall we go lower than this hypothesis, too, and say with Porphyry that the first principle of all things is the father of the noetic triad?[2] (= Damascius *On Principles*, ch. 43, I 86, 3–10 Ruelle)

FROM IAMBLICHUS *On the Soul, De Anima*

§6.[1] Let us now ascend to the consideration of that substance that is of itself incorporeal, distinguishing in order all the opinions about the soul in relation to it also. There are some who maintain that such a substance as a whole is homogeneous and one and the same such that all of it may be found in any part of it, and they place even the individual soul in the intelligible world, and gods and daemons and the Good and all the beings superior to it, and declare everything to be in each thing in the same way but in a manner appropriate to its essence. Numenius is unambiguously of this opinion; Plotinus, not completely consistently; while Amelius is unstable in his allegiance to it; as for Porphyry, he is of two minds on the subject, now dissociating himself violently from this

---

[2] That is to say, the "father" of the Chaldean triad of father-power of the father-intellect of the father (cf. *Or. Chald.* Frs. 3–4 Des Places), the ancestor of the Neoplatonic intelligible triad of Being (Essence)-Life-Intellect. Damascius goes on (ll. 11–5) to condemn this doctrine of Porphyry's as a gross metaphysical oversimplification, but in fact it reveals a most interesting stance on Porphyry's part, which proved most fruitful for Christian Trinitarian speculation.

[1] Iamblichus is here, as throughout his *De Anima*, concerned to distinguish his own position on the soul from that of his immediate predecessors, Plotinus, Amelius, and Porphyry. Iamblichus is here concerned to put all of his immediate predecessors in the same box. Numenius would seem to have been the first to propound the formula, " All things in all things, but in each in a manner proper to its essence." As for Plotinus, a passage such as III 4. 3, 22 ff. (not included in this volume) would support Iamblichus' case, though Plotinus does recognize an ontological difference between soul and the entities superior to it, as made clear, for instance, in V 1. In the case of Amelius, we are precluded, by lack of evidence, from knowing what degree of vacillation Iamblichus is referring to, but in Porphyry's case we can point to, on the one hand, §10 of the *Sentences*, where he virtually repeats Numenius' original formulation; on the other hand, at §30 (not included in this volume) he makes a sharp distinction between the modes of activity of the higher realities, down to and including universal soul. These, however, would probably not be the passages that Iamblichus has in mind.

view, now adopting it as a doctrine handed down from above.[2] According to this doctrine, the soul differs in no way from intellect and the gods and the superior classes of being, at least in respect to its substance in general.[3] (= Stobaeus *Anth.* I 365 W-H)

§17. Do all souls perform the same acts, or are universal souls more perfect, while those of other souls correspond to the appropriate rank of which each partakes? As far as the Stoics are concerned, reason is one; intellection, absolutely identical; right actions, equal; and the virtues, the same in the case of both the individual and the universal souls; Plotinus and Amelius are presumably of this opinion also (for on occasion they define the individual soul as being no different from the universal but as being one with it); but according to Porphyry, on the other hand, the activities of the universal soul are totally distinct from the individual soul.[4] (= Stobaeus *Anth.* I 372 W-H)

§23. There has been much controversy[5] within the Platonic school itself, one group bringing together into one system and form the various types and parts of life and its activities—as, for example, Plotinus and Porphyry—another, exemplified by Numenius, setting them up in conflict with each other, and another, again, reconciling them from a postulated original strife—as, for example, Atticus and Plutarch...

The activities that induce the soul to descend are caused, according to Plotinus, by the "primary difference";[6] according to Empedocles, by

---

[2] Or possibly, "as handed down from former times," since ἄνωθεν could also have that meaning.

[3] As can be seen from *Sent.* §10 (*supra* p. 178), Porphyry is prepared to adopt the formula of Numenius about "all things being in all, but in a manner appropriate to each," but in such a passage as *Sent.* §30, on the other hand (not reproduced here), he does make a sharp distinction between the mode of activity of the higher beings, down to and including universal soul, which generate what is below them without turning their attention towards their products, and particular souls, which are compelled to do this. But Iamblichus may well be relying on other passages from works which are lost to us.

[4] There seems to be some justification for this assertion in *Sent.* §37 (itself largely based on Plotinus VI 4. 40), where Porphyry does assert the distinctness of Soul as a whole from the many individual souls, but we must assume that Iamblichus is relying on works not available to us.

[5] Officially on the subject of the variety of "acts" (ἔργα) attributable to both universal and individual souls, which is the subject of this section of Iamblichus' work, but this section really concerns the question of the essential unity or otherwise of the human soul, and the causes of its descent into matter.

[6] See Plotinus V 1. 1.

the "flight from god;" according to Heraclitus, by the "rest that consists in change";[7] according to the Gnostics, by "derangement and deviation"; according to Albinus, by "the erring judgment of a free will." While of those who are at variance with these thinkers and who would attach evil to the soul from elements that have accrued to it from outside, Numenius and Cronius in many places derive it from matter; Harpocration, also, on occasion, from the very nature of bodies; while Plotinus and Porphyry most of the time derive it from nature and the nonrational life.[8] (= Stobaeus *Anth.* I 378–9 W-H)

§37. Plotinus and his school, on the other hand, champion the opinion[9] that separates the nonrational faculties from the reasoning element, either releasing them into the realm of generation or separating them from the discursive reason. From this opinion arises a choice between two doctrines: either each nonrational faculty is freed into the whole life of the universe from which it was detached, where each remains as far as possible unchanged, as Porphyry thinks; or the whole nonrational life continues to exist, separated from the discursive reasoning and preserved in the cosmos, as the most ancient of the priests declare.[10] (= Stobaeus *Anth.* I 384 W-H)

---

[7] Both these are quoted in Plotinus IV 8. 1, which Iamblichus presumably has in mind.

[8] It is not very clear what Iamblichus is thinking of here, but for Plotinus one might adduce such a passage as IV 4. 44, 31 ff., where Plotinus talks of the "magic of nature" leading us astray; and for Porphyry, *De Abst.* III 27, where we find the remark, "For in many people the motions and the needs of nonrational nature are the first stimulus to injustice."

[9] The subject here is the fate of the rational and nonrational parts of the soul after death. Porphyry's doctrine is that the nonrational faculties are detached from the reasoning element and returned to the ethereal bodies from which they originated.

[10] This is actually the view of Iamblichus himself. Cf. *In Tim.* Fr. 81 Dillon.

IAMBLICHUS

On the Mysteries of the Egyptians

The correct title of this work is The Reply of the Master Abammon to the Letter of Porphyry to Anebo and the Solutions to the Difficulties Raised Therein. *Its customary modern title was conferred upon it by Marsilio Ficino. Porphyry's* Letter, *whether to a real or an imaginary recipient, consisted of a series of critical questions concerning theurgic belief and practice.*[1] *Iamblichus' work (in which he shelters behind the pseudonym of Abammon, Anebo's superior in the Egyptian priestly college) is an extended defense of theurgy and its basis in Neoplatonic theology.*

Book I 1–3

1. Hermes, the god who presides over rational discourse, has long been considered, quite rightly, to be the common patron of all priests; he who presides over true knowledge about the gods is one and the same always and everywhere. It is to him that our ancestors in particular dedicated the fruits of their wisdom, attributing all their own writings to Hermes. And if we for our part receive from this god our due share of favor, such as we are capable of receiving, you, for your part, do well in laying before the priests questions about theology such as they love to deal with,[2]

---

[1] It is unknown whether this letter, is to a real or fictitious recipient. It consists of a series of critical questions concerning both the theurgical practices of popular religion, especially divination, and the gods. Iamblichus' work is an extended defense of theurgy and of its basis in Neoplatonic theology. One of the principal texts that inspired theurgical practices from Porphyry onward is the so-called *Chaldean Oracles*, a collection of verses written, or perhaps collected, approximately during the late 2nd c. C.E. Basically theurgy consists of ritualistic practices aimed at communicating with divinity. It is rooted in the interpretations of Platonic philosophy generally recognized as Middle Platonism (roughly 80 B.C.E.–220 C.E.). At least from the time of Porphyry The *Chaldean Oracles* were generally taken by Neoplatonists as an authentic source of religious and philosophical truth. Cf. *infra* II 11 (p. 356); V 15–17; Proclus *PT* I 25, p.113, 6–10 S-W.

[2] Or, accepting Sicherl's conjecture ὡς εἰδόσι for ὡς φιλοῦσι, "as being the experts."

which pertain to their technical expertise,³ and at the same time it is reasonable for me—assuming the letter sent to my student Anebo to be addressed equally well to me—to grant you a true reply to your enquiries, for it would not be right for Pythagoras and Plato and Democritus and Eudoxus and many other of the Hellenes of old⁴ to have been granted suitable instruction by the scribes of their time, but for you in our time, who have the same purpose as they, to fail guidance at the hands of those who are accounted public teachers in our own time.

So, in view of this, I am presenting myself to take up the discussion, and you, for your part, if you will, imagine that the same person is now replying to you as he to whom you wrote; or, if it seems better to you, posit that it is I who am discoursing with you in writing, or any other prophet of the Egyptians—for it makes no difference. Or, better still, I think, dismiss from your mind the speaker, whether he be better or worse, and consider what is said, whether it be true or false, rousing up your intellect to the task with enthusiasm.

At the outset, perhaps we should identify the number and types of problem that have been set before us. We should also examine from what theological perspectives the questions are being raised and demonstrate what the branches of knowledge are according to which they are being pursued.

Some questions, then, call for the clarification of issues that have been wrongly confused, while others concern the reason why various things are the way they are and are thought of in such a way; others again draw one's attention in both directions at once, since they contain an inherent contradiction; and still others call for an exposition of our whole mystical system.⁵ This being the case, they are taken from many perspectives and from very various branches of knowledge.

Some, in fact, require us to address them on the basis of the traditions of the sages of Chaldea; others will derive their solution from the teachings of the prophets of Egypt; and others again, which relate to the speculations of the philosophers, require to be answered on that basis.⁶ There

---

³ If that is the meaning of εἰς γνῶσιν.

⁴ There are traditions connected with all of these great men visiting Egypt. For Pythagoras, see Herodotus II 81; Isocrates *Bus.* 28; Diodorus Siculus I 69, 4; 92, 2; 98, 2 (from Hecataeus of Abdera). For Plato, see Cicero *Fin.* V 29, 87; *Rep.* I 10, 16; Diodorus Siculus I 96, 2. For Democritus and Eudoxus, see ibid., and, for Democritus, see D.L. IX 35.

⁵ That is to say, system of theurgy.

⁶ The "sages of Chaldea" here is a reference to the *Chaldean Oracles*, while "the prophets of Egypt" will be substantially Hermes Trismegistus, whom

are also some that, deriving from other opinions not worthy of notice, involve one in unseemly controversy, while others are drawn from the common conceptions of men.[7] Each of these problems, then, appear in complex aspects and are variously related to one another and for all these reasons demand a mode of exposition which will organize them suitably.

2. We, then, propose both to transmit to you truthfully our opinion concerning the ancestral doctrines of the Assyrians and to reveal clearly to you our own views, drawing, by reasoning some from the innumerable writings of antiquity, and others from the limited corpus[8] in which the ancients later gathered the totality of their knowledge of things divine.

But if you put forward a philosophical question, we will settle this, too, for you by recourse to the ancient stelae of Hermes, to which Plato before us, and Pythagoras too, gave careful study in the establishment of their philosophies;[9] while we will solve problems derived from alien[10] sources or of a self-contradictory and contentious inspiration gently and harmoniously—or else we will make clear their absurdity. Such, again, as proceed from common conceptions[11] we will try to discuss with both understanding and clarity.

Some of these, such as require experience of actions[12] for their accurate understanding, it will not be possible [to deal with adequately] by

---

Iamblichus quotes later in the work. As for (Hellenic) philosophy, we shall see, on many occasions, "Abammon" exhibiting a good knowledge both of Platonism and of the teaching of other schools.

[7] The identity of these οὐκ ἄξια λόγου δοξάσματα is not clear but could be a reference to the beliefs of vulgar magic; the same would be true of the "common conceptions" (κοιναὶ ὑπολήψεις).

[8] This πεπερασμένον βιβλίον may be a reference to something like our present Hermetic Corpus, as opposed to the fabled 20,000 or 36,525 books of Hermes, of which he makes mention at the beginning of Book VIII.

[9] Proclus also makes reference to στῆλαι—in In Tim. I 102, 20–2 in his comment on the remark of the Egyptian priest at Timaeus 22B: "O Solon, Solon, you Hellenes remain always children"—but he does not explicitly assert that Plato or Pythagoras studied them. On the other hand, in Porphyry's V. Pythag. 7–8, we have quite an elaborate tale of Pythagoras' Egyptian studies, but without mention of στῆλαι.

[10] The precise significance of ἀλλόφυλα here is not quite clear. Does Abammon mean "non-Greek," "non-Egyptian," or just "nonphilosophical"? In any event, it is intended as an arch put-down of Porphyry.

[11] Κοιναὶ ἔννοιαι—presumably the same as the κοιναὶ ὑπολήψεις at the end of the previous chapter.

[12] That is, theurgy.

words alone; others that are replete with intellectual insight[13] [we will not be able] to clarify [completely], but one can reveal noteworthy indications of it,[14] on the basis of which both you and those like you can be led intellectually to the essence of true beings. Of such, finally, as are accessible to processes of logical reasoning, we will spare no effort in making a full demonstration. We will provide, in an appropriate manner, explanations proper to each, dealing in a theological mode with theological questions and in theurgical terms with those concerning theurgy, while we will join with you in examining philosophical issues in philosophical terms.[15] And these last, such as extend to the first causes, we will bring to light by pursuing them in accordance with first principles, while such as concern ethics or the goals of human existence we will deal with, as required, in an ethical mode; and we will deal in similar fashion with all other types of questions, in due order. And now let us turn to your questions.

3. You say first, then, that you "concede the existence of the gods";[16] but that is not the right way to put it, for an innate knowledge of the gods is coexistent with our nature and is superior to all judgement and choice,[17] reasoning and proof. This knowledge is united from the outset with its own cause and exists in tandem with the essential striving of the soul towards the Good.

Indeed, to tell the truth, the contact we have with the divinity is not to be taken as knowledge. Knowledge, after all, is separated [from its object] by some degree of difference.[18] But prior to that knowledge which knows another as being itself other, there is the unitary connection with

---

[13] Νοερὰ θεωρία, a favorite term of Iamblichus in his *Commentary on Aristotle's Categories*. In the lacuna that follows, Iamblichus presumably says that it is *not* possible to clarify fully these problems, either, for the uninitiated.

[14] That is, the νοερὰ θεωρία.

[15] This three-way distinction between theurgical, theological, and philosophical modes of discourse is quite common in Proclus' commentaries and in his *Platonic Theology*. Again we see an elaborate put-down of Porphyry. The truths of theurgy are beyond him because of his skeptical cast of mind, and even the higher truths of theology may be beyond his pedestrian capabilities.

[16] We assume this to be a quotation from Porphyry's *Letter*.

[17] Iamblichus here makes use of two terms basic to the ancient philosophy of mind, κρίσις and προαίρεσις. The argument in favor of natural belief in gods is, ultimately, of Stoic provenance.

[18] This argument recalls that of Plotinus as to why knowledge, even self-knowledge, is incompatible with the absolute unity and simplicity of the One. Cf. especially V 3. For the use of ἑτερότης in this connection, cf. V 3. 10, 24 ff.

the gods, which is natural <and indivisible>.¹⁹ Neither should we accept, then, that this is something that we can either grant or not grant, nor should we admit it as ambiguous (for it remains always uniformly in actuality), nor should we examine the question as though we were in a position either to assent to it or to reject it, for it is, rather, the case that we are enveloped by the divine presence and we are filled with it and we possess our very essence by virtue of our knowledge that there are gods.

And I make the same argument to you also as regards the superior classes of being that follow upon the gods—I mean the daemons and heroes and pure souls. For in respect of them also one should always assume one definite account of their essence and reject the indeterminacy and instability characteristic of the human condition.²⁰ One should also avoid the inclination to one side of an argument rather than another resulting from the balanced antithesis of lines of reasoning, for such a procedure is alien to the first principles of reason and life and tends towards a secondary level of reality such as belongs, rather, to the potentiality and the contrariety of the realm of generation. The higher beings, by contrast, should be grasped with a uniform mode of cognition.

So, then, to the eternal companions of the gods let there correspond also the innate grasp of them. Even as they themselves possess a being of eternal identity, so, too, let the human soul join itself to them in knowledge on the same terms, not employing conjecture or opinion or some form of syllogistic reasoning,²¹ all of which take their start from the plane of temporal reality to pursue that essence which is beyond all these things, but rather connecting itself to the gods with pure and blameless lines of reasoning that it has received from all eternity from those same gods.

You, however, seem to think that knowledge of divinity is of the same nature as knowledge of anything else and that it is by the balancing of contrary propositions that a conclusion is reached, as in dialectical discussions. But the cases are in no way similar; the knowledge of the gods is of a quite different nature and is far removed from all antithetical

---

[19] Accepting Ficino's filling of a small lacuna in the manuscript.

[20] If δόσις here can mean something like "lot" or "destiny"; otherwise, one might accept Boulliau's conjecture—φύσεως for the δόσεως of the manuscripts—though it is not paleographically plausible.

[21] Iamblichus here combines the two modes of cognition proper to the lower half of the line simile in *Republic* VI, εἰκασία and δόξα, with Aristotelian syllogistic, also regarded by Neoplatonists as a mode of reasoning proper only to the physical realm.

procedure and does not consist in the assent to some proposition now nor yet at the moment of one's birth, but from all eternity it coexisted in the soul in complete uniformity.[22]

Book I 10

10. So much, then, for the question of the assignment of the superior classes of being to the various parts of the universe. Next, however, you propose for yourself another division and make a distinction according to "the differentiation of the superior classes in relation to the property of being capable of being affected or not." However, I do not accept this division either. For, in fact, none of the superior classes is capable of being affected, nor yet is any incapable of being affected in the sense of being contrary to what is capable of being affected or as being of a nature subject to passions but it is freed from this through its moral excellence or some other good disposition. It is rather because they completely transcend the distinction between being capable of being affected or not, because they do not even possess a nature that is susceptible to passion, and because they are endowed by their essence with inflexible firmness, that I postulate the incapacity for being affected and inflexibility in respect to all of them.

Consider, if you will, the least of divine beings, the soul pure from contact with body. What need does it have of the generative aspect of pleasure or of the "return to the natural state"[23] that pleasure induces, seeing that it is something supernatural and living a life not subject to generation. And what could be its participation in that pain that leads to destruction or brings about the dissolution of the harmony of the body, when it is external to all body and to that nature that is divided about body and is completely separated from that which descends from the harmony in the soul into bodies? It does not even have need of the experiences that control sense-perception, for it is not at all confined within a body, and not being constrained in any way, it has no need of exercising perception by means of corporeal organs upon any other bodies situated outside itself. And, in general, being indivisible and re-

---

[22] It seems more logical to end the chapter here, though Ficino's chapter division comes after the next sentence.
[23] The word for "restoration" is ἀποκατάστασις. Cf. *MM* B 7, 1204b36–7, where the author alludes to this view of pleasure. This work may or may not be by Aristotle, but that is irrelevant to the point that the view expressed here is an old one.

maining in one selfsame form, being in its essence incorporeal and having no communication with the body that comes into being and suffers, neither would it undergo any experience either through division or through modification nor would it have any element in it that depended upon change or passion.

But even when it [the soul] eventually arrives in the body, not even then does it itself suffer, nor yet do the reason-principles which it imparts to the body;[24] or these, too, are forms and simple and uniform, admitting neither disturbance nor displacement from their proper state. It is the soul, then, in the last analysis, which becomes for the composite[25] the cause of its experiencing passions; and the cause, certainly, is not the same thing as the effect. Just as, then—though composite living beings come into existence and are destroyed—the soul, which is their primary cause of generation, is, in its essence, ungenerated and indestructible, so also—though what participates in soul and does not possess life and being to an absolute degree, but is enmeshed in the indefiniteness and otherness of matter, is subject to suffering—the soul in itself is unchangeable, as being superior in its essence to passion, owing to its incapacity for being affected neither to any mental attitude[26] that might incline in either direction, nor to participation in any state or potency taking on an acquired unchangeability.

---

[24] The first part of this statement is in accord with the doctrine of Plotinus on the incapacity of the soul for being affected (cf. in particular III 6. 1–5), but the assertion that even the λόγοι of soul in body are such goes rather further than Plotinus would wish to go, at least as regards terminology. Plotinus would agree that nothing that was a *form* could be subject to passions, but he recognized a sort of emanation or "trace" of soul in body, which makes up the "composite" (συναμφότερον) that is the living body. This all, in fact, seems embarrassingly discordant with Iamblichus' doctrine in his *De Anima* and *Commentary on Timaeus* (see *infra*), but we must perhaps see a distinction here between the soul in itself (even in the body) and a lower soul, which is more intimately involved with the body. On the other hand, it may just be that Iamblichus is, in each case, wearing a different rhetorical hat. He is, in either case, involved in polemic here against Porphyry on the matter of the capacity of beings superior to us for being affected, elsewhere against Plotinus, Amelius, and Porphyry on the relation of the human soul to entities superior to it.

[25] That is, a σύνθετον of soul (or, at least, life-principle) and body.

[26] Rendering thus προαίρεσις.

Book II 2

2. While the other classes of being[27] are differentiated in this way, secondary to these is the soul, which is situated at the lower limit of the divine orders and which has been allotted partial powers from these two classes while expanding with additional supplements from itself. And at one point or another it projects forms and reason-principles different from one another, and different forms of life while making use of the diverse lives and forms of each region of the universe.[28] It joins with whatever it will and withdraws from whatever it will, becoming like all things and, by difference, remaining separate from them. It selects principles akin both to things really existent and to those subject to generation,[29] allying itself to the gods by harmonies of essences and of potentialities different from those by which daemons and heroes are linked to them.

And though the soul has, to a lesser degree, the eternity of unchanging life and full actuality by means of the gods' good will and the illumination bestowed by their light, it often goes higher and is elevated to a greater rank, even to that of the angelic order.[30] When it no longer abides in the confines of the soul, this totality is perfected in an angelic soul and an immaculate life. Hence, the soul seems to have in itself all kinds of essences and activities, all kinds of principles, and forms in their entirety. Indeed, to tell the truth, while the soul is always limited to a single, definite body, it is, in associating itself with the superior guiding principles, variously allied to different ones.

---

[27] That is, the daemons and heroes, who have just been mentioned in II 1.

[28] That is to say, souls have the characteristic, not shared by the classes of being above them, of involving themselves with a succession of different bodies and their "lives."

[29] This placing of the soul between the realms of true being and of generation emphasizes the median role of the soul in Iamblichean metaphysics, the peculiar nature of which emerges more clearly elsewhere.

[30] Angels as a distinct category of being were not recognized by Plotinus, but certainly were by Porphyry, as evidenced by Augustine CD X 9, 20–35 (= Fr. 290 Smith) and 26, 1–11 (= Fr. 285 Smith). They are clearly distinguished by Iamblichus from daemons and heroes, ranking above them in the universal hierarchy.

Book II 11

11. Your next remarks,[31] in which you express the view that ignorance and deception about these matters contribute to impiety and impurity and in which you exhort us towards true traditional teaching, admit of no dispute, but may be agreed on alike by all. For who would not agree that knowledge that relates to true being is most appropriate to the gods, whereas ignorance that declines towards nonbeing falls very far from the divine cause[32] of true Forms. But since it has not been stated with sufficient accuracy, I will add what is lacking, and because [this suggestion] makes a defense philosophically and logically rather than in accord with the effective skill of priests, I think it necessary to say something more on the theurgic level concerning them.[33]

Granting, then, that ignorance and deception are faulty and impious, it does not follow that the offerings made to the gods and divine works are invalid, for it is not pure thought that unites theurgists to the gods. Indeed, what then would hinder those who are theoretical philosophers from enjoying a theurgic union with the gods? But the situation is not so: it is the accomplishment of acts not to be divulged and beyond all conception, and the power of unutterable symbols, understood solely by the gods, that establishes theurgic union. For this reason, we do not bring about these things by thinking alone. If we did, their efficacy would be intellectual, and dependent upon us. But neither assumption is true. For even when we are not engaged in thinking, the symbols themselves, by themselves, perform their appropriate work, and the ineffable power of the gods, to whom these symbols relate, itself recognizes the proper images of itself, not through being aroused by our thought.[34] For it is neither in the nature of things containing to be aroused by those contained in them; nor in the nature of things perfect, by things imperfect; nor in the nature even of wholes, by parts. Hence, it is not even chiefly through our thinking that divine causes are called into actuality. But it is necessary for these and all the best conditions of the soul and our ritual purity to preexist as auxiliary causes, whereas the things that properly arouse the divine will are the actual divine symbols. And so the

---

[31] Iamblichus is here addressing Porphyry, who is raising these points in his *Letter*.

[32] This is presumably a reference to the One, or to the henadic realm in general.

[33] A reference to his original division of his subject matter into philosophy, theology, and theurgy in Book I, Ch. 2.

[34] This explanation of the efficacy of theurgic rituals is curiously similar to the Christian theory of the efficacy of the sacraments.

attention of the gods is awakened by themselves, receiving from no inferior being any principle for themselves of their characteristic activity.

I have labored this point at some length for this reason: that you should neither believe that all authority over activity in the theurgic rites depends on us nor suppose that their genuine performance is assured by the true condition of our acts of thinking or that they are made false by our deception. For even if we know the particular traits that accompany each kind, we still have not hit upon the truth in regard to the performance of sacred rites. Effective union certainly never takes place without knowledge, but nevertheless it is not identical with it. Thus, divine purity does not come about through right knowledge in the way that bodily purity does through chastity, but divine union and purification actually go beyond knowledge. Nothing, then, of any such qualities in us as are human contributes in any way towards the accomplishment of divine transactions.

Book III 25

25. Let us, then, agree as to that.[35] But thereupon the argument takes us down from inspired frenzy to the displacement of the intellect toward the inferior and claims, irrationally, that the cause of divination is the madness that occurs in diseases. For as much as one is able to fathom, it compares possession to "the excesses of black bile" and to "the aberrations of drunkenness" and to the "raging of rabid dogs." It is thus necessary, initially, to distinguish two forms of ecstasy, as one sort is diverted to the inferior while another is turned towards the higher. One fills its recipients with folly and insanity, while the other furnishes goods more precious than human good sense. And the one degenerates into a disorderly, discordant and material movement, while the other gives itself to the supreme cause which itself directs the orderly arrangement of the universe. And the former, destitute of knowledge, is led astray from good sense, but the latter is united with those beings superior to all our good sense. One is in change, the other, unchangeable; one is contrary to nature, the other, superior to nature; one causes the descent of the soul, the other, its ascent; and one separates it wholly apart from participation in the divine, while the other unites it to it.

---

[35] That is, that divine possession is not a product of emotion or affection (πάθος) but is instilled from without by the gods. The present passage seeks to reinforce the distinction between divine inspiration induced by theurgic practices and any kind of pathological state.

Book V 26

26. Since by no means the least part of sacrificial procedure concerns prayers,[36] and indeed prayers serve to confer the highest degree of completeness upon sacrifices, and as it is by means of them that the whole efficacy of sacrifices is reinforced and brought to perfection, and a joint contribution is made to cult, and an indissoluble hieratic communion is created with the gods, it will do no harm to say a few words on that subject. In fact, it is a subject worthy of study in itself as well one that renders our knowledge of the gods more perfect.

I declare, then, that the first degree of prayer is the introductory,[37] which leads to contact and acquaintance with the divine. The second is conjunctive, producing a union of sympathetic minds and calling forth benefactions sent down by the gods even before we express our requests while achieving whole courses of action even before we think of them. The most perfect, finally, has as its mark ineffable unification, which establishes all authority in the gods and provides that our souls rest completely in them.

According to the distinction of these three levels, then, which measure out the whole range of interaction with the divine,[38] prayer establishes links of friendship between us and the gods and secures for us the triple advantage that we gain from the gods through theurgy, the first leading to illumination, the second to the common achievement of projects, and the third to the perfect fulfilment of the soul through fire.[39] Sometimes it precedes sacrifices, sometimes, again, it comes in the middle of theurgic activity, and at other times it brings sacrifices to a

---

[36] The subject of this section is not really prayer in the traditional Greek form, but rather theurgic prayer, which was doubtless not very different from the formulae prescribed in the magical papyri, including the use of magical names, sacred words, and even strings of vowels. Iamblichus' theory of prayer is set out also in his *Timaeus Commentary apud* Proclus *In Tim.* I 209, 1 ff.

[37] It seems best to construct technical terms for each of the three stages, since they will be explained in what follows. Even so, the exact distinctions are not very clear. The first stage, at least, produces only preliminary acquaintance—it establishes a line of communication, one might say; the second plainly results in joint actions leading to the conferral of benefits; the third, finally, involves some type of mystical union (such as Porphyry asserts that Plotinus attained on a number of occasions, *VP* 23).

[38] This seems to be the sense of τὰ θεῖα here.

[39] That is to say, fire in the Chaldean sense—the immaterial fire of divine power.

suitable conclusion. But no sacred act can take place without the supplications contained in prayers.

Extended practice of prayer nurtures our intellect, enlarges very greatly our soul's receptivity to the gods, reveals to men the life of the gods and accustoms their eyes to the brightness of divine light, and gradually brings to perfection the capacity of our faculties for contact with the gods, until it leads us up to the highest level of consciousness of which we are capable; also, it elevates gently the dispositions of our minds[40] and communicates to us those of the gods, stimulates persuasion and communion and indissoluble friendship, augments divine love, kindles the divine element in the soul and scours away all contrary tendencies within it, casts out from the etherial and luminous vehicle[41] surrounding the soul everything that tends to generation, brings to perfection good hope and faith concerning the light;[42] and, in a word, it renders those who employ prayers, if we may so express it, the familiar consorts of the gods.

If this is how one can describe prayer, and if it works such benefits within us, and if it possesses the connection with sacrifice that we have claimed for it, how would this not cast light on the final purpose of sacrifice—that is to say that it brings us into contact with the Demiurge, since it renders us akin to the gods through acts; and on its good—that it is coextensive with all that is sent down from the demiurgic causes to men? And this in turn will make clear the elevating and efficacious and fulfilling function of prayer, how it is effective, how it produces unification, and how it preserves the common link that is vouchsafed to us from the gods. And thirdly, one could easily grasp from what has been said how sacrifice and prayer reinforce each other and communicate to each other a perfect ritual and hieratic power.

This all serves to reveal the total unity of spirit and action that characterizes the procedure of theurgy, linking its parts to one another with a completely unbroken coherence closer than that of any living being. One should never neglect this nor, by adopting one or another half of it, exclude the rest. Rather, those who aspire to unite themselves absolutely

---

[40] This phrase, τὰ τῆς διανοίας ἤθη, is somewhat odd but may refer to something like the intellectual virtues of the soul.

[41] That is, the pneumatic vehicle. See glossary and Proclus section, n. 184.

[42] This mention of hope (ἐλπίς) and faith (πίστις), together with that of love (ἔρως) just above, completes the enumeration of the Chaldean triad of virtues (cf. Michael Psellus *Hypotyposis*, p. 74, 28 Kroll, p. 199 Des Places, and Proclus *In Tim.* I 212, 19 ff.; *In Alc.* 51, 15 f.).

with the gods should exercise themselves equally in all the branches of theurgy and strive to achieve perfection in all of them.

Book VII 4–5

4. The questions that follow next require a more thorough treatment, if we are to handle them with sufficient logic; yet we should, all the same, set out the truths in our answer with brevity, for you inquire, "What is the point of meaningless names?" But they are not meaningless in the way that you think. Rather, let us grant that they are unknowable to us—or even, in some cases, known, since we may receive their explanations from the gods—but to the gods they are all significant, neither according to an effable mode nor in a way that is significant and indicative to the imaginations of human beings, but united with the gods either intellectually, or rather ineffably, and in a manner superior and more simple than according to intellect. It is essential, therefore, to remove all considerations of logic from the names of the gods, and to set aside the natural affinities of the spoken word to the physical things that exist in nature. Thus, the symbolic character of divine similitude is intellectual and divine, this being implied in the names.

And, indeed, if it is unknowable to us, this very fact is its most sacred aspect, for it is too excellent to be reduced to something knowable.[43] But as for those names of which we have acquired a scientific analysis, through these we have knowledge of divine being and power and order—all in a name! And, moreover, we preserve in their entirety the mystical and arcane images of the gods in our soul. And we raise our soul up through these towards the gods and, as far as is possible, when it has been elevated, we experience union with the gods.

But "why, from among meaningful expressions, do we prefer barbarian ones to our own." For this, again, there is a mystical reason. It is that the gods have shown that the entire dialect of the sacred peoples, such as the Assyrians and the Egyptians, is fitting for religious ceremonies, and so we think that our communication with the gods should be in the proper tongue. Also, such a mode of speech is the first and the most ancient. But most importantly, those who learned the very first names of the gods merged them with their own familiar tongue, and they delivered them to us as being proper and adapted to these things, and forever we preserve here the unshakeable law of tradition, for, whatever else

---

[43] The Greek words are διαιρεῖσθαι εἰς γνῶσιν.

pertains to the gods, it is clear that the eternal and the immutable is connatural with them.

5. "But," so you say, "a listener looks to the meaning, so surely all that matters is that the conception remains the same, whatever the kind of words used." But the situation is not as you suppose, for if the names were established by convention, then it would not matter whether some were used instead of others. But if they are dependent on the nature of real beings, then those that are better adapted to this will be more precious to the gods. It is evident from this that the language of sacred peoples is preferred to that of other men, and with good reason, for the names do not exactly preserve the same meaning when they are translated; rather, there are certain idioms in every nation that are impossible to express in the language of another. Moreover, even if one were to translate them, this would not preserve their same power,[44] for the barbarian names possess weightiness and great precision, participating in less ambiguity, variability, and multiplicity of expression. For all these reasons, then, they are adapted to the superior beings.

So forget these conjectures, which fall short of the truth, "whether he who is invoked either is an Egyptian or uses Egyptian speech."[45] Far better to understand this: that since the Egyptians were the first to be granted participation with gods, the gods invoked rejoice in the rites of the Egyptians.[46] It is not, then, that "all these things are sorcerers'

---

[44] When translation *was* performed, we may note, it required the active assistance of the priestly guardians of the originals, see VIII 5 and X 7 on the Egyptian priest-translator Bitys. Porphyry, as is apparent here, held a very different view of language, seeing it as an agreed set of representative noises and arguing even that we might understand animals if only we could learn and translate their language. See *De Abst.* III 15, 2; III 3, 3–5 Clark. Porphyry's view is represented at *CH* XII 13: "humanity is one; therefore speech is also one, and when translated it is found to be the same in Egypt and Persia as in Greece." The debate as to whether words are natural or conventional originated in Plato's *Cratylus* and was developed by the Stoics, who influenced the later Neoplatonic approach. Proclus *In Crat.* 32, 5–12 argues that various languages can represent a single divine essence, and Greek is included in his list of languages containing divine names. Proclus *In Tim.* I 99, 5 argues that the positing of a name is a form of creation, thereby associating the process of naming with thinking or the actions of the Demiurge.

[45] This is surely a quotation from Porphyry, and a particularly sarcastic comment on his part.

[46] Cf. *PGM* III 120 where the injunction declares, "I conjure you in the Hebrew tongue." The magical papyri are, of course, filled with seemingly meaningless injunctions and lists of names; see, e.g., *PGM* 979–80.

tricks." For how could things most especially linked with the gods, things that join us to them and that possess powers all but equal to theirs, be "imaginary forgeries" when no sacred work could happen without them? But neither are "these arcane devices created through our own passions, and attributed to the gods," for we do not proceed on the basis of our sentiments, but, on the contrary, we take our cue from things allied with the gods and convey declarations in those words according to their nature. And neither do we "make up conceptions about the divine that go against their true existence" but rather, in line with the nature it possesses and according to the truth that those who first laid down the laws of the sacred cult established—in this way do we preserve them; for even if any aspect of the rest of the sacred laws is proper to them, it is surely immutability.

And it is necessary that the prayers of the ancients, like sacred places of sanctuary, are preserved ever the same and in the same manner, with nothing of alternative origin either removed from or added to them, for this is the reason why all these things in place at the present time have lost their power—both the names and the prayers: because they are endlessly altered according to the inventiveness and illegality of the Hellenes; for the Hellenes are experimental by nature and eagerly propelled in all directions, having no proper ballast in them. And they preserve nothing that they have received from anyone else, but even this they promptly abandon and change it all according to their unreliable linguistic innovation.[47] But the barbarians, being constant in their customs, remain faithful to the same words. For this reason, they endear themselves to the gods and proffer words that are pleasing to them. To change these in any way whatsoever is permitted to no man.[48] Such, then, is our answer to you concerning the names, which may indeed be called "inexplicable" and "barbarous," but which are in fact wholly suitable for sacred rituals.

---

[47] This view of the Greek language is expressed in *CH* XVI 2. "Abammon" criticizes the Hellenes *infra* Book VIII.3 for their limited grasp of Ammôn's role, which leads them to name him after Hephaestos. Cf. also Iamblichus *In Tim.* Fr. 11; Plato *Lg.* 656D–657A; *Euth.* 2A1; *Prot.* 310B5.

[48] The injunction not to alter the barbarian names may be found at *Or. Chald.* Fr. 150 Des Places and *CH* XVI 2. See also *PGM* IV 3172 ff; VII 703–26; XII 121–43 and 190–2; Origen *Contra Celsum* I 6; I.24–5; IV 33–4; V 45; *Philocalia* 12; Damascius *In Phil.* 24 Westerink (on Plato *Phil.* 12C); Proclus *In Parm.* 851, 8; *PT* I 44.

Book VIII 2

1. Prior[49] to the true beings and to the universal principles, there is the one god, prior cause even of the first god and king, remaining unmoved in the singularity of his own unity.[50] For no intelligible is linked to him nor is anything else. He is established as a paradigm for the god who is his own father and his own son,[51] and sole father of the true Good; for it is something greater and primary, and fount of all things and basic root[52] of all the first intelligibles, which are the Forms. From this One there has autonomously[53] shone forth the self-sufficient god, for which reason he is termed "father of himself" and "principle of himself";[54] for he is first principle and god of gods, a monad springing from the One, preessential or principle of essence. For from him springs essentiality[55] and essence, for which reason he is termed "father of essence"; he himself is preessential being, the principle of the intelligible realm, for which reason he is termed "principle of intelligibles."[56]

---

[49] We must bear in mind here that Iamblichus is purporting to present not his own metaphysical system but that of the Egyptians, from the mouth of the High Priest Abammon.

[50] In terms of Iamblichean metaphysics, this should be the first One, or the Totally Ineffable; and the "first god and king," the second One, who presides over the triad (identified here, allusively with the "king of all" of Plato's [?] 2nd Ep. [312E]) but this may be pressing the text too far. The alternative would be that this is simply the One, and the second entity the One Being, or monad of the intelligible world.

[51] This is, presumably, the meaning of αὐτοπάτηρ αὐτογόνος. In Neoplatonic terms, the second principle is αὐθυπόστατος "self-generated."

[52] πυθμήν may mean "base," or "root," in the mathematical sense.

[53] An attempt to give due weight to the expression ἑαυτὸν ἐξέλαμψε, — literally, "shone himself forth."

[54] Αὐτάρχης as opposed to αὐτάρκης.

[55] For οὐσιότης in this sense, that is to say, the precondition of essence, cf. Alcinous *Didask.* 10, 164, 34 H., and its occurrences in Hermetic and Gnostic texts (*CH* XII 1; XII 22; Frs. 16, 1; 21, 1 N-F).

[56] All these epithets and descriptions are consistent with the situation of the One-Being, τὸ ἓν ὄν, the first principle or monad of the intelligible realm (which is also the lowest principle of the henadic realm) in Iamblichus' system. Cf. Dillon *Iambl. Frag.* pp. 33–5. νοητάρχης may be a neologism of Iamblichus', though he seems here to attribute it, like the rest of the jargon with which this section is replete, to "the books of Hermes."

Book X 1–8

1.[57] The last subject for discussion concerns happiness, about which you make various inquiries, first proposing objections and then doubts, and after this you start the interrogation. So, taking up these points that you raise, we will answer you appropriately on each one of them. You inquire, then, whether there is not some other road to happiness that we are ignoring; yet what other reasonable mode of ascent to it can there be apart from the gods? For if the essence and accomplishment of all good is encompassed by the gods and their primal power and authority, it is only with us [that is, practitioners of theurgy] and those who similarly attach themselves to the greatest [powers] and have genuinely gained union with them that the beginning and the end of all good is seriously practiced. It is there, then, that there occurs the vision of truth and intellectual understanding, and, with knowledge of the gods, follows a reversion towards ourselves and knowledge of ourselves.

2. It is, then, futile for you to raise the objection that "one should not have regard for human opinions." For what leisure could one whose mind is set upon the gods have to look downwards for human approval? Yet not even in your subsequent statement, that "the soul invents grand things on the basis of chance circumstances," do you raise relevant doubts. For what basis for inventions can there be in things that exist in reality? Is it not the imaginative faculty in us that is the creator of images, even though the imagination is never stirred up when the intellectual life is perfectly active? Does truth not coexist in its essence with the gods—and not merely in harmony with them—based as it is in the intelligible realm? In vain, therefore, are such allegations bandied about by yourself and some others.

And not even those gibes with which some ridicule those who worship the gods as "vagabonds" and "charlatans,"[58] the like of which you have put forward, apply at all to true theology or theurgy. Yet if somehow certain things of this kind do arise incidentally in the sciences of [types of] goods (just as by the side of other crafts evil skills may spring

---

[57] This final section of the work (Book X in the Renaissance division) becomes a significant statement of the mode of the attainment of human happiness (εὐδαιμονία) from a theurgical perspective.

[58] These two terms are probably borrowed by Porphyry from Plato, ἀγύρται from *Rep.* 364B5, and ἀλαζόνες perhaps, from *Rep.* 490A2—though neither term is, admittedly, particularly exotic. If so borrowed, however, Abammon's response may constitute a dig at "regular," nontheurgic Platonism, as represented by Porphyry.

up), they are without a doubt more especially opposed to those [that are true] than to anything else. For evil is more opposed to that which is good than to that which is not good.[59]

3. I would like in the next instance to run through the other slanders that you direct against divine foreknowledge, when you compare it with certain other methods that concern the prediction of future events. For me, not even if there is some instinctive ability from nature for signalling what will be—just as a foreknowledge of earthquakes, wind or storms occurs among animals—does this seem to be any more worthy of respect—for such an innate faculty of divining occurs according to a keenness of perception or sympathy or some other movement of natural powers, containing nothing holy or supernatural—than somebody, who through human reasoning or skilled observation, deduces from signs those things that the signs indicate (just as doctors predict an ensuing fever from a spasm or shivering), nor does he seem to me to possess anything venerable or good. For he conjectures after a human fashion and infers with the aid of our reasoning things that, we all acknowledge, occur naturally and he forms a diagnosis not far removed from the corporeal order. In this way, even if there is a certain natural inkling of the future within us—just as this power is clearly seen to be active in all other animals—this does not, in reality, possess anything that is worthy of celebration. For what could there be that is genuine, perfect, and eternally good among the things implanted in us by generative nature?

4. Only divine mantic prediction, therefore, conjoined with the gods, truly imparts to us a share in divine life—partaking as it does in the foreknowledge and the divine acts of thinking—and renders us, in truth, divine. And this genuinely furnishes that which is good for us, because the most blessed thinking of the gods is filled with all goods. Those, then, who have this mantic prediction do not, as you conjecture, "have foreknowledge, and yet remain without happiness"—for all divine foreknowledge is patently good. Nor do they "foresee the future but do not know how to use this well." Rather, along with the foreknowledge, they receive Beauty itself, and the order that is both true and appropriate. Utility is also present with this, for the gods grant the power of defense against the dangers that menace us from the natural order. And when it is necessary to exercise virtue and an uncertainty over future events contributes to this, then [the gods] conceal what will be for the improvement of the soul. But whenever this [uncertainty] does not matter for

---

[59] Iamblichus has already enunciated this principle at III 31. 178, 1–2 when making a similar point.

this purpose, and foreknowledge, rather, is advantageous to souls for saving and leading them upwards, then the gods implant in the midst of their essences the foreknowledge inherent in divination.

5. But why do I prolong this topic, when I have already shown by many arguments the superiority of divine prophecy over the human? It is better for us, then, to do what you ask of us: to point out to you the road to happiness and where its essence lies, for from this, the truth shall be discovered, and at the same time all doubts may be easily resolved. I say, then, that the man who is conceived of as "divinized,"[60] who once was united to the contemplation of the gods, afterwards came into possession of another soul adapted to the human form and through this was born into the bond of necessity and fate.

Hence, we should consider how one might be liberated and set free from these bonds. There is, indeed, no way other than the knowledge of the gods, for understanding the Good[61] is the essence[62] of happiness, just as obliviousness to the Good and deception concerning evil constitute the essence of evil things. One [way], then, is to unite with the divine, while the other, inferior, destiny is inseparable from the mortal. One measures the essences of intelligibles by sacred methods, while the other, abandoning its principles, gives itself over to the measuring of the corporeal essences. One is the knowledge of the father, the other is a departure from him and obliviousness to the divine father, who is prior to essence and is his own principle;[63] and the one preserves the true life,

---

[60] The uniquely attested term θεωτός seems to refer to the disembodied, "pure" human soul, prior to its descent into body. This concept of a second soul, subject to the laws of fate, is quite remarkable and in line with the doctrine of Numenius (as attested by Porphyry *On the Faculties of the Soul* Fr. 253 Smith = Numenius Fr. 44 Des Places) rather than with that of Iamblichus himself; but on the other hand, the "vehicle of the soul" in Iamblichus' theory, since it survives in the universe after disembodiment, might be seen as filling the role of this "second soul."

[61] We take it that this refers to the Good of Plato's *Republic*, though we cannot be certain.

[62] The word is ἰδέα, which here seems to be used synonymously with οὐσία. Cf. *supra* I 20. 61, 18 and 62, 1.

[63] Preserving the αὐταρχοῦντος of the manuscripts as against Thomas Gale's unnecessary emendation αὐταρκοῦντος ("self-sufficient"). Cf. *supra* VIII 2. 262, 4. This is a fairly clear reference to the Neoplatonic One, though couched in Chaldean terminology.

leading back to its father, while the other drags down the primordial[64] man to that which is never fixed and always flowing. Know, then, that this is the first road to happiness, having for souls the intellectual plenitude of divine union. But the sacred and theurgic gift of happiness is called the gateway to the creator of all things, or the place or courtyard[65] of the good. In the first place, it has the power to purify the soul, far more perfect than [the power] to purify the body; afterwards, it prepares the mind for the participation in and vision of the Good and for a release from everything that opposes it and, at the last, for a union with the gods who are the givers of all things good.[66]

6. And its conjoining [the soul] individually to the parts of the universe and to all the divine powers pervading them leads and entrusts the soul to the keeping of the universal Demiurge and makes it external to all matter and united to the eternal rational order[67] alone. What I mean is that it connects the soul individually to the self-begotten and self-moved god, and with the all-sustaining, intellectual, and adorning power of the universe and with that which leads up to the intelligible truth and with the perfected and effective and other demiurgic powers of the god, so that the theurgic soul is perfectly established in the activities and the acts of thinking of the demiurgic powers. Then, indeed, it deposits the soul in the bosom of the demiurgic god as a whole. And this is the goal of [the soul's] sacred ascent, according to the Egyptians.

7. Good itself they consider,[68] in its divine aspect, to be the god who transcends thinking[69] and, in its human aspect, to be union with him, just as Bitys[70] has interpreted it for us from the Hermetic books. But this

---

[64] The remarkable term γενάρχων ἄνθρωπος would seem to be a reference to a figure such as the "primal man"—'Άνθρωπος—of various Hermetic texts (*Poemandres* (*CH* I), 12 ff.; IV 2; *Asclepius* 7).

[65] For this use of αὐλή, cf. Proclus *In Crat.* 94, 7; *Or. Chald.* Fr. 202 Des Places.

[66] We seem to have here a three-stage process of ascent, "purification—participation—union with the divine," analogous to the three stages of theurgic prayer outlined in V 26.

[67] The word here is λόγος.

[68] "Abammon's" Egyptian mitre has slipped one last time here; he should have said, "we consider."

[69] Or simply, "the god previously envisaged," which would be the normal meaning of προεννοούμενον; but there seems a case for postulating this rather special meaning here.

[70] This personage may be simply an invention of Iamblichus, but he might be connected with a certain Bitos, who is quoted as an authority by the alchemist Zozimus, in his *Commentary on the Letter Omega*, §9.

part [that is, of philosophy] is not, as you suspect, "overlooked" by the Egyptians but is handed down in an appropriately pious manner. Nor do the theurgists "pester the divine intellect about small matters," but about matters pertaining to the purification, liberation, and salvation of the soul. Neither do they "concern themselves diligently with things which are difficult and yet useless to human beings," but rather to things which are, of all things, of most benefit to the soul. Nor are they "exploited by some fraudulent daemon," those men who have conquered the deceitful and demonic nature, and ascended to the intelligible and the divine.

(8) Thus, to the best of our ability, have we responded to the problems you have raised about divine prophecy and theurgy. It remains, then, at the end of this discourse, for me to pray to the gods to grant both to me and to you the unalterable preservation of true thoughts, to implant in us the truth of eternal things forever, and to grant to us a participation in the more perfect conceptions of the gods in which the most blessed end of good things is placed before us along with the sanction of the harmonious friendship between us.[71]

On the Soul (De Anima)

On the Soul (Περὶ ψυχῆς), *only preserved, in extensive fragments, in the* Anthologia *of John Stobaeus, consists of a doxographic survey of philosophical doctrines on the soul, but with the polemical purpose of distinguishing Iamblichus' own doctrine from those of his immediate predecessors, Plotinus, Amelius, and Porphyry.*

§7. The doctrine opposed to this, however, separates the soul off, inasmuch as it has come about as following upon intellect, representing a distinct level of being, and that aspect of it that is endowed with intellect is explained not only as being connected with intellect, certainly, but also as subsisting independently on its own, and it separates the soul also from all the superior classes of being and assigns to it, as the particular definition of its essence, either the middle term of divisible and indivisible <and

---

[71] A final put-down of Porphyry—combined, perhaps, with something of an olive branch?

of corporeal and <in> corporeal[1] classes of being; or the totality of the universal reason-principles; or that which, after the Ideas, is at the service of the work of creation; or that life that has life of itself, which proceeds from the intelligible realm; or again, the procession of the classes of real being as a whole to an inferior substance. It is these doctrines to which Plato himself and Pythagoras and Aristotle, and all the ancients who have gained great and honorable names for wisdom, are completely committed, as one will find if he investigates their opinions with scientific rigour. As for myself, I will try to base this whole treatise, concerned as it is with truth, on these opinions. (pp. 365–6 W-H)

§§18–19

§18. However, another view, which should not be rejected, might be proposed,[2] a view that divides souls according to genera and species, making a difference between the perfect acts of universal souls, the pure and immaterial acts of divine souls, and—different from these—the efficacious acts of daemonic souls, the mighty acts of heroic souls, the acts of a mortal nature proper to animals and men, and so on for the rest. When these have been distinguished, the features that are dependent on them admit of the same sort of distinction.

§19. Those who maintain that the soul is one and the same on every level—either generically or specifically, as is the opinion of Plotinus,[3] or even numerically, as Amelius rashly maintains on not a few occasions—will say that the soul itself is identical with its acts. Others, making a more prudent distinction[4] and insisting that it is by a downward sequence of primary, secondary, and tertiary processions[5] that the different essences of souls continually proceed—such as one would expect of those who enter upon the discussion of these matters with arguments that are novel but unshakeable—will say that the operations of universal and divine and immaterial souls in all cases come to accomplishment in their essences also, but they will by no means agree that individual

---

[1] Completing a small lacuna here in the text.
[2] This is Iamblichus' characteristic way of introducing his own view in this work.
[3] See especially IV 9; Also, VI 4–5; IV 3. 1–8.
[4] Once again, one of Iamblichus' ways of introducing his own opinion.
[5] This seems to be a reference to the "seconds and thirds" of the demiurgic mixing bowl image in Plato *Tim.* 41D.

souls, confined as they are in one single form and divided out among bodies, are to be immediately identified with their acts.

§§37–8

§37.[6] ... Plotinus and his school, on the other hand, champion the opinion that separates the nonrational faculties from the reasoning element, either releasing them into the realm of generation or separating them from the discursive reason.[7] From this opinion arises a choice between two doctrines: either each nonrational faculty is freed into the whole life of the universe from which it was detached, where each remains as far as possible unchanged, as is the view of Porphyry;[8] or the whole of nonrational life continues to exist, separated from the discursive reason and preserved in the universe, as the most ancient of the priests declare.[9]

§38. In the same way, there are very different views concerning the substances intermediate between body and soul; for some join the soul itself immediately to the organic body, as do the majority of Platonists. Others, however, postulate that between the incorporeal soul and the body which serves as its vessel[10] etherial, heavenly and pneumatic

---

[6] The subject of discussion here is the fate of the soul after death, and how much of the soul, or what parts of it, survive. Here Stobaeus has plainly omitted something—presumably, something on the earlier Platonists' views on this topic.

[7] As is often the case in this work, Iamblichus is oversimplifying Plotinus' position. One can, however, refer to such passages as I 1. 2, where Plotinus states that the soul is "a certain form" (εἶδος τι) "having an activity that is natural to itself in itself" (I 1. 9). "For it will perceive nothing nor will there be discursive thinking nor belief in it" (ll. 25–6). Cf. also IV 3. 18, where the soul, on departing the body, no longer employs practical reasoning (λογισμός), but instead employs a kind of reasoning closely connected with intellect (νοῦς); and IV 4. 1–7, where the separated soul does not preserve memories of the lower realm.

[8] Cf. Proclus *In Tim.* III 234, 18–32, where Porphyry's position is set out. He would preserve the nonrational soul and the pneumatic vehicle (ὄχημα) in the universe, but not intact. Rather, just as the faculties involved were gathered from the heavenly bodies in the course of the soul's descent, so they are shed back to their planetary sources during the soul's ascent.

[9] A characteristic way for Iamblichus to introduce his own view. Here he is assimilating himself to either the Egyptian or the Chaldean priestly tradition, or both. For the doctrine, cf. Proclus *In Tim.* Fr. 81 *infra*.

[10] Reading ἀγγειώδους with Ferguson, for the ἀγγελιώδους of the manuscripts, which makes no sense in the context. Once again, this represents Iamblichus'

wrappings surrounding the intellectual life-principle are put forth for its protection, serve it as vehicles, and also bring it together in due proportion with the solid body, joining it thereto by means of certain intermediate common bonds.

LETTER TO MACEDONIUS, ON FATE[1]

This is the longest of a series of letters by Iamblichus, of which fragments are preserved, once again, in the Anthologia *of John Stobaeus.*

Fr. 1

All things that exist, exist by virtue of the One, and indeed the primal level of Being itself is produced in the beginning from the One, and, in a very special way, the general causal principles receive their power of action from the One and are held together by it in a single embrace and are borne back together to the first principle of multiplicity,[2] as preexisting in it. And in accordance with this, the multitude, of causal principles in nature, which are multiform and fragmented and dependent on

---

own view, along with that of Porphyry. Iamblichus, however, as we have seen, maintains the continued existence of the ὄχημα as a whole in the universe after separation from the rational soul.

[1] All of Iamblichus' extant letters are addressed both to various pupils of his, such as Sopater and Dexippus, but also, apparently, to figures of public importance (his correspondent Dyscolius, to whom is addressed a letter *On Ruling*, may be identical with a governor of Syria in the 320's), and Macedonius may have been one of the latter. While a piece of "popular philosophy," it nonetheless contains a good deal of substantial doctrine. Iamblichus here advances a concept of fate of a thoroughly Stoic austerity, at least as regards the physical world. But this, after all, is no different from the view of Plotinus. He also, however, insists on the superiority of the highest part of the human soul to the workings of fate, and the coordination of fate with divine Providence. This is all good Platonist doctrine.

[2] That is, the Indefinite Dyad, which would indeed be the ultimate source of the multiplicity of causal principles. Either the One referred to here is not Iamblichus' higher "One" but, rather, the One that is coordinate with the Dyad; or else the Dyad is to be seen as subordinate to the One. But again, in a work of relatively popular philosophy, Iamblichus may not be concerned to introduce these complexities.

a number of [immediate] sources, also derive from one general causal principle, and all are interwoven with each other according to a single principle of combination and this combination of many causal principles relates back to one source—the most comprehensive controlling principle of causality. Neither is this single chain a mere jumble put together from multiplicity, nor does it constitute a unity formed simply as a result of such combination, nor is it dissipated into individual entities; but, rather, in accordance with the guiding and prearranged single combination of the causal principles themselves, it brings all things to completion and binds them within itself and leads them upwards unitarily to itself. Thus, fate is to be defined as the one order that comprehends in itself all other orders. (= Stobaeus *Anth.* I 80, 11–81, 18 W-H)

Fr. 2[3]

The essence of the soul in itself is immaterial, incorporeal, completely exempt from generation and destruction, possessing of itself existence and life, entirely self-moved, and first principle of nature and of motions in general. This entity, in virtue of being such as it is, also contains within itself free and independent life. And insofar as it gives itself to the realm of generation and subjects itself to the flow of the universe, thus far also it is drawn beneath the sway of fate and is enslaved to the necessities of nature; but, on the other hand, insofar as it exercises its intellectual activity—activity that is really left free from everything and independent in its choices—thus far it voluntarily "minds its own business" and lays hold of what is divine and good and intelligible with the accompaniment of truth. (= Stobaeus *Anth.* II 173, 5–17 W-H)

Fr. 3

It is the life that is lived in accordance with intellect and that cleaves to the gods that we must train ourselves to live; for this is the only life which admits of the untrammeled authority of the soul, frees us from the bonds of necessity, and allows us to live a life no longer mortal, but one that is divine and filled by the will of the gods with divine benefits. (= Stobaeus *Anth.* II 173, 18–24 W-H)

---

[3] This and all the following extracts are from a chapter of John Stobaeus on "What is in our power" (or "What is up to us"). Iamblichus, while admitting the power of fate, asserts nonetheless the autonomy of the rational soul.

Fr. 4

For, indeed, to speak generally, the movements of destiny around the universe are assimilated to the immaterial and intellectual activities and circuits, and its order is assimilated to the good order of the intelligible and transcendent realm. And the secondary causes are dependent on the primary causes, and the multiplicity attendant upon generation, on the undivided substance,[4] and the whole sum of things subject to fate is thus connected to the dominance of providence. In its very substance, then, fate is enmeshed with providence, and fate exists by virtue of the existence of providence, and it derives its existence from it and within its ambit.

This being the case, then, the cause of action in humans has a correspondence with both these causes in the universe. The origin of action in us is both independent of nature and emancipated from the movement of the universe. For this reason it is not implicated in the principle of the universe, for because it is not produced from nature, neither is it produced from the movement of the universe, but it is ranked above it as prior and not dependent on the universe. But because it has taken for itself portions from all the parts of the universe and from all of the elements and because it makes use of all these, it is itself also included in the order of fate, and contributes to it, and assists in the fulfilment of its constitution, and is necessarily involved with it. And insofar as the soul contains within itself a pure, self-subsistent, self-motive, self-generative, and perfective reason-principle, thus far it is emancipated from all outside influences. On the other hand, insofar as it puts forth other levels of life that incline towards generation and insofar as it consorts with the body, thus far it is involved in the order of the universe. (= Stobaeus *Anth.* II 173, 26–174, 27 W-H)

Fr. 5

But if anyone, by dragging in the spontaneous and chance, thinks to abolish the order [of the universe], let him realize that nothing in the universe is unordered or adventitious or devoid of cause or undefined or random or arising from nothing or yet accidental. There is no question, therefore, of abolishing order and continuity of causes and the unity of principles and the domination of the primal essences extending throughout everything. It is better, then, to make a definition as follows: chance is the overseer and connecting cause of a plurality of orders of events or of whatever else—being superior to what comes together

---

[4] That is, of the intelligible realm.

under it, an entity that we sometimes denominate a god and sometimes take as being a daemon. For whenever the higher beings are causes of events, a god is their overseer, while when natural forces are the causes, a daemon [presides].[5] All things, therefore, always come to fruition in conjunction with a cause, and nothing at all unordered obtrudes itself into the realm of becoming. (= Stobaeus *Anth.* II 175, 1–15 W-H)

Fr. 6

Why, then, are deserts apportioned undeservedly?[6] Or is it not even proper to raise this question? For benefits are not dependent on any external cause, but on the individual himself and on his free choice, and these are most properly defined in connection with one's chosen mode of life, and the problems raised by the majority of men arise out of ignorance. There is, then, no fruit of virtue other than virtue itself. This is not to say that the good man is worsted by chance, for his greatness of spirit renders him superior to all accidents of fortune. Nor, I may add, does this come about contrary to nature; for the summit and perfection of the soul is sufficient to fulfil the best nature of man. And, indeed, what seem to be reverses in fact serve to exercise and coordinate and stimulate virtue, and it is not possible without them to develop a noble character. This state of mind of the good man gives particular honor to nobility and regards only the complete fulfilment of reason as constituting the happy life, while ignoring and despising as of no worth everything else. (= Stobaeus *Anth.* II 175, 17–176, 10 W-H)

Fr. 7

So, then,[7] since man's true essence lies in his soul, and the soul is intelligent and immortal, and its nobility and its good and its end repose in divine life, nothing of mortal nature has power to contribute anything towards the perfect life or to deprive it of happiness. For, in general, our

---

[5] It is far from clear what entity Iamblichus has in mind here, but it may be none other than the Sublunary Demiurge, which he postulates elsewhere (*In Soph.* Fr 1 Dillon) as the overseer of the realm of becoming.

[6] Iamblichus here takes very much the same line as that propounded by Plotinus in III 2–3, *On Providence*.

[7] This passage has the air of a peroration, so we may have, more or less, the end of the letter preserved here.

blessedness resides in intellectual life; for none of the median things[8] has the capacity either to increase or to nullify it. It is therefore irrelevant to go on, as men generally do, about chance and its unequal gifts. (= Stobaeus *Anth.* II 176, 12–21 W-H)

COMMENTARY ON PARMENIDES

We have adequate evidence that Iamblichus composed such a commentary, but in his Parmenides Commentary, Proclus avoids mentioning his predecessors by name, so that, although there are nearly a dozen passages where a series of two other commentators lead up to one who is plainly Syrianus, identification with Iamblichus remains less than certain. In Damascius' commentary on the dialogue, however, there is no such problem.

For Iamblichus, Timaeus and Parmenides were the two summits of Platonic doctrine, to be studied after the preliminary cycle of ten dialogues, which began with Alcibiades and ended with Philebus.

Fr. 2B Dillon[1]

21. And that is why each of the things in this realm is both one and many, and for this reason in this order of being there is also pure substance, stripped, one might say, of the One, and the many take their origin from this same order,[2] whereas, prior to this level, multiplicity was present only as an impression in the Unified;[3] and for this reason Iamblichus also maintained that the intelligible remains in the One, because it is more united to it and takes its form from it, rather than from Being. Not, indeed, that there is any distinction within it, neither

---

[8] Presumably, a variant here for the Stoic term ἀδιάφορα, "things indifferent."

[1] This could be seen as part of a commentary on the beginning of the second hypothesis of *Parm.* 142b5–6: "If a one *is*, it cannot be, and yet not have being"—though it must be admitted that it is a fairly general reference to Iamblichus' doctrine.

[2] The reference is to the first intelligible-intellective order, which Syrianus (and possibly Iamblichus before him) saw as the subject of that part of the second hypothesis from 143A4 to 144E8.

[3] "The Unified" is Iamblichus' term for the lowest element of the henadic realm (the product of the union of Limit and Unlimitedness); it also serves as the monad, or summit, of the intelligible realm, which is the subject of discussion here.

substance nor intelligible nor anything else, but its being consists in this—in its being everything in aggregate. And it is really in this respect that is intelligible: "for it is everything, but in an intelligible mode," says the Oracle;[4] for it draws together into one all our acts of thinking and makes of all of them gathered together one complete and undifferentiated and truly unified act of thinking, such as Iamblichus maintains is the thinking of that intelligible.

And if elsewhere Plato or any other divine man declares the summit of the intellectual realm to be substance,[5] there is nothing odd in that; for pure substance manifests itself, in Iamblichus' view as well, at this level of being, too. And this intellective summit would be substance by virtue of being intellective, that is to say, by being distinguished off by itself and subtended to the One, as one distinct entity to another, in virtue of the essential and unitary otherness that manifests itself there.

Commentary on Timaeus

Like Porphyry, Iamblichus composed a commentary on Timaeus, *often disputing positions taken up by his former master and, overall, imposing a more comprehensive view of the subject matter of the work. His commentary plainly had a considerable influence on the exegesis of Syrianus, and therefore on his pupil Proclus.*

Fr. 7 Dillon[1]

But these commentators[2] were corrected in a truly worthy manner, in my opinion, by the most divine Iamblichus. It is his view, and that of my

---

[4] *Or. Chald.* Fr. 21 Des Places.

[5] This would appear to be a reference to *Phdr.* 247C6–D1, where Plato characterizes the "realm above the heavens" (ὑπερουράνιος τόπος) as an οὐσία, which, however, is discernible only by the "helmsman of the soul," which was identified by Iamblichus with the "One" of the soul, that aspect of the soul with which it apprehends the One.

[1] This passage is part of a commentary on the lemma *Tim.* 20D7–9: "Listen, then, Socrates, to a tale that, though very strange, is yet entirely true, as Solon, the wisest of the Seven [Sages], once upon a time declared." Critias then goes on to tell the tale of the Atlantid War.

[2] These are a succession of earlier commentators, going back to Crantor in the Old Academy, who interpreted the conflict between Atlantis and Athens in an inadequately "universalistic" way.

own master,[3] that this conflict should be understood in such a sense as, on the one hand, not to deny the historicity of the physical events—quite the contrary, since it is generally agreed that they took place—but to accord with our practice of referring those parts before the real subject in dialogues to the same aim as that of the dialogues as a whole.[4] It is their view that, in the same way and according to the same general principle, we should raise this conflict from the human level and extend its significance throughout the whole universe, and in particular through the generated part of it, and extend the reference of it to all levels, considering in what respect the universe partakes of opposition by reason of the variety of its powers. For since all things derive both from the One and from the Dyad after the One[5] and are united in a way with each other and have been allotted an antithetical nature—even as among the classes of Being there is a certain antithesis of the Same against the Different, and of Motion as opposed to Rest, and all things in the universe partake of the these classes—so it would be a good idea to view the conflict as extending through all these levels of existence. (Proclus *In Tim.* I 77, 24 ff. Diehl)

Fr. 29[6]

But the divine Iamblichus vigorously opposes this line of argument,[7] declaring the Always-Existent to be superior to the genera of Being and the Ideas and situating it at the summit of the intelligible world, enjoying primary participation in the One.[8] And there is evidence for this theory in what is written in *Parmenides* about the One-Being, and in *Sophist*;[9] for there he ranks the One-Being as prior to the universe and the whole

---

[3] Proclus is referring to Syrianus.

[4] A reference to the Iamblichean principle that a Platonic dialogue should have a single, coherent subject matter, or σκόπος.

[5] That is, the Dyad of Limit and Unlimitedness.

[6] This is part of a commentary on the lemma *Tim.* 27D6–7: "What is it which is always existent and has no becoming, and what is it that is becoming always, and is never existent?"

[7] That is, that "that which always exists" (τὸ ἀεὶ ὄν) of *Tim.* 27D refers to the whole intelligible world.

[8] For Iamblichus, this is the monad of the intelligible realm, which is also the lowest element in the henadic realm, and thus serves to link the two.

[9] That is, in the second hypothesis of *Parm.* 142B ff. and at *Soph.* 244D, 245A–E.

intelligible world, although the universe in its entirety is also intelligible. (Procl. *In Tim.* I 230, 5 ff. Diehl)

Fr. 50[10]

But Porphyry and Iamblichus oppose all these,[11] criticizing them for understanding "the midst" in a spatial and dimensional sense, and confining the soul of the whole universe to some particular part of it, whereas it is present everywhere equally, exerting authority over all alike and leading all things by its own motions. . . .[12]

The divine Iamblichus, on the other hand, holds that we should understand here the soul that is transcendent and hypercosmic[13] and independent and exerting authority over all. Plato, he says, is not here concerned with the soul of the universe but with that Soul that is incapable of being participated in and placed over all the souls in the universe as their monad;[14] for such, he says, is the nature of the primal Soul, and "the midst," in reference to it, denotes its being equally present to all things through neither being the soul of any body, nor yet being relative in any way, both ensouling all things equally and yet preserving its separateness equally from all; for it is not less distant from some things and more from others—it is, after all, free of all relativity—but equally distant from all, even though all things might not be distant from it in the same way; for it is in participating entities that degrees of more and less arise. (Proclus *In Tim.* II 104, 30 ff. Diehl)

[10] This is part of a commentary on the lemma *Tim.* 34B3–5: "and he placed soul into the midst of it, and stretched it through the whole if it, and enveloped its body with it from without."

[11] Various anonymous Middle Platonic commentators who attempted different literal interpretations of this passage.

[12] There follows a passage where Porphyry's interpretation is criticized (presumably, originally by Iamblichus). Porphyry took the soul being described here as the immanent soul of the universe.

[13] The Greek word is ὑπερκόσμιος. Cf. Plotinus IV 3. 4, 14–16.

[14] Iamblichus is here propounding the doctrine of the hypercosmic Soul, occupying the role of monad of the psychic realm. Plotinus had made a suggestion in this direction in IV 3. 4 as a solution to the problem of how the unity of the soul can be maintained; but, so far as we can see, Iamblichus is the first to formalize the theory. In Fr. 54 *infra* we will see him laying down the general principle of which this is a particular application, "every order (τάξις) is presided over by its unparticipated monad, prior to the participated elements." Cf. Proclus *ET* Prop. 21.

Fr. 53[15]

The philosopher Iamblichus, on the other hand, sings the praises of the numbers with all his power, as containing various remarkable properties, calling One the cause of sameness and unity; Two, the organizer of procession and division; Three, the leader of reversion for what has gone forth; Four, the true embracer of all harmony, containing in itself all the ratios and showing forth in itself the second order of the universe; Nine, the creator of true perfection and likeness, being the perfect product of perfect components and partaking of the nature of the Same; Eight, he terms the cause of procession to all levels and of progression through all; and finally, Twenty-Seven, the force stimulating reversion even of the lowest levels; in order that on each side of the Tetrad there might be a stationary, a progressive, and a reversionary principle; on the one side on the primal level, on the other, on the secondary. For Nine has a relation to One, being a "new one";[16] and Eight, to Two, being the cube from it; and Twenty-Seven, to Three, for the same reason. Through the medium of former [numbers],[17] he grants to the simpler entities remainings and reversions and processions, through the latter to the more composite; and the Tetrad—being in the middle—inasmuch as it is a square has the quality of remaining static, while through being even times even, it has the quality of proceeding; and through being filled with all the ratios emanating from the One, it has the capacity to revert. These are symbols of divine and ineffable truths. (Proclus *In Tim.* II 215, 5 ff. Diehl)

Fr. 54[18]

10. It is worth considering what is to be said regarding this "splitting" and the two lengths, or circles. The divine Iamblichus, on the one

---

[15] This passage is part of an exegesis of the lemma *Tim.* 35B4–C2, describing the Demiurge's dividing up of the soul according to numerical ratios: 1, 2, 3, 4, 9, 8, 27. Iamblichus, we may note, arranges them in two triadic systems, each containing a static, progressive, and reversionary element, with Four, or the Tetrad, in a central role, holding the two systems together.

[16] Here Iamblichus indulges in etymologizing, as between ἔννεα, "nine," and ἓν νέον—an etymology that is not attested before him, but which is picked up later by Proclus (*In Remp.* II 4, p. 20 f. Kroll) and Hermeias (*In Phdr.* p. 90, 27 Couveur).

[17] That is, those prior to the Tetrad.

[18] This passage is part of an exegesis of the lemma *Tim.* 36B8–10, concerning the construction of the Soul: "Next, he split all this that he had put together into

hand, "traverses the heavens above," so to speak, and "busies himself with things invisible"[19]—to wit, the one soul and the two proceeding from it; for every order is presided over by its unparticipated monad,[20] prior to the participated elements,[21] and it [the monad] is the number that is distinctive of and naturally related to the unparticipated, and from the One is the Dyad, as in the case of the gods themselves. And Timaeus, indeed, he [Iamblichus] says, having verbally created, in his [Timaeus'] account of the generation of the soul, the one and hypercosmic Soul, from which springs the soul of the universe and the others,[22] produces from it, at this point, the Dyad; for the "splitting" signifies the dividing action of the Demiurge, which goes forth in self-identity and completeness, engendering identical products on secondary levels,[23] and the "division lengthwise" signifies the procession coming down from above from the Demiurge.

And through these are generated two souls after the one, each of which has the same system of principles, and they are combined with each other and are in each other and at the same time are distinguished from each other and preserve unmixed purity along with their mutual unification; for they are united by their very centers, and this is the meaning of the phrase "middle to middle." And since these souls are intellectual and partake of divine Intellect, before even the heaven came into existence the Demiurge "bent them into a circle" and encompassed them "with the motion that moves about the same things in the same way,"[24] making them intellectual and giving them a share in the divine Intellect and placing the dyad of souls into the intellectual dyad which is superior to them in essence. (Proclus *In Tim.* II 240, 4 ff. Diehl)

---

two parts lengthwise; and then he laid the two one against the other, the middle of one to the middle of the other, in the form of a *Chi* and bent them into a circle."

[19] An ironic use by Proclus of an Aristophanic characterization of Socrates, Fr. 672 Kock.

[20] Cf. Proclus *ET* Props. 21, 67, and 101.

[21] This is a basic principle of later Neoplatonic metaphysics, enunciated also by Proclus *ET* Props. 21, 67, and 101, but plainly here attributed to Iamblichus.

[22] That is, the individual souls.

[23] Κατὰ δευτέρους ἀριθμούς literally "according to secondary numbers"; but this seems to be the meaning.

[24] See Plato *Tim.* 36C2.

Fr. 81[25]

See *infra* p. 343, last paragraph for this fragment.

Fr. 87[26]

20. The Circuit of the Different is shaken up by being filled with false notions; for its proximity to the nonrational element [of soul] causes it to take in certain influences from without. Provoked by this, we will address ourselves frankly to Plotinus and the great Theodorus,[27] who want to maintain in us an element that is incapable of being affected and always thinking.[28] For Plato employs only two circles to make up the substance of the soul, and of these he "hinders" the one and "shakes up" the other, so that it is not possible for either that which is hindered or that which is shaken up to enjoy intellectual activity.

The divine Iamblichus is quite correct, therefore, in attacking those who hold this opinion;[29] for what element in us errs when the nonrational element in us is stirred and we chase after a lawless impression? Is it not our free will? And how would it not be this? For by reason of this

---

[25] This passage forms part of an exegesis of the lemma *Tim.* 42D1–2: "For the rest, do ye weave together the mortal with the immortal . . ." The previous two opinions discussed by Proclus are those of (1) Atticus and Albinus and "others like them," i.e., Middle Platonists, and (2) Porphyry, who maintained the continued existence of the pneumatic vehicle but assumed that it dissolved back into its component parts, the various cosmic "garments" that it had picked up on its journey downwards through the celestial spheres. Cf. *De Anima,* §§37–8 *supra.*

[26] This passage is an exegesis of *Tim.* 43C9–D4: "Moreover, since at that time they [that is, sensations] were causing, for the moment, constant and widespread motion, joining with the perpetually flowing stream in moving and violently shaking the revolutions of the soul, they totally blocked the course of the Same by flowing contrary to it, and hindered it thereby from going on its way and governing, while, on the other hand, they shook up the course of the Different . . ." This is made the occasion for a major statement of Iamblichus' doctrine of the soul, in opposition to that of Plotinus. Cf. *De An.* §§6–7 *supra.*

[27] That is, Theodorus of Asine. Theodorus, probably following Amelius, of whom he was a partisan, would seem to have accepted Plotinus' doctrine of an undescended part of the soul.

[28] Cf. Plotinus, IV 8. 8; III 6. 1–5.

[29] Since Iamblichus is unlikely to have been in a position to attack Theodorus, who was a (dissident) pupil of his, it is more likely that it is Amelius, along with Plotinus, who is the object of his criticism, as in his *De Anima, passim.*

we differ from those beings that follow impressions without reflection. If the free will errs, then how would the soul remain without error?

And what makes happy our life as a whole? Is it not when reason is in possession of its proper virtue? We would surely say that it is. But if when the best part of us is perfect, (and then the whole of us is happy), what would prevent us all—the whole human race—from being happy at this moment, if the highest part of us is always thinking and always turned towards the gods? If the intellect is this highest part, that has nothing to do with the soul;[30] if, however, it is a part of the soul, then the rest of the soul must also be happy.

And what is the "charioteer" of the soul?[31] Is it not the noblest and, one might say, most consummate part of us? And how can we avoid this conclusion, if indeed this directs our whole being and, with its own head, views the supracelestial sphere and is assimilated to the "great leader" of the gods, who "drives a winged chariot" and "journeys through the heaven as a first" charioteer?[32] But if the charioteer is the highest element in us, and he, as is said in *Phaedrus*,[33] sometimes is carried up aloft and raises "his head into the region outside," while at other times he descends and afflicts his pair with "lameness" and "loss of wings," it plainly follows that the highest element in us experiences different states at different times. (Proclus *In Tim.* III 334, 3 ff. Diehl)

---

[30] That is, taking the intellect (νοῦς) as distinct from the soul, as all Neoplatonists would. However, this does not seem a very effective point, since Iamblichus wants to assert that no part of us remains constantly "above," in contact with the gods. On the other hand, his argument is against Plotinus, who does wish to assert that the highest part *of the soul* remains above.

[31] A reference, of course, to the myth of *Phaedrus*. Iamblichus, however, as we learn from Hermeias, *In Phdr.* 150, p. 24 ff. Couvreur (= Iambl. *In Phdr.* Fr. 6 Dillon), actually distinguished between the "charioteer" of the soul and the "helmsman" (κυβερνήτης, *Phdr.* 247C7), identifying the former as the intellect of the soul, and the latter as the One of the soul. This does not concord entirely comfortably with what we have here, where we are involved in polemic.

[32] See Plato *Phdr.* 246E.

[33] Ibid. 248A–C.

Commentary on Phaedrus

It is to another pupil of Syrianus, Hermeias, that we owe most of our knowledge of Iamblichus' commentary, along with two mentions in Proclus' Platonic Theology. Phaedrus occupied the eighth place in the preliminary sequence of dialogues to be studied.

Fr. 6 Dillon[1]

The divine Iamblichus takes the "helmsman" as being the One of the soul; its intellect is the charioteer. The term "spectator" is used to signify not that it directs its gaze on this intelligible as being other than it but that it is united with it and derives benefit from it in this way. This shows that the helmsman is a more perfect entity than the charioteer and the horses; for it is the essential nature of the One of the soul to gain union with the gods.[2] (Hermeias *In Phaedrum* 150, 24 ff. Couvreur)

---

[1] This is a comment on the phrase at *Phdr.* 247C7–8: ψυχῆς κυβερνήτῃ μόνῳ θεατῇ νῷ, "visible only to the intellect, the helmsman of the soul," but omitting the word νῷ "to the intellect," which is present in the manuscripts, since Iamblichus' exegesis does not make sense if he read it in this place. Further, it is apparent that Iamblichus read here θεατῇ, the noun in the dative, rather than the adjective θεατή in the nominative, making for a difficult construction but presumably giving the meaning "from the perspective of the helmsman of the soul, its only spectator." This distinction between "the helmsman" and "the charioteer" enables Iamblichus to find for an henadic faculty of the soul, superior to the intellectual faculty, which is able to gain some grasp of the One.

[2] That is to say, with the henads, the "participable" element of the realm of the One.

Commentary on Philebus

We owe our knowledge of this commentary to Damascius' commentary on the same dialogue. Philebus, *as mentioned earlier, occupied the tenth and highest place in Iamblichus' preliminary sequence of dialogues.*

Fr. 4 Dillon

Not even in the second realm[1] is there distinctness in the full sense, for the creation of distinct Forms is a function of the primal Intellect, and the primal Intellect is the pure Intellect.[2] And this is the reason why Iamblichus declares that it is on this level that one may place the monads of the Forms, meaning by "monads" the undifferentiated element in each. For this reason, it [Intellect] is the intelligible for the intellectual realm and the cause of being for the Forms; even as the second element is the cause of life; and the third, the cause of their articulation as Forms. (Damascius *In Philebum*, §105, p. 49–51 Westerink)

Fr. 7 Dillon

Iamblichus also says that the three monads,[3] proceeding from the Good, structure the Intellect. It is not clear, however, to which Intellect he is referring: that which follows on Life, or that which is inherent in Being—the so-called "Paternal Intellect." For some have taken it to be not the latter but the former; and, indeed, he does declare that the three

---

[1] This actually refers to the intelligible order, or order of Being, the highest order of the realm of Intellect. For Iamblichus, the Forms only emerge in an articulated way at the level of Intellect proper, that is, at the third level of the realm of Intellect. Since he also seems to have had a doctrine of henads (see pp. 258–9 *infra*), this makes for a scheme of some complexity; but in fact the monads of the Forms may just be those henads viewed as present at the highest level of Intellect.

[2] That is, Intellect proper, as opposed to the orders of Being and Life.

[3] This is a reference to the three concepts, beauty, proportion, and truth, through the medium of which Socrates suggests, in *Phil.* 65A, the Good must be grasped. That these three constituted a triad of aspects, or "moments" of the hypostasis of Intellect is a notion advanced by Iamblichus and accepted by all subsequent Neoplatonists (though with further refinements from Syrianus on, reflected in the present passage).

monads come to light in the Egg in the mythological system of the Orphic Poems.[4] (Damascius In Philebum §243, p. 115 Westerink)

From Proclus' *Commentary on Parmenides*[1]

1. Necessarily, then, if indeed only the divine is above being and all that is divine is above being, either the present argument could be only about the primal god, who is surely the only entity above being, or else it is about all the gods also who are after him, as some of those we revere would hold.[2] So they argue that since every god, inasmuch as he is a god, is a henad (for it is this element, the One, which divinizes all being)—for this reason, they think it right to join to the study of the primal [god] an account of all the gods, for they are all supraessential henads and transcend the multiplicity of beings and are the summits of beings.

But if we were to say that both the primal cause and the other gods are one, we would have to allot one and the same hypothesis to all of them, for we would have to say that the discussion concerned all the rest of the henads. But if this primal One—as indeed is very much the view of these authorities—is simply and solely one, and unconnected with everything else,[3] and unparticipated—as they say, "snatching itself away"[4] from everything—and unknowable to everything, as being transcendent, whereas each of the other henads is in some degree participated and is not only a unity but participates in the multiplicity proper to it and in some substance either intelligible or intellectual or psychic

---

[4] This would, indeed, seem to settle the argument in favor of Being, the highest element in the noetic realm, since the Orphic "Egg" is equated with Chaldean "Paternal Intellect," which was in turn equated with the highest Intellect.

[1] This and the following two passages, which relate to the question of the true subject of the first hypothesis of the *Parmenides*, involve the attribution to Iamblichus of a doctrine of henads, presumably advanced by him in connection with his exegesis of the first hypothesis, in his commentary on the dialogue.

[2] This must be a reference to Iamblichus, since it is Iamblichus who is credited with the position that the first hypothesis of the *Parmenides* concerns "god and the gods" (Proclus In Parm. 1054, 34 ff. Cousin with scholia ad loc.)

[3] The phrase ἀσύντακτος πρὸς τὰ ἄλλα πάντα recalls the terminology of Iamblichus concerning his second One. Proclus is here seeking to convict Iamblichus out of his own mouth.

[4] Iamblichus uses here a phrase from Or. Chald. Fr. 3 Des Places.

or even corporeal (for participation proceeds down even this far)—why should that One, which is neither reckoned with beings nor ranked at all with the many, be placed in the same hypothesis with henads that are participated in by beings and serve to confer coherence on the many? (Proclus *In Parm.* 1066, 16–1067, 13 Cousin)

2. But if this is true,[5] then how can anyone say that the first hypothesis [of *Parmenides*] treats not only of the first god alone but also of all the other gods? All the henads of the other gods, after all, coexist with being.[6] So each of them is a god, but only the One should be called "One itself" and is above essence and unparticipated so as not to be "a one" as opposed to the simply One. For what is one, together with some other predicate, is "a one"; just as being, together with life, is "a being," and not Being itself; and life, together with Intellect, is intellectual life, not Life pure and simple; and everything taken with some differentiating addition is other than that thing considered as it is in itself and before differentiation. So, One in itself must be before the one that goes with being. For this reason, one cannot say that this hypothesis is about the gods also, as some people have thought. (Proclus *In Parm.* VII 36, 8–28 Klibansky)

FROM PROCLUS' *Platonic Theology*

It is not, then, true, as some authorities [that is, Iamblichus] maintain, that in the first hypothesis the subject is "[the primal] god and the gods." For it was not proper for him [the Platonic Parmenides] to link multiplicity with the One [god] and the One with multiplicity, since the completely primal god transcends in every way the rest of the universe. On the contrary, in the first hypothesis he denies both being and unity itself of the primal [god]; but that this is not appropriate to the other gods must be plain to all. Nor is it true, as they maintain, that Parmenides is treating, in the first hypothesis, the intelligible gods,[1] declaring that it is to those gods that the negations refer, because they are

---

[5] That is, that the first hypothesis concerns the transcendent One.

[6] The henads are the lowest element in the realm of the One—constituting, collectively, the "Unified" (τὸ ἡνωμένον cf. §§10–11 *infra*); so, in Iamblichus' system, they may also be viewed as the highest element of the realm below, that of Intellect—"One-Being" (τὸ ἓν ὄν).

[1] Proclus is here making play with the fact that Iamblichus regarded his henads as also intelligibles (νοηταί), in order to make Iamblichus sound more inconsistent

united to the One and surpass all the divine classes in simplicity and unity; for how could "like and unlike" and "continuous and discrete"[2] and all the other attributes that are denied of the One apply to the intelligible gods? No. While they are right, I think, to say that the attributes being denied are properties of gods, they are wrong to claim that they are all properties of intelligible gods—apart from the fact that, according to this thesis, the subject of the intelligible gods must be treated again in the second hypothesis, because what Parmenides denies in the first hypothesis he affirms in the second. (Proclus *PT* III 23, p. 82, 4–22 S-W)

FROM DAMASCIUS' *On Principles (De Principiis)*

1. After this, let us bring up the following point for consideration: whether the first principles before the primal noetic triad are two in number,[1] the first completely ineffable and that which is unconnected to the triad—as is the view of the great Iamblichus in Book 28 of his excellent *Chaldean Theology*—or whether, as the great majority of those after him preferred to believe, the first triad of the noetic beings follows directly on the ineffable first principle. Or shall we descend from this hypothesis and say with Porphyry that the first principle of all things is the father of the noetic triad? (Damascius *De Princ.* ch. 43, II p. 1, 1–13 W-C)

2. So, then, as a certain person says,[2] one must assume as preliminary the causal principles of both the One-Being[3] and the dyadic structure of the elements inherent in it. The Dyad of first principles has, then, a dis-

---

than he is, in fact, being. The henads may be νοηταί, but they are also members of the realm of the One.

[2] Proclus is actually being somewhat careless here, since these latter attributes are not, in fact, denied of the One in the first hypothesis, though they are asserted of it in the second (*Parm.* 148D5–149D7).

[1] Even this, as we shall see directly, does not reveal the full complexity of Iamblichus' metaphysical position. We must also reckon with a triad of principles depending on the second One, and a system of henads, all within the realm of the One. But this is sufficient for Damascius' purpose here, which is to contrast Iamblichus and Porphyry as two extremes.

[2] This very probably refers to Iamblichus, though it is not clear why Damascius should be so coy about it—he refers to him by name just below. This passage, at any rate, reveals the existence of a Dyad of Limit and Unlimitedness, and their product, the One-Existent, within the henadic realm.

[3] Or: "One-Existent."

tinct existence, prior to the Dyad that has just been mentioned, even as there exists also the One before the Dyad, which Iamblichus postulates, before both, to be the cause of the One-Being. And, in fact, to speak generally, if we divide the totality of beings into what is unified and what is, in one way or another, distinct, even though they are distinguished from one another by a relation of cause and effect, the same result will accrue; for if we start from the principle of two columns,[4] and thus from a single general system of opposition, we necessarily ascend to two principles prior to which there subsists the single summit of both, which is the cause of the fusion of the two principles and of the two sets of things that derive from them, for it is into two that all the channels[5] flowing from them, opposed as they are to each other in every way, come to divide.

Such, at any rate, would be the argument of one who accepts the first principle proposed by Iamblichus, which is situated between the first two [principles] and the Totally Ineffable; and, furthermore, he would add that if the two principles necessarily are participated in by Being[6] (for we must accept that Being is unitary before it is substantial), the processes of participation in it are the primary elements of Being insofar as it is mixed, that is, Limit and the Unlimited. It is for this reason that Being, by its proper nature, is actually "unified,"[7] [because] a multiplicity of elements have come together in it, whereas the elements are everywhere opposed to each other, so that the principles of these elements have an aspect of mutual opposition; and the result of this in turn is that the One is its cause prior to this mutual opposition.

This account, then, claims at once to give support to the hypothesis of Iamblichus and to the mutual opposition, whatever form it may take, of the two principles, since one could very well maintain, as a consequence of this, that the henad prior to these two principles was everything together[8] prior to everything but everything equally, whereas the former of the two principles was itself also all things but, rather, in the mode of limit, while the latter was all things similarly, but, rather, in the mode of unlimitedness. (Damascius *De Princ.* ch. 50, II, p. 25, 1–26, 8, W-C)

---

[4] A reference, presumably, to the Pythagorean Table of Opposites.

[5] A distinctively Chaldean term.

[6] This would be the One-Being, product of Limit and Unlimitedness but also first principle of the noetic realm.

[7] As distinct from being totally one, or unitary.

[8] This Anaxagorean tag is used in Neoplatonism, ever since Plotinus, to characterize the mode of existence of the noetic world. Here the One prior to the Dyad is described as ὁμοῦ πάντα in an anticipatory mode.

3. For, indeed, the single first principle is prior to the two, and this is the "simply One," which Iamblichus postulates in between the two first principles and that Totally Ineffable. These two principles may be termed Limit and the Unlimited or, if one wishes, One and Many—the "One" here to be taken as "one as opposed to many," not the One that is prior to both these and has nothing opposed to it. (Damascius *De Princ.* ch. 51, II, p. 28, 1–6 W-C)

4.[9] And how else could it be that Iamblichus, in expounding the nature of the intelligible, should declare that it subsists in the One and does not proceed from the One, unless he, too, had a concept of what we are just now discussing—namely, the Unified and the One-Being—as being neither yet truly being nor yet still one but, rather, situated as median between the two? (Damascius *De Princ.* ch. 67, II p. 90, 9–13 W-C)

From Pseudo-Simplicius' *Commentary on the Soul (De Anima)*

But if, as Iamblichus thinks, a distorted and imperfect activity cannot proceed from a perfect substance that is incapable of being affected, the soul would be affected somehow even in its essence. Thus, in this way, too, it is a mean not only between the divisible and the indivisible, or what remains and what proceeds or the intellectual and the nonrational but also between the ungenerated and the generated. It is ungenerated in accordance with its permanent, intellectual, and indivisible aspect, while it is generated in accordance with its procession, divisibility, and association with the nonrational. It possesses neither its ungenerated aspect purely—as an intellectual entity does, since it is not indivisible or permanent, nor its generated aspect as the lowest entities do, since these never completely exist. But in its association with generation, it sometimes in some way abandons itself, as it were, and it does not simply remain but simultaneously both remains what it is and becomes. It never leaves what is ungenerated but is always joined to it and holds permanence within and, as it were, flows onward, replenishing what is lost.

---

[9] This passage occurs during a discussion by Damascius of the role and place of "the Unified" (τὸ ἡνωμένον), i.e., the combination of Limit and Unlimitedness, which constitutes, in his system—and in that of Iamblichus before him—both the lowest element of the henadic realm and the transcendent monad of the intelligible realm, for which reason the Unified can also be referred to as "intelligible" (νοητόν).

The generated aspect of it, however, also never proceeds without the stable and ungenerated, while the ungenerated aspect of it is sometimes removed from all association with generation in the life separated from body. Therefore the soul is both immortal and permanent, always having its immortality and permanency inferior to the intellectual life. But our soul is differentiated in itself. It is pure, on the one hand, insofar as is appropriate for it, receiving immortality, permanence, and indivisibility from the separated and intellectual life. For once it has been separated, as he [Aristotle] will say, "it is what it is."[1] In its declension towards the outside, on the other hand, it remains without completely abandoning itself. (This is evident from every rational activity, since such activity does not come into being without reversion to itself, as a result of which there is also belief after assent, when it judges that the thing known is true, and then assents, for this is belief. It is evident also from its restoration from within itself towards what is superior and its perfection by itself.) But it does not preserve its permanence pure, for, owing to its declension outside, as a whole it simultaneously both remains and proceeds, and it does neither completely without the other.

As a result of this, its immortality is, at that time, filled with mortality in its whole self, and it does not remain immortal only. Its ungeneratedness somehow happens to come to be, and its indivisibility is divided. It is no longer activity in essence insofar as is right for it. In accordance with its generated aspect, it is first actuality because of the division of its activity from its essence, and not as a knower (for it is not a composite) but as knowledge or as form. (Simplicius [?] *In De An.* 89, 33–90, 25 Hayduck)

---

[1] Cf. Aristotle *De An.* Γ 5, 430a22.

PROCLUS

Elements of Theology[1]

This work is an attempt to express the main principles of the Platonic system in "geometrical" form (on the model of Euclid's Elements), each theorem being derived from what proceeds it. The subject matter ranges from the One, or Unity, through the various levels of reality and basic processes such as cause and effect, procession and return, down as far as the individual soul, which descends into body.

Prop. 1. *Every multiplicity participates in some way in unity.*[2]

For if it participated in no way, neither would any given whole be one nor would each of the many elements from which a multiplicity is made up, but each of those also will be a multiplicity, and this will continue to infinity, and each of those infinite elements will in turn be an infinite multiplicity; for a multiplicity that in no way participates in any unity, neither in respect of the whole of itself nor in respect of any of the individual components of it, will be infinite in every way and as a whole, for each of the many entities that exist, no matter which you take, will either be one or not one; and if not one, then either many or nothing. But if each part is nothing, then the sum total of these will be nothing; if many, then each of them is made up of infinites infinitely multiplied. These conclusions, however, are impossible. For neither is it the case that any existent thing is made up of infinite-times-infinite parts (since there is nothing greater than infinity, but that which is the sum of all things will be greater than any given part); nor, on the other hand, that anything can be made up of parts which are nothing. Every multiplicity, therefore, participates in some way in unity.

---

[1] "Theology" is here understood as a branch of theoretical philosophy. Cf. Aristotle *Met.* E 1, 1026a18–19.

[2] Proclus begins his most systematic work with the basic principle on which Neoplatonic metaphysics rests, based in its turn on the key texts of Plato *Parm.* 137C–D and 157B–C. Plotinus relies on this basic principle in such a text as VI 9. 1 Cf. also V 6. 3. Proclus elaborates this proof further at *PT* II 1.

Prop. 7. *Everything that is productive[3] of something else is superior to the nature of its product.*

For either it is superior or it will be either inferior or equal. But let us first suppose it to be equal. Then that which is produced by it either has power itself to be productive of something else, or it is completely incapable of generation. But if it were incapable of generation, then by this very fact it would be inferior to its producer, and in its unproductiveness it would be unequal to it, which is productive and has the power to create. And if, on the other hand, it is productive of other things, either it will produce something equal to itself—and this will be universally the case, and so all beings will be equal to one another and none will be superior to any other by reason of the fact that the producer generates what follows upon it as equal to itself—or else it will produce something unequal to it, and so it would no longer be equal to what produced it. For it is a property of equal powers to create what is equal to themselves. But the products of these powers will be unequal to each other, if it is the case that the producer is equal to what is prior to it but that what follows from it is equal to it. Therefore, it is impossible that the product should be unequal to the producer.[4]

But neither will the producer ever be inferior, for if it gives the product being, it must also provide it with the power that goes with its being. But if it were itself productive of all the power that is in what follows

---

[3] Proclus uses the verb παράγειν and its derivatives here, rather than ποιεῖν presumably to avoid the connotation of any sort of temporal creation; this production is an eternal process. The principle enunciated here is basic to the development of the Neoplatonic system. Plotinus states it on various occasions (e.g., V 4. 1; V 5. 13, 37–8: "For the maker is better than what is made, because it is more perfect."). Cf. Porphyry *Sent.* §13. A proof text for the principle could be found in Plato's *Phil.* 27A5–6: "And surely that which produces (τὸ ποιοῦν) has a natural priority, and what is produced follows in its train in coming into being."

[4] The reasoning here is as follows: if we postulate that the primary product—let us say, Intellect, from the One—is equal to its producer, then if (as must be the case) it is also productive, it must in turn produce products equal to itself. But we see that the world is comprised of entities of unequal power; so, plainly, at some stage something has produced something inferior to itself. However, unless this were universally the case, it would be illogical that something that was itself produced as equal to its producer should in turn produce something inferior to itself, since its productive powers would be equal to that of its own producer. Therefore, all productive agents (in the intelligible world) produce entities inferior to themselves.

upon it, then it would have the power to make itself such as that is. And if that were the case, then it could make itself more powerful, for it would not be prevented from this by incapacity, since the creative power would be inherent in it; or through lack of will, since by nature all things strive towards their good. So, if it were able to bring about another thing more perfect than itself, it would perfect itself before it did the same for what follows upon it.

Therefore, since the product is neither equal to the producer nor superior to it, it follows that in all cases the producer is superior in nature to the product.

Prop. 11. *All things that exist proceed from a unique cause, the first.*[5]

For otherwise, either no one among things will have a cause; or alternatively, the totality of existence being limited, the sequence of causes will be circular; or else we will be faced with an infinite regress, cause lying behind cause, so that the positing of prior causes will never come to an end.

But if no thing had a cause, there would be no sequence of primary and secondary, perfecting and perfected, regulative and regulated, generative and generated, active and passive; and so there would there be no scientific knowledge of anything. For the task of science is the recognition of causes, and only when we recognize the causes of things do we say that we know them.[6]

If, on the other hand, the sequence of causes is circular, the same things will be at once prior and consequent and both more powerful and weaker; for every productive cause is superior in power to its product.[7] (It makes no difference whether we connect cause and effect by deriving the one from the other through a greater or a less number of intermediaries, for the cause of all these will be superior to all of them, and the greater their number, the more powerful a cause will it be.)

But if the accumulation of causes is to be continued to infinity, and one comes before the other forever, once again there can be no scien-

---

[5] This proposition in effect establishes that the final cause of all things (as set out in Prop. 8: "All things that participate in the Good are subordinate to that which is primarily Good and which is nothing else than good") is also their efficient cause. Cf. Proclus *In Parm.* 798, 27 ff; *In Tim.* I 228, 11 ff.

[6] Cf. Plato *Men.* 98A; Aristotle *Phys.* A 1, 184a12–14; Plotinus VI 7. 2, 15–19.

[7] This has been argued in Prop. 7 *supra*.

tific knowledge of anything;[8] for there can be no knowledge of anything infinite. And if the causes are unknowable, there can be no scientific knowledge of their consequents.

Since, then, there must be a cause for all things, and causes must be distinguished from effects, and there can be no such thing as an infinite regress, there must be a first cause of all existing things, from which they each proceed as from a root, some closer to it and others more remote (that this principle must be unique, of course, has already been established, inasmuch as the existence of every multiplicity must be secondary to unity).[9]

Prop. 15. *Everything that is capable of reverting on itself is incorporeal.*[10]

For nothing that is a body is of such a nature as to revert on itself, for if that which reverts upon anything is joined to that upon which it reverts, then it is plain that all the parts of any body that reverted upon itself must be joined to every other part; for that is what it means, after all, to revert upon oneself: both elements becoming one—both the reverted subject and that on which it has reverted. But this is impossible for a body and, in general, for any divisible substance. For the whole of a divisible substance cannot be joined with the whole of itself because of the separation of its parts, seeing as they occupy distinct positions in space.[11] No body, therefore, is of such a nature as to revert upon itself in such a way that the whole is reverted upon the whole. If, therefore, there is anything that is capable of reverting upon itself, it is incorporeal and without parts.

---

[8] Cf. Aristotle *Met.* A 1, 994a1 ff.

[9] This has been established in Prop. 5: "Every multiplicity is secondary to unity."

[10] In this proposition and the two following, Proclus wishes to establish the general principle that nothing corporeal can achieve self-reversion and the self-consciousness that goes with it. This particularly concerns the soul (cf. Props. 186–7 *infra*), but the principle is of more general application as a refutation of Stoic materialism. For the doctrine propounded here, cf. Plotinus V 3. 6, 39–43; 13, 13–17; Porphyry *Sent.* §41, but its origins can be discerned already in Aristotle *De An.* Γ 6, 430b22 ff.: "The cognizing agent must be potentially one (of a pair of contraries) and cognize the other. But if there is anything that has no contrary, it is self-cognizing and in actuality and separately existent."

[11] Cf. Plotinus IV 7. 8.

Prop. 16. *Everything that is capable of reverting on itself has being separable from all body.*

For if it were inseparable from any body whatsoever, it could not have any activity separable from the body, since it is impossible that, if a given essence be inseparable from bodies, the activity that proceeds from that essence should be separable,[12] for if that were the case, the activity would be superior to the essence in that the latter would need a body while the former would be self-sufficient, being dependent not on bodies but on itself. Anything, then, that is inseparable in its essence is, to the same or an even greater degree, inseparable in its activity. But if that is the case, it cannot revert on itself. For that which reverts on itself, being other than body,[13] has an activity separate from body and not carried on through the body or with its cooperation, since neither the activity itself nor the end to which it is directed requires the body. Therefore, that which reverts on itself is entirely separable from bodies.

Prop. 17. *Everything that is originally self-moving is capable of reverting on itself.*

For if it moves itself, then its motive activity is directed towards itself, and mover and moved exist together as one. For either it moves in respect of one part of itself and is moved in another; or the whole moves and is moved; or the whole originates motion, but it is moved in respect of a part, or the other way about. But if the mover be one part and the moved another, in itself the whole will not be self-moved,[14] since it will be composed of parts that are not self-moved: it will have the appearance of a self-mover, but will not be such in essence. And if the whole originates a motion that occurs in a part, or the other way about, there will be a part common to both that is simultaneously and in the same respect mover and moved, and it is this part that is the primal self-mover. But if one and the same thing moves and is moved, it will have its activity of motion directed towards itself, since it is a self-mover. But to direct activity towards something is to revert on that thing. Therefore, everything that is primarily self-moving is capable of reverting on itself.

---

[12] Plotinus IV 7. 8, 5–7.
[13] Prop. 15.
[14] Cf. Plotinus V 3. 1.

Prop. 20. *Beyond all bodies is the essence of the soul; and beyond all souls is the intellectual nature; and beyond all intellectual substances, the One.*[15]

For every body is moved by something other than it: it is not of such a nature as to move itself, but by the presence of soul it is moved from within, and it is through the soul that it has life.[16] When soul is present, the body is in some sense self-moved, but when soul is absent it is moved externally, showing that body is naturally moved from without, while self-movement is the soul's portion; for that in which soul is present is endowed with a degree of self-movement. And that which soul bestows by virtue of its mere existence must belong in a far more basic degree to soul itself.[17] Soul is, therefore, beyond bodies, as it is self-moved in its essence, while they come to be self-moved by participation.

Soul in turn, being self-moved, occupies a rank inferior to the unmoved nature that is unmoved even in its activity, for among all things that are moved, the self-moved holds the dominant rank; and among all movers, the unmoved. If, therefore, soul moves other things through moving itself, there must exist prior to it a cause of motion that is unmoved. Now Intellect is such an unmoved cause of motion, being eternally active without change.[18] It is by means of Intellect that soul participates in constant thinking, even as body partakes in self-movement through soul. For if constant thinking belonged primarily to soul, then it would inhere, like self-movement, in all souls.[19] Therefore, it does not belong primarily to soul. Therefore, prior to soul there must be something that is primarily intellectual. Therefore, Intellect is prior to souls.

---

[15] This proposition provides the first exposition within the *Elements* of a logical derivation of the three Neoplatonic hypostases. Proclus (like Plotinus in V 1.) sets out to show dialectically that the existence of objects that move without being self-moving demands an entity that is self-moving, and that in turn demands the existence of something that, while causing motion, is superior to spatial motion (though not to "spiritual motion," i.e., self-thought); but that in turn demands a first principle, the unity of which precludes even self-thought.

[16] Cf. Plato *Lg.* 895C–6C.

[17] This is established by Prop. 18: "Everything that by its existence bestows a character on others itself possesses to a primal degree the character that it communicates to the recipients."

[18] Cf. Aristotle *Met.* Λ 7, 1072a24–6; Plotinus II 9. 1, 29–30.

[19] Cf. Prop. 19: "Everything that inheres primarily in any natural class of beings is present to all members of that class equally and in virtue of their common definition."

But, again, prior to the Intellect there is the One.[20] For the Intellect, even though it is unmoved, is not yet a unity, for it serves as object of knowledge to itself and is object of its own activity. Moreover, while all things, of whatever level, participate in unity, not all participate in Intellect, for to participate in Intellect is to participate in knowledge, since intuitive knowledge[21] is the beginning and first cause of all knowing. Therefore, the One is beyond Intellect.

Beyond the One, on the other hand, there is no further principle, for the One is identical with the Good,[22] and is, therefore, the principle of all things, as has been shown.[23]

Prop. 21. *Every order [of being], beginning from a monad, proceeds to a multiplicity coordinate with that monad; and in the case of any order, the multiplicity is to be referred back to a unique monad.*[24]

For the monad, having the status of a principle, generates the multiplicity proper to it. For this reason, it constitutes a unique series, or order, in that the entire sequence derives from the monad its declension into multiplicity; for if the monad were to remain unproductive within itself, there would no longer be an order or a series.

And conversely, the multiplicity may be referred back to a unique common cause of all the coordinate terms; for the element that is identical in every member of the multiplicity did not proceed from any one of those members. That which proceeds from one out of many is not common to all, but is peculiar to the unique individuality of that one. Since, then, in every order there is some commonality and continuity and identity in virtue of which some things are said to be coordinate and others not, it is clear that the identical element is derived by the whole order from a unique principle. Therefore, in each order or causal chain there exists a unique monad prior to the multiplicity, which determines for the entities ranged within it their unique relation to one another and

---

[20] Cf. Plotinus III 8. 9; V 3. 10–12.

[21] ἡ νοερὰ γνῶσις. Cf. Aristotle *APo.* B 19, where Aristotle calls it simply νοῦς.

[22] Cf. Prop. 13: "Every good is such as to unify what participates in it; and all unification is a good; and the Good is identical with the One."

[23] Prop. 12: "All that exists has the Good as its first principle and cause." Cf. Plotinus V 2. 1, 1; VI 8. 8, 8–9.

[24] Cf. Proclus *In Parm.* 703, 12 ff.; 1069, 23 ff.; Plotinus IV 4. 11.

to the whole. Admittedly, among members of the same series, one may be cause of another. But that which is cause of the series as a unity must be prior to them all. And insofar as they are coordinate, they must all be generated from it, not each of them in their individuality, but as belonging to a particular series.

From this it clearly follows that even at the level of natural bodies unity and multiplicity coexist in such a manner that the one Nature[25] contains the many natures as dependent on it, and, conversely, these are derived from one Nature—that of the whole; that the soul-order, originating from one primal Soul, descends to a multiplicity of souls and again carries back the multiplicity to the one; that to intellectual essence there belongs an intellectual monad and a manifold of intellects proceeding from a unique Intellect and reverting on it; and that for the One that is prior to all things there is the multiplicity of the henads,[26] and for the henads the upward striving towards the One. Therefore there are henads following upon the primal One, intellects following on the primal Intellect, souls following on the primal Soul, and a plurality of natures following on the universal Nature.

Prop. 25. *Everything that has attained its perfection proceeds to generate those things that it is capable of producing, imitating in this the unique principle of all things.*[27]

For even as that principle, by reason of its own goodness, is by a unitary act constitutive of all beings (for the Good is identical with the One,[28] and action that is performed in accordance with goodness is identical with unitary action), so in like manner the principles consequent upon it are impelled because of their own perfection to generate further principles inferior to their own essence,[29] for perfection is a function of the

---

[25] Here we find nature functioning, as in Plotinus (cf. e.g., IV 4. 11), as a sort of fourth hypostasis, presiding over the realm of nonrational living beings.

[26] The concept of "henads" was propounded, probably originally by Iamblichus but in its developed form, perhaps not until Syrianus, to provide a bridge between the absolute simplicity of the One and the multiplicity of the Forms or intellects in Intellect. The henads, though extremely unified, are still multiple and constitute a kind of archetype of the multiplicity of the Forms. See *supra* Iamblichus section Fr. 28 of his *Commentary on Plato's Parmenides*.

[27] Cf. Plotinus V 1. 6, 30–4, etc.

[28] Prop. 13; see n. 23.

[29] Prop. 7.

Good; and the perfect, insofar as it is perfect, imitates the Good. Now we saw that the Good was constitutive of all things.[30] Accordingly, the perfect is by nature productive within the limits of its power. The more perfect is the cause of more, in proportion to the degree of its perfection, for the more perfect participates more fully in the Good. That is, it is nearer to the Good. And that means that it is more nearly akin to the cause of all things; that is, it is the cause of more. And the less perfect, insofar as it is less perfect, is the cause of less; for being further removed from that which produces all things, it is constitutive of fewer things. This is so because that which brings into being—or imposes order or perfection on, or holds together, or gives life to, or creates—all things has a closer kinship to that which does all this to more things, while that which does this to fewer things is more alien to it.

On the basis of this, it is clear that that which is most remote from the first principle of all things is unproductive and a cause of nothing. For if it generates something and has something after it, it is plain that it will no longer be the most remote, but what it produces will be more remote than it, and it itself will be nearer by reason of producing something else, whatever that be, thus imitating the cause that is productive of all beings.

Prop. 35. *Every effect both remains in its cause, and proceeds from it, and reverts on it.*[31]

For if it were simply to remain, it will in no way differ from its cause, being without distinction from it; for distinction arises simultaneously with procession. And if it should proceed only, it will be devoid of conjunction or sympathy with its cause, since it will have no means of communication with it. And if it should revert only, how can that which does not derive its being from its cause revert in its being upon a principle that is alien to it? And if it should remain and proceed, but does not revert, how does it come about that each thing has a natural desire in the direction of its well-being and the Good, and an upward striving towards its generative cause? And if it should proceed and revert, but not remain, how does it come about that after being parted from its cause it strives to be conjoined with it, although before being separated there

---

[30] Prop. 12; see n. 24.

[31] This triad of "moments" within any level of true being is, of course, one of the pillars of Neoplatonic dialectic. Here Proclus sets out to establish it dialectically, by a process of elimination.

was no conjunction? For if it was conjoined with the cause, it certainly remained in it. Finally, if it should remain and revert, but not proceed, how can something revert that has not undergone distinction, since all reversion, after all, resembles resolution into that source from which it has been divided according to being?

So, then, it is necessary that the effect should either remain simply or revert simply, or proceed simply, or combine the extreme terms, or combine the mean term with one of the other two, or else combine all three. The only possibility remaining, then, is that every effect remains in its cause, proceeds from it, and reverts on it.

Prop. 41. *Everything that has its existence in something else is produced entirely from something else; but everything that exists in itself is self-constituted.*[32]

For what exists in something else and is in need of a substratum could never be generative of itself, for that which is of such a nature as to generate itself has no need of anything else as a base, being contained in itself and preserved in itself, without any substratum. On the other hand, that which is able to remain established in itself is productive of itself, since it proceeds from itself to itself, and is such as to contain itself, and is thus in itself as an effect is in its cause; for it is not in itself as in a place or in a substratum. A space, after all, is different from what is in the space, and what is in a substratum is different from the substratum; but this is the same as itself. So, therefore, this is in itself by self-constitution, and in the manner that what derives from a cause is in its cause.

Prop. 53. *Prior to all eternal entities there is Eternity, and prior to all temporal ones there is Time.*[33]

For if, at every level, participated entities are prior to what participates in them, and prior to the participated there are the unparticipated, it is

---

[32] The concept of self-constituted entities, or αὐθυπόστατα, is an attempt to grant a place in the Neoplatonic system to the phenomenon of "emergence," whereby Intellect and Soul are not just emanations from the One but have hypostatized themselves. Such secondary principles proceed from their priors, but also from themselves, and are based in themselves.

[33] This hypotasization of both Eternity (Αἰών) and Time (Χρόνος) as entities transcending and presiding over their respective realms probably goes back to the speculations of Iamblichus but is at variance with the doctrine of Plotinus,

plain that what is eternal is distinct from the eternity immanent in it; and that, in turn, from Eternity on its own, the first as being participant, the second as being participated in, and the third as unparticipated; and likewise, that a temporal entity (which is participant) is distinct from its time (as participated in); and that in turn from the Time prior to it, which is unparticipated. And either of these unparticipated entities is everywhere and in all its participant members to the same extent, while the participated is only in those members that participate in it. For there are as many eternal things as there are temporal ones. And in all of these there are, respectively, an eternity and a time, divided amongst them by participation. But prior to these are the undivided Eternity and unique Time; the former is the Eternity of eternities, while the latter is the Time of times, since they are the generators of their respective participants.

Prop. 57. *Every cause both exercises its activity prior to its effect and generates a greater number of terms following on it.*[34]

For if it is a cause, it is more perfect and more powerful than its effect.[35] And if so, it must be a cause of more things: for greater power produces more effects; equal power, equal effects; and lesser power, fewer; and the power that can produce the greater effects upon similar subjects can also produce the lesser, whereas a power able to produce the lesser will not necessarily be capable of the greater. If, then, the cause is more powerful than its effect, it is productive of more things.

But again, such powers as are in the effect are present to a greater extent in the cause. For all that is produced by secondary entities is produced to a greater degree by prior and more causative principles.[36] The

---

who regards eternity merely as "the state and nature" (διάθεσις καὶ φύσις) of real Being (e.g., III 7. 4), while he takes time to be essentially the life of the soul of the universe (III 7. 11–12).

[34] The principle that the efficacy of a causal principle extends further down the scale of being than those of its consequents is an important axiom of Proclus' system, serving as it does to bind all of creation together in concentric circles emanating from the One. For another good statement of this principle, cf. *In Tim.* I 209, 13ff.

[35] Prop. 7.

[36] As specified by the previous proposition (56): "All that is produced by secondary entities is to an even greater extent produced by those prior and more causative principles from which the secondaries were themselves derived."

cause, therefore, cooperates in the production of all that the effect is capable of producing.

And if it first produces the effect itself, it is presumably obvious that it is active prior to the latter, in the activity that produces it. Therefore, every cause operates both prior to its effect and in cooperation with it and likewise gives rise to further effects posterior to it.

On the basis of this, it is clear that what Soul causes is caused also by Intellect, but not all that Intellect causes is caused by Soul. Intellect operates prior to Soul. And what Soul gives to secondary existents, Intellect gives to them in greater measure. And at a level where Soul is no longer operative, Intellect still sheds illumination with its own gifts on things on which Soul has not bestowed itself; for even the inanimate, insofar as it participates in Form, participates in Intellect or in the creative activity of Intellect.

Again, of those things of which Intellect is the cause, the Good is also the cause of them, but not conversely. For even privations of Form derive from the Good, since all things stem from it. But Intellect, given that it is Form, cannot cause privation to be.[37]

Prop. 64. *Every originative monad gives rise to two series, one consisting of self-complete existents and one of illuminations that have their existence in something other than themselves.*[38]

For if there is a procession by declination through terms akin to the constitutive causes,[39] from the entirely perfect there will proceed in due order things complete in their kind, and through the mediation of these in turn there arise the incomplete. Accordingly, there will be one order of self-complete existents and another of incomplete ones. The latter are such as to already belong to their participants, for, being incomplete, they require a substratum for their existence. The former make the participants belong to them, for, being complete, they fill the participants

---

[37] This is an interesting point. The One, or the Good, is the ultimate source of matter, but it also presented as the cause of privation (στέρησις) of form, a concept derived from Aristotle.

[38] This can be seen as a development of Plotinus' doctrine of the twofold activity of intelligible entities, an internal and an external; cf. e.g., VI 2. 22, especially 26 ff.

[39] This is a development of Prop. 28: "Every producing cause brings things like itself into existence before what is unlike itself."

with themselves[40] and establish them in themselves and have no need of inferior beings for their existence. Accordingly, those existents that are complete in themselves, while by their distinction into multiplicity they show inferiority to their originative monad, are yet in a way assimilated to it in virtue of their self-complete existence. By contrast, the incomplete fall short of the monad that is self-existing, not only owing to their existing in another, but also as they are incomplete in relation to the all-completing. But all processions advance through similars down to the wholly dissimilar. Therefore, each of the originative monads gives rise to two series.

From this it is apparent that, among the henads, some proceed as self-complete from the One, while others proceed as illuminations[41] from unities. And so among intellects, some are self-complete existents, while others are intellectual perfections; and among souls, some belong to themselves, while others belong to ensouled bodies, as being merely appearances of souls. And so not every unity is a god, but only the self-complete henad; not every intellectual property is an intellect, but only the essential;[42] nor is every illumination from Soul a soul; but there are also images of souls.

Prop. 67. *Every whole is either prior to its parts, or made up of its parts, or is in the part.*

For either we contemplate the form of each thing in its cause, and this form preexisting in the cause we say is a whole prior to the parts; or else [we contemplate it] in the parts that participate in the cause, and this in one of two senses: for either we see it in all the parts taken together— and it is then a whole-of-parts, the absence from which of any single part diminishes the whole—or else we see it in each part separately, such that even the part has become <a whole> by participation in the whole, which causes the part to *be* the whole in a partial mode. The whole-of-parts is the whole considered as [an independent existent]; the whole prior to the parts is the whole considered according to its cause;

---

[40] Prop. 25.

[41] Ἐλλαμψις, like ἴνδαλμα and εἴδωλον *infra*, are Neoplatonic terms for the manifestations of a given hypostasis in the level of being below it.

[42] The Greek word is οὐσιώδης. Cf. Plotinus V 3. 5, 37. This term indicates the properties that belong to Intellect insofar as it is intelligible, in contrast to those properties that belong to it insofar as it is the paradigm of life. Cf. Prop. 39.

the whole in the part is the whole considered according to participation.[43] For this last is still the whole, though in an extreme degree of declension, insofar as it imitates the whole-of-parts where it is not any random part, but only [part] of such as can assimilate itself to a whole whose parts also are wholes.

Prop. 123. *Everything that is divine is itself, by reason of its superessential unity, ineffable and unknowable to all things secondary to it, but it may be grasped and known from what participates in it. For this reason, only the first principle is completely unknowable, as being unparticipated.*

For all knowledge that comes through reasoning is of real beings and possesses its grasp of truth in virtue of real beings (for it grasps thoughts and consists in acts of thinking). But the gods are beyond all being.[44] Accordingly, the divine neither is an object of opinion or of discursive reason nor is it intelligible. This is so because all that exists is either sensible, and therefore an object of opinion; or true being, and therefore intelligible; or of intermediate rank, at once being and becoming;[45] and, owing to this, an object of discursive reason. If, then, the gods are superessential, or have an existence prior to beings, we can have neither opinion concerning them nor scientific knowledge nor discursive reason nor yet thinking of them.

Nevertheless, from the beings dependent upon them, their distinctive properties may be cognized, and this with the force of necessity.[46] For it is in accordance with the distinctive properties of the principles participated in that differences within a participant order are determined. And it is not everything that participates in everything (for there can be no conjunction of things that are wholly unlike each other),[47] nor does any chance thing participate in any chance thing, but it is what is akin that is joined to each thing, and from it each proceeds.

---

[43] This important triadic distinction of modes of existence of any given principle has been formally enunciated just above, in Prop. 65. The distinction between a whole made up of its parts and a whole prior to its parts can be observed already in Plato's *Tht.* 204A–205C, and to this Proclus has added the concept of a whole inherent in each of its parts.

[44] Cf. Prop. 115: "Every god is above being, above life, and above intellect."

[45] Such as, presumably, the embodied soul.

[46] Cf. Plotinus V 3. 14.

[47] Cf. Prop. 29: "All procession (πρόοδος) is accomplished through the likeness of secondary entities to their primaries."

Prop. 186. *Every soul is an incorporeal substance and separable from body.*[48]

For if it knows itself, and if anything that knows itself reverts on itself[49] and what reverts on itself is neither body (since all body is incapable of reverting on itself) nor inseparable from body (since, again, what is inseparable from body does not have the ability to revert on itself; for in this way it would be separated from body), the consequence will be that soul is neither a corporeal substance nor inseparable from body. But that it knows itself is plain, for if it has knowledge of principles superior to itself, it is capable that much the more of knowing itself, as it derives self-knowledge from its knowledge of the causes prior to it.

Prop. 187. *Every soul is indestructible and imperishable.*

Anything that can in any way be dissolved or destroyed either is corporeal and composite or has its existence in a substrate; the former kind, being made up of a plurality of elements, is destroyed by being dissolved, while the latter, being capable of existence only in something other than itself, disappears into nonexistence when severed from its substrate.[50] But the soul is both incorporeal and external to any substrate, existing, as it does, in itself and reverting on itself. It is, therefore, indestructible and imperishable.

---

[48] Proclus is here assuming a distinction between the cognitive aspect of soul that is an incorporeal substance and the aspect of soul that is, in fact, inseparable from the body. The latter he calls an "image of soul" (εἴδωλον ψυχῆς). Cf. Prop. 64; *In Tim.* II 285, 27. Plotinus uses the term "living being" (ζῷον) for composite of body plus (inseparable) soul. Cf. e.g., I 1. 5.

[49] This principle is established in Prop. 83: "Everything that is capable of knowing itself is capable of reverting upon itself in every way (πρὸς ἑαυτὸ πάντῃ ἐπιστρεπτικόν)." And this in turn follows from the earlier Props. 15 and 16, above: "Everything that is capable of reverting upon itself is incorporeal (ἀσώματον)," and "Everything that is capable of reverting upon itself has an existence separable from all body." This proposition and the following one simply relate these more general principles to the case of souls.

[50] This is an application of Prop. 48: "Everything that is not eternal either is composite or has its existence in something else."

Prop. 194. *Every soul contains all the Forms that Intellect contains primarily.*

For if Soul proceeds from Intellect, and Intellect is the cause of the existence of Soul,[51] and Intellect, while being itself unmoved, produces all things by its mere existence, then it will give to the soul that takes its existence from it essential reason-principles of all that it contains.[52] For anything that creates by its mere existence implants at a secondary level into its product that which it itself is primarily.[53] Soul, therefore, possesses, in a secondary mode, the irradiations of the Forms in Intellect.[54]

Prop. 195. *Every soul is all things, sensible entities in the mode of an exemplar and intelligibles in the mode of an image.*

For intermediate as it is between the indivisible principles and those which are divided about body,[55] it produces and causes the latter to exist, while at the same time it manifests its own causes, from which it has proceeded. Now those things of which it is the preexistent cause, it pre-embraces in exemplary mode, and those from which it originates, it possesses by participation as products of the primal entities. Accordingly, it pre-embraces all sensible things causally, possessing the reason-principles of material things immaterially, of bodily things incorporeally, of extended things without extension. On the other hand, it possesses as images the intelligible principles and has received their Forms—the Forms of undivided entities divisibly, of unitary entities as a manifold, of

---

[51] The Greek words are: νοῦς ὑποστάτης ψυχῆς.

[52] Cf. Proclus *In Tim.* II 299, 18.

[53] This principle has been established already in Prop. 18: "Everything that bestows some characteristic on others by its existence alone itself primarily possesses that characteristic it shares with its recipients."

[54] This sets up a firmer distinction than Plotinus would maintain between Soul and Intellect. Soul can only attain to ἐμφάσεις, "reflections" or "irradiations" of the Forms in themselves; these constitute its λόγοι, which it then projects upon the material substratum. Cf. Plotinus and Proclus' further criticism of Plotinus' position at *In Parm.* 948, 14–20. Proclus rejects Plotinus' view that a part of the soul—intellect—does not "descend." For this reason, our knowledge of Forms is always indirect. Cf. *infra* Prop. 211 with note.

[55] This role of the soul has already been specified in Prop. 190. The formulation employed here rests upon the description of the composition of the soul in Plato *Tim.* 35A.

unmoved entities as self-moved. Therefore, every soul is all things: the primal orders, by participation; and those inferior to it, in exemplary mode.

Prop. 211. *Every particular soul, when it descends into the realm of generation, descends completely; it is not the case that there is a part of it that remains above and a part that descends.*[56]

For if it is the case that some part of the soul remains in the intelligible [realm], then it will think constantly, either without transition from object to object or transitively. But if without transition, it will be an intellect and not a part of a soul, and the soul in question will be one that directly participates in Intellect. But this is impossible. And if transitively, then there will be a unique substance comprising a part that is thinking constantly and a part that thinks intermittently. But this is impossible, for they differ in kind, as has been shown.[57] And it would, in addition, be strange if the highest part of the soul, being in that case perpetually perfect, did not master the other faculties and render them also perfect. Therefore, every <particular> soul descends <completely>.

PLATONIC THEOLOGY[1]

This is a systematic work (which has come down to us, like the following two works, in incomplete form), on the subject of theology (in the Platonic sense), taking us through, in Proclus' own words, first, general concepts relative to the gods; then, an enumeration of all the degrees of the divine hierarchy; and lastly, a study of the individual gods. The

---

[56] This proposition directly challenges the Plotinian principle that a part of the soul remains "above." Cf. Plotinus III 4. 3. 21–7; IV 8. 8; V 1. 10; V 3. 3–4. The opposition to this Plotinian doctrine was initiated by Iamblichus. Cf. Proclus *In Tim.* Fr. 87, quoted above, p. 254.

[57] This has been shown in the course of Prop. 184, where three orders of souls are distinguished, the divine (which thinks constantly, though even then only by participation in Intellect), the human (or at least that kind subject to "fall" and embodiment), and that which is intermediate between the two (the daemonic).

[1] In order to give some idea of the tone and contents of this largest of Proclus' systematic works, we translate here just the first three chapters of Book I. The work as we have it is incomplete, but six books survive.

project is, in fact, cut off at the end of Book VI, in the midst of the second part, at the level of the hypercosmic gods.

Book I

[Preface]
1. As a whole, Pericles, dearest of friends to me,[2] the philosophical system of Plato made its first brilliant appearance, in my view, through the beneficent will of the higher powers, since it served to reveal the intellectual power hidden within them and the truth that, together with true beings, was bestowed upon souls that have descended into generation, insofar as it is permitted to them to share in such supernatural and vast blessings. It, in due course, achieved a fully developed form, and then, after, as it were, having retreated into itself and making itself invisible to the great majority of those who professed philosophy and aspired to join in the "hunt for true being,"[3] it once again came forth into the light.[4]

But in a very special way, I think, the initiation into the divine mysteries themselves,[5] seated in their purity "on their holy pedestal"[6] and established for all eternity among the gods themselves, has been revealed to those who, in their temporally-bound state, could draw profit from it, by one man alone,[7] whom I would not be wide of the mark in describing as the guide and hierophant of those true rites in which are initiated those souls who have detached themselves from the terrestrial

---

[2] Pericles is a pupil of Proclus, mentioned also in *In Parm.* 872, 18–32, as providing a solution to a problem in the text.

[3] Plato *Phd.* 66C.

[4] This remarkable survey seems to envisage (1) a period of consolidation and codification of Plato's teaching during the period of the Old Academy (347–274 B.C.E.), followed by (2) a period of virtual eclipse of the higher truths of Platonism during the period of the skeptical New Academy (274–80 B.C.E.)—and, it would seem, during the period known to us as Middle Platonism (80 B.C.E.–220 C.E.), down to the emergence of Plotinus. It is interesting that Proclus should so thoroughly dismiss the dogmatic Platonists of the early Empire; this is presumably because they had no true concept of a One above Being.

[5] The comparison of philosophy to initiation into a mystery is a very common image in later Platonism; cf. the elaborate development in Plotinus VI 9, 11; but it goes back to the Middle Platonic period.

[6] Plato *Phdr.* 254B.

[7] The reference is, of course, to Plato.

realm, and of those "perfect and unshakeable visions"[8] of which those souls partake who are genuinely dedicated to the happy and blessed life. However, on this first occasion, he kindled the light with such an aura of solemn secrecy, as if performing holy rites, and placed it in such security in the recesses of the shrine that it remained unknown to most of those who entered in; but then at certain fixed intervals of time, through the agency of certain true priests who had adopted a way of life suited to access to such mysteries, it was brought to light to the extent possible and shed its rays in all directions, bringing about the illumination resulting from such divine visions.[9]

Among these exegetes of the Platonic mystical vision who have laid out for us the hallowed expositions of divine principles, being endowed with a nature akin to their master, I would rank Plotinus the Egyptian: and those who received from him the true vision of reality—Amelius and Porphyry: and thirdly those who were their followers and who attained, it seems to me, such a degree of perfection that they may be compared to statues—Iamblichus and Theodorus[10] and such others as followed in their train to enter this divine choir and elevate their own thought to the ecstatic state induced by contemplation of the doctrines of Plato. It is from them that he who, after the gods, has been our guide in all that is noble and good[11] received undiluted into the recesses of his soul the most authentic and pure light of truth. It is he who has granted us the privilege of partaking in the philosophy of Plato as a whole, and who has taken us as his partner in the traditions that he received in secret from those senior to himself,[12] and in particular who joined us with himself as fellow-celebrants of the mystical truth of divine principles.

---

[8] *Phdr.* 250B–C.

[9] This whole passage constitutes an extraordinary rhetorical elaboration of the theme of the secret doctrines of Plato as a mystery accessible only to the few. It serves to bring home to us the degree to which Platonism was a religion as well as a philosophical system in this period.

[10] Proclus, we may note, is not usually so complimentary to Theodorus of Asine, or to Amelius, for that matter. He more often criticizes them for excessive elaboration in metaphysics.

[11] That is, Syrianus. There is actually something of a mystery as to who relayed the truths of Platonism from Iamblichus and Theodorus to Plutarch of Athens, the mentor of Syrianus.

[12] Here a reference to Plutarch of Athens, and to the secrets of theurgic practice.

If, then, we were to set out to pay him the debt of gratitude appropriate to his benefactions to us, not even the whole course of time would suffice for it. However, if we are ourselves not only to receive from others the outstanding benefit of Platonic philosophy, but also to leave for subsequent generations memorials of the blessed visions of which we ourselves declare that we have been the spectators and, so far as is in our power, the devotees, under the guidance of one who has been, in our time, the most perfect and universally accomplished in philosophy, then perhaps it is right that we should call upon the gods themselves to kindle in our souls the light of truth, and those who follow upon and serve their superiors[13] to direct our intellect and guide it towards the perfect, divine, and exalted goal of insight into the doctrine of Plato; for, in all cases, I presume it is proper for anyone who possesses even a modicum of good sense to take one's start from the gods,[14] and not least when one is involved in expositions concerning the gods; for it is not possible to come to a comprehension of the nature of the divine in any other way than through being perfected by the light emanating from the gods themselves, nor yet is it possible to communicate this knowledge to others other than by submitting to their guidance and by preserving the exegesis of the divine names as something that transcends the variety of opinions and the diversity inherent in words.[15]

Having then grasped this truth, and paying attention to the advice of Timaeus in Plato's dialogue, let us appoint the gods our guides to the teaching that concerns them. As for them, hearkening to us and coming to us "kindly and graciously,"[16] may they take charge of the intellect of our soul and lead it around to the hearthstone of Plato and to the steep summit of this doctrine of his. Once we have arrived there, we will be in receipt of the whole truth about them, and we will gain the best deliverance from these birth pangs which possess us concerning divine matters, yearning as we do to gain some knowledge of them, not only by inquiry from others, but also, so far as in us lies, by seeking within ourselves.

---

[13] A reference, by means of an allusion to *Phdr.* 250B, to the class of daemons and other intermediate beings.

[14] A reference here to Timaeus' beginning of his exposition at Plato *Tim.* 27C. Proclus follows the practice of invoking the gods also at the beginning of his *In Parm* (see *infra*).

[15] A reference here, perhaps, to the proper exegesis of Plato's *Cratylus*, on which Proclus composed a commentary.

[16] *Phdr* 257A.

[The proposed mode of exposition, and the proper preparation on the part of the auditor]

2. But enough now of prefatory remarks. It is incumbent upon me next to set out the mode of my proposed instruction—what one should expect it to be—and to define the sort of preparation proper to those who are going to receive it, by virtue of which they will find themselves suitably disposed to address themselves not so much to my words but to the sublime[17] and divinely inspired philosophy of Plato. In fact, I consider that one must ensure that both the form of the discourse and the dispositions of the auditors are in a favorable state, even as in the rites [of theurgy] the experts prepare suitable receptacles for the gods, and they do not employ always the same inanimate substances nor yet the same animals nor men in order to ensure the manifestation of the gods, but in each case they introduce into the rite in question that which is naturally capable of serving as an intermediary.[18]

First of all, then, it is my intention to divide this treatise into three parts. At the beginning I will assemble all the general concepts concerning the gods that Plato conveys to us, and I will examine in each case the significance and the value of the axioms propounded. In the middle section I will enumerate all the orders of the gods; define, in the Platonic manner, their attributes and their processions;[19] and relate everything to the basic principles laid down by the theologians.[20] In the final section I will treat of the gods, both hypercosmic and encosmic, who have been celebrated in an individual way in the Platonic writings, and I will connect their study with the universal classes of divine orders.[21]

---

[17] The word used here, ὑψηλός, is a verbal reminiscence of *Phdr.* 270A1–2.

[18] This point is also made by Iamblichus in *De Myst.* V 23. It is interesting that Proclus here combines the rather widespread introductory theme of the necessity for a suitable disposition in the auditor of philosophical discourses with an explicit reference to theurgical practice.

[19] Meaning by this the various lower levels of being that depend upon them.

[20] That is to say, such figures as Orpheus, Musaeus, Homer, and Hesiod.

[21] These divisions correspond, respectively, to: (1) Book I, Chs. 13–29, in which he enumerates all the divine attributes set forth in *Laws, Republic, Phaedrus,* and *Phaedo*; (2) Books II–VI, in which he goes through the various divine orders, beginning with the One (Book II), and continuing with the henads (Book III 1–6), the intelligible gods (Book III, Chs. 7–28), intelligible-intellective gods (Book IV), intellective gods (Book V), and the hypercosmic gods (Book VI). At this point the treatise breaks off, but he still would have had to cover the encosmic gods, universal souls, and "higher beings," such as angels, daemons and heroes. After that would have come Part 3, in which he would presumably have

In all cases, I will give precedence to what is clear, distinct, and simple over their opposites. What is transmitted through symbols I will transform into straightforward doctrine; truths purveyed in images I will refer back to their originals;[22] that which is presented in too categorical a manner I will buttress with "reasonings concerning the cause";[23] that which is composed by means of demonstrations I will subject to examination, providing a root-and-branch exposition[24] of the form of truth that it contains, and putting it in terms familiar to my audience; of those things that are set forth in riddles I shall uncover the clear meaning through making appeal to other data not drawn from alien sources but, rather, from the most genuine works of Plato himself; while that which falls immediately within the understanding of the audience I will examine in accordance with the realities themselves. It is by all these means that there will be revealed to us the unique and perfect form of Platonic theology, the truth that extends throughout all of its divine insights, and the one unique intellect that has generated the whole beauty of this system and the mystical unfolding of the theory behind it.

Such, then, will be the nature of my exposition, as I have said. Now as for the auditor of the doctrines that be set forth, it is axiomatic that he be adorned with the ethical virtues, having repressed all unworthy and unharmonious motions of the soul through the rational direction of virtue and having brought them to harmonious unity in the form of practical wisdom. "For it is not right," as Socrates says, "that the impure enter into contact with the pure,"[25] and certainly every wicked man is, in all cases, impure, even as his contrary is pure.

Secondly, the auditor should be trained in all the procedures of logic and present himself as someone who has worked his way through many irrefutable propositions both in the area of analysis of concepts and in that of the method of the division that is its contrary, even as, I think, Parmenides counseled Socrates to do.[26] In fact, until one engages in

---

dealt with particular deities in a series of individual studies. It would have been a truly monstrous work, if it was ever completed.

[22] This distinction between symbols (σύμβολα) and images (εἰκόνες) is identified by Proclus at *In Tim.* I 29, 31 ff. as being of Pythagorean provenance. He expands on this distinction in Ch. 4.

[23] A reference to Plato *Men.* 98A.

[24] Proclus here uses, significantly, the compound verb ἐπεκδιηγέομαι, which Plato uses in *Phd.* 97E1 to describe what Socrates expected (but was disappointed of) from Anaxagoras.

[25] *Phd.* 67B.

[26] See *Parm.* 135C–136C.

such a "tortuous path"²⁷ through logical reasonings, the intelligent grasp of the divine classes and the truth that resides in them remains difficult and, indeed, unachievable.

Thirdly, over and above these qualifications, the auditor should not be ignorant either of the science of nature or of the opinions of all sorts that relate to it,²⁸ in order that, having investigated in a suitable way in [sensible] images the causes of existent things, he may more easily advance to an understanding of the real nature of transcendent and primordial substances. Let him not remain backward, as we have said, in discerning the truth present in phenomena, or yet the "paths of technical knowledge"²⁹ and the teachings inhering in them; for it is through these teachings that we come to know in a more immaterial manner the essence of divinity.

If the auditor has united in himself all these qualities under the direction of his intellect—if he has familiarized himself with the dialectical method of Plato, if he has immersed himself in activities that are immaterial and transcend corporeal powers, and if he has striven to contemplate true reality "by thought with the aid of reasoning"³⁰—then let him apply himself avidly to the explication of the divine and blessed doctrines, "unfolding through love the depths of his soul," in the words of the Oracle,³¹ since one cannot have any better helper than Love for the acquisition of this insight, as indeed is asserted in the text of Plato.³² And having been schooled in the truth that extends throughout all things, he will raise the eye of the intellect to absolute truth itself. And having established himself at the level of the stable, immobile, and sure form of knowledge of divine things, he will be persuaded³³ no longer to harbor admiration of anything else nor to turn his gaze towards other things but rather to strive towards the light of the divinity with a serene

---

²⁷ Ibid. 136E.

²⁸ The auditor should thus be proficient in all three main divisions of philosophy—ethics, logic, and physics, enumerated in that order.

²⁹ Plato *Tim.* 53C.

³⁰ Ibid. 28A.

³¹ This is not included as such in Des Places' edition of the Chaldean Oracles, but the phrase "depths of the soul" (ψυχῆς βάθος) occurs in Fr. 112. The auditor is now to be endowed with the three Chaldean virtues—love, truth, and faith, which correspond to the divisions of philosophy, ethics, logic, and physics (including metaphysics).

³² Plato *Symp.* 212B.

³³ This verbal form is a reference to the third Chaldean virtue of faith (πίστις), which corresponds to the knowledge of metaphysical reality.

intellect and the power of indefatigable life. And, in a word, he will set himself as an objective that state that unites activity and repose, such as one should possess who wishes to be that sort of "leader" of whom Socrates makes mention in *Theaetetus* (173C).[34]

[The Nature of Theology]

3. Such, then, is the magnitude of our theme; and such the mode of discourse proper to it, and of such a sort, at least in my opinion, should be the preparation of those who wish to study it. But before beginning the exposition of the topics with which I propose to deal, I want to say a few words about the topic of theology in general[35] and about the modes in which it is presented; and also to specify which of these theological modes Plato himself adopts and which he rejects in order that, armed with this advance knowledge, we may the more easily be able in what follows to grasp the first principles behind our demonstrations.

All those, then, who have ever occupied themselves with theology have termed "gods" the first principles in nature and have declared that it is with these that the science of theology is concerned. There are some who have considered only corporeal substance as qualifying for existence, regarding all the classes of incorporeal things as secondary in respect of substantiality. They have concluded from this that the first principles of beings are by nature corporeal and that the faculty in us that cognizes them is itself corporeal.[36] Others again, postulating that all bodily things are dependent on incorporeals and defining primary existence as residing in souls and in the faculties of soul, denominate as gods, I believe, the best class of souls and call theology the science that raises itself to the cognition of these.[37] Then, there are those thinkers

---

[34] That is to say, a true philosopher, "who does not even know his way to the market-place, or to law-courts, or to the assembly."

[35] We must bear in mind here that, for Proclus, θεολογία, which may be rendered "discussion of the nature of god and the gods," can be regarded as a branch of philosophy, not as its rival. In fact, of the topics here mentioned, only the first is addressed in Ch. 3; the latter two are dealt with in Ch. 4, which we do not include in this volume.

[36] These are the Stoics, as is made clear from a parallel passage in Proclus' *In Parm.* 1214, 7–15, and this begins a sequence that continues with Anaxagoras, the Peripatetics, and the Platonists.

[37] If this, as just mentioned, refers to Anaxagoras (as is plainly indicated by *In Parm.* 1214, 10–11), it is a remarkable attribution. Presumably, Proclus is understanding Anaxagoras' Νοῦς, or Intellect, as being really a soul of the universe, and the heavenly bodies as souls also.

who see the multiplicity of souls as deriving from another principle superior to them and postulate intellect as the leader of all things: these assert that the finest aim in life is the union of the soul with intellect, and they consider that the type of life that is in accord with intellect exceeds all others in value. And that is why, presumably, they come to identify theology with the exposition of the essence of intellect.

All these, then, as I have said, call "gods" the most primal and self-sufficient principles of reality, and "theology" the science concerned with these. Only the divinely-inspired philosophy of Plato, disdaining as it does to rank anything corporeal as a principle (for the good reason that nothing that has parts and extension can by its nature either produce itself or preserve itself in being, but [what has parts and extension] possesses being and the capacity of acting and being acted upon only by the agency of a soul and the motions inherent in that soul), and revealing that the essence of the soul, though superior to that of bodies, is nonetheless dependent upon the existence of intellect (since everything that is subject to temporal motion, even if it is self-moved—while being superior to those things that are moved by something else—is yet secondary to what enjoys eternal motion), asserts, as has been said, that Intellect is the father and causal principle of both bodies and souls, and that everything that exercises its life in conditions of progression and unfolding possesses its being and its actualization in dependence on Intellect. But, then, it advances to another first principle, completely transcending Intellect, yet more incorporeal and ineffable than it, from which all—even if you include the lowest order of things—must derive their existence.[38] For it is not all things that are of such a nature as to participate in Soul, but such as possess in themselves life of some sort, whether clearer or dimmer; nor yet can all things enjoy the influence of Intellect or Being, but only those that have some degree of formal existence, while it must be that that the first principle of all should be participated in by all existent things, if, indeed, it is the case that "it will never be separated from any of them,"[39] being the cause of anything that exists in any manner whatever.[40]

---

[38] For what follows, compare the doctrine enunciated in ET Prop. 57, *supra*.

[39] It is interesting that Proclus should here use a phrase from the second hypothesis of Plato's *Parm.* (144B1–2) to reinforce his point, since the subject of that hypothesis is normally regarded by Neoplatonists as being Intellect rather than the One.

[40] Cf. *In Parm.* 56, 3–6 Klibansky.

This principle that is absolutely first in the universe and superior to Intellect, Plato, divinely inspired as he was, discovered hidden in secret recesses,[41] and, as a consequence, has presented as being superior to the corporeal realm these three causal principles or monads—namely Soul, the primal Intellect, and that Unity that is above Intellect—and he has drawn out from these the numbers [of existents][42] proper to them—that proper to the One, that proper to Intellect, and that proper to Soul (for in every case a monad is at the head of a multiplicity coordinate with it)[43]—and even as he attaches bodies to souls, so, it would seem, he attaches souls to the Forms in Intellect, and these in turn to the henads of beings,[44] and finally he relates all things to the single imparticipable Henad [that is, the One].

And when Platonic philosophy has ascended to this point, it considers that it has attained the highest limit of theoretical consideration of the universe and that this is the truth about the gods, which concerns itself with the henads of beings and details their processions and their properties, the kinds of linkage that beings have with them, and the orders of Forms that are dependent on these unitary existents. As for the area of study concerned with Intellect and the genera and species it contains, this it considers to be secondary to the science that is concerned with the gods themselves, and it considers that this seeks to attain the knowledge of Forms that are still intelligible and capable of being grasped by the soul through a direct intuition, while the science that is superior to it goes in pursuit of ineffable and unutterable realities, both so far as concern their distinction from one another and their emergence from a single cause.

From this it follows, I think, that it is the strictly intellectual function of the soul that is capable of grasping the Forms in Intellect and the distinctions between them, while it is the summit of the intellect, and, as

---

[41] This image harks back to the initial point made in Ch. 1, that the deepest truths of Platonism, after being revealed by Plato, lay long buried until brought back into the light by Plotinus and his followers. Cf. Plotinus V 1. 8, 8–14.

[42] Proclus says only ἀριθμοί, "numbers," but this is what he must mean. Cf. *ET* Prop. 113: "The whole divine ἀριθμός has the character of unity," where ἀριθμός refer to whole sum of henads dependent on the One. It is henads that Proclus is about to discuss here.

[43] Cf. *ET* Prop. 21. This principle seems to go back to Iamblichus, *In Tim.* Fr. 54 Dillon (in Proclus *In Tim.* II 240, 6–7).

[44] That is to say, the henads of the Forms, in the realm of the One.

they say, its "flower"[45] and its mode of existence, which unites itself to the henads of beings and, by means of these, to the hidden Unity behind all the divine henads; for of the many cognitive faculties within us, this is the only one that permits us to enter naturally into relation with the divine and to participate in it. For the divine is not graspable by sense-perception, seeing as it completely transcends all body; nor yet by the faculties of opinion or discursive reasoning, for these make distinction of parts and are suited to the apprehension of multiform entities; nor yet by "thinking involving an account,"[46] since this type of knowledge relates to the realm of true beings, whereas the essence of the gods "rides above"[47] true beings and is defined as the very unity behind all things.

If, then, the divine is to be known at all, it remains only that it be graspable by the [corresponding] mode of existence of the soul, and be knowable by this, so far as that is possible at all, for at every level we say that "like is known by like";[48] that is to say, the sensible realm is known by sensation; the opinable world, by opinion; the dianoetic, by discursive reason;[49] and the intelligible, by intellect; so that it is by the One [in us] that the most unitary realm is known, and by the ineffable element [in us], the ineffable. That is why Socrates in *Alcibiades*[50] was right to declare that it is by entering into itself that the soul can gain the vision not only of all other things but also of god; for it is through turning itself towards it own unity and the center of its whole life and shaking itself free of multiplicity and the variety of multifarious powers within it that the soul may raise itself to the highest "vantage point"[51] from which to view the whole of existence.

---

[45] A distinctively Chaldean term for the suprarational aspect of intellect, by which the One is cognized. Cf. *Or. Chald.* Fr. 1, 1 Des Places: "There is an object of intellection, such as must be discerned by the flower of intellect"—a line much quoted by Proclus.

[46] Borrowing here a phrase from *Tim.* 28A1.

[47] Another Chaldean term (cf. Fr. 193 Des Places), also used by Plotinus I 1. 8, 9.

[48] This is a very widespread Platonist principle, actually going back to Empedocles Fr. B 109 D-K.

[49] These latter two levels of reality should refer to the heavenly realm (identified first by Xenocrates in the Old Academy as cognizable by δόξα ("belief"), and the realm of Soul.

[50] *Alc.* 133B–C.

[51] Employing here a significant term from the myth of Plato's *Sts.* 272E.

In the most sacred of the Mysteries, they say that the initiates first of all come up against beings of myriad shapes and forms that precede the gods,[52] whereas, when they have entered into the sanctuary and are standing hedged about by the rites, they receive into themselves in all purity the divine illumination and, as those men would say, partake "in the nakedness"[53] of the divine. In the same manner, I think, the soul, in contemplating the universe, when it considers what comes after it, sees only the shadows and the images of true beings, but when it turns towards itself, it uncovers its own essence and its own reason-principles.[54] Initially it is as if it sees itself alone, but then, in deepening its own insight into itself, it discovers in itself Intellect and all the orders of true beings and, lastly, when it has passed into the interior of itself and, as it were, into the secret sanctuary of the soul, there it contemplates "with eyes shut"[55] the race of gods and the henads of beings. For all things are within us in a manner proper to soul, and by reason of that we have the natural capacity to know everything through awaking the powers within us and the images of all beings.

And it is this that constitutes the best form of activity: in the quietude of one's faculties to extend one's attention to the divine; and to join in the dance around it; and always to gather together all the multiplicity of the soul towards this unity; and, casting from one all that comes after the One, to establish oneself in it and to join oneself with this ineffable entity that transcends all existent things. Indeed, it is up to this that it is proper for the soul to ascend until it reaches the culmination of its ascent at the [first] principle of beings. Once it has arrived there and contemplated the place where it is and then has descended from there, passing through the realm of being and spreading out before it the multiplicity of Forms, surveying not only their monads but also the numbers proper to them and discerning intellectually how each of them depends upon its proper monad, it will have reason to believe that it has come into possession of the most perfect knowledge of divine matters, having contemplated in a unitary manner both the processions of the gods into beings and the distinctions of beings in relation to each of the gods.

---

[52] This actually seems to be a reference to the Eleusinian Mysteries, rather than to anything theurgic.

[53] A Chaldean term (cf. Fr. 116, 1 Des Places—quoted by Proclus In Crat. 88, 4–5 Pasquali)—so "those men" are the theurgists.

[54] That is to say, the projections within it of the Forms resident in Intellect.

[55] This is perhaps also a Chaldean reminiscence, though not attested in surviving fragments; but it also used by Plotinus I 6. 8, 25, so Proclus may have borrowed it from there.

COMMENTARY ON PARMENIDES

Of this vast work only the first seven books are extant (the last only in the Latin translation of William of Moerbeke), which takes us as far as the end of the first hypothesis of the second part of the dialogue (142A). That it continued further is indicated by the fact that Damascius later bases his own commentary, which continues to the end of the dialogue, on a critique of that of Proclus.

Book I

(i) Introductory Invocation[1]

[617] I pray to all the gods and goddesses to guide my mind in this that I have undertaken—to kindle in me a shining light of truth and enlarge my understanding for the genuine science of being; to open the gates of my soul to receive the inspired guidance of Plato; and, in anchoring my thought in the full splendors of reality, to hold me back from too much conceit of wisdom and from the paths of error by keeping me in intellectual converse with those realities from which alone the eye[2] of the soul is refreshed and nourished, as Plato says in *Phaedrus*.[3]

I ask from the intelligible gods[4] fullness of wisdom; from the intellectual gods, the power to rise aloft; from the supercelestial gods guiding the universe, an activity free and unconcerned with material inquiries; from the gods to whom the universe is assigned, a winged life; from the angelic choruses, a true revelation of the divine; from the good daemons, an abundant filling of divine inspiration; and from the heroes, a generous, solemn, and lofty disposition. So may all [618] the orders of divine beings help to prepare me fully to share in this most illuminating

---

[1] The only other work of Proclus to begin with a comparable dedicatory preface (with prayer) is *Platonic Theology*, though he does invoke divine help elsewhere on occasion (e.g., *PT* III 1; *Dub.* 10.1–2) following Plato's example at *Tim.* 27C (cf. *In Tim.* I 214, 26 ff.).

[2] Plato actually says πτέρωμα, "wing," not ὄμμα, "eye," at *Phdr.* 246E2, but all manuscripts of Proclus have ὄμμα, and it is not an exact quotation, so ὄμμα may stand.

[3] 246E–251B.

[4] We find here a complete Procline hierarchy set out: intelligible, intellectual, transcendent (ἀπόλυτοι), and encosmic gods, and then angels, daemons, and heroes, each bestowing gifts appropriate to their natures.

and mystical vision that Plato reveals to us in *Parmenides* with a profundity appropriate to its subject and that has been unfolded to us, with his own very lucid applications, by one who was, in very truth, a fellow Bacchant with Plato and filled entirely with divine truth and who, by leading us to the understanding of this vision, has become a true hierophant of these divine doctrines.[5] Of him I would say that he came to men as the exact image of philosophy for the benefit of souls here below, in recompense for the statues, the temples, and the whole ritual of worship, and as the chief author of salvation for men who now live and for those to come hereafter. So may all the higher powers be propitious to us and be ready with their gifts to illuminate us also with the light that comes from them and leads us upwards. And you, Asclepiodotus,[6] who have a mind worthy of philosophy and are my very dear friend, receive these gifts that come from that worthy man, all of them in full measure, and store them in the most intimate folds of your mind.

(ii) Dramatic Setting

But before beginning the consideration of this vision, I will set forth the dramatic setting of this dialogue for the sake of those who are interested in such things. It was the festival of the Great Panathenaea, celebrated [619] by the Athenians of that time with more elaborate preparations than the Lesser, which they called by the same name in honor of the goddess, thus celebrating her with both longer and shorter processions. It was while this festival was being observed, as I said, that Parmenides and Zeno had come to Athens, Parmenides being a teacher and Zeno his disciple. Both were citizens of Elea and, what is more, had been members of the school of Pythagoras, as Nicomachus somewhere relates.[7] They had come then from Elea in Italy to honor the goddess and help any at Athens who were interested in knowledge of divine things. They lodged outside the Ceramicus,[8] inviting anybody to come and converse with them.

---

[5] This fulsome praise of Syrianus recurs frequently in Proclus' writings and acknowledges a very real dependence. Cf. *PT* I 1, pp. 7–8 S-W; *In Remp.* I 71, 21 ff. Kroll.

[6] A pupil of Proclus, born in Alexandria, sometime resident of Aphrodisias in Caria (presumably after Proclus' death).

[7] The Pythagoreanizing Middle Platonist Nicomachus of Gerasa in his *Life of Pythagoras*, now lost but drawn on copiously by both Porphyry and Iamblichus in their extant *Lives*.

[8] Or rather "outside the walls, in the Ceramicus," to accord with the text of Plato (127C1). But it is not clear that the manuscript reading should be changed.

Among those who came to see them was Socrates, who was then a young man, but of outstanding natural abilities. On one occasion, Zeno was reading to the assembled visitors a book in which he tried to show the numerous difficulties that are encountered by those who maintain a plurality of things as primary; for Parmenides put forward as his peculiar teaching, it is said, that Being is one. Those who took these words in a rather irreverent sense assailed the doctrine with witticisms, such as that if Being is one, then Parmenides and Zeno do not both exist at the same time, but if Parmenides, then not Zeno, and if Zeno, then not Parmenides; and on these and other similar grounds they tore his doctrine apart, seeing nothing of its truth.

Now Zeno, Parmenides' disciple, did not care to plead directly for his master's doctrine, since he thought it needed no additional confirmation, but attempted to give it secret aid by writing a book in which he ingeniously showed that those who suppose that beings are many encounter no fewer difficulties than were alleged against those who say Being is one. For he showed that the same thing [620] will be both like and unlike, both equal and unequal, and in general that there will result the abolition of all order in the world, and everything will be thrown into confusion.

And if I may interpolate my opinion, I think he did so plausibly. For Being must be both one and many. Every monad has a plurality correlative with it, and every plurality is comprehended under some appropriate monad. But since in every case the ground of plurality is tied up with the monad and cannot exist without it, these men of Elea were focusing their attention upon the incomprehensible unifying causality of the monad when they made the "One Being" primary. Seeing that every plurality exists in unity, they declared that the "One Being" is prior to the many; for what primarily is, is one, and from it the plurality of beings proceeds.

Now Parmenides did not see fit to descend to plurality, having anchored himself in the contemplation of the One Being and ignoring everything that would direct his thought to particulars. But Zeno was not his equal, and though he, too, made the One Being the goal of his thinking, he still wished to separate himself from plurality and gather himself into that One that is, as it were, the center of all things; so he refuted the proponents of the view that Being is many in order to purge their understanding of its propensity towards plurality. For refutation is purification, i.e., a removal of ignorance and a way towards truth. Thus he showed that when the One is taken away, there is complete confusion and disorder among the Many, for what is without a share in unity cannot possibly be a whole, or a totality, or endowed with form. All of these characters depend surely upon participation in unity, but when form and wholeness are taken away all order and arrangement depart, and nothing is left but disorderly and discordant [621] movement.

He who removes the One is unwittingly doing the same as one who removes god from things, for with unity absent, things will be "as it is probable they are when god is absent," as is said somewhere in *Timaeus*.[9] It is god who provides unity to things separated, order to the disordered, wholeness to the parts, form to material things, and perfection to the imperfect; and in each of these cases unity is unquestionably conferred. This, then, is the way in which Zeno refuted the proponents of the Many and brought himself to the conception of the One Being. Hence, the necessary consequence: if Being is not a many, either nothing at all exists or Being must be one. Thus in the end Zeno espoused the teaching of his father, Parmenides, seeing that plurality exists in the One as in its center and that the One cannot be preserved in mere plurality; for this exists in itself prior to plurality, and plurality is what it is entirely from the One.

These are the contents of the book that he reads to the company. When Socrates had listened to the reading of it and to all the absurdities that Zeno said result for those who posit that Being is many, he shifted the discussion from the examination of unity and plurality in things to that of the unity and diversity of Forms. There is nothing remarkable, he said, in showing that the same thing is both like and unlike, both equal and unequal. For the same thing is both right and left, and there are many things in this condition in the sensible world, that is, together with their plurality they possess also unifying Forms by which each thing is at the same time many and One. Rather, he said, it ought to be shown that among intelligible species the same is equal and unequal, like and unlike; for he saw there the unmixed purity of the Forms, and thought that plurality as thus distinguished was being maintained. So, he thought it necessary to shift the inquiry from sensible to intelligible [622] things and to look there for mingling and separation in each case, since in sensible things these characteristics are abundantly evident because of the nature that is their substratum. These are the same questions that he discusses in later life in *Philebus*,[10] where he says that to affirm the same thing to be one and many is a commonplace when applied to composite things, but the sight of this among the monadic Forms would be something to marvel at.

---

[9] 53B3–4.
[10] 14D.

At these words of Socrates, Parmenides takes over the discussion and asks Socrates whether he really believes there are intelligible Forms and what his reasons are for this belief. When Socrates replies that he holds firmly to this hypothesis of Forms, Parmenides raises difficulties about them. Are there, or are there not, Forms of all things? How do sensible things participate in Forms? How are the Forms related to us? Thus, the fundamental difficulties connected with the Forms are brought up by Parmenides.

When Socrates shows his bewilderment in the face of these problems, Parmenides advises him, if he is really enamored of the truth about Being, to exercise himself in dialectic before undertaking this larger inquiry—meaning by dialectic that method that Socrates himself teaches us in other works, such as *Republic*, *Sophist*, and *Philebus*. When Socrates asks what this method is and shows himself ready to accept these visitors' teaching, Parmenides expounds the method whose praises Socrates also has sung on many occasions.

In *Phaedo*,[11] for example, in distinguishing the function of dialectic from that of eristic, he says that one must, at every step, assume a hypothesis and continue an inquiry in this way until from many hypotheses we come up to "something adequate," which he calls "the unhypothetical."[12] As Parmenides recommends, we must first posit the object of our inquiry and then divide this hypothesis by the employment of antitheses. That is, we assert that the object exists or that it does not exist; and, assuming its existence, we inquire what follows from this assumption, what is excluded by it, [623] and what neither follows from it nor is excluded by it, for in each case, some attributes are completely alien to the object under inquiry, some necessarily belong to it, and some may or may not be present in it.

And then we must divide each of these three classes into four, for we should inquire, assuming its existence, what consequences are implied for it—both with reference to itself and with reference to other things—and what are implied for the other things with respect to one another and with respect to our subject. And again, we should ask what is excluded from it with respect to itself and with respect to other things, and for other things with respect to one another and with respect to it. Thus, our inquiry should proceed through these twelve modes and through an equal number more when the nonexistence of our subject is assumed. So, from one hypothesis two arise at first; then, for each of them, three

---

[11] 101E1.
[12] *Rep.* 510B7.

other hypotheses; and, for each of the three, four more; making twelve hypotheses in all for each of the initial alternatives. And, if you like, you could divide each of them again and thus obtain a great many others, indefinite in number. It is through these hypotheses that we must make our way in accordance with the numbers mentioned—by twos, threes, fours, and twelves, until we come to the unhypothetical principle itself that is prior to all hypotheses.

When this method has been described, Socrates expresses his admiration for its scientific precision and for the intellectual quality of the visitors' teaching. (This is said to be a special feature of the Eleatic School, just as another trait, discipline through mathematics, is characteristic of the Pythagorean, and another of the Heraclitean, viz., the use [624] of names for obtaining knowledge of things.) After expressing his admiration, Socrates demands to have the method fixed in his mind by an example of its use, by Zeno's taking one of his hypotheses and showing how it works in this particular case, as is done in *Sophist* when the Stranger in that dialogue explains the method of division by using it to find the angler and the sophist. But Zeno says the task is beyond his powers. It requires Parmenides himself, and he invites the leader of the discussion to make such an exposition.

Parmenides then takes the floor and asks upon what hypothesis he shall exercise his method. "Shall we," he says, "take my hypothesis of the One, asking what consequences for it follow respectively from its being and its not being, what consequences do not follow, and what consequences may or may not follow, both for itself with respect to itself and with respect to other things, and to other things with respect to one another and to it?"[13] This is agreed upon, and so he examines each of his alternative hypotheses following the twelve modes. In view of these, some persons have thought that the sum total of the hypotheses is twenty-four, but we shall dispute their interpretation when we come to speak of the hypotheses,[14] where we shall make a distinction between the dialectical modes and the hypotheses that are called such. Now, however, let us proceed with matters immediately before us.

Such was the teaching given, as I have said, by Parmenides and Zeno to the young and gifted Socrates and certain others. Pythodorus, the son of Isolochus (a pupil of Zeno, as we have learned from *Alcibiades*),[15]

---

[13] *Parm.* 137B.

[14] He does not in fact deal with these critics when he comes to give a survey of previous views later, in Book VI.

[15] 119A.

was one of those present at this conversation, but he was [625] silent throughout and made no contribution to the discussion, as was done by Socrates, in part asking questions and in part serving as respondent. But he [Pythodorus] heard what was said and, like Aristodemus, who recalled the discourses about Eros in *Symposium*, reported the discussion to Antiphon and his friends. This Antiphon was an Athenian, one who prided himself on his noble ancestry (this is why he was interested in horses, a tradition of long standing among well-born Athenians), and a brother of Plato by the same mother, as Plato himself tells us. Antiphon took in these arguments and himself recounted them to another group, certain Clazomenaeans who cultivated philosophy and who had come to Athens from the School of Anaxagoras; and this is obviously the third account of this conversation.

On this occasion, a certain Cephalus was present, himself a citizen of Clazomenae; and hearing the discussion from Antiphon, he arranged it in narrative form for some future persons not identified, transmitting a fourth account of the meeting. It is not even said who the persons are to whom Cephalus communicated his narrative. He simply recounts the arguments he has heard from Antiphon, who has got them from the Pythodorus mentioned above, who had listened to the words of Parmenides. We have, then, first, the original conversation between the principal personages at the scene where it took place; second, the account of Pythodorus recalling the original conversation and presumably narrating everything as it had occurred; third, the account given by Antiphon of the arguments that Pythodorus had expounded to him and that he transmitted, as we have said, to Cephalus and the philosophers from Clazomenae; and fourth, the account by Cephalus of the arguments transmitted to him by Antiphon, ending up with an indeterminate audience.

(iii) Allegorical Interpretation of the Conversations

Of these four conversations—for we must speak now of the [626] analogies to reality that this series presents, taking our point of departure for the present from the inquiry about Ideas, which is so prominent in the dialogue that some persons have entitled it "On Ideas" [16]—the last is analogous to the procession of Forms into sense-objects. For Cephalus is presenting his narrative to no determinate person for the reason that

---

[16] It seems to have been Thrasyllus, the first-century C.E. editor of the Platonic corpus, who first gave subtitles to the dialogues (cf. D.L. III 56–61).

the receptacle of sensible reason-principles is indeterminate, unknown, and formless.

The preceding conversation resembles the establishing of the Forms in natural essences, for prior to sensible things, all natures, both general and particular, have received from the intelligible world the reason-principles by which they guide sensible things, generating them endlessly and preserving them as living beings. Analogous to them are the visiting nature-philosophers, the followers of the teaching of Anaxagoras.

The still earlier conversation resembles the procession into souls of the varied world of Forms from the Demiurge, for the reason-principles exist psychically in souls, and it is these with which the Demiurge fills up their essence, as *Timaeus*[17] teaches us. To them we may plausibly liken the words that go forth into Antiphon; for souls are likened to the winged pairs of horses and charioteers.[18]

And the first of all the conversations represents the organization of the Forms in the realm of the truly real, for there reside the primary *tetraktys*[19] and all the number of the divine Forms, intelligible and intellectual. These are the ultimate source from which souls receive their complement of appropriate reason-principles, the source from which also the natures are supplied with active forms and from which corporeal bodies are supplied with sensible forms. Just as the same arguments are present in all four conversations but in a special way in each—primarily in the first conversation, for there we have the original discussion; secondarily in [627] the second, for here their transmission is accompanied by memory and imagination; in a tertiary way in the third, for here there is memory of memory; and in the lowest fashion in the fourth, which is the lowest stage of memory—so, likewise, the Forms are everywhere, but in a special way in each grade of being.[20]

Those [Forms] that exist primarily exist in and for themselves, Socrates says, and are in the rank of intelligibles, at which level there is

---

[17] 41A ff.

[18] *Phdr.* 246A.

[19] This is originally the Pythagorean term for "fourness," a fundamental mathematical principle in their system. It represents the musical-numerical order of the universe. The concept enters Platonism through its application to the structure of the Indefinite Dyad.

[20] Application of a basic Neoplatonic principle, "All things are in all, but in a manner proper to the essence of each," going back at least to Numenius (Fr. 41 Des Places); found in Plotinus IV 9. 5; Porphyry *Sent.* §10; Iamblichus *In Phil.* Fr. 5 Dillon; and Proclus *ET* Prop. 103, etc.

no imaging of anything higher, just as in the original conversation the argument was not transmitted through imagination or memory (memory is a likeness of things remembered). The forms in souls have their being in a secondary way, in respect of perfection; and thus are likenesses of the intelligibles, even as the second exposition is secondary because it uses memory and imagination. The forms in nature are likenesses even more, i.e., they are likenesses of likenesses; for it is through the forms in souls that the reason-principles in nature come to be and are. The forms in sensible things are last of all and they are images only, for the Forms end their procession at what is unknowable and indeterminate.

There is nothing after them, for all the reason-principles reach their final term in sensible things. And this is the remarkable thing: the author of the second account gives us not only the bare discourse but also brings in the persons and the actions. The author of the third rehearses all the details of the first as well as those of the second. And the author of the fourth gives us what is in the first as well as what is in the second and what is in the third, both the persons and the actions. So, the primary realities are present at all stages, down to the last. The realities of secondary rank have their causal ground in the former and in turn pervade all the ranks below them (here it is Pythodorus who edited the second conversation); and likewise the third version (of which Antiphon is the author) has its causal ground in the second and in turn passes on the activity of the primary realities to the very last.[21] So much, then, as a preliminary statement about these likenesses, as we begin our study of the dialogue.

(iv) Allegorical Interpretation of the Characters

[628] If we should be required to give a likely analogy for the characters involved,[22] it seems to me that Parmenides himself should be ranked as an analogue to the unparticipated and divine Intellect that is united to real Being in respect of its thinking, or perhaps to Being itself, which was his special concern and which he declared to be one. Zeno

---

[21] This is an application of the principle enunciated at *ET* Prop. 57. See *supra*. pp. 274–5.

[22] What we find here is a panorama of the various levels of being in the intelligible world, which is the proper subject of *Parmenides*. In Proclean (and Iamblichean) theory, this should be reflected, symbolically, in the details of the prooimion, or prefatory portion, of the dialogue. The same will hold true of *Timaeus*.

is an analogue to the Intellect, which is participated in by the divine Soul, filled with all the intellectual Forms that he has received into his essence from the immaterial and unparticipated Intellect. This is why he, too, strives to "snatch himself away"[23] from plurality towards the One Being, imitating the Intellect above him, to which he refers his own perfecting. Or, if you wish, we may liken him to Life—I mean Life that is immediately subsequent to Being—for he delights in assembling contradictions and arguing both for and against a thesis, just as the Life that comes after Being is the first to furnish an expression of contraries, of rest and motion together. And Socrates could be compared to the particular intellect, or absolutely to Intellect, whereas of the other two, the former (Parmenides) is ranked analogically with Being, the latter (Zeno) with Life. This is why he is associated so closely with Parmenides and Zeno, and together with them makes up the first conversation, which we said bears the likeness of genuine being, as Intellect is itself the fullness of indivisible being. Socrates is also portrayed as especially confident of the theory of Forms; and what other role is more fitting for the particular intellect than to see the divine Forms and declare them to others? So, these three personages seem to me to satisfy the analogy: the first, to Being; the second, to Life; the third, to Intellect—or the first, to complete and unparticipated intellect; the second, to intellect that is participated; the third, to the individual and participated intellect. Indivisible nature stops with these grades of being, for intellect is either universal and unparticipated, or universal and participated, or particular and participated; for there is no intellect that is particular and unparticipated.

Of the three narrators of the conversation, Pythodorus is analogous [629] to the divine Soul, for he is present at the original meeting and is filled with blessed words, just as the divine Soul is filled with intellectual forms (for the divine Soul, as Plato tells us in *Phaedrus*[24] goes up to "banquet and festival" in the train of great Zeus). But he is a silent member of the group, for that kind of discussion belongs to beings with indivisible nature. But he might also be likened to the angelic order, as being the first to expound the whole theory of those divine beings. Antiphon resembles the daemonic soul, which lays hold of nature and spurs it to action. For this reason, he wants to be a horseman, as the daemon soul wants to guide and lead according to its will the nonrational steed. But he is filled with words from Pythodorus in the second

---

[23] *Or. Chald.* Fr. 3, 1.
[24] 247A.

conversation and with them he fills the men who have come from Clazomenae, since this kind of soul occupies a middle position, being filled from the higher powers and filling nature with its own forms.

Cephalus and the philosophers from Clazomenae are like individual souls that are conversant with nature. And they have a similar role in this work, because the philosophers from Clazomenae are themselves students of nature. This interest in nature is characteristic of the whole Ionian school, as contrasted with the Italian; for the latter was always striving to apprehend the being of intelligibles, in which it saw all other things causally, whereas the Ionian school occupied itself with nature, i.e., with physical actions and effects, and regarded this study as being the whole of philosophy. The Attic school, being midway between the two, corrected the Ionian philosophy and developed the views of the Italians.

Thus, Socrates in *Phaedo*[25] charges Anaxagoras with making no use of Intellect and invoking airs and [630] dispositions and various other like things as causes of natural events, and in *Sophist*[26] he invites the wise man from Elea to impart to him the philosophy cultivated there. But in those dialogues, as I have said, he brings in both schools, keeping their roles distinct; whereas, in this case, the plot involves bringing to Athens the men from Italy to impart to the Athenians their traditional doctrines and brings the men from Ionia that they may share in the Italian teachings.

Clazomenae is in Ionia and Elea in Italy. Just as all events in nature share in intelligibles through the mediation of the forms in souls, so this setting shows how the Italian philosophy was imparted to the Ionians. It brings them to Athens and through the Attic philosophers enables them to share in these esoteric doctrines.

(v) The Subject of the Dialogue

But we have said enough about the setting of the action—about the four conversations, the rank of the personages involved and their analogy to the grades of things in the universe—to satisfy those with the desire and the ability to contemplate the realm of beings, each in its proper place, from the perspective of the theory of Ideas, from which some of our predecessors, as I have said, have given it its title; for just as we must proceed upwards from sensible appearances to the intelligible cause, so we must ascend from the circumstances presupposed in this dialogue to the unique purpose and the unique end of the whole trea-

---

[25] 98C.
[26] 217C.

tise and relate to this, so far as we can, the other details—the persons, the occasion, the setting—that we have previously considered on their own account.

(a) An Exercise in Logical Method: Aporetic

Some of our contemporaries and predecessors have referred the purpose of this dialogue to logical exercise.[27] In doing so, they discount the [631] title "About Ideas," though it is very ancient, for they say it is relevant to only a small part of the dialogue, and to the aporetic, not the expository part of it. There are some, then, who say the purpose of the dialogue is argumentative—as in *Theaetetus*,[28] where Plato writes against Protagoras, quoting "Man is the measure of all things," and showing that man is no more the measure of all things than a pig or a dog-faced baboon. And they dismiss its theory of reality, regarding the arguments from the implications of saying that the One is and those [implications] that follow from asserting that it is not as mutually destructive. And of these interpreters (I mean those who say the purpose is argumentative), some suppose that Plato wrote it against Zeno to put to the test the working of his subtle new methods of argument on a more difficult theme—that of the intelligibles—for Zeno had been occupied with applying these techniques to the sense-world and showing the clash of antithetical arguments about sense-objects.

It is Plato's custom, these interpreters say, when he writes a controversial dialogue, to do it in one of three ways: sometimes he composes an imitation of what his rival has written, but carries the imitation to greater perfection by adding what his rival's discourse omits. For instance, in *Menexenus*, which he composed in rivalry with Thucydides, the oration written for a public funeral has the same purpose as his rival's; but in the arrangement of its main points, in its invention of supporting reasons, and in the clarity of its exposition, he constructs a much nobler discourse than that of Thucydides. Sometimes he composes arguments counter to those of his rival, as he does here against Zeno, for while Zeno produced a rich and varied show of arguments [632] aimed at catching out the partisans of the Many and brought forth in his refutation not less than forty arguments revealing contradictions

---

[27] For example, Albinus, who in his *Prologue to the Platonic Dialogues*, Ch. 3 presents it as "elenctic."
[28] 152A.

in their position, Plato himself, they say, in rivalry with this energetic opponent of plurality, produced this varied show of arguments with reference to the One, showing, in the same way as he, contradictions about the same subject.

As Zeno refuted the many by showing that they are both alike and unlike, the same and different, equal and unequal, so in the same way Plato shows that the One is like and unlike, not like and not unlike, the same and not the same, different and not different, and so for all the other contradictory predicates, both affirming and denying the contradictory propositions and not, like Zeno, simply affirming them. In this way, he exhibits a far more varied wealth of arguments than Zeno, who had so amazed the world that the Sillographer called him "double-tongued" and, in admiration of his ability, spoke of "the great and unwearied force of Zeno."[29] If he called Zeno double-tongued, what could he have called the man who increased manyfold Zeno's inventions in method?

Thirdly, they say Plato sometimes constructs a controversial piece by using both imitation and antithesis (the remaining alternative). Thus, in his discourse against Lysias, the sophist,[30] he takes for demonstration the same theme as Lysias, but instead of throwing his thoughts together pell-mell, as Lysias does, he introduces the logical order necessary to make the discourse like a living being. Instead of beginning without method, he shows the scientific way of starting from definitions and proceeding in his inquiry from qualities to essence. And instead of ornamenting the discourse with a multitude of phrases that mean the same thing, he adds all sorts of color and [633] variety of thought. All this shows how the sophist should have handled his discourse on behalf of the nonlover. And when Plato goes over to the contrary task and enters into competition with him in pleading for the lover, he leaves his competitor far behind. He uses definitions, divisions, demonstrations, and every sort of means in his rival discourse, going even beyond the customary bounds of exposition, so that by the grandeur of his words he overwhelms the leanness of his opponent's style, and by attributing the difference to divine inspiration, he conceals the cause from the ordinary hearer.

(b) An Exercise in Logical Method: Gymnastic

Such are the contentions of this group of interpreters. But there are some[31] who say that the polemic alleged is inconsistent both with the

---

[29] Timon *Silloi* Fr. 45 D.

[30] *Phdr.* 243D ff.

[31] Alcinous, for instance, in *Didask*, Ch. 6, no doubt reflecting at least one strand of Middle Platonist thinking, treats it as a logical exercise.

contents and with the persons in the dialogue. It is inconsistent with the contents because Zeno has the same purpose as Parmenides in confuting those who, while positing that there are pluralities of beings, have no conception of that unity in virtue of which the many are many and from which they derive their being and have this designation. It is as if someone, seeing the multiplicity of men and saying that they are men, should overlook the one Form, Man, through which these beings are men and are called such; for if he had noted this, he would have said that the men as men are not many but one, as being of the same species. And it is inconsistent with the persons; for it is most incongruous to describe Parmenides and Zeno as lover and beloved, one the teacher and the other a disciple trained by him, and then make the lover and teacher swim through such a sea of controversy with his beloved, the [634] person whom he has trained. And it is also most discordant (as one can most truly call it) to say that the one [Zeno] had prepared the book he wrote as an aid to Parmenides' doctrine, while the other [Plato] is arguing against this aid that Zeno had given by working out these numerous arguments.

Although discounting, then, the interpretation of the dialogue as polemic, some say that its purpose is logical exercise, for there are three main parts, speaking generally, of the dialogue, as these interpreters analyze it: one part puts forward the difficulties in the doctrine of Forms, another contains a concise statement of the method in which it is thought lovers of truth must practice themselves, and the third works out an example of this same method as applied to the One of Parmenides. All these parts have one end—to afford practice in the exercise of logical disputation. For the first shows that such a study is necessary by demonstrating that for those who turn to the study of being without having mastered it, even true hypotheses are overturned, since Socrates, through his lack of practice in this method, is presented as helpless to defend the theory of Forms and that, although he has a "divine impulse," as Parmenides says (135D), and the hypothesis is of the truest . . .[32] And the third part is nothing else but an example, as is plainly stated (137B), to illustrate how this method works so that we may be able to exercise ourselves in this way in all our inquiries. It does

---

[32] There appears to be a lacuna here containing Proclus' remarks on the second part of the dialogue. These are summarized below, at 635, 24–5 Cousin, in the phrase, "another serves to clarify its general rules," referring to the bridge-passage 135B3–137C3, the subject of Book V of the *Commentary*.

somewhat the same thing as the example of division in *Sophist*;[33] as *Sophist* makes known the method of division by using it to find the definition of "angler," so here dialectic is explained by applying it to the One of Parmenides.

From all this they conclude that dialectic is the aim [635] of the dialogue throughout. They say it differs, however, from the method in Aristotle's *Topics*[34] in that the latter divides problems into four kinds and devises a wealth of methods of attack for each kind, even though Theophrastus condenses this fourfold division and restates the method, dealing with two species of problems only—one concerned with definition, the other with accident—counting problems about genus with those concerned with definition, and problems about property with those about accident. But the method described here is a brilliant invention for examining any problem in a variety of ways and bringing the truth to light, since possible conclusions follow as necessary consequences from possible premises, and impossible from impossible.

So, it is the case that a method of this sort does not fall outside the compass of philosophy—as does the method of the *Topics*, which is suitable for those who are seeking only probable conclusions—but rather contributes to the quest for truth itself. Nor, on the other hand, does it allow us to speculate about any more esoteric doctrine beyond itself, seeing that one part of the dialogue shows dialectic to be necessary, another serves to clarify its general rules, and another illuminates the working of the method itself through these rules. These are the objections brought by interpreters who agree that the purpose of the dialogue is logical but discount as implausible the views of those who look for an explanation in personal references.

(c) Metaphysical: A Study of Being

Some say, however, that the intent of the dialogue is directed towards matters of substance and that the logical exercise is introduced for the sake of these substantive questions, although these interpreters do not import the more recondite doctrines to explain the method. [636] Some of them have said that the inquiry is about Being:[35] Plato proposes to

---

[33] 221B.

[34] *Top.* A 4, 101b11 ff., where Aristotle makes a division into "property, definition, genus, and accident." Theophrastus, in his *Topics* (Fr. 124B FHSG), reduces these four to definition and accident.

[35] This may refer to Origen the Platonist, Plotinus' fellow-student with Ammonius, who is known to have taken the first hypothesis to have a purely negative

confirm, through the agency of these persons themselves, how they asserted Being to be one, and by means of the methods they were accustomed to use, Zeno vigorously criticizing the many and Parmenides expounding the One Being; for cathartic discourses must precede perfective ones. They say that Plato himself lauds Parmenides and testifies of the arguments here that they have a most noble depth in them. At least in *Theaetetus*[36] Socrates says that when he was very young he met Parmenides, then quite an old man, and heard him philosophizing about Being—not logical gymnastics, but profound conceptions—and he fears that they will not understand his words and will fail completely to grasp what he means. By all this he shows that the purpose of the inquiry now under way is an important one, and that the method introduced serves that important purpose and is understood as a necessary preliminary to the inquiry about Being, and that the difficulties connected with the Ideas are additional incitements to us to apprehend the One Being, for the plurality of Forms has its foundation in the One Being, as the corresponding number does in its monad.

Consequently, if we analyze the dialogue and range in order its various segments, we would say that what is most aimed at is its final end, viz., to expound the truth about Being in the Parmenidean sense. And since this had to be established by the use of these visitors' favorite method—the method of logical gymnastics—it was necessary beforehand to understand what this method is and by what rules it proceeds. And since the method could not otherwise be introduced than by showing the need for it, and this in turn could not be shown except by impressing upon those who embark on the study of things without it the unavoidable difficulties involved in their opinions—for this reason, the [637] discussion of the doctrine of Forms is taken up first, together with the difficulties whose consideration, by the use of the method, would introduce the discussion of the knowledge we were wanting, viz., the knowledge of Being as Parmenides conceived it.

Nowhere do we find Plato producing a work that is principally a study of method; rather, we find him employing different methods at different times according to what each subject requires and always adopting his method for the sake of the object of his inquiry. Thus, in *Sophist* he brings in the method of division not in order to teach his hearers division (though this is an incidental result), but in order to

---

role with no positive subject matter, and to have rejected the concept of a One above Being.

[36] 183E.

catch and bind the many-headed sophist. This procedure is in accordance with the nature of things, for it is nature's way to adopt means for the sake of ends, not ends for the sake of the means necessary to bring them about.

A method is a necessary means when we want to exercise it in gaining knowledge of things, but not worthy of earnest attention for its own sake. An attentive look at the arrangement of the set of hypotheses would clearly confirm that Plato did not introduce the theory of being for the sake of the gymnastic method that is proposed before it, for that method requires that we posit both the existence and the nonexistence of our subject, then consider what follows and what does not follow for the subject, whether posited as existing or not existing, both in relation to itself and in relation to other things, and for the other things likewise both in relation to themselves and in relation to the subject of the hypothesis. But in developing the hypotheses, he does not always follow the patterns of his method, but omits some and alters others. Yet if he introduced the doctrine of One Being as an example of the method, would it not have been ridiculous not to follow the method and handle his example according to its announced rules and say at every stage what inferences do not follow? As we make our [638] way through the so-called hypotheses, we shall see that he does not altogether follow his method as he goes through them, but takes away some, adds others, and alters still others.

(d) Metaphysical: A Study of all Things Which Derive from the One

What has been said should convince us that we should not say that the aim of the dialogue is logical exercise; we must look for a substantive theme. Some interpreters contend, as we have said, that the theme is Being, and they cite the declaration of Parmenides at the beginning—that he will take for argument his own One—and this is, they say, Being. Such is the common interpretation of Parmenides' doctrine. And the Stranger in Sophist[37] makes this clear, they say, when he criticizes Parmenides as not meaning the genuine One when he speaks of Being.

Others,[38] agreeing with them in supposing that the aim of the dialogue is metaphysical, say that we should regard him as examining not merely the One Being, as the others affirm, but all things that get their reality from the One. Indeed, although the hypotheses do actually take

---

[37] 245A.

[38] This could be a group comprising Plotinus, Porphyry, and Iamblichus, all of whom certainly regarded the One as being the subject of the first hypothesis.

their departure from Parmenides' One, which is identical with the One Being of the dialogue, yet as they proceed from this point they sometimes fix upon the notion of One apart from Being and develop the implications of genuine unity, purged of all plurality and therefore as transcending Being and repudiating that predicate. At other times, the hypotheses apply to both One and Being alike and bring into view the whole intellectual universe, containing both Being, in its genuine sense, and the One, self-sufficiently participating in Being.

Then, again, taking being and attaching to it alone essential oneness, they show there is a nature that exists through the One but is third in rank from the genuine One. Then shifting to the examination of the others than the One, they show that these things, by participating in the One, posit all other things along with themselves and, by not participating in it, are deprived of all qualities. Since all these results cannot be applied to the One Being, [639] they conclude with plausibility that the discussion is not only about it but also about all things from the primary cause down to the lowest, in which there is privation of all things. (These are thus likened to the primary cause by dissimilarity,[39] for that which is deprived of all qualities by its nonparticipation in the One is, in a sense, like that which transcends all things by its nonparticipation in Being.)

In fact, how can we reconcile with the One Being things that are so at odds with one another? For if the hypothesis is true—i.e., that the One Being is—and expresses exactly what Parmenides meant, then—and he proves that the consequences are necessary consequences of the true hypothesis—according to him everything demonstrated from the hypothesis that the One Being is would be true. So, all negative and all positive consequences would be truly affirmed of the same thing—the One Being—and this is of all things the most impossible. And if all the consequences of positing that the One Being is not are in any way true [i.e., valid], they also will be predicates of the One Being; not to mention that, as the argument shows, all the properties uniquely predicated of the One cannot belong to this same thing, i.e., the One Being, for how can the One Being be infinite plurality when the One itself, according to him—I mean Parmenides—repudiates infinity in number? How can there even be infinite number—the very thing he is always so eager to unify that he appears to eliminate every plurality of beings?

---

[39] For the concept of the "similarity of dissimilarity" (ἀνόμοιος ὁμοιότης), cf. *PT* I 12, p. 57, 20 S-W, and *infra*, p. 645, 6–7 Cousin. It arises ultimately from *Parm.* 159E2–6, and is first to be found in Syrianus *In Met.* 153, 5–6.

How can the eternal participate in time? For such is the One Being according to Parmenides, which, as he says, "remains in the same state."[40]

If, then, our remarks are true, we clearly cannot say that the purpose is to inquire simply in regard to Being in the Parmenidean sense (for not all that he affirms—and still less, all that he denies, as well as everything that he both affirms and denies—is consistent with this interpretation), [640] but to inquire in regard to all beings, some of which will accept the affirmations and the denials. So, it was both reasonable and accurate for Parmenides to say that he would start from his own doctrine of the One (137B), for he did make this his point of departure, but, in revealing its consequences, he set forth the whole nature of beings.

Suppose someone wished to apply the same procedure to the soul, saying that he was going to start from the One Soul [the primary soul], and then, from this hypothesis, he showed the plurality of souls and all things that participate in them. We would not in this case say that though he began with the One Soul he was not discoursing about that alone but about both that hypothesis and all the consequences that follow from it. In general, when anyone lays down a hypothesis, the hypothesis has the status of a starting point; but the inquiry is not about it but about its consequences, according as it remains fixed or is modified.

(e) Metaphysical: Doctrine of Syrianus and Proclus

These are the differences of opinion among the ancients with respect to the purpose of *Parmenides*. Now we must say what our master has added to their interpretations. He agrees with those of our predecessors who thought the aim of the dialogue is metaphysics and dismisses the idea that it is a polemic as implausible. That Zeno should ask Parmenides to practice his method before the company and that Parmenides in exhibiting it should defend himself against the treatise of Zeno is altogether incredible in the light of what has been said; and to make its purpose an exposition of method is as silly as the idea that it is a polemic. For if he had to have an example in order to make his method clear, he would have taken some other readily-available topic as an illustration instead of making the most august of all his doctrines incidental to the teaching of method, though he considered this method appropriate only to young men. To understand that august doctrine requires the intellect of an older man and, indeed, an intel-

---

[40] Fr. B 8, 29 D-K.

lect more than human, as he says in his poem, and rather that of a nymph, Hypsipyle.[41]

[641] Considering such to be the dialogue's purpose, our master denied that it was about Being, or about real beings alone. He admitted that it was about all things, but insisted on adding "insofar as all things are the offspring of one cause and are dependent on this universal cause" and, indeed, if we may express our own opinion, insofar as all things are deified. For each thing, even the lowest grade of being you could mention, becomes god by participating in unity according to its rank. For if god and One are the same, because there is nothing greater than god and nothing greater than the One, then to be unified is the same as to be deified, just as, if the Sun and god were the same, to be illumined would be the same as to be deified; for the One gives unity, the Sun, light. So, as Timaeus does not simply inquire about nature in the usual manner of the natural scientist but insofar as all things get their cosmic ordering from the one Demiurge, so also Parmenides, we may say, in conducting an inquiry about beings, is himself examining these beings insofar as they are derived from the One.

Now this One, we may say, exists otherwise in the gods than in the beings that come after the gods. In the one case, it is self-sufficient, not like something existing in a substratum (for every god is god by virtue [642] of the One, though the supreme god is one purely and simply, having no multiple aspect, while each of the others is more than unity, one thing because it has these entities dependent on it, another, those. The beings that are nearer the pure One are fewer in number, those further away are more numerous, just as those nearer have a nature more akin to it and those further away are less akin; addition and plurality come about because of their descent in the scale of being). So, in the former case the One truly is, while in the latter case it exists as a character in something; for every form, every soul, every body participates in some unity, but this unity is no longer a god, although, if I may say so, it is an image of god, a divine seed—as form is a likeness of Being, knowledge, a likeness of Intellect, even in the lowest of things, and as self-motion is an image of Soul.

Then, just as every self-moving thing is Soul, or ensouled; as every knowing thing is Intellect, or possessed by Intellect; as every form is either essence or possessed by Essence; so, every unity is either a god or

---

[41] It is not quite clear from Proclus' terminology whether he is giving this as a name for Parmenides' divine guide in his poem. The goddess' name is not elsewhere mentioned.

possessed by God. Timaeus, then, traces all things back to the Demiurge, Parmenides traces them to the One; and there is an analogous relation between the Demiurge and the contents of the universe, and the One and all things whatsoever, <the Demiurge [643] being a kind of one>[42] but not One in the absolute sense; for he is a god, not God, and the god that is the One is not a god, but God simply. So, the Demiurge is a god, since demiurgy is a property of a god, and there are other divine properties that are not demiurgic.

As there is this analogy between the dialogues in respect of their purposes, so they agree in the temporal settings of the actions they portray. One presupposes the Lesser Panathenaea, the other the Greater, as I said before;[43] and in the latter, the Athenians would carry the peplos[44] of the goddess that pictured her victory over the Giants. As a background for the presentation of the unity pervading all things, this scene of the Giants is highly appropriate, for Athena is said to prevail over the Giants by bringing knowledge and unity to the divisible and material regions of her administration, making the intelligent elements prevail over the nonrational; the immaterial, over the material; and the unified, over the pluralized. This peplos, then, was the symbol of the power of Athena transcendent over cosmic things, by virtue of which she is one with her father and with him overcomes the Giants. And the so-called Lesser Panathenaea exalted her rank in the universe, making it coordinate [644] with the period of the Moon. For this reason, it seems fitting to a dialogue revealing to us the whole of the cosmic genesis.

The time is thus in agreement with the purpose of *Parmenides*. And this conversation that Cephalus narrates, being the fourth from the original one (whoever his audience may be), is in harmony with the procession of all things, from the One down to the last. For the things that proceed from that source are either henads, which have their reality immediately from the One; or essences that proceed from the One through these henads; or intermediates between these essences and the generations produced by them (and before them by the henads and the One); or the generated beings that proceed from all the foregoing.

If, therefore, the procession of all the beings that are, in diminishing degrees of perfection and likeness to the supreme goal, ends at the fourth stage of descent, is not this account of the descent of all things from the One, being fourth, in perfect agreement with the theory pre-

---

[42] Accepting Thomas Taylor's supplement for a lacuna in the manuscripts.
[43] At 618, 24 ff. Cf. also *In Tim.* 84, 12 ff.
[44] A cloak or robe.

supposed in the dialogue? And if in generated beings there exists a formless receptive capacity, the persons who receive the words uttered in this fourth account would bear a likeness to this capacity, being themselves [645] nameless in accordance with their analogy to the indeterminate; for a name is the sign of a form.

We could summarize all this by saying that every existence is either essence or generation, or neither essence nor generation; and in the last case is either prior to essence and generation or subsequent to them; for all the material element is neither of the two and resembles (unresemblingly, as they say)[45] the beings that are prior to generation and essence.

(f) Style of the Dialogue

We must remark further that the style of the dialogue is most appropriate to the subject it treats and to its method of inquiry. Its subjects are divine beings that have their foundation in the simplicity of the One and who fervently rejoice in "unadorned beauty"[46] (as one of the experts in divine matters says) and extend it to those capable of looking at the divine. The method proceeds by using the most exacting capacities of reason, careless of adornment, abjuring all artifices extrinsic to its subject, and intent only on finding with accuracy the objects it is looking for and tying them fast by geometrical necessity, so that, to both the subject and the method, its form is well and nicely adapted; the leanness of its style befits its dialectical procedure, and its naturalness and lack of exaggeration and adornment go with the divine matters it expounds, so that any trace of Socratic charm, or any middle style of discourse appropriate to median forms of life, or any rich and elevated [646] invention suited to and arising from the fancy of divinely possessed enthusiasts—all this is naturally alien to the style adopted here, and nothing of that sort should be expected in this dialogue.

For my part, while I admire those who have allied themselves to the critical acumen of their predecessors,[47] which has led them to applaud the entire type of diction of this dialogue—which in its sparseness marvellously preserves the character of true Being, adequately mingles fullness with restraint, and weaves harmoniously together intensity with

---

[45] See n. 39 *supra*.

[46] Perhaps a phrase from a lost work of Iamblichus.

[47] This sounds like a backhanded compliment to Porphyry; those with whom he is contrasted just below would then be Iamblichus and Syrianus. Cf. the discussion of the style of *Timaeus* at *In Tim.* I 7, 17–18, 29, and the remarks about Longinus, ibid. 86, 19–25.

precision—still more do I admire those who in their instructions regarding the correct mode of theological discourse have pointed out that many parts of *Sophist* are phrased in this way and that the whole of *Parmenides* falls into this class. This much, however, should be added to what they have said: when we say this style befits theology, we do not mean that it alone is suitable for discussing divine matters, but that these terms and this style are especially adapted to teaching divine truth dialectically, as is done in a discourse of this nature. Divine truth can be expounded in a variety of ways.[48] The poets under the inspiration of Phoebus will use a richer style, filled with terms from mythology; others, abstaining from dramatic or mythical garb but otherwise speaking in inspired language, will express themselves in an elevated style and priestly terms; others aim at presenting divine matters through images, using mathematical terms—those used either in arithmetic or in geometry.

Quite different from all these is the exposition through dialectical [647] terms, a method especially suitable for members of the Eleatic school, even as of the former, the one is specifically Pythagorean—as Philolaus reveals[49] in his use of numbers to expound the existence and the genealogy of the gods, while another is the priestly style—which gives the names of the gods according to the secret doctrines of their sect, such as those current among the Assyrians[50]—Zônai and Azônoi, Pêgai, Ameiliktoi, Synocheis—for interpreting the divine hierarchy. And yet another is the Orphic style, characteristic of Hellenic theology, which assigns the names Kronos, Zeus, Ouranos, Nyx, Cyclopes, and Hundred-handers to the highest principles of the world. But instead of all these, the dialectical exegesis of the divine employs, as I said, such dialectical terms as "One" and "Being," whole and parts, same and other, like and unlike—the terms with which dialectic mostly operates and here uses for interpreting divine things. This, therefore, is the kind of discourse that Parmenides follows here, a style appropriate to such terms as these and taken from ordinary speech, not grandiloquent but restrained, not overly contrived but natural.

---

[48] Cf. *PT* I 4, where the various modes of theological discourse found in Plato are set out.

[49] Probably in his Περὶ Φύσεως. Cf. Frs. 44 B 1–16 D-K.

[50] That is, the Chaldean Oracles. Again, this is possibly Iamblichus, the previous category referring to Porphyry, and the following (Orphic) to Syrianus (cf. Hermeias *In Phdr.* p. 148, 17 ff. Couvreur, presenting Syrianus' exegesis).

(g) Parmenidean Dialectic and Platonic Dialectic

[648] This is as much as we had to say regarding the expository style of the dialogue. But since I have heard many interpreters of Plato's doctrine attempt to distinguish the method that Parmenides presents here from the dialectical method so highly prized by Plato, I think it desirable to state my opinions on this point. According to some, there are three statements made by Parmenides himself that show this method is different from Plato's.

Socrates says in *Republic*[51] that dialectic ought not to be given to young men, lest they acquire a bent towards lawlessness through using their skill in argument to upset the unperverted concepts in us. But Parmenides urges Socrates, a young man, to use this method and exhorts him to do so for this reason especially—that he is young—for, he says, the cultivation of this method is appropriate for the young, yet Plato's legislation excludes them from dialectic. Secondly, this method is called by Parmenides an exercise, which implies that it uses arguments both for and against a thesis, like [649] Aristotle's dialectic, which Aristotle, in teaching it, says contributes to logical exercise. But Plato's dialectic is described in the dialogues as leading to the highest and purest stage of knowledge and insight, since its activity is based on intelligible Forms, through which it advances to the very first member of the intelligible world, paying no attention to human opinion but using irrefutable knowledge at every step. A third point, in addition to these two, is that the method of reasoning here is explicitly called "babbling" by Parmenides himself,[52] whereas dialectic is called by Socrates "the capstone of knowledge"[53] and indeed is said by the Eleatic Stranger to be suitable only for genuine philosophers;[54] and clearly we would not venture to rank among the babblers those who are striving to apprehend being.

So say those who think that this method is different from dialectic. And, indeed, Socrates never appears to have adopted it in his own philosophy, although as a young man he practiced it on the advice of Parmenides. But he is always using dialectic, following it by preference on all occasions and saying that he would "follow in his footsteps as if he were a god"[55] any man who is able to divide one into many and collect

---

[51] 537E–539D.
[52] *Parm.* 135D5.
[53] *Rep.* 534E.
[54] *Soph.* 253E.
[55] Homer Od. V 193, quoted at *Phdr.* 266B.

many into one. For this is the real function of dialectic, he says in *Phaedrus*[56]—not, as the method here prescribes, to make a hypothesis and discover what follows from affirming it and from denying it, nor to find hypotheses for hypotheses and the positive and negative implications of their consequences.

But why speak of Socrates and argue that what he describes as appropriate to the dialectician is quite [650] different from the method that Parmenides presents in this dialogue? Even the Eleatic wise man—though himself a member of the group around Parmenides and Zeno, nevertheless, when expounding the procedure of dialectic in *Sophist*[57]—see what he says: "He then who is capable of this"—he means capable of not mistaking the same kind to be other or the other the same—"perceives distinctly a unique form pervading many, each of them posited as distinct, and many forms different from one another included under one embracing idea, and again a unique form pervading many others but united into one, and many forms altogether distinct in every way." Can he be saying here that the dialectician's task is to make his way through such hypotheses as Parmenides' method goes through—to hunt for the consequences, positive and negative, both for itself and for other things, of affirming a hypothesis and the corresponding consequences of denying?

And yet the four parts in the above statement are consonant with the two aspects of dialectic mentioned in *Phaedrus*. One of them was to divide the one into many. This is the property of diaeresis—to separate a genus into its species. The genus is the "unique form" spread through many separate things and existing in each of them. For the genus is not an assemblage of species, like a whole of parts, but is present in each of the species as existing before them and participated in both by each of the separate species and by the genus itself. The species are the many forms different from one another but comprehended by one unique embracing form, which is the genus: though it is outside them, as transcending the species, yet it contains the causes of the species; for to all those who posit Forms, real genera are thought to be both older and more essential than the species ranged under them. The realities existing prior to species are not identical with the characters that exist in the species by participation.

Thus we see that to distinguish between these two kinds is the task of the diaeretic part of dialectic; the distinction between the remaining

---

[56] *Phdr.* 266B.
[57] 253C.

two belongs to the definitional aspect. This art (1) perceives a unique unified Form pervading many wholes—collecting the many Forms, [651] each of which is a whole, into a unique definition, weaving them together, and from all these apprehended wholes bringing about a unique Form by grasping the many as one; and further (2) looks upon the many Forms it has collected as distinct both from one another and from the whole which arises from them. This is what we should expect; for how could it make one out of many if it had not previously seen the many as separate from one another?

Since Parmenides makes no mention of such functions of dialectic when outlining to us his method of hypotheses, and since Socrates almost everywhere hotly pursues them but does not mention the method of Parmenides, how could one accept the view that they are the same as each other?

The answer is, to begin with, that the first point mentioned (that Parmenides recommends his method to the young, and Socrates forbids young men to practice his) is not sufficient to differentiate them; to give advice in a personal instance is not the same as to formulate a general rule. The latter envisages a variety of unruly natures and in view of them necessarily puts the general requirements of what is proper ahead of advice to individuals. For the legislator is giving guidance not to one man but to many and therefore considers not what is fitting for the best of natures but what is incumbent alike upon the best, the middling, and the worst; so that he takes cognizance of reversals of fortune and takes care not to prescribe what would injure any of the persons whom he is educating. Even if he selects to the greatest extent possible the class of superior individuals, he knows that even in them there is a great deal of irregularity, as is to be expected in human beings. But if he is advising an individual on his occupation, he looks at the special character of the man whom he is counselling, especially if he is himself such a man as to be able to discern the fitness of the recipient to receive his advice, and in this case he advises him to select or [652] ignore some particular of his occupation. For this reason, this manner of legislation regarding dialectic was appropriate to be given to Socrates. And it also goes with the character of Parmenides, who was looking only at the divine impulse towards philosophy that, as he says,[58] he observed in Socrates and knew that no damage would be done to any youth who practiced this method if he had a character like that of Socrates. Socrates himself, after all, if he knew that all the natures for whom he was giving advice were of the

---

[58] *Parm.* 130B1.

highest type, would not have hesitated to give his dialectic to young men, knowing they would get no harm from it nor suffer any of the consequences which led to his withholding it from all for fear that some, whose bent for such dialectic he was not sure of, would be injured.

In general, we observe that all legislation is aimed at what is usual, not at the rare occurrences; it considers the general nature of the kind, not the particular individual, whether it be laws about the gods to be honored, or the studies and occupations to be chosen, or the selection of duties to be observed. These prescriptions are not necessarily incumbent on those who fall outside the legislation, i.e., who are endowed with a different nature higher than the common. So, there is no reason why Socrates and Parmenides, in laying down prescriptions about one and the same occupation, should not say different things about its use and both be speaking truly, the one having in mind the common human nature, the other, the individual.

Nor is it true that when Parmenides calls his method an "exercise" he is using a different term from those that Socrates uses. This is evident to any one who has followed carefully the laws that Socrates lays down for dialectic. He says that his young citizens who have gone through the studies prescribed in mathematics must exercise themselves (this is the expression he uses)[59] in dialectic, and appoints a definite limit of time for such exercise. Either, then, his dialectic must be regarded as identical with the exercise on probable premises, or it cannot be reduced to dialectic merely because [653] of the word "exercise," although Parmenides declares that his "exercises" will "with difficulty" enable one to see the truth—which is *not* the purpose of the arguments in the so-called *Topics*.

Why, then, did both these men call the primary use of this method "exercise"? I shall tell you. This method of trying to attain genuine knowledge, looked at as a whole, contains three sorts of activities. One, which is suitable for young men, is useful for awakening the reason that is, as it were, asleep in them and provoking it to inquire into itself. This is actually an exercise in training the eye of the soul for seeing its objects and for taking possession of its essential ideas by confronting them with their contradictories. It explores not only the path that leads, as we may say, in a straight line towards the truth, but also the bypaths that lie alongside it, trying them also to see if they reveal anything trustworthy. Thus, it brings all the soul's varied conceptions to the test.

---

[59] *Rep.* 526B.

In another form of its activity, dialectic places the mind at the outset in the region of thought where it is most at home, looking at truth itself "sitting on a sacred pedestal,"[60] which Socrates says unfolds before the mind the whole intelligible world, making its way from Form to Form until it reaches the very first Form of all, sometimes using analysis, sometimes definition, now demonstrating, now dividing, both moving downwards from above and upwards from below until, having examined in every way the whole nature of the intelligible, it climbs aloft to that which is beyond all being. When it has safely anchored the soul there, it has reached its goal, and there will no longer be anything greater to be desired. You could say these are the functions of dialectic spoken of in *Phaedrus* and in *Sophist*, the former dividing dialectical procedures into two, the latter into four parts; and this is why the method is referred to the genuine [654] philosopher, who no longer has need of mental gymnastics but nourishes the reason in his soul on pure thoughts.

There is another and third kind of dialectic: that which is "tentative"[61] in the proper sense and which purges "double ignorance" when directed against men falsely confident of their opinions. *Sophist*[62] also speaks of this kind of dialectic; for as the philosopher is compelled to use refutation as a method of catharsis on men obsessed by their conceit of wisdom, so also the sophist, when engaged in refutation, was thought to assume the guise of the philosopher—like a wolf pretending to be a dog, as the dialogue puts it. For he who truly refutes another and not merely appears to do so, since he is truly a purger of false opinion, is a philosopher; for how could one purge another's soul if his own is unpurged?

Of these three kinds of dialectical activity—arguing on both sides, expounding truth, and exposing error—it is the first alone that is called gymnastics by our two philosophers. This is the method by which Socrates trains his young men, as for instance Theaetetus, by examining both sides of the question—e.g., whether what a man thinks is true for him or not; whether or not knowledge is perception—and then in turn examining the difficulties in true beliefs, or rapping them against one another and showing up any that give a hollow ring. Young Lysis is another of these [and Socrates trains him] by enquiring: "What is a friend? Can only persons who are alike be friends? Or is friendship a relation between opposites? And is it the lover, or the beloved, who is a friend to

---

[60] *Phdr.* 254B.

[61] Reading πειραστική for παραστατική of the manuscripts. Cf. Aristotle's use of the term, e.g., at *Soph. El.* 169b25; *Met.* Γ 2, 1004b25.

[62] 231A.

the other?"[63] — in this way constantly exposing him to the difficulties latent in his opinions.

Such exercise is a good thing for young and ambitious persons enamored of knowledge, to strengthen them against weariness in inquiry and giving up through not having the initial . . .[64] since when he [Socrates] is contending with sophists masquerading, [655] as they always do, as experts and masters of wisdom, all the methods of dialectic are ready to hand to show his adversaries where they contradict themselves, and since these dialectical methods are in some way cathartic of overweening self-opinion, his adversaries may eventually, after being pounded from all sides, be brought to a recognition of their own false pretences. Many examples of this kind of Socratic dialectic are found in *Gorgias* and *Protagoras* and in other dialogues that attack the theses of the sophists, for example, the arguments Socrates puts together in *Republic* against the ingenious Thrasymachus.

But obviously if the dialectician is reasoning with himself, having to do with men who are neither adversaries needing to be trounced nor pupils needing to be exercised, he employs the highest form of dialectic, that which reveals the truth in its purity. Thus, Socrates in *Phaedo* lays down certain hypotheses, deduces their consequences, and shows that the soul is incapable of receiving the opposite of the quality that it confers on that in which it is present, and after proving this he once again demands that we examine whether the initial hypotheses themselves are true, and he outlines certain rules of procedure agreeing with the method of *Parmenides:* at each hypothesis you should look only at the consequences that follow from it but make no defense of the hypothesis itself until you have adequately gone over its implications. Then, give a reason for the hypothesis itself, conducting your search in due order by assuming another hypothesis, the best of those above until, going upward step by step, you come to "something [656] adequate" — meaning by this, obviously, the unhypothetical principle — that which is, not by hypothesis but in fact, the first principle of what has been demonstrated.

And when the Eleatic sage uses diaeresis to make many out of one and definition for getting one from many, he, too, is employing the highest form of dialectic, as if to show that he divides and defines by himself as well as when reasoning in the presence of others. For in this dialogue he is holding forth neither before unpracticed novices — his

---

[63] Not exact quotations. See Plato *Lys.* 212E6; 214B3.
[64] There is a lacuna here, unnoticed by Cousin. When the text resumes, the subject is Socrates.

hearers have already been exercised through arguments with Socrates, have been trained in mathematics, and thus have been prepared for the theory of Being—nor before sophists hampered by their double ignorance and incapable of receiving scientific reasoning because of their self-conceit.

This, then, is why he called training in dialectic "gymnastics." That dialectic was commonly called "babbling" and those who practiced it, "babblers" hardly requires illustration, seeing that the comic poets called Socrates a "beggarly babbler" and gave the same name to all others who presumed to be dialecticians.

> I despise Socrates also, that beggarly babbler.
> Either Prodicus, or one or other of those babblers.[65]

This is why Parmenides does not simply call his method "babbling" but adds "what the many call babbling." Furthermore, Socrates [657] himself in *Phaedo*[66] implies that in his earlier life the name had been applied to him in comedy:

> Now at least I don't think any comic poet would say that I am babbling and talking about what does not concern me when, being about to go to dwell in Hades, I discourse about my transfer of residence thither.

And in *Theaetetus*,[67] when he has examined the Protagorean thesis from all sides and thinks he has proved the point at issue, then it is that he prepares to raise objections to what he has concluded. "A babbling man," he says, "is surely a terrible thing." When Theaetetus asks the reason for this preamble, he replies, "Because I am about to dispute with myself." Clearly, what he here calls babbling is this very characteristic of dialectic—the practice of raising difficulties, of turning the same propositions this way and that and not being able to leave them alone. In short, those who were derisively called babblers are those men who do not find it easy to stop going over the same arguments.

It was, then, as I said, the multitude who gave this name to dialectic, and that is why Parmenides says it is what "the many" call the method

---

[65] The former of these quotations is from Eupolis (Fr. 352 Kock), the latter from Aristophanes, Ταγηνισταί ("The Broilers," a lost work, Fr. 490 Kock). In both cases, Proclus is doubtless dependent on an intermediate source, perhaps an earlier commentary on *Phd.* 70B.
[66] 70B.
[67] 195B.

he is going to expound. But if we look at the classification of arts in *Sophist*[68] we shall find that even the Eleatic Stranger there puts dialectic under the rubric of babbling. He divides sciences into two classes — one creative, the other acquisitive — and of the latter, one part acquires by combat, the other, by other means; and of the combative class one part is competitive, the other, pugnacious; and of pugnacious acquisition, one species uses violent and bodily conflict, the other, verbal controversy; and under this clearly we must place dialectic; for it is not creative, but acquisitive, like mathematics, and acquisitive in no other way than through competition.

And when the art of disputation is divided into the kind that makes long speeches and that which [658] proceeds privately by questions and answers, it is clear that dialectic belongs under the latter. This art of "antilogy," as it is called here, is again divided into a species that is concerned with particulars of contracts and another that inquires into general principles that admit of controversy (as he says, about the just and the noble and their opposites); and clearly dialectic will find its place here. He calls it eristic, not meaning that it is disreputable strife or antilogy but indicating only its activity of controverting and raising objections, for there is a correct way of carrying on controversy, just as there is good and bad strife, if, as the poet says, there are two forms of strife:[69] "There is, then, more than one species of strife."

And so of eristic there is one species that makes money (this brings in our ingenious sophist) and another species that wastes money, which neglects private affairs for its insatiable interest in discussion. Under this we shall obviously place the dialectician, for he clearly does not belong in the other class, since that is sophistry. And when he gives a name to this money-wasting eristic he says it can be called nothing else than babbling. If, then, Plato himself gives this name to dialectic, how can it be maintained that the method in *Parmenides* differs from dialectic because it is called babbling, and dialectic cannot possibly deserve this appellation.

(h) The Significance of Plato's Prologues

But we have said more than was necessary on this point. Let us return to the project we have undertaken, with only this additional observation. The ancient commentators have held varying opinions regarding the prologues to Plato's dialogues. Some have not condescended [659]

---

[68] 219B–225D.
[69] Hesiod *Works and Days* 11.

to examine them at all, saying that hearers who are genuinely interested in the doctrines must come with a previous knowledge of these preliminaries. Others do not take them as irrelevant, but see their use as being for the presentation of moral attitudes and present their relevance to the central problems addressed in the dialogues on this basis. Others demand that the interpreter bring the matter of the prologue into relation with the nature of the dialogue's subject.[70] We agree with the last group and shall begin by showing how the subject of the dialogue relates to the matter in the introduction. Not that we shall neglect the moral stances represented, but in studying any Platonic dialogue we must look especially at the matters that are its subject and see how the details of the prologue prefigure them. In this way we should show that each of them is perfectly worked out, a living being harmonious in all its parts, as Plato says in *Phaedrus*,[71] and bring into harmony with this also what belongs to the outlining of moral attitudes. When the preludes are completely irrelevant to what follows, as in the dialogues of Heraclides of Pontus and Theophrastus, it offends every critical ear.[72]

Book VI

On Principles and the First Principle: Doctrine of Henads[73]

[1043] So, then, as I said, this line of inquiry[74] is more concerned with the underlying realities, while the previous one is of a more logical nature. But before I turn to its refutation, I must say a few words about the [first] principle, such as will suffice for the elucidation of our present problem. When we say that the One is the principle of things existent and nonexistent (since being unified is for all things a good and

---

[70] From parallels in the *Timaeus* commentary (cf. *In Tim*. I 87, 6 ff.), it is plain that Iamblichus is the protagonist of this last view, at least in its developed form. The second view is that of Porphyry, the first that of Middle Platonic commentators, such as Severus (cf. *In Tim*. I 204, 16 ff.). Porphyry's tendency to refer the contents of the preludes to τὰ καθήκοντα is mentioned at *In Tim*. I 19, 24 ff.

[71] 246C.

[72] It sounds from this remark as if Proclus had access to these works.

[73] This passage comes just after the beginning of the book, the first section having dealt with the number of the hypotheses (1039, 1–1043, 4).

[74] The subject of this criticism is probably Origen the Platonist, who seems to have maintained that all the hypotheses concern the One in one or another of its aspects, and specifically that the first hypothesis has no positive subject matter at all.

indeed the greatest of goods, while to be sundered completely from the One is an evil and the ultimate of evils; for such a separation becomes the cause of Unlikeness and disconnectedness and of departure from the natural state), the principle of everything, then, as being the provider to all things of the greatest of goods, we term it unifier of all and for this reason One and, owing to this, we say also that every principle, insofar as it has a share of this honor among beings, is a henad of some class and the most unitary of things in each class.

First of all, we place this entity that has the status of principle, not on the level of parts but of wholes, nor in any single one of the many, but in the monads that hold together the multiplicity, and further, among those monads, we see as being particularly in the summits that which is most unitary in them insofar as these are themselves united to the One and are divinized and do not depart from that unique principle.

For instance—to transfer our discussion to the realities themselves— we [1044] see many causes of light, some in the heavens, others below the moon; for different types of light are projected into this realm in various ways from material fire and from the moon and from the other stars. But if one were to inquire after the unique monad of all the light in the universe, from which all the other objects derive that are lighted or productive of light, he will not fix upon any other candidate than this visible circuit of the sun. For this entity, proceeding forth from some higher level, from the "hidden," as they call it,[75] and supracosmic realm, has distributed to all the cosmic entities the light that is suitable to them. Or where else would both the heavenly bodies and the lightlessness of matter derive their share of light? Well, then, are we to call this visible body a principle of light? But it is spatially extended and divisible, and projects different light from each separate part of it. We, however, are seeking the unique principle of light.

Perhaps, then, it is the soul, that "leads the body to [separate] existence,"[76] that we may take to be the generative principle of light? This generates light, certainly, but not primarily, for it is itself a multiplicity, while light gives the impression of arising from a simple and unitary source. Perhaps, then, it is Intellect, the cause of Soul? But this, too, though it is more unified than Soul, is not yet a principle in the proper and primal sense.

---

[75] *Or. Chald.* Fr. 148.
[76] Plato *Lg.* 899A.

What is left, then, is for the One, the cause of existence and, as it were, the "flower"[77] of this Intellect, to be the first principle of this light also; for this is the true sun "ruling in the visible realm,"[78] "offspring of the Good."[79] Every henad derives from this source, and every divinity, [1045] from the henad of henads and the fount of gods. And even as that is the principle of light there in the intelligible realm, so the henad of the solar order is the principle of light here in the visible realm, so that if one is to choose the unique cause and principle of all light in the universe, one must take this henad, analogous as it is to the One, established hidden within it and never departing from it.

Since this henad is established above the solar intellect, there is also in Intellect, insofar as it is Intellect, the One participated in by it, like a seed sown in it, through which it is joined to the henadic realm; and not only in it, but in the solar soul as well. For this, too, is drawn up to it in virtue of its own One, through the mediation of the One in Intellect. In the same way, even in the solar body there is at least some echo of it, for this, too, must participate in what is above it: in Soul by virtue of the life that is sown into it, in Intellect by virtue of its form, and in the henad by virtue of the unity in it, since Soul, too, participates in both Intellect and the henad, and things participated in are different from what participates in them. You might actually say that the immediate cause of the solar light is this one, which it possesses through its participation in that henad.

Even thus, if we were to seek for the root, as it were, of all bodies, from which have sprouted all those both in the heaven and beneath the moon, both wholes and parts, we would not unreasonably say that this was nature, which is "the principle of motion and rest"[80] for all bodies, established in the things themselves that move and are at rest (I mean by "nature" the unique life that permeates the whole universe, participating after Intellect and Soul, and by means of Intellect and Soul, in unity). This we would say is the principle rather than any of the many particular things.

And yet not even this is a principle in the true sense, for it has a multiplicity of powers, and by means of different ones it [1046] controls different parts of the universe. We are, however, at present seeking the

---

[77] ἄνθος, a Chaldean term (Or. Chald. Fr. 1.1, etc.), much used by Proclus, e.g., In Tim. I 419, 9 and III 118, 26; In Crat. 47, 15 ff.; PT I 3. p. 15, 3 ff. S-W.
[78] Plato Rep. 509D.
[79] Ibid. 507A.
[80] See Aristotle Phys. B 1, 192b21–2.

unique common principle of all things, not a multiplicity of separate principles. But if we are to discover that unique principle, we must ascend to the most unitary element of nature and its "flower," in virtue of which nature also is a god, which is dependent upon its own fount and which holds together the universe and unifies it and renders it sympathetic with itself. That, then, is the One, the principle of all generation both for the manifold powers of nature, and for particular natures, and for all those things under the sway of nature.

Thirdly, we may take the case of knowledge. We say that there is a principle of knowledge, by which we certainly do not mean imagination and sense-perception, for there is no object of knowledge in these that is partless and immaterial and without shape. Nor yet will we call knowledge derived from opinion and discursive intellection a principle, for the former kind does not have knowledge of causes, but is without an account, as Diotima says;[81] for it only investigates the fact of things. The latter, again, even if it knows the cause also, yet it grasps facts part by part and does not comprehend the whole, nor the eternal and invariable aspect of reality, nor the simultaneous and noncomposite and simple. Therefore, these likewise are not to be postulated as principles of knowledge.

Might Intellect, then, be the first principle of knowledge? The knowledge inherent in it, after all, is simultaneously omnipresent and nontransitive and incessant and partless. If the knowledge of Intellect were without multiplicity, so as to be totally nonmultiple and one, perhaps we would have postulated it as the principle of knowledge. Since, however, it is not only one but also variegated, and there are a multiplicity of acts of thinking within it, and that which is the thinking of something else is not necessarily also that of the rest of the intelligibles (for as intelligibles are distinguished from one another, so, too, are acts of thinking), necessarily none of these are the principle of knowledge; for they are all equally acts of thinking.

[1047] If, however, we are to state the unique principle of knowledge, we must fix upon the One, which generates Intellect and all the knowledge, both within it and what is seen on the secondary levels of Being. For this, transcending the many as it does, is the principle of knowledge for them and is not the same as them as is Sameness in the intelligible realm. This is coordinate with its Difference and inferior to Being. The One, on the other hand, is beyond intellectual Being and

---

[81] Plato *Symp.* 202A. Plato, like Proclus, uses the word ἄλογος ("without account") in the special sense pertaining to someone who has the right answer without understanding why it is right.

grants coherence to it, and for this reason the One is god and so is Intellect, but neither by reason of Sameness nor Being. And, in general, Intellect is not god *qua* Intellect, for even the particular intellect is an intellect, but is not a god.

Also, it is the proper role of Intellect to contemplate and think and judge true being, but of god to unify, to generate, to exercise providence, and suchlike. By virtue of that aspect of itself that is not intellect, the Intellect is god;[82] and by virtue of that aspect of itself that is not god, the god in it is Intellect. The divine Intellect, as a whole, is an intellectual essence along with its own summit and its proper unity, knowing itself insofar as it is intellectual but being "intoxicated on nectar," as has been said,[83] and generating the whole of cognition, insofar as it is the "flower" of the Intellect and a supraessential henad.

So once again, in seeking the principle of knowledge we have ascended to the One. And not in the case of these only, but in every other case we would likewise discover the monads being the most proper principles of things; for everywhere the principle is the One. It would be about this principle that Socrates in *Phaedrus*[84] is speaking when he says, "the first principle is ungenerated," for if it is impossible for any species to be wholly extinguished, far more so, surely, is it necessary that the unique principle of each of them should be preserved and remain eternally, in order that around it there should come into existence the whole multiplicity that proceeds properly from each one.

[1048] It is the same to say "henad" as to say "principle," if, in fact, the principle is in all cases the most unifying element. So, anyone who is talking about the One in any respect would then be discoursing about principles, and it would then make no difference whether one said that the thesis of the dialogue was about principles or about the One. Those men of old,[85] too, decided to term incorporeal essence as a whole "One," and the corporeal and, in general, the divisible, "Others"; so that in whatever sense you took the One, you would not deviate from the contemplation of incorporeal substances and the ruling henads; for all the henads are in each other and are united with each other, and their unity is far greater than the community and sameness among beings.

---

[82] Cf. *ET* Props. 120, 134.

[83] Cf. Plotinus VI 7. 35, where we find the reference to "intoxication with nectar"; Proclus *PT* I 14. p. 67, 2–5 S-W.

[84] 245D.

[85] That is, the Pythagoreans. Cf. *PT* V 39, pp. 143, 13 ff. S-W, and Damascius *In Phd.* I 154, 3.

In these, too, there is compounding of Forms and likeness and friendship and participation in one another. But the unity of those former entities, inasmuch as it is a unity of henads, is far more unitary and ineffable and unsurpassable, for they are all in all of them, which is not the case with the Forms. These are participated in by each other, but they are not all in all. And yet, in spite of this degree of unity in that realm, how marvelous and unmixed is their purity, and the individuality of each of them is a much more perfect thing than the otherness of the Forms, preserving as it does unmixed all the divine entities and their proper powers distinct, with the result that there is a distinction between the more general and more particular, between those associated with Continuance, with Progression and with Return, between those concerned with generation, with induction to the higher, and with demiurgic administration, and, in general, the particular characteristics are preserved of those gods who are respectively cohesive, completive, demiurgic, assimilative, or any of the other characteristics of theirs that our tradition celebrates.[86]

Whereas, then, there exist there both indescribable unity and, yet, the [1049] distinctness of each characteristic (for all the henads are in all, and yet each is distinct), we gain knowledge of their unity and their distinctness from things secondary to them and dependent upon them; for in the case of the visible gods we discern a difference between the soul of the sun and that of the earth, seeing that their visible bodies have a large degree of variety in their essence and their faculties and their rank in the universe. So, then, even as we take our start from sense-perception in acquiring understanding of the differentiation of incorporeal essences, so it is on the basis of the variation in incorporeal essences that we cognize the unmixed distinctness of the primal, supraessential henads and the particular characteristics of each. For each henad has a multiplicity dependent upon it,[87] in one case intelligible, in another intelligible-and-intellectual, in another intellectual simply, and within this one having an unparticipated multiplicity, another, a participated one, and within this latter one having a supracosmic one, another, an intracosmic. And thus far extends the procession of the henads.

So, then, as we contemplate the extent of the whole incorporeal realm that is spread out beneath them and the measured series of variations down from the hidden level to that of distinctness, we declare our belief that there exist particularity and order even in the henads them-

---

[86] The various orders of gods, or henads, are dealt with at *ET* Props. 150–159.
[87] This doctrine is set out at *ET* Props. 135–140, and in *PT* III 1–7.

selves, along with their unity. For it is on the basis of the differences in the participants that we discern the distinctions within the participated. For things that participated without variation in the same thing could not have exhibited such differences relative to each other.

So much, then, may be said concerning the situation of the primal henads and their communion with and distinction from one another, of which we are accustomed to call the one particularity, the other unity, distinguishing them thus also by name from the sameness and difference manifested at the level of real Being. For these henads are supraessential and, to use technical terms, are "flowers" and "summits."[88] Since, then, as we have said, there is within them both unity and distinctness, it is to this that Parmenides is addressing himself, that he may make [1050] clear their whole progression, right from the summit of the transcendent henad, and he thus takes for his hypothesis his own One, that is the One that is seen at the level of Being, and he considers this now as one, now as participated.

The antecedent he preserves always the same by taking it in various senses, while the consequent he keeps changing, so that through the identity of the antecedent he may demonstrate the unity of the divine henads; for whichever of these you take, you can assume the same for the rest, because all are in each other and are rooted in the One. For even as trees by their "topmost" parts are fixed in the earth and are earthy in virtue of that, so in the same way the divine entities also are by their summits rooted in the One, and each of them is a henad and one through its unmixed unity with the One. Through the changing of the consequent, on the other hand—taking it now as a "whole," now as "shape," now as something else again, and this both affirmatively and negatively—he seeks to demonstrate their distinctness and the particular characteristics of each of the divine orders. By means of the whole syllogism, in turn, he seeks to show both the communion of the divine entities and the unmixed purity of each.

For these reasons, then, the antecedent is one, the consequents are many, the syllogisms are many, and the hypotheses are more than two, since Parmenides, through his hypothesis of the One Being, at one stage ascends to the One that is prior to the participated henads, and at another passes through the whole extent of those that are on the level of beings, and at another reveals the existence of those of them that are inferior to Being. And, in general—since it has been stated previously

---

[88] These are both distinctively Chaldean terms; cf. (for ἄνθος) Or. Chald. Fr. 1, 1; 34, 2; 35, 3, etc. Des Places; (for ἀκρότης) Fr. 76, 2; 82, 1.

about this method that its purpose is to postulate a given entity or proposition and then see what follows for itself in relation to itself and to others, and what does not follow, and again for the others, both in relation to each other and to the postulate—we shall see how he himself in the first hypothesis examines what does not follow for the One, both in relation to itself and to others; in the second, what follows; and in the third, what [1051] follows and does not follow; and how in the two following hypotheses he examines what follows for the others in relation to themselves and to the postulate and what does not follow; and how in the remaining four sections he varies his hypotheses similarly.

So one should neither be disturbed at contemplating the multiplicity of hypotheses nor think that he is going beyond the proper limits of his proposed method nor that he is deviating from the study of the henads in their capacity as first principles, but that it is demonstrating simultaneously both their unity and their distinctness, for they are all united, insofar as they "remain in one"[89] while they are distinguished according to the different degrees of progression that they have accomplished from the One.

And do not be astonished if we say this about the divine henads. Even at the level of intellectual essences we are accustomed to call the whole intellectual realm a partless and unique essence, and all the intellects one, and the one Intellect all, by reason of the sameness that draws and holds together the intellectual hypostasis as a whole. If we can talk of this level of being in this way, what should we think about the actual henads in the sphere of Being? Should it not be that they are unified to an especial degree? That they are in one another? That their mingling is unsurpassable? That they do not proceed forth from the One? That they all have the imprint of the One upon them? Certainly, at every level primal entities have on them the imprint of their own causes. Even in the case of bodies, the primal is most full of life, like Soul, and the first among souls has the character of Intellect, and the primal Intellect is a god. So, also among numbers the first is of the nature of One and henadic and supraessential, even as the One is. If, then, the henads also constitute a number, then there is both multiplicity and unity in that realm.

---

[89] Plato *Tim.* 37D.

COMMENTARY ON TIMAEUS

This work (which Proclus' biographer Marinus tells us was one of his earliest works, completed by the age of 28, i.e., by 440 C.E.) comes down to us likewise in incomplete form—five books, ending with the exegesis of Timaeus 44C–D—though it is not necessary to suppose that Proclus commented on the whole dialogue. Unlike the case in the Parmenides Commentary, Proclus is here generous in his mentioning of previous commentators, which makes it a most valuable source for the history of commentary on the dialogue as well as for his own doctrine.

1. The Prologue

(i) Subject Matter

That Plato's *Timaeus* has as its subject of investigation the totality of the science of nature, and that it is devoted to the study of the universe, which it treats of from its beginning to its end, seems to me obvious to all but those thoroughly blinded to rational procedure. In fact, the treatise of the Pythagorean Timaeus is itself also entitled, in the Pythagorean manner, *On Nature*—"whence taking his start," Plato "turned his hand to composing a *Timaeus*," as the Sillographer has it[1]—and consequently we have prefixed it to our commentary, so that we may be able to discern where Plato's *Timaeus* is in agreement with that work, where he has made additions, and where he is in disagreement, and in order that we may investigate closely the cause of such disagreement.

The present dialogue has as its overall subject the science of nature, viewing the same topics both through images and original models,[2] both as regards wholes and parts, for it is made up of all the finest principles of natural science, taking on simple subjects for the sake of

---

[1] Timon of Phlius (c. 325–235 B.C.E.). Timon cannot, it is generally felt, be referring to the extant Neopythagorean pseudepigraphon *Timaeus Locrus, On the Nature of the Soul and the World* (though Proclus assumes that he *is*) since that is agreed to date from considerably after his time (probably 1st century B.C.E–1st century C.E.) He must be referring to a rumor, perhaps emanating from the Peripatos, that Plato bought certain Pythagorean books on his first visit to Sicily, and borrowed doctrines from them.

[2] There is a contrast being made here between εἰκόνες and παραδείγματα— the former referring to the allegories being discerned in the prefatory portion of the dialogue.

complex ones, parts for wholes, and images for the sake of their originals, leaving uninvestigated none of the dominant causes of natural phenomena.

That the dialogue in fact deals adequately with such an objective, and that Plato, in his subtle and detailed treatment of the subject, is preserving to a unique degree the Pythagorean approach to the study of nature, is something [2] that merits examination at the outset by persons of superior acuity, for if we accept that the science of nature, broadly speaking, comprises three divisions, of which the first concerns matter and material causes; the second adds to that an inquiry as to the formal cause and identifies that as the more important factor; while the third in its turn makes clear that the former two do not have the status of causes, but only of contributory cause, and postulates as causes of natural phenomena in the strict sense yet others—that is, the creative, the paradigmatic, and the final—we can see that the majority of students of nature prior to Plato directed all their attention to matter, some postulating one element as basic, some another.

Anaxagoras, for instance, who, "while all others were sunk in slumber,"[3] appears to view Intellect as the cause of all things that come to be yet in his expositions makes no use of Intellect but declares the causes of things to be rather some sort of "air" or "ether," as Socrates says in *Phaedo*.[4] And, on the other hand, the leaders of philosophical schools after Plato—not all, but at least the more exact among them[5]—deemed it right that the theoretician of nature should reckon in the formal cause along with matter, thus tracing back the first principles of all things to matter and form. And, indeed, if they ever make mention of a creative principle, as when they say that "nature is the principle of motion,"[6] they nonetheless deprive it of its efficacious and properly creative function, since they do not grant that it contains within it the reason-principles of those things that are created from it but concede that often things are generated spontaneously. And, as well as that, they do not even recognize a preexistent efficient cause of all natural beings whatever but only for those borne around in the realm of generation, for they declare that there is absolutely no cause of those things that are eternal, by which move they quite fail to see that they either make the whole heaven a

---

[3] A verbal reminiscence of *Rep.* 390B6, where Plato's reference is to Zeus planning while all the other gods and mortals slept.
[4] 98C.
[5] Proclus seems to have in mind here primarily Aristotle and the Stoics.
[6] A reference to Aristotle *Phys.* B 1, 192 b13 ff., and *Met.* Δ 4, 1014b16 ff.

product of chance or postulate that the corporeal realm is such as to generate itself.

Plato, following the lead of the Pythagoreans, is the only one, on the other hand, to present [3] both the contributory causes of physical things, in the shape of the "receptacle"[7] and the form-in-matter, as putting themselves at the service, for the purposes of generation, of the causes in the true sense; and, on the other hand, to investigate, prior to these, the primal causes, such as the efficient, the paradigmatic, and the final. It is in that connection that he establishes, above the universe, a demiurgic intellect and an intelligible cause, in which the universe is primarily situated, and then the Good, which is preestablished in the role of object of desire for the creative cause; for since that which is moved by some external force is dependent on the force that moves it, it is obviously not of such a nature as to produce itself, nor to bring itself to perfection, nor yet to preserve itself in being, but in the case of such entities there is need of a creative cause by which they are given coherence.

And, likewise, the contributory causes of natural objects may be properly seen as depending upon the true causes from which they are derived, in accordance with which they are fashioned by the father of all things, for the sake of which they have come into being.[8] It is with good reason, then, that we may take Plato as handing down to us an accurate exposition of all these causes, while presenting as dependent upon these the remaining two, form [that is, form-in-matter] and the substrate; for this world is not in the same case as the intelligible or intellectual worlds, which are constituted by pure Forms only, but there is in it one element fulfilling the role of reason-principle and form, and another that of substrate.

But we will have the opportunity to go into all this more fully on a later occasion. For the moment we may simply assert the manifest truth: that Plato has transmitted to us all these causes of the creation of the world, the Good, the intelligible paradigm, the creative principle, form, and the substrate. If, on the other hand, we were discussing the intelligible gods, he would have specified the Good as their only cause, for it is from this cause alone that there arises the sum total of the intelligibles.[9]

---

[7] Presented at *Tim.* 51A.

[8] Proclus manages in this sentence to include the efficient, paradigmatic, and final causes. We may note throughout this passage Proclus' determination to credit Plato with the initial formulation of the (Aristotelian) system of four causes.

[9] See *Rep.* 509B7–8.

Again, if our topic were the intellectual realm,[10] he would have postulated as the cause of this both the Good and the intelligible realm, for the intellectual multiplicity proceeds both from the intelligible henads and from the unique fount of beings.[11] And if discussion had centered on the supracosmic gods, he would have derived them both from the universal demiurgic intellect and from the intelligible gods and from the cause of all things, for of all things of which secondary entities are the causes, that cause, too, is generative on a primal and ineffable and incomprehensible level.[12] But since now he is proposing to discuss encosmic realities and [4] the universe as a whole, he will grant it both matter and form—the latter of these coming to it from the supracosmic gods—and he will portray it as dependent on the universal demiurgic intellect and will liken it to the intelligible living being, and he will identify it as a god by reason of its participation in the Good, and thus he will represent the world as a whole in its perfection as "a god possessed of intellect and soul."[13]

(ii) Structure of the Dialogue

This, then, is the subject of *Timaeus*, as we see it, and it is such as we have declared it to be. That being so, then, it is fitting that in the beginning portion,[14] the order of the universe is indicated through the medium of images; in the middle section,[15] we are presented with the whole composition of the world; and in the final section,[16] particular beings and the final details[17] of creation are woven together with the

---

[10] That is to say, the realm of Soul.

[11] That is to say, from the lowest element of the henadic realm (though it is interesting that the henads are here presented as "objects of intellection"), to the highest element of the intelligible realm, One-Being, of the Intelligible Monad.

[12] This principle is enunciated in *ET* Prop. 56: "All that is produced by secondary beings is in a greater measure produced from those prior and more determinative principles from which the secondary were themselves derived."

[13] See *Tim.* 30B and 34B.

[14] That is, 17A–27D, the προοίμιον or "prologue," of which all Neoplatonist commentators after Iamblichus gave an allegorical interpretation.

[15] 27D–76E, comprising the whole account of the composition of the universe and of man in general.

[16] That is to say, 76E–92C, where we find a more particular discussion of the composition of human beings. The surviving portion of Proclus' commentary, we may note, breaks off at 44D2.

[17] This seems to be the meaning of τέλη here.

general principles. In fact, the résumé of *Republic*[18] and the tale of Atlantis[19] provide a view of the universe through the medium of images. If we were to direct our attention to both the unity and the plurality of the contents of the universe, we could say that Socrates' recapitulation of *Republic* is an image of unity, since this work has set before it as its aim the community that pervades the whole structure, while the war of the Atlanteans against the Athenians, as it is related by Critias, provides an image of division and, in particular, of opposition into two classes of thing,[20] for whether we have regard for the heavenly realm or that beneath the moon, we will say that *Republic* may be likened to the order of the heavens—for Socrates declares that the model of it is laid up in the heavens[21]—while the Atlantid War resembles, rather, the realm of generation, which is based on conditions of opposition and change. This, then, is how this section serves as a prologue to the whole exposition of nature.

There follows upon this the description of the creative cause of the universe as well as the paradigmatic and final causes. Once the existence of these types of cause has been postulated, the creation of the universe can proceed, both as a whole and with respect to its parts; for its bodily component is constructed through being carved up by forms and demiurgic sectionings and divine numbers,[22] and the soul [of the universe] is, then, produced by the Demiurge and filled with harmonic reason-principles and divine, creative symbols,[23] and the whole Living Being [5] is woven together in accordance with the unified plan of the universe present in the intelligible realm. And the parts within it, in turn, such as are corporeal and such as are living, are arranged as they should be within the whole, for the individual souls are settled within it,

---

[18] At 17A–19B. Strictly speaking, this is not what this is, but rather the résumé of a quite separate account of an ideal state (very like that of *Republic*) with which Socrates has been on the previous day regaling the present company (together with a fourth guest, absent today).

[19] 19B–27B.

[20] A reference here to the Pythagorean Table of Opposites.

[21] Cf. *Rep.* 592B. A rather tendentious use of this passage, it must be said! Socrates' real point, after all, is that his ideal state is probably an unrealizable ideal but one to which one can at least refer intellectually.

[22] The reference is to the five Platonic figures set out in *Tim.* 53C–55C and the process by which the combinations of triangles are imposed upon the Receptacle.

[23] These σύμβολα are an importation from the Chaldean, theurgic tradition, rather than anything present in *Timaeus* itself.

and ordered in the train of their leader-gods,[24] and become embedded in the universe by reason of their vehicles, imitating those who lead them; and mortal beings are fashioned and given life by the agency of the heavenly gods.

And it is here also[25] that consideration is given to the constitution of the human being and the causal principles of his being, this entity before all others, either because such a study is appropriate to us, since we always have before us the concept of a human being and live in accordance with this concept, or because a human being is a universe on a small scale, and in him all things are present on the particular level, such as exist in the universe in a divine and holistic mode; for there is present in us actualized intellect,[26] and a rational soul that proceeds from the same father and the same life-giving goddess[27] as the soul of the universe, and an ethereal vehicle with affinity to the heavens, and an earthly body molded from the four elements, with which it is classed. If, then, the task was to consider the universe both in its intelligible and its sensible aspect, both as paradigm and as image, both from the aspect of the whole and of the parts, then, indeed, the account of the nature of the human being would have a good claim to be given a thorough treatment in the course of a study of the universe as a whole.

And you might also add the following argument: that it is in accordance with Pythagorean custom that one should relate the mode of discourse of the researcher to the object of research. Thus, since we have as our subject the nature of the universe, we should, I think, subjoin to that our knowledge of the nature of the entity that researches that and that obtains a rational grasp of it. And, indeed, that it is this that he has in mind he has shown clearly by saying near the end of the work[28] that he who wishes to attain a happy life "should strive to assimilate the thinking subject to the object thought." The universe as a whole, after all, is permanently happy. And we also will be happy when we have assimilated ourselves to the universe, for in this way we will have reconnected ourselves with our cause. For in fact a human being in this realm has the same relationship with the universe as Human Being in the

---

[24] A reference to the myth of *Phdr.* 247A ff.

[25] *Tim.* 69C–76E.

[26] This is probably a reference to the "active or agent intellect" of Aristotle *De An.* Γ 5.

[27] Again, a Chaldean reference. The goddess in question is Hecate.

[28] 90D4.

intelligible realm[29] has with [6] the Living Being itself, and, since in the intelligible world the secondary beings are always dependent upon the primary, and parts are inseparable from their wholes and fixed within them, when a human being in this realm comes in turn to assimilate himself to the universe, he will imitate his own model in the appropriate manner, becoming orderly by reason of his assimilation to the order of the universe and happy by reason of his likeness to that happy god.

Following on the topics just mentioned, the final details of the creation are specified according to their genera and species, both those in the atmosphere and those established in the earth and, in living beings, both what is contrary to nature and what is in accordance with it. It is in this connection that the first principles of medicine are given an airing, for the inquirer into nature does not stop before this point, since he has as his object the whole of nature; for what is in accord with nature goes along with nature, while what is against nature is a deviation from this.[30] The variety of ways, then, in which deviation occurs and how the organism is to be returned to a normal and natural state are a proper study for the theoretician of nature, and there follows upon this the development of the art of medicine.

It is in this part of the work above all that Plato aligns his concerns with those of other natural philosophers, for they concerned themselves with the lowest and most material aspects of nature, neglecting the whole heavenly realm and the arrays of the encosmic gods, inasmuch as they looked to matter and dismissed the Forms and the primary causal principles. As regards the inspired[31] Aristotle, it actually seems to me that he has arranged his whole treatment of nature, as far as possible, in rivalry with that of Plato.

On the one hand, [he does this] when he is considering the general principles of all natural things—form, substrate, the source of the principle of motion, motion itself, time and place—all things that Plato has

---

[29] That is to say, the Form of Human Being.

[30] This seems to cover the text from 76E to 92C, 76E–81E being concerned broadly with the process of respiration in living beings, 81E–90A with medical questions, including the causes of disease ("that which is contrary to nature"), and 90E–92C with the generation of animals.

[31] Δαιμόνιος, we may note, is a term of qualified respect, in contrast to θεῖος, "divine," which would be accorded to Plato himself as well as to Plotinus and Iamblichus. What follows here is a critical overview of the doctrine of Aristotle's physical treatises, starting with *Physics*, but including also *De Caelo*, *De Generatione et Corruptione*, and even *Meteorologica* (with all of which we may assume Proclus to be acquainted), challenging their originality and/or accuracy.

dealt with here, in his teaching on space; on time as being an image of eternity and beginning its existence along with the heavens; on the various types of motion and the contributory causes of natural phenomena. And, on the other hand, [he does this] when he turns to consider the particular properties of beings distinguished according to their essence and, of these, firstly those that belong to the heavens, in a manner conformable to Plato, insofar as he makes the heavens uncreated and composed of the "fifth essence"—for what difference [7], after all, is there between talking of a fifth element and a fifth world or fifth figure, as Plato has termed it?[32]—and, secondly, the elements common to all structures involving generation, an area in which one can only admire the degree of accuracy with which Plato has investigated the essences and powers of these same elements and has correctly maintained both their harmony and their oppositions.

Further, in the case of those aspects of the realm of generation that pertain to meteorology, of which Plato has laid down the principles, Aristotle has extended the range of his teaching beyond what was proper, while as regards what pertains to the study of animals, which in Plato's case has been clearly set out in relation to all types of causal principle, both final and accessory, Aristotle has barely and in only a few cases considered this from the perspective of the formal cause. In most cases, he stops at the level of matter and goes no further, and in basing his explanations of physical phenomena on that, demonstrates to us how far he falls short of the teaching of his master. So much, then, for that.

(iii) Genre and Character of the Dialogue

Let us turn next to discuss the literary genre and the character of the dialogue. It is universally acknowledged that Plato, after having acquired the book of the Pythagorean Timaeus *On the Universe*,[33] set out to compose his *Timaeus* on Pythagorean lines. It is also, however, recognized by anyone who has even the least acquaintance with Plato that the tone of the dialogue is Socratic, exhibiting as it does a spirit of benignity and a willingness to present proofs. Indeed, if ever it was true that Plato blended together the Pythagorean and the Socratic modes of

---

[32] Cf. *Tim*, 55C—where, however, Plato only raises the possibility of declaring that there are five worlds (κόσμοι), one corresponding to each of his basic figures (σχήματα).

[33] That is to say, the pseudepigraphic work of Timaeus Locrus, which Proclus accepted as genuine. The idea that Plato is borrowing from, or even transcribing, some such book goes back at least, as we have seen (*supra*, n. 1, p. 331, to Timon of Phlius, in the early third century B.C.E.).

discourse, it is clearly the case in this dialogue. From the habitual practice of the Pythagoreans the work borrows sublimity of spirit, intellectuality, an inspired mode of discourse, and a tendency to establish the dependence of everything on the intelligible realm, to give a definitions of all things by means of numbers, to express truths by means of symbols and secret formulae—a mode of discourse conducive to elevation, such as rises above partial insights—and a tone of confident affirmation.

From the benign practice of Socrates there is derived social graciousness,[34] good humor, receptiveness, [8] the tendency to represent reality by means of images,[35] the moral tone—all such traits as these. And so it comes about that, though the dialogue is solemn in tone and draws its conclusions from above, from the very highest principles, yet it nonetheless mingles a demonstrative character with the dogmatic, and it disposes us to comprehend natural phenomena not just from the perspective of physics but from a theological point of view as well. For in fact this nature that guides the universe gives unerring direction to the corporeal realm in dependence upon the gods and inspired by them—although not itself in the position of a god, it is yet not entirely deprived of divine properties by virtue of being pressed into service by those who are truly gods.

So, if, indeed, modes of discourse should be assimilated to the subject matters "of which they are the expounders," as Timaeus himself will remark below,[36] it would be fitting that this particular dialogue should exhibit both a physical and a theological aspect, in imitation of the nature of which it presents a study.

Further, since, according to Pythagorean doctrine, reality is divided into three levels—namely, the intelligible, the physical—and the level intermediate between these, which they are accustomed to term the mathematical, and since it is possible to view all three in a manner appropriate to each[37] in fact, the median and the lowest levels preexist in the intelligible in a primordial way, while both of the other two are manifested at the mathematical level, the first in the form of copies, the third of exemplars, and there exist at the level of natural things reflections of the realities that precede them—it is certainly reasonable that Timaeus, in his composition of the soul, should have explained its

---

[34] Translating the otherwise unattested compound adjective εὐσυνουσίαστον.
[35] By contrast with the Pythagorean σύμβολα mentioned above.
[36] *Tim.* 29B.
[37] A utilization, here, of the originally Numenian formulation, "All things are in all, but in a manner appropriate to each," cf. Porphyry *Sent.* §10, *supra* p. 178.

powers, its ratios, and its elements in mathematical terms, while Plato should define its properties on the basis of geometric figures and postulate that of all these things[38] the causes preexist primordially in the intelligible realm and the demiurgic intellect.

But that is enough on that subject, since the examination of the details of the text will be better suited to acquainting us with the character of the dialogue.

(iv) The Occasion of the Dialogue

The occasion[39] of the dialogue is the following: Socrates, having taken himself down to the Piraeus for the festival and procession of the Bendideia, entered on a discussion there with Polemarchus, son of Cephalus, [9] Glaucon, Adeimantus, and, last but not least, Thrasymachus the Sophist. The day after that, in the city, in the company of Timaeus, Hermocrates, Critias and, as a fourth, another unnamed person, he gave an account of the conversation in the Piraeus, which is presented in *Republic*. At the conclusion of this, he has invited the others to offer him, on the following day, a feast of discourse in return for his. They have, accordingly, gathered both to hear and to deliver discourses on the third day after the conversation in the Piraeus. In *Republic*,[40] after all, we find the statement, "I came down yesterday," and now it is said: "of those whom I feasted yesterday, and who now will feast me." However, all of those are not present at this session; the fourth member is absent through illness.

(v) The Characters of the Dialogue

What can be the reason, one might ask, why, on the present occasion where the discussion concerns the universe as a whole, the auditors are three? Because, I will say in reply, it is fitting that the father of the discourse should bear an analogy to the "father of works"[41] — the construc-

---

[38] This would seem to refer not only to the composition of the soul, but also to that of the whole universe.

[39] This seems to be more or less what ὑπόθεσις means here. What we get in fact, is "the story so far," based on the assumption that the previous day's conversation followed directly upon that recounted in *Republic* — which, as we have remarked above, is something of an oversimplification of the relation between the two works.

[40] 327A2.

[41] A reference to *Tim.* 41A7: "gods of gods, those works of which I am the craftsman and father are indissoluble except by my will."

tion of the universe in discourse is an image of the construction of the world in intelligible reality[42] — and that, on the other hand, the triad of those who "receive" the discourse is analogous to the demiurgic triad that receives the unique and universal creative activity of the father.[43] Of this triad, the summit is Socrates, who, because of kinship in way of life, attaches himself directly to Timaeus, even as, in the paradigmatic triad, the first term is united to that which transcends the triad. But all these matters we will explore in more detail in what follows, if the gods so will. (*In Tim.* I 1 4–9, 24 Diehl)

2. Creation of the Universe: Temporal or Nontemporal?

"*Has it existed always, having no beginning of generation, or has it come into being, taking its start from some beginning?*"[44]

Such being the question, Plutarch, Atticus, and many others among the Platonists have understood this "coming into being" in a temporal [277] sense,[45] and, according to them, the question posed is this: is the universe uncreated in a temporal sense, or is it created? For prior to the creation of the world, they say, there exists a disorderly motion, and along with the motion there is inevitably also time, with the consequence that time also existed prior to the [ordered] universe. What is born along with the universe is that time that is "the numbering of the movement of the universe,"[46] while that other time was the numeration of the disorderly motion that existed prior to the creation of the world.

---

[42] This must be the sense here of the expression κατὰ νοῦν.

[43] This demiurgic triad subordinate to the demiurgic father is a feature of Proclus' metaphysical scheme, which is further developed in Book V of *Platonic Theology*.

[44] *Tim.* 28B7–8. The answer to this question, "It has come into being (γέγονεν)," is reserved for the next lemma, but the discussion as to the true sense in which the universe is to be regarded as "created" (γενητόν) begins in the present lemma, of which the following is an extract. It sets out the interesting array of answers to this conundrum proposed by previous Platonists.

[45] On this question, the Middle Platonists Plutarch and Atticus constituted a notorious "heresy" from the perspective of later Platonists.

[46] A reference to *Tim.* 38B6: "Time, then, came into existence along with the heaven," supplemented by Aristotle *Phys.* Δ 11, 219a33 ff., where Aristotle declares time to be the number of motion (ἀριθμός κινήσεως).

The commentators on Plato who are of Crantor's persuasion,[47] on the other hand, declare that the world is called "created" as being produced from a cause external to itself and not being self-generating or self-substantial. Plotinus, however, and the philosophers after Plotinus, Porphyry, and Iamblichus, say that it is its compositeness that is here called "created," and to this is subsidiary the fact of being generated from an external cause.[48] (*In Tim.* I 276, 30–277, 14 Diehl)

3. Which Parts of the Soul Are Immortal?

"For the rest, do ye weave together the mortal with immortal . . ."[49]

What is meant by "immortal" here, and what, by "mortal" has been the subject of much discussion among the exegetes of Plato. Some allow the rational soul alone to be immortal, and consign to dissolution both the whole of nonrational life and the pneumatic vehicle of the soul,[50] since they grant an existence to these latter only in relation to the declination of the soul towards generation, and they preserve as immortal only the intellect, inasmuch as it alone is permanent and likened to the gods and not subject to destruction. This is the opinion of the more ancient commentators, who consider themselves to be following the letter of the

---

[47] It is hard to see that the turn of phrase οἱ περὶ Κράντορα here means any more than Crantor himself. Crantor (c. 345–290 B.C.) was a member of the Old Academy, contemporary with Xenocrates and Polemon, and is credited by Proclus (*In Tim.* I 76, 1–2) with being the first to comment on *Timaeus*, whatever we are to understand by that.

[48] We have here two stages of what was plainly a long-running debate within the Platonist School as to the real meaning of γενητός in the context of the *Timaeus* account, of which the fullest recorded version is that of L. Calvenus Taurus in the mid-second century, who lists four possible senses (other than the literal one), of which these are the fourth and the second, respectively. The nearest that Plotinus seems to come to discussing this question is V 9, 3, 24 ff., but even there, though this position is presupposed, his point is a different one.

[49] *Tim.* 41A1. This lemma is part of the address of the Demiurge to the young gods, *Tim.* 41A–D. Proclus makes it an occasion to review the opinions of his predecessors on the "mortal" and "immortal" parts of the soul. We present just the first segment of this.

[50] The "pneumatic vehicle," a natural but not visible body, is a concept developed in later Platonism to provide a kind of bridge between the immaterial soul and the material body.

text, in which Plato postulates destruction for the nonrational element by calling it "mortal"—I mean such figures as Atticus and Albinus.[51]

Others, more moderate and more benign than this first group, like Porphyry and his school, decline to extend so-called "destruction" to both the vehicle and the nonrational soul but declare that these two are broken up and dissolved in some way into the spheres from which they were constituted, that they are mixtures derived from the heavenly spheres, and that the soul collects them as it descends, so that they both exist and do not exist but do not exist any longer as individual entities, and that there is no permanence to their individual nature. They seem in this to be following the [Chaldean] Oracles,[52] which say that, in its descent, the soul assembles the elements of its vehicle by taking on "a portion of ether and of the sun and the moon, and all such things as float in air."[53] But we must adduce in opposition to these the text of Plato himself, who does not describe in any clear way the destruction of the whole nonrational element.

Third, in turn, come those who remove all destruction from both the vehicle and the nonrational soul, and combine [235] the survival of the vehicle and that of the nonrational, and explain the term "mortal," in this case, as referring to the element that is corporeal and that is fascinated by matter and concerned with mortal things, such as is the view of Iamblichus and those who are inclined to agree with him, and not simply granting it [that is, the vehicle] an existence dependent on the divine [that is, heavenly] bodies, lest, coming into existence from mobile causes, it also may be changeable of its own nature, but deriving it from the gods themselves who organize the universe and perform all their acts eternally.[54] (In Tim. III 234, 8–235, 9 Diehl)

---

[51] Prominent Platonists of the second century C.E., also mentioned by Iamblichus in his De An §§23 and 28.

[52] Fr. 67 Des Places.

[53] That is, the other planets. The soul, on this theory, acquired a "garment" (χίτων) from each of them, which bestowed upon it one or other of the passions. It then shed these in turn on its ascent through the spheres after death.

[54] The last paragraph here = Iambl. In Tim. Fr. 81 Dillon. It was the view of Iamblichus that the vehicle survived in the universe as a coherent entity after separation from the rational soul, to be available for reactivation on the soul's return to the universe.

Commentary on Book I of Euclid's Elements

The Nature of the Objects of Mathematics and Their Relation to Soul[1]

The next thing for us to decide is what sort of reality can properly be attributed to mathematical genera and species. Are we to accept that they are derived from sense objects, either by abstraction, as is commonly said, or by the assemblage of particulars under one common definition; or should we instead grant them an existence prior to sense objects, as Plato thinks right, and as the order of procession of things indicates?

First of all, if we say that mathematical forms derive their existence from sense objects—that the soul, on the basis of having viewed material circles and triangles, derivatively shapes within herself the Form of Circle and the Form of Triangle—whence arise the exactness and certainty that are characteristic of our concepts? For it is necessary that they arise either from sense objects or from the soul itself. But they cannot come from sense objects, for in that case sense objects would be endowed with far more precision than is in fact the case; they must therefore come from the soul, which adds perfection to the imperfect sense objects and accuracy to their imprecision.

Where, after all, among sensible things is there to be found anything that is without parts or without breadth or without depth; or where, the equality of the lines from center to circumference? Where are the regularly fixed ratios of the sides, or where, the rightness of angles? Do we not see that all things in the sense realm are mixed up with one another and that no element in them is pure and free of its opposite, but that all are divisible and extended and changing? How, then, are we to attribute actual stability of essence to the unchangeable reason-principles, if they are derived from things that are always in a process of change from one state to another? For it must be admitted that anything that arises from changing beings receives from them a changeable mode of existence.

---

[1] This passage concerns a doctrine of great importance for Proclus, and for Neoplatonists generally—the true status of the objects of the mathematical sciences. For Proclus, they are actually reason-principles (λόγοι) in the soul (primarily in the soul of the universe, but also in the soul of the individual), projections (προβολαί) of Forms primarily resident in Intellect. What is being countered here is the alternative (Aristotelian) view that they are simply concepts derived by the soul from its observation of sense objects.

And how can we derive the exactness of the precise and irrefutable Forms from things that are not precise? For whatever is the cause of steadfast knowledge possesses that quality itself to greater degree. We must, therefore, postulate the soul as the generator of mathematical forms and reason-principles. And if we say that the soul generates them by having their models in her own essence and that these offspring are the projections of Forms previously existing in her, we shall be at one with Plato and shall have discovered the true essence of mathematical being.

If, on the other hand, she weaves such a vast immaterial structure and gives birth to such a science without possessing or having previously grasped these ideas, how can she judge whether the offspring she bears are fertile or wind eggs, whether they are not phantoms instead of truth? What standards could she use for measuring the truth in them? And how, if she did not possess their essence in herself, could she even produce such a great variety of reason-principles? After all, by accepting this line of argument we should be making their being come about by chance, without reference to any standard. If, therefore, mathematical Forms are products of the soul and the reason-principles of what the soul produces are not derived from sense-objects, mathematicals are their projections, and the soul's birth pangs and her offspring are manifestations of eternal Forms established within her. (*In Eucl.* p. 12, 2–13, 26 Friedlein)

THE NATURE AND ORIGIN OF EVIL

This monograph, which survives in complete form only in the Latin translation of William of Moerbeke (as well as in a pirated adaptation by Isaac Comnenus), is the last of three essays on providence and its working, the existence of evil being a problem within that context in particular. The solution presented here is that pure evil is absolute nonbeing, but that evil, so far as it is mingled with individual things, is a necessary part of the structure of the universe, and thus, a kind of good.

§1. The nature and origin of evil was investigated by some of our predecessors[1] <who did so neither superficially nor incidentally in the

---

[1] Especially Plotinus I 8; also, Porphyry *De Abst.* 2, 38–40; Iamblichus *De Myst.* IV 6–10. Proclus apparently produced a separate discussion of Plotinus' work.

course of treating another subject>;[2] rather, they took as the object of their study evil itself, that is, whether it exists or not and if it does, how and from where it came into existence or reality. <We in turn can do no less, and, since we have the leisure, we are recording what each of them has to say, especially> what the divine Plato has thought about the nature of evil; <we will understand what they are getting at more easily> and we will be much closer to a grasp of the matters sought if we uncover Plato's views and then use them as a sort of light to guide our investigations.

The first thing that should be examined is whether evil exists or not; then if it does, whether it exists among intelligibles or not; and lastly if it exists [only] among sensibles, whether it subsists according to a prior cause or not.[3] But if it does not exist, we must inquire whether it should be counted as having some essence or should be supposed to be altogether without an essence. And if the former is the case, we must examine how it came to exist—its principle being different from it[4]—and from what it originates, and how far up the scale of reality it extends. And further, we must examine how evil exists and where it can be found, given that providence exists. <In short, we must examine all the matters related to evil that we are accustomed to examine in our commentaries>.[5] But above all else we must take account of the doctrine of Plato on this subject, for if we deviate from Plato's thought, we will rightly be regarded as having accomplished nothing.

§2. The starting point of our discussion, then, should be the natural one, namely, the question of whether or not evil is something real. For how is it possible that that which has no share in the principle of all things [the Good] is a real thing? For even as darkness is not able to partake of light, nor is vice able to partake of virtue, nor evil of good, <so, just as, if light were the first principle, there could be no darkness in the second, presuming that the second did not come to be by chance or from anywhere but the first principle>, in the same way, <since the Good is the principle of everything>, evil should not be among the things that are real. For either evil comes from the Good, in which case how can that which produced the nature of evil be the cause of all

---

[2] The words in brackets are a translation of the Latin translation of Proclus' text by William of Moerbeke in 1280. It is used to supply the parts missing from the Greek text.

[3] See Proclus *ET* Prop. 65 on the various ways in which something can exist.

[4] See Proclus *In. Tim.* I 392, 20–5.

[5] See Proclus *In Parm.* III 829, 23–831, 24; *In Remp.* I 37–8; 97–100; II 89 ff; *In Tim.* I 373–81. Also, see *PT* I 18.

valuable and good things? Or else it did not come from the Good, in which case the Good is not, after all, the cause of all real things nor their principle, since evil, though counted among things real, has avoided inclusion in the procession from the Good. In general, if everything whatsoever that exists only exists by partaking of being, that which partakes of being necessarily partakes of the One, <for something is and is one at the same time because the One is prior to being>.[6] And it is not proper, and never will be proper, for secondary entities to produce anything otherwise than with the cooperation of that which is prior to them, i.e., Intellect with Life, Life with Being, and everything with the One.[7]

It must be, then, that for evil, one of two possibilities obtains: either it did not partake of being at all, or else in whatever way it did partake of being, at the same time it partook of the transcendent cause of being [the Good or the One]. <Or again, the following alternatives would pertain>: either there is no such principle, or evil does not come to be nor does it exist, <for that which does not partake of being does not exist, and that which comes from the first cause is not evil>. In both cases we must conclude that evil exists nowhere. If, however, <as we maintain>, the Good transcends Being and is the source of all that is real, <because all that in any way is or becomes desires the Good by nature,>[8] how will evil be one of the things that are real if it is to be excluded from such a desire?

<It is, therefore, hard to make the case that evil exists because the Good must have an opposite.[9] If it is totally opposite, how can it desire the opposite nature? It is, however, impossible that a being does not desire the Good; for everything that exists and has come to be does so

---

[6] That is, the One is prior to finite being. See Proclus, *PT* II 4, 12–19, p. 31 S-W for an emphatic statement that the One exists, though it transcends being or essence.

[7] See Proclus *ET Props.* 56 and 57, for this principle. According to Proclus, in the intelligible world, the One is above Being (i.e., that which has limited or finite being) and is perfect unity. Being is caused by the One and is perfect being. Life is caused by the One and Being and is perfect life. Intellect is caused by the One, Being, and Life and is perfect intellect. Soul is caused by the One, Being, Life, and Intellect, and is perfect discursive reasoning. In the sensible world, (embodied) life is causes by the One, Being, Life, and Intellect, and it possesses minimal cognition. Plants are caused by the One, Being, and Life and have minimal life. Inanimate bodies are caused by the One and Being and have minimal unity and minimal being. Matter is caused by the One and has minimal unity.

[8] See Proclus *ET* Prop. 8. See Plato *Gorg.* 499E, *Phil.* 20D; Aristotle *EN* A 1, 1094a3; Plotinus I 8. 2, 2–3.

[9] See Plato *Tht.* 176A; Plotinus I 8. 6, 32.

owing to that desire and is preserved in existence owing to it.[10] Therefore, if evil is the opposite of the Good, evil is not among things that are real>.

§3. <What more need one say? For if the One or that which we call the nature of the Good transcends Being, evil itself transcends Non-Being.[11] I mean that it transcends Non-Being itself, for the Good is better than Being itself. There are, therefore, two possibilities: if Non-Being in no way has being, then evil is non-being to an even greater degree because it is even more insubstantial than Non-Being, as our argument makes clear: Evil, then, is even further from the Good than is Non-Being.>[12]

<This is what those mean who place Non-Being prior to Evil-Being>, namely, that something that is more removed from the Good is more insubstantial than something that is closer to it.[13] Therefore, that which is absolutely nonbeing exists even more than does that which is called "evil."[14] <Evil is, therefore, more non-being than any non-being.

If, however, according to Plato's account, not only does the father of this universe[15] make exist the nature of the goods in it, but also he wills that there be no evil at all in it,[16] what is the device whereby evil came into existence unwilled by the Demiurge? For it is not proper that he should will some things [to exist] but in fact make others; in fact, his will and his making are the same with respect to divine beings.[17] So, not only is evil unwilled by him, but it is also nonexistent, not because he did not make it (that is not proper to conceive), but because he made it as nonbeing. For it was not his will not to make evil, but rather that evil should absolutely not exist.

---

[10] See Proclus *ET* Prop. 13. Proclus' point is that since the Good is the cause of the existence of everything, everything partakes of the Good in some way. Things variously partake in the Good by having the natures they are endowed with and by striving to fulfill these. This striving to attain the fulfillment of their natures or their own good is another name for their existence.

[11] Proclus here means the Form of Non-Being (i.e., the Form of Difference). See Plato *Soph.* 255C and 256D–E on the identity of Difference with Non-Being.

[12] See Proclus *In Tim.* I 374, 13.

[13] If Evil-Being is a type of Non-Being, it is more limited or qualified than Non-Being and so more removed from the unqualified first principle.

[14] See Plato *Soph.* 237B–239C. Presumably, evil is more nonbeing than absolute nonbeing, because the latter is unqualified.

[15] See Plato *Tim.* 28C; 37C.

[16] Ibid. 30A.

[17] See Proclus *In Tim.* I 371, 4; Plotinus VI 8. 13, 5–7.

What else, then, could that which makes evil be, if it is the father and maker of the existence of everything there is who consigns it to non-being? What is opposed to this, and where would it come from? For the [putative] maker of evil did not come from him—that would not be proper for him. But if it came from somewhere else, that would be absurd, for everything that is in the universe comes from the father, both those things that are said to derive directly from him and those that are to a certain degree the result of the activity of others.>

§4. The line of thinking, then, that defines evil out of existence is something like this, and those who offer such arguments do so in order to persuade us of this. He who raises his voice against this view <requires us first to look at reality and, in doing so, to say clearly whether evil exists or does not, especially in the cases of intemperance and injustice and the rest of those things that we customarily call "vices" of the soul. And in each case, we must say if we will allow that it be called "good" or "evil," for if we call any one of them "good">, we must necessarily say one of two things: either that virtue is not the opposite of vice—neither the entirety of it [to the entirety of vice] nor, analogously, any part of it [to any part of vice]—or else that that which is in conflict with good is not altogether evil.

But, indeed, what could be more paradoxical or more out of line with the nature of things than either of these alternatives? For vices are, in fact, in conflict with the virtues. And that they are in conflict is clear from various areas of human life—where the unjust are in conflict with the just, the unrestrained are opposed to the temperate and, if you will, from the dissension within the individual soul. For instance, in the souls of those who are imperfect, reason leads in a direction other than that towards which passions compel one, and, reason and passion being in conflict, the better part is bested by the worse; for in these souls, what else is it but the temperate character of the soul that is in disaccord with the unrestrained?[18] <And what else is it in the souls of those struggling against their anger> and what else is it with the other vices in which we perceive the soul to be in disaccord with itself? For generally, the modes of opposition of the evil to the good are apparent much sooner in invisible souls.[19] And it is the ultimate ignorance and sickness of the soul whenever the better part in us and the good reasoning operating in it are overcome by earthly and dishonorable passions.

---

[18] See Plato *Rep.* 435B–444A.

[19] That is, evil (as vice) is noticeable within people prior to its being noticed among people.

<But would it not be truly stupid to continue with this any longer?> If vices are opposed to virtues, as we say, then evil is in every way opposed to good, for the nature of the Good is not by nature in disaccord with itself, but since good originates from a unity and from one cause, it is related to that by its likeness and unity and love, and the greater goods preserve the lesser, and the lesser are ordered by the more perfect ones. It is necessary, then, not only that the vices be evil in theory, but also that each of them be evil in reality, and not [merely] a lesser good, for the lesser good is in no way opposed to the greater good, just as lesser heat is not opposed to greater heat, nor less cold opposed to more cold. But if it should be agreed that the vices of the soul have the nature of evil, it has then been shown that evil is among the things that are real.

§5. And this is so not only for the above reason but also because evil is the destructive element in each thing. <That this is evil, Socrates demonstrates in *Republic*,[20] showing neatly>, that "the good of each thing is that which preserves each thing." For this reason, the desire of everything is for the Good. It is owing to that that each thing exists and is preserved in existence, just as each thing does not exist and is destroyed because of the nature of evil. It is necessary, then, either that evil exist or that there is nothing that destroys anything. <But in the latter case, "all generation will collapse and cease">,[21] for if destructive forces do not exist, destruction is not possible. But if destruction does not exist, then generation does not, since all generation arises owing to the destruction of something else. And if there is no generation, the entire universe will be imperfect. For then "the universe will not have types of mortal living beings in it, which it must have if it is to be as perfect as possible," according to *Timaeus*.[22] If, therefore, the universe is to be a "happy god,"[23] it must preserve perfectly in itself a likeness of "the Perfect Living Being."[24] If this is the case, types of mortal living beings must fill up the universe. If this is the case, it must be that destructible and generable things are among the things that exist, and there must be [destructive forces working on] some and [generative forces working on] others; for in all things, neither generation nor destruction occur as a result of the same [forces]. Rather, given that there are destructive forces that have come to be within things and that destroy their power, evil

---

[20] 608E3–4.
[21] See Proclus *In Parm.* 998, 29; Plato *Phdr.* 245E1.
[22] 41C1–2.
[23] Ibid. 34B8.
[24] Ibid. 31B1.

must exist, for this is what evil was [assumed to be]—the destructive force itself in each thing from the moment that it is generated. The forces that are destructive of soul are one sort of thing and the forces that are destructive of body another, and that which is destroyed is different from [that which destroys].[25] And the manner of destruction is not the same; rather, one is of the essence, and one is of the life.[26] In the first case, the essence is led to nonbeing and destruction; in the second, it is the life that flees entirely from being towards the other, namely, nonbeing.

The same line of reasoning, therefore, will serve to explain the preservation of the entire universe as perfect and will place evil among the things that exist. So, it is the case that not only will evil be owing to the Good, but also it will be good by existing. This is the most paradoxical [result], and it will be more understandable from the following.

§8. <If, then, as we have said,[27] we wish to explain the existence of evil not only on the basis of the above arguments but also in line with what Plato says, what we have already said should be sufficient for those who have difficulty following his thought. But as in court, where it is necessary not only that the parties be heard, but also that a penalty be proposed by them, so, if you like, let it be in the present case. Evil exists in two forms. Let us say it at once: there is an evil that only exists in a pure state and is not at all mixed with good, and there is an evil that is neither in a pure state nor unmixed with the nature of good, for similarly in the case of good, there is a primary Good, which is in itself nothing but good—neither Intellect nor thinking nor true Being—and there is a second good, which is mixed with other things.> And in the first case, it is a good unmixed with any privation, while in the second it is already mixed with privation. For that which sometimes partakes of the primary Good is filled up with the entanglements of that which is not good. This is also the case since that which is Being itself and the nature of Being in the intelligible world is really real and is being alone, whereas in subsequent [sensible] things, nonbeing is somehow mixed in with them; for that is in one way being and in another nonbeing, and at

---

[25] See Plato *Rep.* 609A9.

[26] Plato, in Rep. 610E5–8, argues that in general a thing is destroyed by its proprietary evil. Since the proprietary evil of soul is injustice, and soul is not destroyed by injustice, then soul is immortal. Proclus, therefore, makes a distinction between destruction by proprietary evil ("of the essence") and destruction of life. It is the latter type of destruction that applies to soul.

[27] See §6, 35–6.

one time being and then is forever nonbeing [it exists contingently], and is "this" being but not all the other beings. Someone would say that it has some being rather than that it is nonbeing that is in every way filled up with nonbeing.

Also, as for nonbeing itself, there is absolute nonbeing deprived of that which is of the lowest nature, namely, that which is [has being] only incidentally, and which is not able to be in itself or to be incidentally, for it is not, in one way, absolute nonbeing and, in another, not absolute nonbeing. But there is also that which is both nonbeing and being, whether it is correct to call it privation of being, or Difference.[28] And [the first] is in every way nonbeing, and [the second] in the intelligible world "is no less than Being," as the Eleatic Stranger says.[29] [The second] is in the things that sometimes are and sometimes are not, "more obscure"[30] than Being, though, since it exists in a certain way, is itself under the aegis of Being.

§9. So, then, if someone should ask whether nonbeing exists or does not exist, we would say that that which is absolutely nonbeing, which in no way partakes of being, is absolutely not, whereas we concede to the one who says [that nonbeing exists] that that which in a certain way is nonbeing is to be counted among the things that exist.

The same considerations apply to evil—since this is twofold: that which is strictly evil and that which is not unmixed with goodness—so that in the first case we will suppose it to transcend nonbeing altogether, <to the same extent that the Good transcends Being,> and in the second case we will put it among the things that exist, for this [type of evil] is not able to remain any longer bereft of being, owing to the intervention of the Good, nor bereft of the Good, owing to [the intervention of] Being, for it exists and is good simultaneously. But that which is in every way evil, which is a falling away from the first of all goods and a sort of exile, is, reasonably enough, deprived of all being; for how could that which is not able to partake of the Good have an entrée to the things that exist? But as for that which is not in every way evil, since it is opposed to good in some way and not in every way, it is made good owing to the superabundance of all goods. And it is evil for the things to which it is opposed, but dependent on others as goods. For [evil] must not be in conflict with these; rather, it must follow all according to what is just on pain of not being altogether.

---

[28] See Plato *Parm.* 160D.
[29] *Soph.* 258D1-2.
[30] See Plato *Rep.* 533D6.

§30. <Before we proceed to a consideration of matter itself, having been led there by our own train of thought,> we must say in regard to matter whether it is evil or not. That evil should be incidental to it is not at all possible, since in itself it is without qualities and is formless and a substrate (though not in a substrate), and simple, not one thing in another.[31] But if it is wholly evil, as some say,[32] it is evil essentially, as they say, making matter primary evil and "what the gods hate."[33] For what else is evil but lack of measure and limitlessness and all such privations of the Good?[34]

For the Good is the measure of all things and the definition and limit and perfection. So, evil is lack of measure and limitlessness itself and imperfection and lack of definition. But these are all in matter primarily, not being other than it, but [identical with] matter itself, that is, what the being of it is. Therefore, matter is primarily evil and the nature of evil and the lowest of all the things that are.

If, however, good is twofold—the one the Good itself and nothing else but good, the other in another and a qualified good and not primarily good—so evil will be twofold—the one in a way evil itself and primarily evil and nothing else but evil, the other in another and a qualified evil and evil owing to that [the primary evil] by partaking of it or evil by similarity [to it].[35] And just as the Good itself is first, so evil itself is last, among the things that are real, for nothing is able to be better than the Good nor worse than evil; for we say that all other things are somehow better or worse owing to these. But the last among things that exist is matter, for everything else acts or experiences by nature, but matter does neither, being deprived of this ability. Therefore, matter is evil itself or the primary evil.

§31. If, however, what happens contrary to nature in bodies does so when matter rules in them, as was said,[36] and there is evil and weakness in souls[37] <owing to their falling into matter>, in fact, by becoming

---

[31] For matter as a substrate see Aristotle *Phys.* A 7; *Met.* Λ 10, 1075b22.

[32] Proclus seems to have Plotinus especially in mind. See Plotinus I 8. 3, 35–40; 5, 8 ff.

[33] A reference to Homer *Il.* XX 65.

[34] Cf. *infra* §51.

[35] See Plotinus I 8. 3, 23.

[36] At §28, 9.

[37] See Plotinus I 8. 14, 49: "matter is the cause of the soul's weakness and the cause of its vice."

intoxicated[38] with the limitlessness surrounding matter, they become like it, why should we, rejecting this, seek for another cause for evils and the source of their reality?

But if matter is evil <—here we need to move on to another aspect of the question—> one of two things is necessary: either this makes the Good the cause of evil or there are two principles of things that exist; for it is necessary that everything whatsoever that exists either is a principle of everything or comes from a principle. But since matter is from a principle, it comes from the Good, that is, it has its arrival in existence [owing to the Good]. But if it is a principle, then we must suppose two principles among things that exist in conflict with each other, that is, primary Good and primary Evil.

But this is impossible. For primacy cannot be double. For where would everything come from if it were not from unity? And if each of the [supposed] two is one, it is necessary that prior to them both there be the One, owing to which these are both one; that is, there must be one principle.[39]

Neither can evil come from the Good, for as the cause of goods is superlatively good, so too, the generator of evil would be superlatively evil. And if this is so, then the Good will no longer have its own nature [good], since it is introducing the principle of evil. <If, however, it is everywhere the case that that which is generated loves to assimilate itself to its generator, then evil itself will be good, since it makes itself good by taking on the nature of its cause>. In this way, the Good will be evil, since it is the cause of evil; and evil, good, as produced from the Good.

§32. If, however, matter is necessary for the All or the universe—and it would not be the great thing it is and a "happy god"[40] if matter were absent from it—how, then, can the nature of evil be added to it?[41] For evil is one thing and necessity, another; the latter is that without which it is impossible [for the universe] to exist, the former is the privation of being.[42] If, then, matter offers itself for the making of the entire universe,

---

[38] See Plato *Phd.* 79C for the idea that embodiment is a sort of intoxication.

[39] See Proclus *ET* Props. 1 ff.; *In Parm.* 696, 32–697, 21. Cf. Plato *Parm.* 137C; Plotinus VI 9. 1, 1: "All real things are real owing to the One."

[40] *Tim.* 34B4.

[41] See Plato *Tim.* 47E3 ff.; Plotinus I 8. 7, 3: "This All would not exist if matter did not."

[42] See Aristotle *Phys.* A 9, 192a4 ff. for the distinction between matter and privation.

and if it appears as a sort of "nurse"[43] and "mother,"[44] how could one go on to say that it is evil—indeed, the primary evil?

If we speak of [matter] as lack of measure and limitlessness and indefiniteness and each of the things of this sort in various ways—for it is as each opposes measure and is an absence of it and a removal of it and as underlying substrate to it and a lack of measure and definition—but matter is not by nature in conflict [with anything], nor does it in general make anything, nor is it capable of experiencing anything according to nature, owing to its lack of the ability to experience. Again, if it is not the elimination of measure and limit because it is not the same thing as privation,[45] since privation does not occur when these [measure and limit] are present, whereas matter is present and receives their imprint, then it is necessary that the indefiniteness and unmeasuredness of matter is a lack of measure and of definiteness.

But how would the lack of these be in opposition to them? How can that still be evil that is in need of the Good? For evil flees the nature of the Good and generally so for everything that is opposed to its opposite state.[46] <But if matter "assists" [like a nurse]> and "conceives " [like a mother] the realm of generation, and, as Plato himself says, nurtures it, nothing evil comes from it, since it is the mother of the things that come from it—more precisely, of the things that come to be in it.

§33. <But if it is true that souls are susceptible to weakness and decline, it is not owing to matter, since these existed prior to [entrance into] the body and matter and since the cause of their evil existed in their souls in some way prior to matter. If this is not so, from where would the incapacity come that exists among the souls that follow Zeus, when he is no longer able to lead the charioteer and make them turn their heads to the heavenly place and they fall, finding themselves unable to have that vision?[47] How could there be forgetfulness and misfortune and heaviness in them?[48]

The absence of matter does not prevent the horse, which partakes of evil, from becoming heavy and inclining with its weight to the earth.[49]

---

[43] *Tim.* 49A6.

[44] Ibid. 50D3; 51A4.

[45] See Plotinus I 8. 5, 20–5; I 8. 11, 1–7; II 4. 16, 3–8 for the opposing view that evil, matter, and privation are identical.

[46] See Aristotle *Phys.* A 9, 192a13–25, where Aristotle argues similarly against Plato that matter and privation are not identical.

[47] See Plato *Phdr.* 248A.

[48] Ibid. 247C.

[49] Ibid. 247B.

When the soul has fallen to earth, it is then that it is associated with matter and with its attendant darkness. But before that, weakness and forgetfulness and evil already exist, for we would not fall if we were not weak, since even if we were distant from the sight of true being, we would desire to have it. If, then, there was weakness prior to the "drinking,"[50] and if being enmattered and coming to matter only occurs after the flight from that place, therefore matter is not the cause of weakness and, generally, of the evils from which souls suffer.>[51]

Further, what could have an effect on other things when it is unable to do so? How will that which is without qualities in itself be able to do anything? Is it that matter leads soul to itself or that souls lead themselves to matter and are separated from it by their own power and lack of it? If they are led by themselves, then this is what was their evil—namely, their impulse and desire for what is worse—not matter. For all things, the flight from what is better is evil, and the flight to evil is even worse. And those [souls] who choose badly must suffer the sort of things they suffer, owing to their weakness.

But if they are led by matter, where is its property of being a self-mover,[52] and where are the souls' choices <if we grant that the cause of generation [embodiment] is the attraction of matter, operating like a magnet on the soul? Or how could we explain that, among the souls in matter [embodied], some of them look to the intelligible and the Good while others look to becoming and to matter>, if it is indeed the case that matter leads all souls to itself and troubles them all and does them violence so long as they are here?

<Here, then, is the conclusion to which this line of reasoning leads us: matter has been shown not to be evil; rather, by negating the contrary argument that it is evil, we show that it is good.>

§36. <Perhaps someone will ask us, "What is your view about matter? Do you reckon it to be good or evil? And what is the basis of your view?" Our view is>: matter is neither good nor evil. For if it is good, it will be a goal—and that on account of which things are done—or an object of desire, and not [as it is in fact] the lowest of all things. For everything that is good is like this, since the primary Good is a goal, and that on account of which all things are done, or an object of desire, for all things. But if matter is evil, there will be, in addition to god, another principle of all things, one that is in conflict with the cause of goods; and there

---

[50] See *Rep.* 621A, for the drinking of the "cup of forgetfulness" in the Myth of Er.
[51] See Plotinus I 8. 14, 49 for the contrasting view.
[52] See Plato *Phdr.* 245C ff.

will be "two sources released to flow forth"[53] in opposition to each other. One will be the source of goods and the other, the source of evils; and there will not be for the gods themselves the carefree life exempt from mortal sorrow; rather, there will be in their life something hard and alien and in a way a burden.

But if matter is neither [good nor evil], what is it, then, in itself? Or should that which has been said many times be said of it now: that it is that which is necessary?[54] For the nature of good is one thing and the nature of evil, another; and these are opposed to each other. But there is a third [nature] that is neither unqualifiedly good nor evil, but is, rather, necessary; for evil leads away from the Good and flees its nature. But that which is necessary is altogether what it is on account of the Good and has its reference to it and has whatever sort of generation it has because of that.[55] If, however, <matter's> generation is on account of something, and there is no generation of anything else on account of matter such that we would then say that it is a goal and a good, what we should say about it is, evidently, that it is necessary for generation, and not evil that it has been generated from god as necessary and to be necessary for the forms that in themselves would not be able to be situated [here].

For it had to be the case that the cause of all goods brought forth not only goods from things like themselves, but also other things and that nature that is not simply good in itself but that desires good and, desiring that, gives to others their generation into existence and whatever else goes with that. For its lack of any of the goods contributes to the making of sensibles, since Being not only makes beings exist but also things that desire partaking in existence, things whose existence follows according to their desire for being.

So, that which is the primary object of desire is one thing, and that which desires it and has its good in this, is another. Yet another is that which is in between, that which is the object of desire of some things and itself desires others, that is, of course, the things that are prior to it and on account of which it exists.

§37. We would conclude, then, that matter is neither good nor evil, at least on the basis of this line of argument, but that it is only necessary.

---

[53] Proclus here borrows a phrase from Plato *Lg.* 636D7–8, where, however, the reference is to pleasures and pains.

[54] See Plato *Tim.* 47E where Plato distinguishes the works of Intellect (i.e., the Demiurge) and the things that come to be "by necessity." Cf. also Aristotle *Phys.* B 9, 199b34ff. on matter as (hypothetical) necessity.

[55] On the question of the generation of matter see Plotinus II 4. 5, 24–8; IV 8. 6, 18–23.

And, in the sense that it came to be on account of a good, it is good, though it is not good unqualifiedly. And, in the sense that it is the lowest of the things that exist, it is evil, if that which is separated as far as possible from the Good is evil, though it is not unqualifiedly evil. Rather, as it was said, it is necessary.

Generally speaking, it is not, I suppose, true that evil exists in itself. For neither unmixed nor primary evil exists; for if evil has to be opposed to every good, and prior to the good in another there is the Good itself, which exists primarily, evil also is twofold—that which is Evil itself and that which is in another. But if evil is opposed to those among the goods that have their being in another, evil will be even more so in another and not exist itself.

For it is not the Good to which evil is opposed, but the good that is in another and is not separate. For what could be opposite to the primary Good, not in the sense of evil, but in the sense that it is any thing that exists? For all things that exist do so because of that and on account of that. But it is impossible for the opposite to exist because of the opposite nature, since the opposite itself does not exist, for opposites are destroyed by each other and, generally, all opposites are connected to one supreme genus. But what would the genus of the primary Good be? For what would transcend the nature of the Good? What among things that exist would be in the same genus as that? For that would require that there be something different prior to both of them, of which each would be a part. But in that case, the Good would no longer be the principle of things that exist, but that which is common to the two would be the principle. Therefore, there is nothing opposite to the primary Good, nor is there [an opposite of] that in which all things partake [Being] but [only an opposite of] that in which the participation is not the same in each case.

§51. We must now say what evil itself is. It would seem to be the hardest thing of all to know the nature and form of evil in itself, since all knowledge is a contact with form, whereas evil is without form and, in a way, privation. Perhaps what it is would become clear if, looking at the Good itself <and to the number of goods>, we considered in this way what evil is itself;[56] for just as the primary Good transcends everything, so evil itself has no part in any goods; I mean, insofar as something is evil, it is a lack of and privation of those goods.

<The extent of the Good and the manner of its existence and its organizing role have been discussed elsewhere>.[57] As for evil, if it is a

---

[56] Plotinus I 8 1, 7.

[57] See *ET* Props. 8–13. This is perhaps also a reference to *In Phil.* (not extant) and *In Remp.* I 269 ff.

privation of all that is good insofar as it is evil, it has no part in the source of goods, just as the unlimited has no part of the limit of everything; and as weakness has no part in the <intelligible> power; and as the absence of proportion, falsity and ugliness have no part in beauty and truth and proportion, <owing to which the mixtures are made and where is found the unity that things that exist have>.[58] As unsettled in its own nature and unstable, it thus has no part in that eternity abiding in unity and in its power; for its absence of power makes it not to be thus. As privation and absence of life, it has no part in the primary unity of Forms of the life in the intelligible world. As destructive and divisive for the things to which it is present, it is also imperfect in relation to the perfective goodness of wholes [Forms]; for that which produces destruction goes from being to nonbeing; and the divisive eliminates the connectedness and unity of being; and the imperfect removes from the natural disposition of each thing its own characteristic perfection.

Further, the indeterminateness <of the nature of evil> is a lack and failure to achieve the highest unity, as barrenness is a failure to produce offspring and idleness a failure of productive activity. For the removal and weakness and indeterminateness are privations of these goods, I mean of the unitary causes and of the generative power or productive activity.

And if evil is the cause of the absence of likeness and of division and of absence of order, then it is clear that, in this way, it lacks the goods that make things like and that it necessarily lacks the providence of the undivided for the divided and the order in the things that have been divided. <And if the Good does not reach down to here but it is the kind of thing that is pure and productive of great things in the intelligible world>, then evil will be ineffective and dark and enmattered.

How could these things and things like them be true of it if it did not have the privations of these goods? For in the intelligible world are the primary goods, of which the good in us is a part and an image. And the privation of these is evil. So, it is a privation of those things of which the good in us is an image.

What should one say further, since the evil in bodies is the privation of not only their good but also of that in souls that is prior to this? For the good in bodies is an image of the good in souls. <The corruption and privation of form are nothing else but the decay of intelligible power, since form is the product of the Intellect, and that which is form is essentially intellectual>. But that evil is that which is in every way privation and lack of goods has already been stated.

---

[58] See Plato *Phil.* 64A–66A.

Glossary

abstraction (*aphairesis*, ἀφαίρεσις):   also, removal. Indicative of a separation in thought or reality.

action (*praxis*, πρᾶξις):   also, practicality. Refers specifically to rational beings but broadly to all beings with a principle of motion.

actuality (*energeia*, ἐνέργεια):   also, activity. An Aristotelian term employed generally by Neoplatonists to indicate the dynamism of reality without motion (*kinesis*, κίνησις), which implies imperfection. The product of actuality or activity is *energēma*, ἐνέργημα.

always (*aei*, ἀεί):   also, eternally, continuously. See everlasting (*aidios*, ἀΐδιος).

appetite (*epithumia*, ἐπιθυμία):   also, desire. A state of the lowest part of the embodied soul. Sometimes the more general word *orexis*, ὄρεξις is used equivalently.

apprehend (*antilambanō*, ἀντιλαμβάνω):   also, grasp. A general term for the cognition of something real, whether by sense-perception or by intellect.

apprehension (*antilēpsis*, ἀντίληψις):   also, grasp. The term *katalēpsis* (κατάληψις) is often used synonymously and translated accordingly.

appropriate (*oikeios*, οἰκεῖος):   also, proper, assimilated to. Broadly used for something that is compatible with or promotes the achievement or fulfillment by an entity of its nature.

audacity (*tolma*, τόλμα):   according to Plotinus, the characteristic of souls that led to their separation from the intelligible world, and the characteristic of Intellect that led to its separation from the One. Originally a Neopythagorean term indicating the separation of the Indefinite Dyad from the One.

awareness (*sunaisthēsis*, συναίσθησις):   the activity of cognizing one's own cognitive or affective states. The prefix *sun-*, συν-, indicates a level of cognition over and above *aisthēsis*, αἴσθησις, which generally has something "external" as an object.

being (*on*, ὄν):   the most general term for what is real, usually implicitly including the fact of existing as well as the nature or essence that exists. Also, "[real or true] things" (*onta*, ὄντα), usually referring to the things Plato called "really real," that is, to the Forms or the intelligible world generally.

belief (*doxa*, δόξα):   also, opinion. A cognitive state dependent upon sense-perception and distinct from the types of cognition that have purely intelligible objects. Belief admits of falsity; the higher forms of cognition do not.

cause (*aitia*, αἰτία, αἴτιον):   also, explanation. The term used both for the four Aristotelian causes and for the Platonic paradigmatic cause.

choice (*proairesis*, προαίρεσις):   also, intention. An Aristotelian term meaning deliberate desire or the state after deliberation has been completed.

composite (*to koinon*, τὸ κοινόν): the state in which body and soul are joined; also, the totality of these. Synonyms: *sunamphoteron*, συναμφότερον; *suntheton*, σύνθετον. Also, common, indicating a sum or union of parts.

concept (*ennoia*, ἔννοια): the intellectual residue of sense-perception, distinct from the activity, which is not dependent upon sense-perception.

conscious, be (*parakoloutheō*, παρακολουθέω): a word used both as a contrary to nonconscious or unconscious and, more consistently, as indicating self-awareness or self-consciousness. The noun "accompaniment" (*parakolouthēma*, παρακολούθημα) reflects this latter sense.

contact (*epibolē*, ἐπιβολή): the immediate relation of an entity usually with another at a higher level. The relation is generally cognitive.

contemplation (*theōria*, θεωρία): also, (mental) seeing. Primarily, the relation between intellect and Forms, or intelligible reality.

conviction (*pistis*, πίστις): also, persuasion. Sometimes, a pejorative term indicating something like gullibility. More often, in Neoplatonists, a settled (true) belief that is the basis for moral and intellectual improvement. The virtue of faith in late Greek religion and in Christianity.

corporeal (*sōmatikon*, σωματικόν): also, bodily. The term used for things in the sensible realm that indicates three-dimensionality and solidity.

demonstration (*apodeixis*, ἀπόδειξις): technical term for a formal argument generally in syllogistic form, which reveals something nonevident.

difference (*heterotēs*, ἑτερότης): see sameness. A fundamental principle within intelligible reality, accounting for the reality of distinct natures cognized by Intellect. Along with its contrary, sameness (*tautotēs*, ταυτότης), a principle necessary for thinking.

discernment (*krisis*, κρίσις): also, judgment. The fundamental property of all cognitive powers; the ability for or state of distinguishing samenesses and differences among things.

discursive power (*dianoētikon*, διανοητικόν): that faculty in virtue of which we engage in nonintuitive cognition. This is the lowest part of intellect and the highest part of the soul. The activity of this faculty is called "discursive thinking" (*dianoia*, διάνοια).

distinct (*diakekrimena*, διακεκριμένα): term used to describe Forms in Intellect; Forms are *not* distinct in the One. The distinction among Forms is different from the distinction among physically separate entities.

error (*hamartēma*, ἁμάρτημα): error, mistake, usually with a moral connotation.

essence (*ousia*, οὐσία): also, being, substance. A term indicating a Form, or the totality of Forms, or the totality of Forms and Intellect. The term connotes limitedness or definiteness. The One is beyond essence.

essence itself (*autoousia*, αὐτοουσία): a Form itself, considered according to its nature.

eternity (*aiōn*, αἰών): characterization of everything above the principle Soul.

everlasting (*aidios*, ἀΐδιος): continuously existing.

evil (*kakon*, κακόν): also, bad. The state arising from attachment to the opposite of the Good. Also, the principle producing this state. Evil describes the trajectory away from the Good.

excellence (*aretē*, ἀρετή): usually used with a moral connotation, referring generally to the ideal human achievement.

exemplary mode, in (*paradeigmatikōs*, παραδειγματικῶς): characteristic of Forms in Intellect in relation to their instantiations or images.

existence (*einai*, εἶναι): verbal noun that indicates the fact of a thing's realness as distinct from (but including) the nature or essence or character of what is real.

existence (*huparxis*, ὕπαρξις): also, mode of existence or being. A term used widely in Proclus, indicating separate or nondependent existence or reality. The term *kath huparxin*, καθ' ὕπαρξιν, indicates a consideration of an entity according to its (separate) mode of existence as opposed to that in the entity which is dependent on or caused by something else.

expressed principle (*logos*, λόγος): the product or expression of a higher principle at a lower level. See reason.

form (*eidos*, εἶδος): also Form, figure, kind, class. A term that may refer either to Platonic Forms or Aristotelian (enmattered) forms or to the intelligible principle of any group.

freedom from disturbance (*ataraxia*, ἀταραξία): in Epicureanism and Skepticism, the removal of disturbance in the body, the principal impediment to happiness.

function (*ergon*, ἔργον): refers to a defining activity of an entity according to its essence.

generation (*genesis*, γένεσις): indicates the beginning of anything that exists in time, or the entire realm of that which is in time. Forms of the word can also refer to dependence in the eternal intelligible world. This includes "offspring" (*gennēma*, γέννημα).

god (*theos* θεός): used for principles of the intelligible world, often virtually as an honorific adjective. Seldom if ever used as a proper noun, hence, the inappropriateness of translating the term as "God." The term is used of the first principle of all, which is by definition unique, though this use does not preclude its application simultaneously to other principles.

Good-like (*agathoeides*, ἀγαθοειδές): being an image of the Form of the Good in some way.

grasping (*katanoēsis*, κατανόησις): also, understanding. Usually refers to a purely intellectual state, but sometimes to a cognitive state dependent upon sense-perception.

happiness (*eudaimonia*, εὐδαιμονία): the ideal human achievement. For Neoplatonism, this involves reversion or identification of the person with the highest part of the soul, the intellect.

henad (*henas*, ἑνάς): a unitary or unifying principle. See monad (*monas*, μονάς).

human being (*anthrōpos*, ἄνθρωπος): the composite of soul and body, distinct from the person or self, which can exist apart from the body.

imagination (*phantasia*, φαντασία): an Aristotelian term indicating the presence of the form of a sensible in a subject without the presence of the physical sensible that caused it. Also, sensory image (*phantasma*, φάντασμα).

imitation (*mimēma*, μίμημα): also, reproduction. One of the family of terms expressing the relationship between sensibles and Forms. The term is also used to express the dependence relation within the intelligible world, between Soul and Intellect and between Intellect and the One. Also, likeness (*homoioma*, ὁμοίωμα).

immaterial (*aulon*, ἄυλον): that which is separate from matter or incorporeal, in distinction from that which is *enulon*, ἔνυλον, or dependent on matter.

impression (*tupos*, τύπος): also, type. The intelligible residue of a higher principle in a lower, or of a sensible composite in the intellect. An archetype (*archetupos*, ἀρχέτυπος) is that higher principle in relation to the lower expression or representation of it.

in fact (*ē*, ἤ): in Plotinus, the word typically used to indicate the beginning of his answer to a question raised or his determination of the solution to a problem.

incontinence (*akrasia*, ἀκρασία): the inability to control the appetites or passions against one's better judgment.

intellectual insight (*noera theōria*, νοερὰ θεωρία): in Iamblichus, a term indicating the ability to see the inner meaning of an observed subject.

intelligible world (*ekei*, ἐκεῖ): literally "there," used generally for the realm of Intellect and the One, and for other components of intelligible reality.

interval (*diastēma*, διάστημα): space between bodies.

intuitive knowledge (*noera gnōsis*, νοερὰ γνῶσις): nondiscursive cognition.

know (*gignōskō*, γιγνώσκω): be acquainted with, recognize, cognize. The verb is used widely for cognition above the level of sense-perception. Related terms are "cognizing" (*gnōrizō*, γνωρίζω) and the noun "cognition" (*gnōsis*, γνῶσις).

lineage (*genos*, γένος): generally, a dependence relation with respect to causality.

lineage, same (*suggenes*, συγγενής): also, kinship. A term used to indicate the connectedness of souls or persons with intelligible reality. Also, congenital (*sumphuton*, σύμφυτον).

living being (*zōon*, ζῷον): any bodily entity possessed of a soul, that is, of a principle of motion in it.

manifestation (*deixis*, δεῖξις): also, symbol. Used for a representation of a higher principle at a lower level.

moderation of the passions (*metriopatheia*, μετριοπάθεια): a technical term based on the Aristotelian idea of moral virtue as a mean between the extremes of affective response.

monad (*monas*, μονάς): a unitary or unifying cause of a series or order. See henad (*henas*, ἑνάς).

multiplicity (*plēthos*, πλῆθος): the general term for the opposite of unity; therefore applying to everything besides the first principle of all. The term connotes complexity when quantity is not necessarily meant.

nature (*phusis*, φύσις): also, principle of growth. Used by Plotinus in two ways: as a synonym for essence or form or intelligible structure, and as the lowest part of the soul of the universe — that which is variously present in plants, animals, and human beings. In both senses, nature is prior to the corporeal or sensible and determinative of it. As a sort of ontological principle, nature is both distinct from and the cause of the individual natures of organic individuals.

necessity (*anankē*, ἀνάγκη): used of both physical and logical necessity.

order (*taxis*, τάξις): in later Neoplatonism any intelligible series headed by a unifying principle. Synonym: series (*seira*, σειρά).

participate (*metechō*, μετέχω): the verb indicating both the dependence relationship between the sensible world generally and the intelligible world and a similar relationship within the intelligible world.

passion (*pathos*, πάθος): in general, a state; specifically, an affective or emotional state.

perceptible (*aisthēton*, αἴσθητον): a direct or indirect object of sense-perception.

perfection (*teleiōsis*, τελείωσις): closely related to the terms "actuality" and "goal" (*telos*, τέλος).

pneumatic vehicle (*ochēma*, ὄχημα): also sometimes referred to as an astral body. In Porphyry and Iamblichus, a means of connecting the soul with the body, though neither itself a three-dimensional body nor incorporeal, as is the soul itself. Also, the seat of the imagination.

power (*dunamis*, δύναμις): also, virtuality, potency, ability. Used both in the Aristotelian sense, where it is translated as "potency" or "ability" and where it is contrasted with "actuality"; and in the Neoplatonic sense, where it indicates what, in a higher principle, is manifested in some way in a lower. The One is virtually all things in the sense that it is the cause of all multiplicity and essence.

power (*exousia*, ἐξουσία): roughly equivalent to the Platonic conception of *dunamis*, δύναμις, with an added moral connotation.

principal (*kurios*, κύριος): also, authoritative, proper, in charge. Generally, refers to that which in a system determines its direction or structure.

principle (*archē*, ἀρχή): also, first principle, source, starting point. Refers to that which ultimately explains as well as to the beginning of a demonstration, that is, a definition or axiom.

privation (*sterēsis*, στέρησις): an Aristotelian term; along with form and the underlying subject, one of the three principles of change. For Plotinus and Proclus, privation is in some way identified with evil; but Plotinus, unlike Proclus, equates evil and matter.

procession (*proodos*, πρόοδος): the derivation of an order from its monad or unifying principle.

providence (*pronoia*, πρόνοια): literally, "forethought," and generally exercised by the intelligible and intellectual realm on that which is below. In Neoplatonism, the term is influenced by the Stoic notion of providence as equivalent to the rational, causal order of nature.

pure (*katharos*, καθαρός): specifically referring to detachment from the body and identification with the intelligible realm.

reality (*hupostasis*, ὑπόστασις): also, existent, existence.

reason (*logos*, λόγος): also, statement, argumentative procedure, argument, theory, rational discourse, account, rational principle, expressed principle, etc. A general term for any unit of intelligible communication. Also, the expression of a higher principle at a lower level. A lower principle, e.g., Soul, is itself a *logos* of a higher—namely, Intellect.

reasoning (discursive) (*logismos*, λογισμός): also, argument, calculative reasoning. Refers to the activity of the highest part of the embodied soul. The part itself is called "reasoning power" or "rational part of the soul" (*logistikon*, λογιστικόν).

reflection (*eidōlon*, εἴδωλον): also, representation, image, phantom. In general, the manifestation of an intelligible principle at a lower level, entailing some diminution of intelligible or unity. The word *eikōn*, εἴκων is used similarly.

reflection (*indalma*, ἴνδαλμα): an imperfect representation of a higher principle at a lower level.

restoration (*apokatastasis*, ἀποκατάστασις): in moral psychology, the return to a "neutral" state after a painful one; in physics, the return to a natural state of a body.

reversion, return (*epistrophē*, ἐπιστροφή): literally "turning towards." The process or result of the reconnecting of what is at a lower level with a higher level.

sameness (*tautotēs*, ταυτότης): see otherness. Also, the property of being self-identical.

self-constituted (*authupostaton*, αὐθυπόστατον): refers to the characteristic of intelligible entities which is owing to their own natures and not to a higher principle.

self-determining (*autexousios*, αὐτεξούσιος): indicating the accord of the soul with intellect. A narrower term than "up to us" (*eph hēmin*, ἐφ' ἡμῖν), which indicates that the person "could have done otherwise."

self-evident (*enargēs*, ἐναργής): what is cognized without inference.

self-transcending experience (*ekstasis*, ἔκστασις): literally a "going out of a stable position." Usually indicates the process or activity of "ascent" from a lower to a higher level of being.

sense-perception (*aisthēsis*, αἴσθησις): sense-perception, sensation. Also, (intellectual) awareness, having immediacy analogous to sense-perception.

series (*seira*, σειρά): synonym of "order."

share in (*metalambanō*, μεταλαμβάνω)): the basic verb expressing the relationship between sensibles and the Forms that explain such intelligibility as they have.

source (*pēgē*, πηγή): literally, a spring or well; metaphorically, the origin of everything, that is, the One or the Good.

spirit (*daimōn*, δαίμων): a supernatural power, including, but also extending beyond, the gods to "intermediate" beings of various sorts.

state (*katastasis*, κατάστασις): refers generally to a psychic or intellectual state.

state (*pathēma*, πάθημα): also, condition. Closely related to *pathos*, πάθος.

statue (*agalma*, ἄγαλμα): also, image.

stillness (*hesuchia*, ἡσυχία): also, tranquility. A psychic state achieved through attainment of balance.

subject (*hupokeimenon*, ὑποκείμενον): also, underlying subject, substrate. An Aristotelian term employed by Neoplatonists to indicate matter in relation to form or the composite of matter and form in relation to predicates or to the underlying assumption of an argument.

substance (*ousia*, οὐσία): also, essence, being. The term is taken from Aristotle and used, after him, for basic entities as well as for their nature or essence. However, for Neoplatonism, the basic entities are unequivocally, purely intelligible entities. Also, the adjective οὐσιώδης, translated as "essential character" is used as the general description of the natures of the primary entities.

think (*noeō*, νοέω): the activity of intellect, νοῦς, closely related to thinking (*noēsis*, νόησις). That in virtue of which the activity occurs is intellect (or Intellect) (*nous*, νοῦς). The intentional object of thinking is an intelligible (*noēton*, νοητόν), translated sometimes simply as "object of thinking." This object is sometimes referred to as an object of thinking, as opposed to what it is in and by itself. In that case, it is called "that which is thought" (*nooumenon*, νοούμενον). The result or product of thinking is a thought (*noēma*, νόημα) or sometimes a concept. The activity of thinking is characterized as intellectual or thought-like (*noeros*, νοερός).

transcendent (*epekeina*, ἐπέκεινα):   literally, "beyond," indicating the relation of a higher principle to a lower. The term is used especially of the One, the first principle of all which transcends all multiplicity or plurality.

unaffected (*apathēs*, ἀπαθής):   also, incapable of being affected. Not subject to change or alteration; especially applied to the soul. Opposite of *empathēs* (ἐμπαθής), capable of being affected or subject to affective or emotional states.

understanding (*epistēmē*, ἐπιστήμη):   also, knowledge, scientific knowledge. Cognition through (first) causes. The plural, *epistēmai*, ἐπιστῆμαι, is used to refer to specific areas of knowledge.

understanding (*katalēpsis*, κατάληψις):   see "apprehend."

understanding (*sunesis*, σύνεσις):   an intellectual virtue and an Aristotelian term indicating the cognitive ability to grasp a point or see the central issue.

union (*henōsis*, ἕνωσις):   the act or activity of identification, mainly with a higher principle. The One, the first principle of all, is in a state of perfect union with itself.

unity of sensibility (*sumpatheia*, συμπαθειά):   indicating a sameness of states via the process of assimilation or identification (*homoiōsis*, ὁμοίωσις) with a higher principle.

universe (*kosmos*, κόσμος):   the (organized or structured) world.

unparticipated (*amethekton*, ἀμέθεκτον):   a monad in its aspect of separateness from that which participates in its nature.

venerable (*semnos*, σεμνός):   also, revered, majestic, solemn. A standard honorific term, generally applied to the intelligible realm and to the soul in an elevated state.

vice (*kakia*, κακία):   a state of the soul resulting from attachment to bodily appetites.

virtuous (*spoudaios*, σπουδαῖος):   also serious, worthy. A term used for a person of elevated character.

voluntary (*hekousion*, ἑκούσιον):   that which is done without force and with awareness. Animals and children can act voluntarily, but what they do is not "up to them," since they, having no reason, could not have done otherwise.

will (*boulēsis*, βούλησις):   the power, in virtue of which something can be "up to us." In practice, what is "up to us" is usually equivalent to what is voluntary, though they are not the same in definition.

INDEX

accidents, 215–16
actuality and potentiality, 144
Albinus, 220, 343
allegorizing, 249–50, 298–302, 340–1
Amelius, 218–19, 242, 282
Ammonius, 197
Anaxagoras, 79, 332
angels, 200, 228
animals: in intelligible world, 136
Antiphon, 298
appetite(s), 6, 161
archetype: contrasted with image, 120
Aristotle, 80, 214–15, 242, 306, 315; and Plato, 337–8
ascent, 28–9, 178; *see also* soul
Atticus, 219, 341, 343

barbarians, 233; and Hellenes, 235
beauty, 18–30, 146, 159; and Forms, 20–1; and Good, 151; of Intellect, 150; intelligible, 20, 22–3; and matter, 24–5; physical, 18–20; of soul, 23–5, 29; and ugliness, 24
Being/being, 73, 121, 248, 261, 306–11, 357; and beauty, 25; and the One, 208–10; one and many, 294–5; and stability, 77
Being-Life-Intellect, 200, 212–13, 301
Bitys, 240
body, 49–50; moved by soul, 269; *see also* soul
bravery, 164; *see also* courage

calculation, 161
calculative reasoning, 122–3, 126
categories, 215

cause(s): coordination of, 275; relation to effect, 265–6, 272–3, 274–5; *see also* contributory cause
Cephalus, 298
chance, 168–9, 246–7
cognitive powers, 189–92
contemplation, 36–44, 142; and action, 39–41; and nature, 37–9; as productive, 38, 44; and soul, 40–1
contributory cause, 332–3
courage, 181–2; *see also* bravery
Crantor, 342
Cronius, 220

daemons, 225
definition, 216
Demiurge, 232, 240, 299; and evil, 348–9
demiurgic intellect, 333
descent, 178, 219–20; *see also* soul
desert: and virtue, 247
desire(s), 6, 147–8, 161, 163
dialectic, 296, 306, 314–22; and "babbling", 321–2; and definition, 317; and division, 316; and eristic, 322; kinds of, 318–21
Difference, 73, 140, 209
difference: in Intellect, 145
discursive power, 93
discursive thinking/reasoning, 3, 9, 87–90, 104, 123
divination, 230, 238–9
divine foreknowledge, 238–9
divine beings: impassibility of, 226
divine names, 233–5
division (method of), 315–17, 320
dreams, 197
Dyad, 74, 133, 260–1; and Demiurge: 253

Egyptians, 240–1
elements: in intelligible world, 136–7
Empedocles, 57, 62, 80, 142, 219
Essence/essence, 213; and Intellect, 180; and "why?", 124, 170
eternity: and intellect, 194; as principle, 273–4
evil, 30–5; 65, 345–59; and destruction, 350–1; and the Good, 347–8, 354–5; knowledge of, 30–1; and matter, 33–4, 353–4; mixed vs. unmixed, 351; and nonbeing, 32, 348, 352; and privation, 31, 34, 358–9; reality of, 346–7, 350; and sensibles, 32; in the soul, 33–5, 356; no unmixed, 358; and vice, 349
expressed principle, 37–8, 41–3, 74, 78, 93, 95, 103, 128–31, 134, 136–7, 141, 145; *see also* reason-principle
expression (in predication), 214

false belief, 8–9
fate, 244–8; and free choice, 245; and human action, 246; and providence, 246
Father (divine), 239
first cause argument, 266–7
Form(s), 74, 125, 142–8, 289, 295–6, 307, 327–8, 333; of Beauty, 26; and Being, 143; and division, 317; Good-like, 143, 147–8; in Intellect, 144; and mathematical objects, 344; and nature, 300; and One, 144; and sense-objects, 298–300; and souls, 299–300
free will, 159–177, 254–5; distinguished from related concepts, 160–1; and evil actions, 163; and Good, 163–4, 167–8; human, 175; and imagination, 162–3; in Intellect, 163–7; in soul, 164, 167; and virtue, 164–6; and will, 160, 165

generation, 179
genus, 214–16
god: above being/essence, 207; knowledge of, 206–7; and One, 236; as principle, 236; *see also* Good, Intellect/intellect, One
gods, 229; of Assyrians, 233; of Egyptians, 234–5; immutable, 234–5; knowledge of, 224–6, 277; language about, 233–5; *see also* god
Good, 31–2, 103–4; activity in, 171; and Being/being, 153–4; above being/essence/thought, 155–6, 170, 174, 240; and evil, 346–7; freedom in, 168–9; and Good-like, 143; and Intellect/intellect, 48, 143–4, 146, 153; object of desire/love, 26–7, 174; and the One, 271; no opposite, 358; participation in, 64; as principle/cause, 144, 151–2, 174–5; priority of, 169; self-sufficient, 49, 154, 158, 175; simplicity of, 152–5, 157, 159, 171; (no) thinking in, 152, 154–8; volition in, 172; *see also* god, One
Good-like, 142–3

happiness, 12–17, 237, 336–7; awareness of, 13–14; and body, 17; and chance, 247–8; and god(s), 239–40, 337; nonhuman, 12–13; and pleasure, 13–14; and reason, 14–16, 255; and theurgy, 240; and virtue, 17
Harpocration, 220
henads, 276, 289–91, 324–5; "flowers" and "summits", 329; and the One, 258–9; 271; 330; as principles, 327–8, 330; procession of, 328
Heraclitus, 56, 62, 79, 220
Hermes (god), 221
heroes, 225

human being, 7, 89; essence of, 170; in Intellect, 130; soul vs. composite, 127–30; and thinking, 172–3
hypothesis, 296–7

Iamblichus, 217, 282, 342
Ideas, 211, 242; *see also* Forms
ignorance, 229
illumination(s), 11, 276
image: *see* archetype
imagination, 161, 190–1, 237
individual, 215–16
infinite regress, 266–7
infinity, 264
Intellect/intellect, 31–2, 311; activity of, 139–41; in actuality, 92, 139; and beauty, 25–6; and Being/being, 72, 84; and body, 189; not deliberative, 126; and descent, 65–6; eternity of, 217; and ethics, 245; and evil, 359; and externals, 87; and Forms, 74, 82, 125, 257; freedom in, 165, 167; and god, 327; Good-like, 146, 149–50; and henads, 325; and human being, 7–9, 90–1; identity with intelligible object, 43, 91–2, 189–92; indestructible, 120; knowledge of, 46, 291; limited, 145; nonrational entities in, 134–7; and One/Good, 44, 46, 48–9, 72–3, 76–7, 104, 144–5, 189, 217; "one-many", 101, 141, 145; and paradigmatic virtues, 184; and place, 85; and planets, 213; and plurality, 45, 133, 189, 192; practical, 94; as principle/cause, 275, 288; and self-knowledge, 88–9, 91, 94–5; simplicity and complexity in, 140–2; and Soul/soul, 54–5, 70–2, 85, 269; and thinking, 12, 158; timeless, 193; universal, 45, 59–60; unmoved mover, 269; variegated, 139; contains "why", 124–7; *see also* Form, Good, One, Soul/soul, thinking
intelligibles: internal to intellect, 108; and place, 198
intelligible world: as archetype, 142; and place, 121; multiplicity in, 121; one and many, 248; sensibles in, 132–3; and sensible world, 138–9; substantiality of, 214

justice, 182

knowledge, 180; and Intellect, 326; and One, 326; and sense-perception, 328; and theurgy, 229–30

language: about gods, 233–5
legislation: aimed at general case, 317–18
life: Good-like, 146, 149; in Intellect, 144–5, 149–50
light, 144, 175, 324; in Intellect/intellect, 96–7, 150, 151; and thinking, 157
Limit and Unlimited, 261–2
living being: unity of, 195–7
love, 142, 150, 174, 176, 286
luck, 172–6
Lysias, 304

mathematical objects, 344–5; *see also* numbers
matter: and evil, 33–4, 353–6, 358; and Good, 354; neither good nor evil, 356; and necessity, 357
moderation, 182
monads, 289; and multiplicity, 270–1, 294; as principles, 275
Moon, 213
Motion, 73, 134
motion, 37; in Intellect, 139–41, 144

nature, 36–7, 271; in Aristotle, 332;

INDEX   371

and causes, 332; and One, 325–6; science of, 332; and soul, 84
necessity: and evil, 354; freedom from, 245
nonbeing, 180–1, 351–2
nonrational faculties, 220
numbers, 73–4, 252; *see also* mathematical objects
Numenius, 218–20

offerings (to gods), 229
One, 248; ascent to, 67; contemplation of, 44; and Being/being, 208–10, 347; above being/essence, 47, 81, 100, 177, 250, 258–9, 326; and Dyad, 250; no form, 210; and Good, 270; and henads, 258–9, 329–30; and human being, 8; impassible, 211; and Intellect/intellect, 49, 74, 211, 270; knowledge of, 100, 104–5, 180, 277, 290–1; principle of knowledge, 326–7; and light, 325; and nature, 326; and number, 252–3; in *Parmenides* (Plato), 294–5, 297, 308–13; and place, 175–6; and plurality, 47, 74, 85, 100–3, 259; as principle/cause, 46–7, 72–4, 82–4, 244, 262, 271, 289, 323–7; as power, 102; self-caused, 176; self-sufficient, 99; simplicity of, 99, 103, 211; and soul, 256; transcendence of, 98; unmoved, 74; (no) thinking in, 99–100, 210; virtual plurality/totality, 76, 102; *see also* Good, god, Intellect/intellect
One-Being, 208–10, 250, 260–2, 294–5, 307–10, 329

Parmenides, 79, 293–5
Parmenides (Plato): allegory in, 298–302, 312–13; not aporetic, 303–4; characters and dramatic setting, 293–8; dialectic in, 314–22; division in, 321; not logical exercise, 304–6; method in, 306–8; prologue, 322–3; study of Being, 306–8; study of One, 308–10; style and content, 313–14; Syrianus' interpretation, 310–12
passion(s), 161, 165–6, 188
perceptual power: sensible vs. intelligible, 130, 132
perfection: generative, 271–2
persuasion: vs. necessity, 155
Pherecydes, 81
place, 109–21, 199
planets: circuits of, 212–13; intellects of, 213
plants, 13, 84–6; in intelligible world, 136
Plato, 56–9, 78–82, 126, 129, 137, 142, 154–5, 159, 196, 201–2, 209, 212, 242, 249, 251, 254, 281–9, 344, 346, 348, 351, 355; on the One/Good, 202–3, 207; on principles, 203–4; unwritten teachings, 81; *see also Parmenides, Timaeus* (works)
play, 36
Plotinus, 202, 218–20, 242–3, 254, 282, 342
Plutarch, 219, 341
Porphyry, 243, 251, 282, 342–3
powers: and place, 119–20
practical wisdom, 181
prayer, 231–2, 235
principles, 217–18; incorporeal, 288
privation: and matter, 355; *see also* evil
providence, 122–3
pure souls, 225
purification(s), 52, 182–8, 199–201; *see also* Soul/soul, virtue
Pythagoras (*and* Pythagoreans), 56, 81, 242; *see also Timaeus* (Plato)
"really real", 23

random: *see* luck

reason, 14–16, 175, 188
reason-principle, 227–8, 247, 279, 291, 299–300, 332; 344–5; *see also* expressed principle
recollection, 88
Rest, 73, 133
reversion, 237, 278; *see also* self-reversion
rites, 199–200
rituals, 235

sacrifice, 231–2
Sameness, 73, 140
scientific knowledge: of causes, 266–7
self-constitution, 273
self-evidence, 105–8
self-reversion, 267–8; and incorporeality, 267; and self-movers, 268; and separation from body, 268
sense faculties: and body, 189
sense-perception, 3, 5–8, 83, 87–9, 96, 98, 106, 122, 127, 132, 162, 179, 187, 190–1
sensible world: imitation of intelligible world, 64, 110; substantiality of, 214
species, 214–16
substance: incorporeal, 218; and predication, 216; primary, 214–5; secondary, 215–16
substratum, 273
slavery, 164
Socrates, 285
Soul/soul, 245; ascent of, 67, 240; and beauty, 25; and being, 51; and body, 3–7, 10, 51–2, 54–5, 57–9, 61–2, 70, 109–10, 112, 114–18, 186–7, 195–8, 226–7, 243–4, 269, 278; as cause, 275; descent of, 11, 61–3, 65–7, 122, 219–20, 280; eternity of, 228; fallibility of, 10–11; and Forms, 279; generated and ungenerated, 262–3; and god, 240; and Good, 150–1; and

human being, 9, 12, 247; immortality of, 2, 53–5, 120–1, 263, 278, 342–3; impassivity of, 2, 226–7; and Intellect/intellect, 60, 62, 70–2, 76–8, 81–2, 95, 97, 145, 219, 241, 255, 269, 279, 288; kinds of, 242; and life, 50, 53; and magnitude, 115, 118; and mathematical objects, 345; multiplicity of, 114; and nature, 39, 84; non-human, 55, 85, 131; and place, 82, 116–18, 198–9; purification of, 52, 182–3; and reason-principles, 179, 279; and self, 50; self-knowledge, 87–9, 291; self-moved, 269, 311; of stars, 59; transmigration, 202; twofold nature, 64; universal, 219; of universe, 58–9, 65–6, 68–9, 113, 131, 253; variegated, 139; whole soul, 67; *see also* Intellect/intellect.
spirit: and human being, 131
Stoics, 36, 207, 219
Sun, 213

Theodorus, 212–13, 254, 282
theology, 287–8
Theophrastus, 306
theurgy, 200–1, 229–32, 237, 241
thinking, 7, 9, 12, 72–4, 134, 155–8, 211; complexity in, 157; and essence, 156; and images, 179; in Intellect, 91–2, 192–3; kinds of, 156; in One/Good, 99, 152, 154, 166; reflexive, 86–7, 90, 94–5; and sameness and difference, 154–5; in soul, 93
Thucydides, 303
Timaeus (Plato), 331–43; allegory in, 249–50, 340–1; characters, 340–1; genre and character, 338–9; mathematics in, 339–40; and Pythagoreans, 331–2, 336, 338–9; setting, 340; Socrates in, 338–9; on soul, 342–3; structure,

334–8; subject matter, 331–2, 334;
on temporal creation, 341
time, 193–5; future and present, 124; motion of soul, 194; as principle, 273–4
Totally Ineffable, 261–2
translation, 234
truth, 108–9

unity: prior to multiplicity, 264, 267
universe, 125; and place, 110–12; creation of, 341–2; true vs. visible, 110
"up to us", *see* free will

vice, 349–50

virtue, 181–8; and beauty, 25; civic, 181; contemplative, 182–3; and freedom, 164–5; four classes, 181–6; fruits of, 247; and intellect/Intellect, 166; intellectual, 184; paradigmatic, 184–5; and philosophy, 285; and purification, 25, 182–6
voluntary actions, 160–1; and knowledge, 161

wholes and parts, 119, 276–7

Zeno, 293–5, 303–5